The Empire Strikes Back

Race and racism in 70s Britain

Centre for Contemporary Cultural Studies

London and New York

in association with

the Centre for Contemporary Cultural Studies
University of Birmingham

First published 1982
by Hutchinson & Co. (Publishers) Ltd

Reprinted 1992, 1994
by Routledge
11 New Fetter Lane, London EC4P 4EE
29 West 35th Street, New York, NY 10001

© Centre for Contemporary Cultural Studies,
University of Birmingham 1982

Typeset in Times by Donald Typesetting, Bristol
Printed and bound in Great Britain at
Redwood Books, Trowbridge, Wiltshire

British Library Cataloguing in Publication Data
A catalogue record for this book is available from the British Library

Library of Congress Cataloging in Publication Data
A catalog record for this book is available from the Library of Congress

ISBN 0-415-07909-8

Contents

Preface

There are many reasons why issues raised by the study of 'races' and racisms should be central to the concerns of cultural studies. Yet racist ideologies and racial conflicts have been ignored, both in historical writing and in accounts of the present. If nothing else, this book should be taken as a signal that this marginalization cannot continue. It has also been conceived as a corrective to the narrowness of the English left whose version of the 'national-popular' continues to deny the role of blacks and black struggles in the making and the remaking of the working class.

This book is the overdue result of three years' collective work. It contains few definitive statements. We hope it will be read as a contribution to political and intellectual debates over the problems it indicates. We started work in the autumn of 1978 as a new subgroup at the Centre for Contemporary Cultural Studies. After a year spent surveying the field of 'race relations' we were appalled by the myopia and parochialism which characterize this 'discipline'. Our own investigations took us through the major sociological problematics, the work of non-European radicals, and the often Eurocentric 'Marxist' debates on late capitalism and migrant labour. It was the frustrating search for an interdisciplinary, historical approach which was geared to the contemporary struggle against racism which forced us to turn our own hands to analysis. If at times what we have written seems too firmly in a critical mode, we feel this is a small price to pay while the predicament of the black communities is professionally obscured by those who make a living on the back of black sufferings. We have tried to address the principal areas of concern to the communities whose struggles we aim to service. A chronicle of our omissions is pointless here, but two points must be raised to avoid misunderstanding. We have not dealt satisfactorily with the struggles of black women, and have struck an inadequate balance between the two black communities. We opted to remain within the bounds of our own historical resources rather than make pronouncements on things that were unfamiliar. Only one of us has roots in the Indian subcontinent whereas four are of Afro-Caribbean origin. This accounts for the unevenness of our text. We would have liked to include material on black, waged workers and their relation to the political institutions of the white working class. We had also intended to produce chapters on housing and health care; all these disappeared under the burden of the tasks we had set ourselves. Our book is therefore incomplete, but it is a first rather than a final step and we hope the work will be continued both inside and outside CCCS.

The weaknesses of working collectively are more than a matter of missed deadlines. Precisely because the collective whole is greater than the sum of its individual parts, it has been sad to watch the numbers of our group dwindle as we put our ideas on to paper and real conflicts began to emerge. We were always divided by 'racial' and gender differences, and it was unusual to be able to work together at all. The same political differences which took their toll on group membership, were also part of the creative process of production. The truce our final text represents does not imply that the war is over. None of us agrees with every formulation or opinion, and in recognition of this the chapters which follow are credited to their authors. This is no reflection on the depth of collective processes involved.

Those of us who completed the course wish to thank all those who dropped out for their energy and time: Robin Doughty, Duncan Eastoe, Andy Green and Ann Shabbaz. Raghib Ahsan's job at the Rover factory in Solihull prevented him from taking a greater part, and Robin Wilson returned to live in Ireland just as we were nearing the end. All these people are a big part of this book. The internal structure of CCCS makes it easy to spread the blame.

Rajinder Bhogal is far more than just a secretary to the centre; she translated and transcribed interviews which were crucial in the development of our work. The staff at the Institute of Race Relations, particularly Jenny Bourne, were patient over our library demands, always supportive and good-humoured. This book would not have been possible without Stuart Hall's tuition. We have other debts to CCCS where we were always able to have a good argument. It is an exceptionally stimulating place to study. We therefore want to say an extra 'thank you' to those students and staff, past and present, who took us seriously, and provided sisterly and comradely debate – in particular Richard Johnson, Sue McIntosh, Chris Griffin, Bob Willis, Janet Batsleer, Maureen McNeill, Janice Winship and Paul Willis. Claire L'Enfant at Hutchinson was always helpful and patient. Cyrille, Remi, Brendon and Laurie restored on Saturday afternoons the momentum we lost in midweek.

Finally, the 'alien' members of our collective wish to thank their families for substantiating our claim that immigrant households are not pathologically disorganized, and that even if they are this can be productive.

This book is dedicated with love to Rachel Lawrence whose tender years mean that she has a better chance of seeing Babylon queendom fall than the rest of us.

Paul Gilroy
For the Race and Politics Group, November 1981

1 The organic crisis of British capitalism and race: the experience of the seventies

John Solomos, Bob Findlay, Simon Jones and Paul Gilroy

We are witnessing and passively acquiescing in a quiet but hardly bloodless revolution. The induction of general social disorder, uncensored crime and personal negligence have replaced more warlike conduct as the painless way to undermine the stability of the state.

JAMES ANDERTON

The combined assault on English identity and values is neither planned nor fully understood by its participants; its roots often lie deep in the unconscious. Its main force stems from the lack of coherent opposition. Too many people are frightened off by accusations: 'racialist', 'elitist' or simply 'old-fashioned', which make cowards of nearly all.

ALFRED SHERMAN

Introduction

The central theme of this book is that the construction of an authoritarian state in Britain is fundamentally intertwined with the elaboration of popular racism in the 1970s.[1] * The aim of this introductory chapter is more modest. It offers a framework for examining the relation of 'race' to British decline, and attempts a periodization of state racism during the seventies. We hope to provide a more detailed morphology of these transformations in future work.[2]

The parallel growth of repressive state structures and new racisms has to be located in a non-reductionist manner, within the dynamics of both the international crisis of the capitalist world economy, and the deep-seated structural crisis of the British social formation. This idea links the various chapters which follow. Some aspects of it have already been developed by others,[3] but the argument is far from complete. What concerns us, therefore, is not to outline a theory of racist ideologies, but to scrutinize the political practices which developed around the issue of race during the seventies. We have chosen this approach for two basic reasons. First, we believe that it is not possible to understand the complex ways in which state racism works in British society without looking closely at the ways in which it is *reproduced* inside and outside state apparatuses. Second, we feel that it is not possible to see racism as a unitary fixed principle which remains the same in different historical conjunctures. Such a static view, which is common in many sociological approaches,

---

* Superior figures refer to the Notes and references which appear at the end of chapters.

DAILY EXPRESS   JULY 10, 1981

"We'd better do something quick or WE'LL be unemployed..."

London Express Service

Source: Daily Express, 10 July 1981
Reproduced by permission of *Daily Express*

cannot explain how racism is a *contradictory* phenomenon which is constantly transformed, along with the wider political-economic structures and relations of the social formation.[4]

The function of this chapter is twofold – first, to introduce at a more general, and therefore theoretical level, themes which will be covered later on, and second, to explain the way in which certain key concepts have been used. In the second and third sections we shall attempt to analyse, albeit briefly and schematically, some of the main shifts in the relation between the various types of state intervention and the wider organic crisis. Although a number of recent Marxist studies have analysed the deep *economic* roots of the present crisis, we think that this is only part of the story. This is why we emphasize the *organic* nature of the crisis, meaning by this that it is the result of the combined effect of economic, political, ideological and cultural processes. A full historical account of these issues has not been attempted in this book, partly because we feel that this is one area where the recent revival of Marxist political economy has made a substantive contribution.[5] Nevertheless, as a contribution to this debate, we will introduce some discussion of race around which a fuller historical account may be constructed. In the fourth and fifth sections we attempt to show how official thinking on violence, law and order, and race has been closely connected. We establish the origins of these interconnections in debates about violence which began in the sixties and argue that they have assumed a particularly sharp and pernicious form during the seventies. This is because race has increasingly become one of the means through which hegemonic relations are secured in a period of structural crisis management. Although as Chapters 2 and 8 emphasize, we see race as a means through which other relations are secured or experienced, this does not mean that we view it as operating merely as a mechanism to express essentially non-racial contradictions and struggles in racial terms. These expressive aspects must be recognized, but race must also be approached in its autonomous effectivity.

Racism as it exists and functions today cannot be treated simply from a socio-logical perspective: it has to be located historically and in terms of the wider structures and relations of British society. The historical roots of racist practices within the British state, the British dominant classes, and the 'British' working class, go deep and cannot be reduced to simple ideological phenomena. They have been conditioned, if not determined, by the historical development of colonial societies which was central to the reproduction of British imperialism.[6] This process generated a specific type of 'nationalism' pertinent in the formation of British classes long before the 'immigration' issue became a central aspect of political discourse.[7]

We are arguing for a conception of racism which is historical rather than socio-logical. Just as Marxist accounts of the historical links between the specific political structures concentrated in the 'capitalist state' and the course of capitalist develop-ment have emphasized the dynamic nature of political relations, so we would argue that the links between racism and capitalist development are complex, and con-ditioned by the specific socio-political circumstances in which they function. We want to emphasize that ethnic and racial forms of domination are shared not by *exogenous* mechanisms, but by the *endogenous* political economic forces which are dominant in the specific societies under study.[8] It follows from this basic proposition that racial forms of domination do not develop in a linear fashion but are subject to breaks and discontinuities, particularly in periods of crisis which produce qualitative changes in all social relations.

This is how we see the period of the seventies in Britain.

The reorganization of the international division of labour and black workers in Britain

It is important to situate the question of racism in Britain today in a broader international context.[9] Although these links are often ignored in studies of 'race relations' we refuse to study them at our peril. A recent report from the OECD is worth mentioning in this respect, since it points out in a very clear way the need for 'supporting policies' to be instituted to help out national states facing acute social problems. The message contained in this report was tellingly summarized in a *Financial Times* leader called 'Searching for consensus':

Not only the pre-summit row over U.S. interest rates, but also the eight days of street fighting in London, Liverpool and Manchester, have shown that consensus, whether on the international stage or at home, is becoming in dangerously short supply.[10]

It should be made clear that what happened in Britain over the period 1979–81 cannot be reduced to some immutable laws of history which apply to every society at every point of time. Such a reduction avoids difficult problems by attributing the type and direction of the changes occurring to an outside force, some inevitable determinant of all social relations. It is as methodologically distant from a critical Marxist account as the liberal-democratic pluralist framework which dominates the research on race relations in Britain.[11] In opposition to it, we suggest that while the specific forms of racism which exist in Britain today have been shaped by endogenous political-economic forces, they have also been transformed in ways which can only be understood as the result of the qualitative changes in Britain's international position over the last three decades.

Although the disarticulation in labour demand and supply in most European countries since 1973–4 has shown how fragile the position of migrant workers really is,[12] there is a much longer history of decline which underlies the experience of these workers in the period after 1945. Indeed, from a longer-term perspective 'the end of the migrant labour boom'[13] does not look as surprising as it may have done a few years back.

The reproduction of racial and ethnic divisions has been a central feature of accumulation in the post-war period precisely because of the requirement that labour from the colonies and other peripheral economies be used to reorganize the main industrial sectors of the advanced industrial economies. This is a proposition which has received strong support from a number of historical and sociological studies of specific societies,[14] and from a theoretical perspective.[15] But it has tended to be used as a mechanical model of explanation, with the assumption that it is applicable to every situation, and therefore very little advance has been made in substantiating *historically* the variable patterns of absorption and exclusion of migrant labour as they have taken shape in the main European societies. We still have no clear idea of how a 'historically-concrete and sociologically-specific account of distinctive racial aspects'[16] can help us to develop a more critical perspective towards the analysis of racism and its modalities in late capitalism. The elements of such an approach exist in abstract formulations but the process of applying them to concrete situations in an experimental fashion has hardly begun.

Take, for example, recent advances in developing critical accounts of how, in their specific modalities, imperialism, the state and the restructuring of the labour process have shaped the articulation of the different levels of the accumulation process.[17] A number of these approaches, notably those of the debate on the state, have been usefully applied to the study of migration and the processes through which the segmentation of the working class takes place. Yet no attempt has been made to link such studies to issues such as racial/ethnic divisions, which have tended to be consigned to the study of ideologies rather than political economy. Because of this neglect, the field of race has been dominated by narrow sociological studies, and no grounded attempts to locate it within a political economy framework have materialized.

The reorganization of the international division of labour has only belatedly been analysed from the perspective of its implications for migrant workers, although a number of general accounts of a shift from 'labour-import' to 'capital-export' strategies have been written.[18] Such accounts have, however, not been balanced by a parallel attempt to draw out the mediations between the international environment and the operation of individual nation states. A few illuminating remarks have been made by Stuart Hall,[19] Immanuel Wallerstein,[20] Sivanandan[21] and Marios Nikolinakos.[22] But their accounts have tended to remain at too general a level of abstraction to be directly applicable to the contemporary transformations of the politics of migration and ethnic/racial divisions. What they do suggest, however, is the need to apply criteria of historicity and of combined though uneven development to the study of ethnic/racial patterns of domination in late capitalism. Wallerstein, in his historical account of capitalist development, argues correctly that Marxists have too often failed to locate racial, national, or regional divisions materially, and consigned them all too simply to the ubiquitous superstructure. He himself proposes that such divisions are not *exogenous* but *endogenous* to the rearticulation of nation and class which capitalist development brought about:

The development of the capitalist world-economy has involved the creation of all the major institutions of the modern world: classes, ethnic/national groups, households, and the 'state'. All of these structures postdate, not antedate, capitalism; all are a consequence, not cause. Furthermore, these various institutions in fact create each other. Classes, ethnic/national groups and households are defined by the state, and in turn create the state, shape the state and transform the state. It is a structured maelstrom of constant movement, whose parameters are measurable through the repetitive regularities, while the detailed constellations are always unique.[23]

This conception of the interplay between the state and the reproduction of ethnic/ racial differences is important because it situates the operation of the international context within the complex reality of the political and economic forces in each national formation. Moreover it firmly locates the capitalist state as a central mechanism for the articulation and reproduction of such divisions. It thus problematizes both narrow sociological models which take the nation state for granted, and reductionist frameworks which only 'explain' race through displacing it on to economic forces. In his work on mugging, and the position of race and class in the Caribbean, Stuart Hall has developed a similar account of how the reproduction of hegemony is not a stable process but is constantly reshaped and undermined by the operation of the wider socio-economic structures.[24]

It would be against the line of thought developed in this book to think that these general arguments are directly applicable to the complex history of black labour in Britain, both before and after 1948. A number of mediations have to be introduced if we are to analyse how the patterns of 'inclusion' and 'exclusion' of black workers have been transformed over time. Certainly a global view of labour migration is important if we are to break down the idea that racism is an 'aberrant epiphenomenon introducing a dysfunction into the regular social order'.[25] It is also a means by which one can counter what has been called a 'loss of historical memory' and understand the way in which the imperialisms of the past and present secure the transformation of racist practices. According to Stuart Hall the development of racism as a political force has to be understood *sui generis*:

It's not helpful to define racism as a 'natural' and permanent feature – either of all societies or indeed of a sort of universal 'human nature'. It's not a permanent human or social deposit which is simply waiting to be triggered off when the circumstances are right. It has no natural and universal law of development. It does not always assume the same shape. There have been many significantly different *racisms* – each historically specific and articulated in a different way with the societies in which they appear. Racism is always historically specific in this way, whatever common features it may appear to share with other social phenomena. Though it may draw on the cultural and ideological traces which are deposited in a society by previous historical phases, it always assumes specific forms which arise out of the present – not the past – conditions and organisation of society. . . . The indigenous racism of the 60s and 70s is significantly different, in form and effect, from the racism of the 'high' colonial period. It is a racism 'at home', not abroad. It is the racism not of a dominant but of a declining social formation.[26]

This is an argument which will be developed at length, and with reference to con-crete issues, later on. But from the perspective of this section it is important to emphasize the issue raised in the last sentence, about the *specificity* of the sixties and seventies – the period of decline and restructuring. In the context of black settlement in Britain this conceptualization allows us to locate the shaping of racial segmentation in the labour market, residential segregation, legislation to control immigration, and the policing of black working-class areas, as related aspects of organic crisis in the present period. Racisms structure different areas of social life. It is the development of new forms of racism in a phase of relative decline that a materialist analysis of the current situation must explain.

In broad terms, the post-1948 experience of black workers in Britain can be periodized according to three phases: (a) the period of immediate response by the state to the wave of black settlement, leading up to the control of immigration strategy promulgated by the 1962 Act; (b) the articulation of various policy packages to deal with the 'problems' which were seen as associated with a black presence, e.g. in education, the social services, employment, which dominated official thinking up till the early seventies; (c) a period of 'crisis management' which has operated since the early seventies and which prioritizes the option of control and containment of forms of black resistance against racial domination. These phases cannot be said to be discrete, and there is clearly a case to be made that there was a fair amount of overlap between them. Nonetheless, it seems useful to think of the post-war period as one of contradictory changes in the economic and political forms of racial domination, rather than as one of linear patterns of sociological integration.[27] This periodization is also helpful because it elucidates links with changes in other aspects of social life, and with the trans-formation of Britain's economic position in the international arena.

During the latter two periods, as public concern has focused increasingly on the complex definition of social problems and the management of the crisis, we have seen quite fundamental redefinitions of the racial dimension of politics and a reshaping of the national and urban political economy. Although these processes must be given some degree of autonomy, it is still possible to look at the mechan-isms which have secured an articulation between the different levels. In rejecting reductionist forms of analysis we do not believe that it is at the same time necessary to construct race as a *completely* autonomous factor, with no relation to other areas of social reality. We contend that the international context, the material reality of a 'declining social formation', and subsequent transformations in the role of the state, have contributed to the form and trajectory of racisms which have in turn, shaped these relations during the seventies. The following sections concen-trate on these issues, and introduce the main themes which govern the concrete historical analyses presented in the rest of the book.

Racism and authoritarianism in the seventies

The period which this book covers cannot easily be abstracted from what went on before or, more importantly, from the developments which we are witnessing in the first phase of the eighties. Yet there is little doubt that the seventies was a period of major changes in a number of areas, not least in the political field, which will have profound implications for the position of black people in British society. The struggles around the policies of the Conservative Government during 1971–4, the breakup of the 'unity' of the Labour Party during the late seventies, the series of expenditure cuts imposed by both Labour and Conservative administrations, the massive rise in unemployment since 1976, and the imposition of a neo-conservative politics since 1979, may all seem to be issues which are only tangentially related to race as such. But they all have to be looked at as part of the wider politico-economic environment which has conditioned the ways in which race has been experienced.[28] Take for example the role of the state in its various attempts to control vital areas of the economy, social welfare expenditure and the repressive apparatuses. All of these changes have been shaped by the uneven development of political and economic relations during the seventies, and also by changes in the balance of the state apparatuses themselves. Economic policies have been framed around the various stages of the developing organic crisis of accumulation which Britain experienced during this period. But they have also been shaped by a variety of political struggles and other factors which cannot be reduced to a simple reflection of the accumulation processes. The history of 'the cuts' in state expenditure, an uneven process which went through various stages throughout the seventies, illustrates these twin processes,[29] as does the articulation of legal mechanisms in the field of industrial relations to the management of organized labour.[30] We shall discuss later how both policing and the 'race-relations industry' have undergone a parallel process of restructuring.

Most late capitalist states have gone through a period which Poulantzas and others[31] have defined in terms of two shifts: first, a progression from the interventionist *state* of the post-war period to the *technocratic state* of today, which not only acts to meet the needs of processes of production and reproduction but is a constituent element of these processes; and second, the articulation of more specific and organized forms of politically orchestrated domination in every field of social life, and the development in embryonic form of a *state authoritarianism*. This analysis is of course abstract and is not meant as an explanation of what has actually happened to every national state formation. As an analytical tool, however, it can be productive, at least in trying to make sense – from a theoretical perspective – of what has actually happened in Britain over the last decade, and although this approach has been criticized for being determinist, this criticism does not hold for all the applications of this model to concrete situations.[32] Against the backdrop of the fundamental changes which the last two decades have wrought on the political realm, it is important to analyse such developments theoretically as well as historically. The first problem with using a term like *authoritarianism* is that it carries a conspiratorial connotation. Although it should be clear from the concrete analyses of specific state agencies which are contained in later chapters that such a viewpoint could not be further from our own, it may be a useful exercise to state our theoretical distance from it here.

We see the period of the seventies as one in which there was a rapid development of rational forms of direct state control as opposed to more indirect forms of social control. In other words, it is the articulation of an 'all-pervasive state regulation of social and economic processes',[33] rather than partial and intermittent forms of state intervention, which characterizes this period. This has been shown in relation to race-relations legislation by John Lea, who argues that even in the sixties there was a shift in emphasis from integration to social control.[34] In a wider theoretical and comparative framework this has also been substantiated by the work of Poulantzas, Offe and Habermas.[35] Offe argues that the current form of the state can best be characterized by the term the 'crises of crisis management':

Such a definition predisposes one to favour a processual concept of crisis. Crises, then, are developmental tendencies that can be confronted with 'counteracting tendencies', which means that the outcome of crises is quite unpredictable. More-over, this processual form of crisis concept has the advantage of making it possible to relate the crisis-prone developmental tendencies to characteristics of the system; in other words, such developmental tendencies need not be seen as catastrophic events of contingent origin.[36]

In addition, this model allows us to see the specific nature of the state's role today, which is by no means monolithic. Just as the economic crisis of the seventies has taken a unique form – stagflation – so state authoritarianism is a novel phenomenon in capitalist democracies (though as a tendency it has a long history), corresponding neither to the normal liberal-democratic state form, nor to fully exceptional forms like Fascism. Democracy has not been recomposed on a new basis, but neither has the crisis been resolved through the wholesale elimination of democracy. What we have seen, as Poulantzas puts it, is:

Intensified state control over every sphere of socio-economic life combined with radical decline of the institutions of political democracy and with draconian and multiform curtailment of so-called 'formal' liberties, whose reality is being discovered now that they are going overboard.[37]

This schematization of the recent history of the state serves to demonstrate that as hegemony becomes contested, in its various sites of operation in civil society and state, power becomes more concentrated and centralized as the dominant bloc seeks to insulate itself from popular struggles. Since the state is structured by the capacity of one or several classes to realize their specific interests, it is to be expected that policies will not be uniform, but result from a sometimes contra-dictory series of decisions and non-decisions taken to meet perceived or real dangers.

Because political authority in late capitalism is structured so that it selects specific outcomes from an infinite number of possibilities, the state is able to construct a hierarchy of 'political needs' that have to be dealt with. In the case of the restructuring of the social services and the nationalized industries in the period since 1971, what we have seen is not a uniform reduction of levels of expenditure but a hierarchical ordering of priorities in relation to the twin axes of 'reducing inflation' and 'increasing profitability'. Of course, this process has not taken place in a linear manner but has taken shape through a series of negotiations and retreats which have involved shifts and relocations in the formulation of 'needs'.

The state has not been totally successful in its attempt to harmonize contra-dictory social and economic processes. We can see this from its growing interventions in the processes by which crisis is *ideologically* constructed. The state which in 1945 presented itself in the guise of a more humane and socially responsible capitalism, has been pulled into the processes of crisis management. Ravaged by a crisis it cannot control, it is in a sense boxed in, between the inner limit of inadequate response and the outer limit of excessive response. The case of unem-ployment is a clear example of how this politicization of the state tends to over-flow from the political system as such. The state responds to the issue of unemployment reactively rather than positively: it attempts to prevent a 'problem' from becoming too 'serious' rather than to actually produce solutions. This has produced fresh contradictions within the state itself:

Increasingly the state has appeared to absorb all the pressures and tensions of the economic and political class struggle into itself, and then been torn apart, by its conspicuous lack of success – progressively, the various crises take the form of a general crisis of the state as a whole, and rapidly reverberate upwards from their initial starting-points to the higher levels of the legal and political order itself.[38]

This tendency for the state structures to become ensnared by the processes which they themselves set in motion has a long history – but what makes it so pervasive in the current situation in Britain is an overall historical legacy of economic failure and social disintegration. It is this relative paralysis of the state and the fracturing of mechanisms of social control which has produced a new articulation between the state and racism today. But before we examine this in detail, it is necessary to say something more about the ways in which the sharpening of the crisis, and its articulation to more precise and extensive forms of intervention, has been experienced at the ideological level.

We have argued that the current phase of restructuring the state has to be looked at against the background of the intractable and organic nature of the crisis facing British capital, and that the difficult relationship between class power, class conflict and political forms must be understood from a perspective on the inter-national nature of the crisis and the specific ways in which it is reproduced in Britain. These observations point to the fact that the state cannot rely on some simple form of economic intervention to overcome it. This is confirmed by the ways in which neo-conservative ideologies are shifting the locus of crisis causation to the social and political sphere, and by the general inability to develop policies which allow Britain to 'live within its means'.[39] Precisely because 'depression, inflation or other disasters can bring down a government',[40] the organizing principles underlying state intervention cannot ignore the need to maintain the conditions of accumulation, but neither can the state ignore for long the necessity to organize consent. The problem of how to negotiate a balance between economic needs and legitimacy has become the central issue of neo-conservative thinking. Thus according to Lord Hailsham:

The symptoms of our malaise may be economic, may show themselves in price rises, shortages and industrial disputes. But underlying the symptoms is a disease which has destroyed democracies in the past, and the causes of that disease are not economic. They are moral and political and constitutional, and in order to cure it we must reorganise them as such.[41]

The simplicity of this argument is a bit misleading: the medical metaphor not only betrays a fear of the depths of the British crisis, it also indicates a suspicion of the social elements which make up the society. The economic crisis is seen as a symptom with much deeper roots in the social fabric of the 'nation'. So, on the one hand, we have to look at the metaphors which make the crisis comprehensible and, on the other, the periodization of the elements of the crisis as such.

One of the threads which connects the progression from more secure forms of political regulation and technocratic control is the position of 'race' and the practices which it has generated in the experience of crisis. This is why we need to see how the politico-social field has been structured by shifts in material and ideological relations which have constructed race as a pertinent, political force. Precisely because the state has extended its areas of functioning to cover 'moral', 'political' and 'constitutional' issues, it has become possible to bring about a *racialization* of state policies in all areas of social life. We shall see that labour market policy is not the only area in which the issue of race has taken on a central role in planning.

The restructuring of the state is not disconnected from the contradictions immanent in and between structures, neither does it have a predictable outcome. It is part of an ongoing struggle to impose cohesion in the face of contestation. The substantial transformations of the state during the seventies are not simply an outcome of the changes in the economy. To say this would be to confuse long-term tendencies with the immediate causes of change within the state. So it is important to see that the crisis which Britain faced during the seventies, and faces today, is a crisis of hegemony, an 'organic crisis' to use Gramsci's terminology.[42] Its content is not reducible to a cyclic economic crisis in the traditional sense, or a 'crisis of the political system' in the narrow sense. It consists rather of profound changes in the balance of forces, in the class struggle and in the configuration of the class alliances. It is visible in the emergence of new social forces and a specific representation of these changes in the form of crisis management *within* the state itself. This is demonstrated by recent work on the reorganization of state policies during the seventies which[43] discusses the complex ways in which the recognition of

Britain as a 'declining social formation' has affected the development of official responses to real and perceived problems. It is important to understand, therefore, that in terms of both its ideological construction and its material functioning, the state itself is becoming a factor in the reproduction of the organic crisis. Consequently, it is difficult to substantiate the idea that the state can act as a liberal-democratic arbitrator sorting out problems and providing remedies for dysfunctions. This is clearest in the field of economic interventions, and the protracted battle to restructure the relation between the state and the economy which has taken place over the last two decades. It can also be viewed in the areas of education, urban and social policy.[44] Here too the state is increasingly having to cope with a situation which requires a transformation of its own powers to deal with changes in society as a whole: it is in this sense that it is wrong to see the incipient form of authoritarianism which is taking shape as a 'strong state', since it is the outcome of a dialectical interplay between changes in the political field as well.

Following arguments developed by Poulantzas, Jessop and Foucault,[45] we see the seventies as a period during which the following tendencies become manifest (though it should be emphasized that they have by no means reached maturity). First, there has been a rapid concentration of political power in the executive coupled with confusion over the roles of executive, legislative and judicial powers. This has entailed constant intrastate wrangling over the competence of apparatuses associated with these power centres. Second, the decline in the role of bourgeois political parties and the ideological basis on which these parties were founded has accelerated. Third, the political freedoms which have been associated with the ideology of liberal democracy have been severely qualified. This has required shifts in the ideological and repressive apparatuses of the state, but also a reorganization of what Foucault has called the 'micro-physiology of power' or symbolic force. As Poulantzas argues:

We know that the process corresponds to a considerable redeployment of the *legal–police* network, which, in a new form, duplicates, props up, supports and extends the capillary diffusion of the circuits of social control: the power of the police, preliminary administrative investigations, control by the various measures of assistance and surveillance, interpenetration of these circuits and the police apparatus . . . centralisation of files and intelligence thanks to advances in electronics, duplication of the official police by private surveillance networks. In a certain sense, this involves a lifting of the traditional boundaries between the normal and the abnormal (i.e. supposedly 'anti-social' elements); thus, control is shifted from the criminal act to the crime-inducing situation, from the pathological case to the pathogenic surroundings, in such a way that each citizen becomes, as it were, an a priory suspect or a potential criminal.[46]

These transformations cannot be documented in detail here. But it is sufficient in this context to point out that the history of policing and legal relations in the seventies substantiates the claims made by Poulantzas and Foucault. We have witnessed not a simple extension of repression, but a recomposition of relations of power at all levels of society.[47] Although the more overt forms of 'social control' are orchestrated by the police, it is important to note that the whole of society is constituted as a field of social relations structured in dominance. What were once tendencies have taken institutional form during the last few years.

Political debates over the July 1981 uprising have introduced a new range of possible outcomes which demand reassessment of the balance between social control and reform. However, given the objectives of this book we shall not analyse this question further in the abstract. Instead we shall attempt to show the mechanisms through which the presence of black people in Britain has become constructed ideologically as a national problem, thereby rendering them subject to specific and intense forms of control and repression. These themes must be related to the ways in which the developing organic crisis has been expressed as, and defined by, a 'crisis of race relations'. The power of racial symbols and signification has had a profound impact on how the 'crisis of society' is perceived.

Political violence, law and order and the 'enemy within'

The construction of race as a 'problem' has not come about by evolutionary means. It has emerged from a whole series of events: struggles, breaks, and discontinuities[48] which have characterized the development of organic crisis. Before we move on to the specific ways in which race articulates or does not articulate to specific phases of the crisis, we must comment on the ideological axis of these struggles – law and order.

In a recent discussion of the policing of the working-class city Phil Cohen argued that: 'The current crisis in the policing of the working class city has become a crisis of legitimacy for the bourgeois public realm as a whole.'[49] The experience of the various debates over the growth of a violent society, the breakdown of law and order, and the erosion of trust in legitimate order demonstrate this.

Since the sixties, these debates have functioned less as a way of actually changing the situation, i.e. by getting rid of the problem, than as a way of negotiating a more fundamental contradiction: the apprehension of crisis itself.[50] The concern with violence and law and order is easier to understand if we avoid a simple social control model, and see political and legal institutions as arenas in which the balance between social classes is constructed.[51] It would be a mistake to interpret popular concern with violence and law as a simple diversionary measure designed to secure legitimacy by creating a 'false consciousness'. As we have argued above, the development of common-sense images of social phenomena is best understood from a historical perspective, since they are always discontinuous and contradictory. This is because we treat ideology as a material relation which is both determined by and reacts upon the wider social relations. We therefore distance ourselves from manipulative conceptions of ideological relations and emphasize the need to understand the links between 'popular' concerns and the everyday experience of reality. This is how we see the function of ideologies of race and law in the context of the present crisis.[52] The detailed account of the changes in police practices over the last decade has been left for a later chapter, but a few preliminary remarks are necessary at this stage.

The sixties provided a complex of new issues which has rightly led people to see them as a watershed in the development of British society.[53] It is striking how in this period 'violence', 'law and order' and 'permissiveness' became central features of the discourses of all political parties and of the media, eventually being articulated in common sense as threats to 'British' society.[54]

In his discussion of the role of the media in the representation of violence Chibnal periodizes the sixties in the following way:

The notion of the 'violent society' is to be seen to result from the convergence of a criminal violence theme, originating in the mid-sixties, and a political violence theme which developed a few years later.[55]

The construction of these themes in political discourse is only partly reducible to the role of the media; we must relate them to transformations in the wider politico-economic framework. In this perspective, the sixties represent what Gramsci called a condensation of contradictions at all levels of society. This placed violence, permissiveness and later race on the agenda of popular politics. This was also the period in which the post-war consensus over the role of the state in economic and social policies began to break down. It presents a clear example of a crisis of hegemonic relations at the political level.[56] As Stuart Hall and his colleagues have shown, although the sixties are sometimes represented as the high points of the 'permissive society', they are also a period which saw important changes leading to greater separation of decision-making from popular control, and a shift towards an authoritarian response to so-called 'threats' to society. 'Permissiveness' in this sense was a double-edged development, which contained the seeds of authoritarianism even within a liberal discourse. It was one aspect of a new popular politics which *defined* both 'the people' and their desires: 'permissiveness' was not what 'the people' wanted.

The period of Wilsonism from 1964 to 1970 is perhaps the most interesting from this angle, since it is also during these years that race became a core theme in wider political discourse. The 'Wilson experiment', with its detailed plans for transforming the economy, developing further social provisions, and bringing Britain through a new technological revolution, has always been difficult terrain for political historians of the left.[57] It was, after all, a period which the left had welcomed as the dawn of a new era in 1964, and which ended in a dismal defeat in the 1970 election. It seemed to represent the end of the road for the post-war model of social-democratic change, and yet, ironically, it confirmed the fact that the basic dilemmas which Britain faced could not be overcome by the implementation of technocratic models from the top. The Heath Government learned this bitter lesson when in 1971-3 it attempted to run the country on the basis of a concerted attack on the 'power' of the trade unions.[58] But it was Wilson's earlier failures which introduced the notion that ours was not simply an economic problem, but a deep malaise which had taken root in the whole of society.

The idea that 'the nation' is diseased and slowly destroying itself is not new; it has been a recurrent theme in British political discourse. What was new in the sixties was that the threat came to be conceptualized as the 'enemy within' rather than a model of subversion from without.[59] This shift had profound implications for the way black people were perceived, and it reverberated right across the political field. The period 1964–70 witnessed three developments which had brought it about: (a) a growth in forms of extra-parliamentary organizations, particularly among the young, which were outside the traditional channels of political participation, e.g. the student movement, the anti-Vietnam war movement, and on a wider scale the development of mass-based youth subcultures;[60] (b) the development of rank-and-file movements within the trade unions which took up a more combative position in both traditional trade union struggles and in wider political issues;[61] (c) from 1969 the situation in Northern Ireland developed in the direction of a fundamental polarization between the Catholic and Protestant communities, and the British army was used directly as a mechanism of control.[52] Each of these developments had its own specific impact. At a more general level, the categories of crime, sexuality and youth were the raw materials from which the image of the violent society[63] was constructed. These three issues can be used to organize thinking about the transformations that took place in the sixties, and which were to condition how the theme of 'enemies within' would develop in the seventies.

The threat posed to the nation by trade union 'militants'[64] emerged into popular politics during the sixties. Its growing resonance reflects the development of class struggle during this period, particularly when compared to the long boom from 1948 to 1963. More than that, it embodies the decline of the hegemonic political institutions of social democracy, which had achieved a relative class peace during the immediate post-war period. Political representation of the Seamen's Strike of 1966 and the struggles over the reform of trade union legislation during 1968–9 are two clear cases of this process, which is also visible in numerous localized cases.[65] The general trend is clear:

Time and again, in the succeeding decade, the class struggle was to be reconstructed, ideologically, in these terms: the conspiracy against the nations; holding the nation to ransom; the stark contrast between the subversive clique and the innocent worker and his family – the seducers and the seduced.[66]

The unspoken meaning of this discourse on trade unions was that they had come to exercise too much 'power' and, in doing so, to threaten the legitimacy of the state itself. These ideas governed the electoral campaigns of 1970 and 1974 ('who rules the country?'). They have also been a crucial element in the appeal of neo-conservative ideologies in the late seventies. However, terms such as 'militants' and 'agitators' have become vehicles for a more generalized phobia about who the 'enemies of society' actually are.

The fundamental move away from the social-democratic consensus was not limited to the field of working-class struggles. It involved strategic shifts at a number of other levels, including the role of parliamentary institutions, the bureaucracy, the police, and the local authorities. The breakup of the post-war coalition demanded a wholesale rethinking of the function of democratic institutions. This was urged on by the fear that 'too much' democracy could lead to an overload of demands on a state already weakened by both the period of relative economic instability, and the disturbances experienced in the late sixties. In a double sense the years leading up to the seventies were a time of transition:

Politically, in Britain, as elsewhere, the 1968–69 period represents a watershed: the whole fulcrum of society turns, and the country enters, not a temporary and passing rupture, but a continuous and prolonged state of semi-siege. Its meaning and causes, then, and its consequences since, have been neither fully reckoned with, nor liquidated. The political polarisation which it precipitated fractured society into two camps: authority and its 'enemies'.[67]

This 'prolonged state of semi-siege' extended far beyond the shores of Britain, and indeed in the period 1968–70 it took on a more virulent form in countries such as France and Italy. But the oppositions were the same, as the well-known report of the Trilateral Commission on *The Crisis of Democracy* makes clear:

Everywhere one discovers a complete dissociation between the decision-making system, dominated by traditional and often quite rhetorical political debate, and the implementation system, which is the preserve of administrative systems quite often centralised and strong, but usually even more irresponsive when they are centralised and strong. This dissociation is the main cause of political alienation among citizens. It continually nourishes utopian dreams and radical postures and reinforces opposition to the state.[68]

Despite numerous appeals to the good old 'common sense' which the British are supposed to believe in, the fear that political violence (i.e. opposition to the state) would be a reality for some time to come was shared by the major political forces. Their responses differed, but the fear remained the same.

The beginning of the seventies saw not only the self-recognition of a society firmly caught in the grip of 'violence', but general fears of a further slide into lawlessness. The stark choice was between authority and disorder, and there were calls for immediate action. The prevention of further violence, and the comforting realization that even within the existing political structures the limits to change were not firmly set, became the guiding principles of a moral backlash against 'liberalism' and later on against the 'socialism' of the Labour Party.[69] The crisis of the British way of life came to be seen as pervading the economy, social welfare, the schools, the prisons, on the streets, and above all the family. Everywhere there were moles at work. Commenting on 'the red badge of revolution that is creeping across Britain' after the Angry Brigade trial, the *Evening Standard* for once gave form to the hitherto amorphous threat:

These guerrillas are the violent activists of a revolution comprising workers, students, trade unionists, homosexuals, unemployed and women striving for liberation. They are all angry. . . . Whenever you see a demonstration, whenever you see a queue for strike pay, every public library with a good stock of socialist literature – anywhere would be a good place to look. In short there is no telling where they are.[70]

This siege mentality shaped the seventies, in much the same way that the fear of the future had helped to construct the image of violent society in the sixties. Even as the crisis took shape, a new range of political possibilities had been created by the realization that *these* enemies could not be countered by traditional methods. A new range of strategies and of political outcomes developed with the awareness that the consensus which had been taken for granted for so long had broken down.

During this period, transformations in the *form* of state power were secured through a political discourse which emphasized the drift of British society into 'violence' and 'disorder' as a way of securing and reordering the relative balance between the ideological and repressive roles of the state. This is particularly true of the ways in which the policing role came to be defined but it was also a clear tendency in the fields of industrial relations, social welfare, and race relations.[71] Both the Heath Government from 1971–4, and the period of the Labour Government (1974–9) saw a popularization of these themes. Though there was simultaneously a marked increase in the level of racist violence against black communities – particularly in the form of 'Paki-bashing' – the 'violent society' and the consequent threat to the existing order of things was not redefined by these crimes. The issue of the day became 'political violence' rather than the 'criminal violence' of the train robbers and Kray twins. There was a concerted attempt to counteract the tendency for political action to take a 'violent' form.

In his study of these developments, *Britain in Agony*, Richard Clutterbuck provides a clear statement of this position:

The 1970s were agonising years for the British people, who felt frustrated, humiliated and insecure. By British standards they were exceptionally violent years. Economic performance was dismal. British society, instead of drawing together as it has more often done in past crises, seemed to become more cantankerous, less generous and less compassionate.[72]

From an explicit social control perspective, Clutterbuck moves on to explore the relation of merely criminal violence to its subversive counterpart:

Political violence should be treated more seriously than criminal violence, not only because it has a more arrogant motivation, but also because it affects the lives of more of the community. . . . Crimes of violence have increased alarmingly and, for robbery with violence and rape, the courts will send a man to jail for several years. But some magistrates seem to regard political violence as more morally forgivable than violence for personal gain.[73]

He attempts to rationalize a *perceived* change in the 'social basis' of violence during the seventies.[74] This required commensurate shifts in official discourse and in the legal–police apparatuses which proceed to counter the danger of 'violence' being used to change the nature of society. Clutterbuck's notion of political violence is predictably elastic. It includes various forms of dissent which, by their very nature, involve physical contact with symbols of authority, but which are not intrinsically violent nor illegal, for example picketing, demonstrations etc. Hall *et al.* have shown in their study of 'mugging'[75] that changes in the use of language can be indicative of wider shifts in the balance of power in society. The passing of notions like the 'violent society' and 'the breakdown of law and order' into common parlance reflected transformations in the form of authority, political participation and social relations which undermined the legitimacy of the state. This process has taken place while the system has been under severe pressure to 'deliver the goods'.[76] These shifts, more than anything else, conditioned the development of the crisis of political authority which Britain experienced in the seventies.

The battle lines between 'society' and its 'enemies' were more clearly drawn by the end of the seventies than they had been for decades. This was because responses to the crisis had taken a specific course, with hegemony being secured on the basis of ever more loose definitions of the 'enemy within'. The cause of the crisis was constructed through ideas about externality and criminality which supported a view of blacks as an 'outside' force, an alien *malaise* afflicting British society.

It was a short step from seeking to explain the crisis through the unions, to linking the unions with violence and terrorism.[77] By the mid-seventies it was possible to present blacks as the main danger to society. Anything could be blamed, so long as it was not capitalism itself. This is a common feature of all legitimation crises:

Official discourse on law and order confronts legitimation deficits and seeks discursively to redeem them by denial of their material genesis. Such denial establishes an absence in the discourse. This absence, the Other, is the silence of a world constituted by social relations, the reality of which cannot be appropriated by a mode of normative argument which speaks to and from its own self-image via an idealised conception of justice.[78]

The processes by which this 'denial' came to operate by racial differentiation constitute the main concerns of this book. We aim to show how the material conditions which have reorganized state racism over the seventies are deeply rooted in the *present*, and gain power from the ways in which the organic crisis of British capitalism is being experienced. This is the argument we want to outline in the last section of this chapter.

Making sense of the crisis: the centrality of race

In the wake of the election of the Conservative Government in 1979 an important official debate has taken place about the position of black people in Britain.[79] In *Hansard* one can find many humorous, and some not so humorous, attempts to produce watertight definitions of exactly who is 'British' and who 'is not'. It is important that we are clear what such debates are about: they are an aspect of a much broader attempt to bring some kind of order into a society which is widely perceived to be falling apart. They are part of a struggle to 'make sense' of a conjuncture where all that is good and wholesome seems to be under threat.[80] It should be no surprise that the management of 'good race relations' has assumed a central and expressive role in the context of this deep-seated crisis. For what is seen to be at stake in the arena of race is the survival of the existing order of things. Alfred Sherman, a key figure among right-wing ideologists, has articulated these fears:

The imposition of mass immigration from backward alien cultures is just one symptom of this self-destructive urge reflected in the assault on patriotism, the family – both as a conjugal and economic unit – the Christian religion in public life and schools, traditional morality, in matters of sex, honesty, public display, and respect for the law – in short, all that is English and wholesome.[81]

The convergence of these fears around the idea of a threatening black presence (always codified as 'immigration') cannot be reduced to economic factors. Economic decline preceded popular acknowledgement of crisis, and the expulsion of blacks as a solution to national problems has a long history in British political thought. There is a lot to learn about how material conditions in urban areas have been affected by the crisis, how youth have been affected by unemployment, etc. But none of these areas can properly be understood if we do not acknowledge the ways in which 'race' is used to construct explanations and therefore consent, where crisis management is the goal of popular politics.

There is no one-to-one correspondence between the 'crisis of race' and the economic crisis. Yet race is always present, whether the issue under discussion is the growth of unemployment, the role of the police in inner-city areas, or the recent 'riots' in a number of major cities. The complexity of this signification demonstrates that the history or racisms in British society cannot be grasped by a simple formulaic reduction of races to some immutable economic base. There are many political/historical factors which condition the relation of race to the current crisis; all need careful study. The specific circumstances which have generated a new racism are not the result of autonomous racial conflicts any more than they are the outcome of some abstract laws of capitalist development. The contextualization of racism today demands analysis of both the racial and non-racial elements which constitute the complex totality within which it functions:

At the economic level, it is clear that race must be given its distinctive and 'relatively autonomous' effectivity, as a distinctive feature. This does not mean that the economic is sufficient to found an explanation of how these relations concretely function. One needs to know how different racial and ethnic groups were inserted historically, and the relations which have tended to erode and transform, or to preserve these distinctions through time – not simply as residues and traces of previous modes, but as active structuring principles of the present society. Racial categories alone will not provide or explain these.[82]

The new morphology of racism which has developed in the seventies needs to be located against the background of these social relations, which have been drastically reorganized by overall conditions of crisis. In every field of social life there is talk of a crisis, whether it be a temporary fiscal problem or a much deeper crisis of confidence in the existing order. As far as 'solutions'[83] are concerned, there is a tendency for *ad hoc* interventions to be proposed, only to be superseded by new 'problems'. The crisis is insoluble. In this context, race relations have become the central aspect of attempts to orchestrate politically – and therefore to manage – the effects of organic crisis. We must locate the pertinence of 'race' within this *hegemonic* struggle and assess its articulation by and with the processes which secure economic, ideological and political power and domination. A few tentative propositions follow as to how this should proceed.

The first point is that the term 'articulation' needs to be used precisely: as a concept which means that race *joins together* the various elements of the organic crisis and the ways in which they are experienced, but also that it *gives expression* at the political and ideological levels to specific forms of control aimed at black people.[84] The meshing of these two meanings can be most clearly seen in relation to issues of rising unemployment, cuts in welfare expenditure, the crisis of the local state, and the reorganization of the forces of law and order. It can be seen at work in the common-sense neo-conservatism of Sir Keith Joseph, who has been known to explain the relative decline of the inner cities and some regions 'through' race.[85] Popular representation of the recent 'riots' in Bristol, Brixton and July 1981 shows how racial and therefore cultural conflict systematizes and 'explains' both what is happening, and what might happen in the future.[86] In any discussion of unemployment, for example, race 'slips' in, whereas ten years ago the issue would have been ignored. Keith Middlemas, a critical Tory thinker, expresses some of these linkages very clearly:

What will Britain look like after even three years of 2 million unemployed? Divisions, which for half a century governments have tried to abolish will show nakedly, between the two geographical Englands, with Scotland, Wales and North Ireland on the periphery, like the Italian Mezzogiorno, between those in work and unemployed; between the mature and the young, between white and black.[87]

The seamless location of 'white and black' among a wide variety of other divisions shows the way in which the crisis of the seventies was lived through race. By situating race amidst the new realities of structural change and economic uncertainty that characterize the present conjuncture, it also provides a glimpse of the meaning of what we have called the new racism.

The quotation from Middlemas reflects one of the main strands of thinking about race in the seventies. It places a number of seemingly 'non-racial' phenomena on a par with race; with the implication that a solution to the problem of the divisions between white and black must be sought in the wholesale transformation of the wider conditions which produce and maintain consensus. The other strand in the dominant approach to 'race' in the seventies has been to present the 'race problem' as comprised of the black communities themselves. The earlier quotation from Alfred Sherman is a good example of how this argument operates, as is the following from the Nationality Bill debate:

On the issues dealt with by the Bill we are in the grip of forces which, because of the large influx of immigrants into Britain, we now seem unable to control. Racial violence is occurring with increasing frequency. The British people are sick at heart about it all. We badly need honest and forthright politicians to express their feelings without fear of being condemned on moral grounds.[88]

This image of forces beyond the control of ordinary 'British people' is a recurrent theme in neo-conservative racist 'theory', particularly since it fits in with the common-sense notion that 'enemies within' – subversive moles – are undermining the structures of society. It connects with common-sense ideas about *why* racial 'problems' arise by identifying 'racial violence' as a result of an illegitimate alien presence. The unseen 'illegal' immigrants are central to this political discourse. Their very illegality ensures that the British resentment which perpetrates violence on 'Pakis' is scarcely more than rough justice provoked by foreign interlopers. In the context of mass unemployment, deindustrialization, and major outbreaks of social violence, old-style 'Powellism' was not an adequate mode through which the crisis could be rendered intelligible. The late seventies saw a transformation of racist ideology which took account of these new realities, and provided a more adequate though nonetheless racist interpretation of what was happening. Those reworkings have taken place along two main lines.

First, there has been a consistent attempt to pin down the dangers posed by specific groups of the black population: the illegals, the young, the militants, the unemployed, and even the white traitors who identify with an 'alien culture'.[89] This involves recognition of the 'deep social problems' revealed by black poverty, as well as a concerted attempt to control the antisocial disruption which is considered to be a consequence of the encounter between 'deprivation' and pathological 'immigrant' cultures. Second, a reworking of the concepts of 'nation' and 'citizen' has taken place which aims to deny even the possibility that black people can share the native population's attachment to the national culture – God, Queen and country. This presents the common-sense logic of repatriation or 're-emigration':

The United Kingdom is the national homeland of the English, Scots, Welsh, Ulster-men. . . . They wish to survive as an identifiable national entity . . . they have been willing to work, suffer and die for it. By contrast, for the jet-age migrants, Britain is simply a haven of convenience where they acquire rights without national obligation.[90]

In crisis conditions, these ideas accord with a mythology which has very deep roots in English popular culture. The essence of this culture has, after all, depended on a kind of historical forgetfulness which reworks the whole meaning of 'Britishness' in powerful images of the purity of nation, family and way of life, now jeopardized by the alien, external wedge. For this culture, even the imagery of the 'enemy within' has a particular resonance in terms of race. Subversion is un-British. The overall context of a society rapidly becoming conscious of its own shortcomings, of an entropy of political thought, and the consequent need to 'pull together' in order to survive made the issue of race an important signifier of the crisis. This may be clearer now that the post-Bristol 'riots' have placed the issues of race and political violence explicitly on the political agenda. But the roots of the inferential interconnections go much deeper than the recent events. For over a decade now, race has been situated, primarily through the discourse of Powellism, as a specific social problem which has been imposed from *outside*.[91] As the bastard children of Empire set up 'camps' in the heartlands of the mother country, a degree of *internalization* has been forced on the reluctant Briton. The blacks are now a home-grown problem. They are in Britain but not of Britain.

Since the first signs of disturbances in major inner-city black areas, the response of the state has been (a) to prepare the police forces to deal with 'the fire next time', and (b) to inject fiscal resources into the depressed areas to help with specific social problems by initiating schemes to deal with what are seen as the 'causes' of increasing violence and a breakdown of law and order.

This is not crude monolithic state strategy, and these two elements of a response have not always been successfully integrated, nor been applied equally in every case of locally centred 'race' disturbances. At a macro-level, however, one should not underestimate the extent to which the preventive/ameliorative measures are being backed by a steady strengthening of security forces. Where admitted, this has been presented as an insurance measure, rather than the frontline of defence. But, since the 1979 police riot in Southall, it should be clear that this insurance policy is flexible if not tactical. A leading political commentator on *The Sunday Times* recently assessed the risks of the present situation in the following way:

What are the risks to British society? It is fanciful, no doubt, to envisage brown shirts and red brigades coming out on the streets. It may be tendentious to predict that Britain might join these nations whose most successful members must protect themselves and their population behind barbed-wire and armed guards. All this is no doubt a worst-possible scenario. But it is one the government should be thinking about.[92]

The reality of the 'worst-possible scenario' is precisely what has concerned the state over the last few years. Of course there is still an important gap between Powellism, the extreme right, and state racism – but with the concept of 'humane repatriation' looming ever more centrally in official thinking on race it need not be conspiratorial to talk of a shift in the balance of state responses from amelioration to repression. At the level of everyday practices the oppressive aspects of the state's role have been felt throughout the seventies: by black youth, by black workers engaged in industrial disputes, and at the territorial level by whole black communities.[93] What has happened over the last period, particularly since 1976, is a qualitative strengthening of these repressive measures. This has been demonstrated time and time again by numerous official and academic studies,[94] as well as in the anger of blacks themselves.

These moves can only partially be explained by the tendency for racism to show a close relation to the tempo of crisis management. Race must be given its own autonomous effectivity in any account of the present; it makes every black person a priori a suspect, a potential criminal, a potential agitator. During the series of 'riots' from early 1980 to July 1981 the fixing of a number of 'causes' to these events within official explanations, located race as one variable among others , including social, economic and local issues.[95] Yet within the popular consciousness, and not just the media, the issue of race came to occupy the central role in common-sense accounts of *why* the riots have taken place in specific areas. The press coverage of the events took a number of forms, some of which will be looked at more carefully later on in the book. But there can be no denying that race, even at the level of metaphor, was a crucial variable in explanations of the Bristol, Brixton and the July 1981 'riots'.[96]

When Enoch Powell asked in a House of Commons debate 'in which town or city does the honourable Gentleman (Mr Whitelaw) expect the next pitched battle against the police to be fought?', he did not need to make the race dimension overt for everybody to understand what he meant.[97] Coverage by the *Daily Mail, Sun, Daily Express* and *Daily Telegraph* during July 1981 needs no elaboration. Even the more 'liberal' views of *The Financial Times* and *Guardian* place race supreme among numbers of other factors as the common denominator of the riots.[98] *The Financial Times*, for example, under the banner headline 'Outbreak of an alien disease', reflected on the events in a typical manner:

Like an epidemic of some alien disease, to which the body politic has no immunity, street riots have erupted in different parts of England during the past ten days. . . . It is in a way all the more disturbing that there are so many conflicting explanations of the past week's violence. Riots in different towns seem to have been sparked off by rather different factors: in Southall by racial fear and racial hatred; in Liverpool perhaps by a tradition of lawlessness and rivalry between police and idle, frustrated youngsters; in Manchester apparently by imitation of their Liverpool neighbours; and perhaps worst of all, in parts of London, by what appears to be pure criminality and greed. For if there are so many forces which are capable of sending hundreds of youths onto the rampage – youths of all races, and living in relatively prosperous areas such as London, not just suffering from desperate deprivation – then the problem of restoring order and respect for law may be all the greater.[99]

It is worth taking note that this 'alien disease' theme is shared by openly racist political groups, which have given it an extra edge by greater emphasis on the cure – repatriation.[100] However, even when the social problems of unemployed or poor inner-city people are discussed rather than the 'immigration problem' *per se*, racial signification and explanations gain the upper hand. It should be understood that there is no necessary contradiction between the institutions of the welfare state, and the intensification of social control required by crisis management. The details of the police response to this situation will be discussed later, but it is useful to outline the state's political responses to the post-Bristol situation.

After the Southall events of April 1979, the crisis management approach to race has taken two forms. One, generally associated with the Labour Party, the Liberals and a section of the Conservative Party, prioritizes 'social engineering' experiments aimed at improving the urban environment as well as strengthening law and order; a second, which is upheld by the majority of the Conservatives and the fringes of the political right, holds that law and order must come first, and that any reforms should proceed through the due process of law.[101] In the House of Commons debate on Civil Disturbances held on 16 July 1981 the basic features of these approaches were presented in some detail.

It is important to avoid a binary counter-position where at the level of political strategies there is either a conspiratorial attempt to control black people or a policy of social reform.[102] For throughout the sixties and seventies race-relations legislation has been neither completely 'progressive' nor 'socially controlling'. It reflected both a reform and a control element, which attempted to secure the 'problem' of race as part of an overall political agenda. It is in this complex, and ultimately contradictory, way that the response to the growing activism and self-organization of black people is likely to develop over the next decade. As such it is likely that it will also be subject to contradictory outcomes.[103] Nevertheless, it is important to look seriously at the *popular* alternative which is being advocated by the right in Parliament and by racist organizations on the streets; that is, the issue of repatriation. The discourse of repatriation is rooted in the reality of the present crisis, even though some elements of its ideological construction have been carried over from the past. It has been restructured and reorganized by the materiality of the employment crisis, by the thematization of violence, and by the rapid decline of inner-city areas. The pivot of this rearticulation is the location of 'racial problems' as historical invariables to the extent that remaking history itself becomes a method of ideologically constructing the need for re-patriation. The 'facts' are taken as given because the last two decades are supposed to have 'proved' that as the black population grew, violence and disorder became the order of the day. Traces of black life have been removed from the British past to ensure that blacks are not part of the British future.

It is precisely the weight of this history which allows Powell to penetrate the walls of official thinking even when his 'solutions' are specifically rejected. After the July 1981 riots he spoke of the inevitability of 'civil war' if the black population rose in line with his predictions.[104] In rebutting both the Conservative and Labour strategies he voiced an alternative view of causation:

The Government and the House will not be serving the country unless they address themselves to the ultimate reality, the ultimate cause, the *sine qua non*, without which what we have witnessed and are witnessing could not and would not have happened. . . . [Mr Hattersley] gave three causes – poverty, unemployment and deprivation. Are we seriously saying that so long as there is poverty, unemployment and deprivation, our cities will be torn to pieces, that the police in them will be the objects of attack and that we shall destroy our own environment? Of course not. Everyone knows that, although those conditions do exist, there is a factor – the factor which the people concerned perfectly well know, understand and apprehend, and which unless it can be dealt with – unless the fateful inevitability, the inexorable doubling and trebling, of that element of a population can be avoided – their worst fears will be fulfilled.[105]

We have quoted this argument at length because it is important to note the ways in which even when race is not mentioned in so many words, it is the 'element' which cements common-sense notions of why violence is increasing, and why the existing order is under stress. Powell's idea of an 'ultimate cause' intersects with popular racist notions at the level of everyday experience and becomes a central means of explaining why the country is 'going to the dogs'.

Repatriation is not a political strategy that can be put into large-scale practice at this particular time, not least because blacks will not countenance it. As the task of policing and managing black working-class areas becomes even more difficult, calls for a final solution to the 'problem' of race are likely to increase. Sections of the Conservative Party have already debated the appropriate financial inducement. But the outcome of these struggles cannot be judged from here. Options for state responses to the 'alienation of black youth' supposedly revealed by 'the riots' are already taking shape. It would clearly be false to argue that the state will respond simply through either greater repression or ameliorative measures of social control. There *is* a strong element of both these approaches in proposals being considered in policy-making channels.[106] The unsteady terrain on which the police have been operating has already led to a reworking of their tactics in inner-city areas.[107] No doubt, in time, we shall see the development of policies for all areas of social life which aim to control and contain the 'social' problems which government policies have done much to reproduce.[108] Piecemeal responses should not be seen as the guiding principle of all the state's actions in this field. It is incorrect to maintain a modified pluralist framework, whereby each of these responses is seen as liable to negotiation on its own terms, e.g. the current attempts to reform policing and the development of 'new' policies for the inner-city areas. The transformations in the role of the state are structural, and should not be confused with the *ad hoc* policy alternatives which appear in the political arena. The fundamental reworking of state policies which took place in the sixties, and accelerated during the seventies, secured a new balance of hegemonic relations, a tendency which we have called *authoritarian statism*. It is foolish to think of the state as some kind of immobile object which suddenly awakens to the riots, and could be swayed either way by sound arguments. Such a situation, if it has ever existed, is not the one which confronts us today. We are faced with a state that is in the process of fundamental change, which cannot be reduced to a conscious will, and which is the outcome of complex determinations at all levels of British society.

As shown in later chapters (particularly Chapters 2 and 8) the restructuring and strengthening of state racism in the current period has been periodized and punctuated by the operation of racist practices and by the contradictory effects of crisis management. The aftermath of the recent 'riots' undoubtedly represents a watershed in the development of state racism, but we should avoid the temptation to think about it in outdated categories. The response of the state to the perceived and real 'dangers' of this period will take novel forms which cannot be understood through a simple dichotomy of reform/repression. We are likely to see policies which display a fluid combination of preventive and repressive options, which will be moved one way or the other according to the balance of forces. The accelerated pace of development in the 'race-relations industry' over the past few years is therefore a sign of things to come, as is the intensified policing of working-class black areas. This is why the choices of resistance and struggle which black communities are making must not be fitted into narrow models of political action which assume that liberal-democratic forms of government are the only forms possible in late capitalism. They must be seen for what they are: a response which has been conditioned by popular racism, state racism and the intensity of the racist attacks against black communities in many inner-city areas.[109]

The everyday struggles of blacks against the racism of capitalist command are the ground on which the state and its agencies will attempt to develop mechanisms of containment and counter-insurgency. They also supply 'facts' from which new elements of racist ideologies will be constructed, at the level of official discourse and on the streets. They raise issues which have a wider importance than the immediate scope of the struggles themselves. As Stuart Hall remarked, in his account of the recent riots:

The police–black front is the front line: policing and the drift into authoritarian social control are front-line issues. Nevertheless, responding to the riots is not a matter of defending civil rights or of 'being nice to black people'. Rioting and civil disorder grow out of and reflect back on what is happening to the working class as a whole and to society as the crisis cuts into the latter at all levels. The riots are only the outward, if dramatic, symptoms of this inner unravelling of our social, political and community life.[110]

In this wider, deeply social sense, the long-term implications of recent events are likely to be profound. They show that the articulation of race to the organic crisis has resulted in important contradictions for the state, which will sharpen as the crisis involves more and more groups in the front line. The problems this poses for the state are being assessed within various state agencies, with the help of the race-relations industry. The left has hardly attempted to sift the complex issues involved, let alone think about them. Yet without carefully working through the issue of race and crisis, it is inconceivable that they will come up with an adequate response to the development of repressive policies, and popular authoritarianism.

Conclusion: stepping into the eighties

Whole histories remain to be written about the experience of black workers in this country. In this book we aim to produce some elements of that history, which we hope will form a basis for further research. Because of our deep dissatisfaction with the dominant approaches to 'race-relations theory', which tend to concentrate on either narrow empirical studies or descriptive interview surveys, we have attempted to locate our own work within a broader theoretical framework which derives much from recent Marxist discussions on the nature of contemporary capitalism. We are aware that this approach has its own problems, but we feel it to be a necessary step in the current context of debates on racism.

Broadly speaking, there are four conclusions which can be drawn from our discussion so far, some of which will be elaborated in the chapters which follow. The first step in breaking down the dominant conceptions of 'race relations' is to locate histories of racism firmly within a framework which establishes that it is reproduced by endogenous political-economic forces, not by exogenous mechanisms. Second, it is important to see that the changes in the *form* of racism during the seventies were forged in the crucible of the struggles waged by black people against the patterns of domination imposed by the manner of their incorporation into the relations of production, as well as by the practices involved in their political and cultural forms of resistance. Third, we have argued that although the ways in which the 'crisis of race relations' has been conceptualized cannot be separated from the general crisis of hegemony which has afflicted British capitalism, it would be wrong for analysis to stop there. We need to analyse race in terms of its *specific* forms at *different* periods of time in order to see how it articulates – or not – with other social relations. Fourth, we argue that in a context of emerging authoritarianism and a strengthening of repressive agencies, there is little hope that reformist strategies will fundamentally improve the material conditions which confront black people in their daily struggle to survive in British society.

The full development of these arguments is beyond the scope of this book, but we do believe that individual chapters have developed them to a sufficiently high level to sponsor new areas of concrete investigation and to illuminate a number of important phenomena articulated to the structural position of black people in the dominant social relations. We would not claim to have 'finished' this discussion, but it does seem to us that the questions we raise need to be considered more seriously than they have been in the past. If this discussion takes place we will have served a useful role in sensitizing others to an understanding of both the deep roots of racism in Britain, and the need to move beyond simple reform in order to overcome racism. This is why in the midst of the depressing story we tell, we feel able to maintain some optimism about what can be achieved if the oppressed organize to change the conditions of their daily existence. The experience of the black masses during the decade of the seventies has alerted us to what underlies the superficial appearance of the British state: namely that the normal processes of political authority, when they cannot proceed by co-operation, proceed through confrontation, and, at a higher level, through the state's orchestration and legitimation of repression. This is a very dangerous time, and those who are interested in transforming the material conditions of contemporary capitalism must not mistake a situation of crisis for the collapse of capitalist relations of domination. As Friedrich Pollock once remarked, albeit in a different historical context: 'What is coming to an end is not capitalism but its liberal phase'.[111] This may be a more fruitful way of looking at current realities than the rather dubious attempts to develop modes of political action which are premised on the continued existence of a liberal-democratic state.

Acknowledgments

In writing this chapter we have incurred a number of debts which we would like to acknowledge. Apart from helpful discussions over a number of months with other members of the group, we have benefited especially from detailed discussion with Robin Wilson and Errol Lawrence. Robin Wilson co-operated with us in the early stages of writing this chapter. Outside the group we would like to thank the following for various types of support and help: Martin Barker, Ann Walters and Mike Cowen. In addition the late Neil Williamson was instrumental in helping us develop some ideas expressed in the chapter. Christine Dunn and Rose Goodwin were helpful in typing successive drafts with patience. In addition our common enthusiasm for West Bromwich Albion was important in showing us the value of good teamwork.

Given the nature of recent political developments it is important to note that the final version of this chapter was completed in July 1981.

Notes and references

1   On the links between racism and authoritarianism the classic texts are those of Stuart Hall and his colleagues, in addition to the work represented by the journal *Race and Class*. But see the following for a general outline of these positions: S. Hall *et al.*, *Policing the Crisis* (Macmillan 1978); S. Hall, 'The law's out of order', *Guardian*, 5 January 1980; A. Sivanandan, 'Race, class and the state', *Race and Class*, vol. 17, no. 4 (1976), pp. 347–68.

2   We envisage this work developing along a number of axes, which are difficult to specify at this stage. But, in particular we would like to look further at the

historical background of black workers in Britain, the complex morphology of legal-administrative organization of race relations, and the development of common-sense racism in the context of crisis management.

3 For a summary presentation of the basic aspects of Hall's approach see: 'Race, articulation and societies structured in dominance', in UNESCO, *Sociological Theories: Race and Colonialism* (Paris 1980). In addition a useful intervention in this debate has been made by G. Carchedi in his: 'Authority and foreign labour: some notes on a late capitalist form of capital accumulation and state intervention', *Studies in Political Economy*, no. 2 (Autumn 1979), pp. 37–74.

4 Here we should not be seen as arguing that there is a one-to-one correspondence between the transformation of racism and the changes in the wider economic framework. But we would wish to maintain that there is a relationship between the two and that this involves relations of detérmination. In this sense we would take issue with the approach popularized by Hindess and Hirst which relies on a notion of necessary non-correspondence. In the field of race this is associated with the work of John Gabriel and Gideon Ben-Tovim which we discuss in Chapter 7. An outline of this approach can be found in their article on: 'Marxism and the concept of racism', *Economy and Society*, vol. 7, no. 2 (1978), pp. 118–54.

5 An outline of these debates can be found in: John Urry, *The Anatomy of Capitalist Societies: The Economy, Civil Society and The State* (Macmillan 1981). But for more critical accounts see: E. Wright, *Class, Crisis and the State* (New Left Books 1978); B. Jessop, 'Recent theories of the capitalist state', *Cambridge Journal of Economics*, vol. 1 (1977), pp. 353–73; H. Gintis and S. Bowles, 'Structure and practice in the labour theory of value', *Review of Radical Political Economics*, vol. 12, no. 4 (1981), pp. 1–26.

6 These issues are usefully discussed by: K. Post, *Arise Ye Starvelings: The Jamaican Labour Rebellion of 1938 and its Aftermath* (The Hague 1978); P. S. Gupta, *Imperialism and The British Labour Movement* (Macmillan 1975; W. R. Louis, *Imperialism at Bay 1941–1945: The United States and the Decolonisation of the British Empire* (Oxford University Press 1977).

7 See: R. Benewick, *The Fascist Movement in Britain* (Allen Lane 1973). For a longer historical perspective see: D. A. Lorimer, *Colour, Class and the Victorians* (Leicester University Press 1978).

8 For a detailed analysis of this argument see: Hall, 'Race, articulation and societies', particularly pp. 336 ff.

9 This is an argument developed in greater detail in: J. Solomos, 'Urban social policies, migrant workers and political authority', in J. Solomos (ed.), *Migrant Workers in Metropolitan Cities: A European Perspective* (North Holland Press 1982).

10 *The Financial Times*, 11 July 1981.

11 In the field of race the pluralist framework tends to be an underlying theme in most debates rather than a conscious theoretical effort. But precisely because it remains unspoken and relies on common-sense notions of the relations of power in our society its tendency is to foster debates about the role of policy changes which take the possibility of reform for granted. In this sense it fits into the traditional pluralist power framework, albeit with a racial

dimension. For criticisms of the pluralist paradigm see: R. Benewick, 'Politics without ideology: the perimeters of pluralism', in R. Benewick *et al.* (eds.), *Knowledge and Belief in Politics* (Allen and Unwin 1973); W. Connolly, *The Terms of Political Discourse* (D. C. Heath 1974).

12   See: Carchedi, *passim*; S. Castles, 'Structural racism: ethnic minorities in Western Europe', paper prepared for World Council of Churches Programme to Combat Racism, 1980.

13   R. Cohen, 'The end to the migrant labour boom', *Newsletter of International Labour Studies*, no. 10 (April 1981).

14   Two of the main studies are: S. Castles and G. Kosack, *Immigrant Workers and Class Structure in Western Europe* (Oxford University Press 1973); G. Freeman, *Immigrant Labour and Racial Conflict in Industrial Societies* (Princeton University Press 1979).

15   M. Nikolinakos, 'Notes towards a general theory of migration in late capitalism', *Race and Class*, vol. 17, no. 1 (1975), pp. 5–17; M. Castells, 'Immigrant workers and class struggles in advanced capitalism: the West European experience', in R. Cohen *et al.* (eds.), *Peasants and Proletarians* (Monthly Review Press 1979).

16   Hall, 'Race, articulation and societies structured in dominance', p. 336.

17   All of these debates are very complex and it is not feasible to take account of them in detail within the terms of reference of this book. But in specific cases we have referred to these debates to support our own analysis of events during the seventies. A useful attempt to apply some of these theoretical advances historically can be found in: M. Reich, *Racial Inequality: A Political-Economic Analysis* (Princeton University Press 1981).

18   For a summary presentation of these arguments see: F. Froebel *et al.*, 'The world market for labour and the world market for industrial sites', *Journal of Economic Issues*, vol. 12, no. 4 (1978), pp. 843–58; A. Sivanandan, 'Imperialism and disorganic development in the silicon age', *Race and Class*, vol. 21, no. 2 (1979), pp. 111–26.

19   Hall, 'Race, articulation and societies structured in dominance', *passim*.

20   I. Wallerstein, *The Capitalist World Economy* (Cambridge University Press 1979), particularly Part 2.

21   A. Sivanandan, 'Imperialism and disorganic development in the silicon age'.

22   M. Nikolinakos, 'The new dimensions in the employment of foreign workers' (Berlin 1975).

23   I. Wallerstein, 'The state in the institutional vortex of the capitalist world economy', unpublished paper 1980, pp. 3–4.

24   S. Hall, 'Pluralism, race and class in Caribbean society', in UNESCO, *Race and Class in Post-Colonial Society* (Paris 1977).

25   D. Lecourt, 'Marxism as a critique of sociological theories', in UNESCO, *Sociological Theories: Race and Colonialism* (Paris 1980), p. 284.

26   S. Hall, 'Racism and reaction', in Commission for Racial Equality, *Five Views of Multi-Racial Britain* (CRE 1978), p. 26. The notion that the racism of the seventies is historically specific is important to our own understanding of what we have come to see as the 'new racism'. We would also wish to place special emphasis on Hall's remarks concerning links between the present and cultural and ideological traces from the past. This forms the subject matter

of part of the next chapter.

27   This is a view which we attempt to substantiate in a number of chapters in this book and one which needs much more work done on it. This is because in general the development of a race-relations sociology during the last decade has relied on notions of society which are liable to sociological investigative techniques, thus pushing historical and structural issues into the background. Where historical and political analyses do make an entry into the debates they do so either in a minor way or they tend to be narrow case studies of specific issues. Although we do not claim to have redressed this situation, it is important to stress that this is the area on which much more serious and critical theoretical work remains to be done.

28   S. Hall, 'The whites of their eyes: racist ideologies and the media', in G. Bridges and R. Brunt (eds.), *Silver Linings: Some Strategies for the Eighties* (Lawrence and Wishart 1981).

29   I. Gough, *The Political Economy of the Welfare State* (Macmillan 1979).

30   On the history of state attempts to orchestrate trade union reform in the sixties and seventies see: L. Panitch, *Social Democracy and Industrial Militancy: The Labour Party, The Trade Unions and Incomes Policy 1965-1974* (Cambridge 1976); L. Panitch, 'Profits and politics: labour and the crisis of British capitalism', *Politics and Society*, vol. 7, no. 4 (1977), pp. 477-507.

31   N. Poulantzas, *State, Power, Socialism* (New Left Books 1978), especially Chapters 1 and 2; C. Offe, 'The separation of form and content in liberal democratic politics', *Studies in Political Economy*, no. 3 (Spring 1980), pp. 5-16.

32   This is the reply we would make to the arguments put forward by Paul Hirst and Barry Hindess, and taken up by a number of other writers. See: B. Hindess, 'Democracy and the limitations of parliamentary democracy in Britain', *Politics and Power*, no. 1 (Routledge and Kegan Paul 1980); M. Prior (ed.), *The Popular and the Political: Essays on Socialism in the 1980s* (Routledge and Kegan Paul 1981).

33   C. Offe, 'Political authority and class structures: an analysis of late capitalist societies', *International Journal of Sociology*, vol. 2, no. 1 (1972), p. 78.

34   J. Lea, 'The contradictions of the sixties race relations legislation', in National Deviancy Conference (ed.), *Permissiveness and Control* (Macmillan 1980).

35   A good summary of the shifts in modes of social control, using the theoretical framework of Habermas and Offe in particular, can be found in: J. Keane, 'The legacy of political economy', *Canadian Journal of Political and Social Theory*, vol. 2, no. 3 (1978).

The impact of Poulantzas's work is clear in the work of Adam Prezworski who provides an illuminating account of the transformations of the state in his: 'Material bases of consent: economics and politics in a hegemonic system', *Political Power and Social Theory*, vol. 1 (1980). See also: V. Burris, 'The structuralist influence in Marxist theory and research', *Insurgent Sociologist*, vol. 9, no. 1 (1979), pp. 4-17.

36   C. Offe, 'Crises of crisis management: elements of a political crisis theory', *International Journal of Sociology*, vol. 6, no. 3 (1976), p. 32.

37   Poulantzas, *State, Power, Socialism*, pp. 203–4.

38   Hall *et al.*, *Policing the Crisis*, p. 214.

39   The articulation of these themes over the period of the seventies and the construction of the Thatcher strategy are closely related. Some of the important contributions to the debate about the post-1974 experience, and also the post-1979 experience, of austerity policies are discussed in: C. Leys, 'Neo-conservatism and the organic crisis in Britain', *Studies in Political Economy*, no. 4 (Autumn 1980), pp. 41–64; L. Panitch, 'Trade unions and the capitalist state', *New Left Review*, no. 125 (1981), pp. 21–44.

40   This is an argument which was developed at length in: C. Lindblom, *Politics and Markets* (Basic Books 1977). More recently it has been debated and further developed by: G. Therborn, 'Enterprises, markets and states', unpublished paper 1975; C. Offe, 'The attribution of political status to interest groups', in S. Berger (ed.), *Interest Groups in Western Europe* (Cambridge University Press 1980).

41   As reported in *The Times*, 3 December 1973.

42   Gramsci develops this concept in the *Prison Notebooks* and applies it in a number of historical contexts, particularly in relation to Italy. For a full discussion of the origins, development and usefulness of this concept see: C. Buci-Glucksmann, *Gramsci and The State* (Lawrence and Wishart 1980), especially Chapters 2, 3, and 6.

43   On the overall issue of the reorganization of the state in Britain see: N. Johnson, 'Quangos and the structure of government', *Public Administrations*, vol. 57 (Winter 1979), pp. 379–96; D. Coates, 'Politicians and the Sorcerer: the problems of governing with capitalism in crisis', in A. King (ed.), *Why is Britain Becoming Harder to Govern?* (BBC Publications 1976). The comparative aspects of this process are analysed in: D. Coombes and S. A. Walkland (eds.), *Parliaments and Economic Affairs* (Heinemann 1980).

44   On these links see: M. Castells, 'Urban crisis, political process and urban theory', in *City, Class and Power* (Macmillan 1978).

45   Poulantzas, *State, Power, Socialism*; B. Jessop, 'Capitalism and democracy: the best possible shell?', in (ed.) G. Littlejohn *et al.*, *Power and the State* (Macmillan 1978); M. Foucault, *Power/Knowledge: Selected Interviews and Other Writings* (Harvester 1980).

46   Poulantzas, *State, Power, Socialism*, pp. 186–7.

47   This is an argument which has been taken up by Alain Touraine in his: *The Voice and the Eye: An Analysis of Social Movements* (Cambridge University Press 1981). In this work Touraine attempts to look at the implications of these shifts for the development of social movements within the contemporary context and thereby attempts to widen the issue to cover oppositional forces.

48   These breaks are dealt with in somewhat more detail in the later chapters, but it may be useful to comment briefly on the whole notion of discontinuous histories. This way of thinking through the complex levels of determination involved in any specific historical conjuncture has developed as a measured response to economism within Marxist theory. But it cannot as yet be said to have been fully articulated, since in some contexts it has tended to be used simply as another way of saying that reality is 'complex'. To

leave the issue at this level would be to accept a more or less relativist approach, which cannot tell us very much about actual mechanisms of determination. What we have attempted in this book is to use the idea of discontinuous histories in a concrete manner to explain how race articulates to the organic nature of the crisis.

49   P. Cohen, 'Policing the working class city', in National Deviancy Conference/Conference of Socialist Economists, *Capitalism and the Rule of Law* (Hutchinson 1979), p. 136.

50   For an account of this crisis and the ways it was experienced at the level of official thinking see: S. Blank, 'Britain: the politics of foreign economic policy, the domestic economy and the problem of pluralist stagnation', *International Organisation*, vol. 31, no. 4 (1977), pp. 673–722; B. Jessop, 'Corporatism, parliamentarism and social democracy', in P. Schmitter and G. Lehmbruch, *Trends Towards Corporatist Intermediation* (Sage 1979).

51   On the issue of negotiation in relation to moral and legal relations see: P. Corrigan, 'On moral regulation: some preliminary remarks', *Sociological Review*, vol. 29, no. 2 (1981), pp. 313–37. On the wider issue of the collective negotiations between capital and labour see: C. Offe and H. Wiesenthal, 'Two logics of collective action: theoretical notes on social class and organisational form', in M. Zetlin (ed.), *Political Power and Social Theory*, vol. 1 (Jai Press 1980).

52   This is the argument which Paul Gilroy develops in the chapter on policing, where he attempts to show the kind of options which the repressive apparatuses are opening up for handling working-class black communities.

53   For a concise account of the transformations which led to this conception of the sixties see: S. Hall, 'Reform and the legislation of consent', in National Deviancy Conference, *Permissiveness and Control* (Macmillan 1980).

54   Detailed accounts of these processes can be found in: Hall *et al.*, *Policing the Crisis*, especially Chapters 8 and 9. But see in addition: S. Cohen, *Folk Devils and Moral Panics: The Creation of the Mods and Rockers* (Martin Robertson 1980).

55   S. Chibnall, *Law and Order News* (Tavistock 1977), p. 75.

56   The best account of this breakdown can be found in: B. Jessop, 'The transformation of the state in postwar Britain', in R. Scase (ed.), *The State in Western Europe* (Macmillan 1980).

57   These issues are discussed in some detail in: J. Solomos, 'The political economy of energy policy in Britain', unpublished D. Phil. thesis, University of Sussex, February 1980, especially Chapters 3 and 4.

58   On the chronology of the Heath experiment see: A. Barnett, 'Class struggle and the Heath Government', *New Left Review*, no. 77 (1973), pp. 3–41.

59   The orchestration of this shift has to be located firmly within the state itself because it is within its own apparatuses that the technocratic world view of a Britain rejuvenated by the application of 'new technologies' arose and took shape. In addition, however, one must bear in mind that during this period the legitimacy of social democracy had yet to be seriously brought under question.

60   See the various accounts of youth and other subcultures that are contained

in: S. Hall and T. Jefferson (eds.), *Resistance Through Rituals* (Hutchinson 1976); J. Clarke *et al.* (eds.), *Working Class Culture* (Hutchinson 1979).

61   For a comparative account of these transformations in the role of unions see: C. Crouch and A. Pizzorno (eds.), *The Resurgence of Class Conflict in Western Europe Since 1968*, 2 volumes (Macmillan 1978); S. Berger, 'Politics and antipolitics in Western Europe in the seventies', *Daedalus* (Winter 1979), pp. 27–50.

62   These developments are carefully analysed in: P. Bew *et al.*, *The State in Northern Ireland 1921–72: Political Forces and Social Classes* (Manchester University Press 1979).

63   See: Hall *et al.*, *Policing the Crisis, passim*; Chibnall, *Law and Order News, passim*. Also see the discussion in Chapter 2.

64   In a number of specific contexts the themes of trade union 'militants' and 'race' have been connected, notably in the struggles at Grunwick and Imperial Typewriters. But clearly both these themes have operated in an autonomous manner as well, even when the specific ways in which they have been presented have produced wider resonances. What is likely to happen, however, as levels of black unemployment reach a higher peak is that the industrial struggles waged by black workers in defence of jobs will take on a more general form.

65   For a careful account of all these struggles see: Panitch, *Social Democracy and Industrial Militancy*.

66   Hall *et al.*, *Policing the Crisis*, p. 238.

67   ibid., p. 238.

68   The Trilateral Commission, *The Crisis of Democracy* (New York University Press 1975).

69   Jessop, 'Corporatism, parliamentarism and social democracy'.

70   As quoted by: T. Bunyan, *The History and Practice of the Political Police in Britain* (J. Friedmann 1976), p. 47.

71   These points are developed in greater detail in Chapters 6 and 8.

72   R. Clutterback, *Britain in Agony* (Penguin 1978), p. 19.

73   ibid., p. 311.

74   The treatment of 'violence' in relation to recent 'race riots' is an example of this trend, and we discuss the specific meaning of these developments in Chapters 2 and 6.

75   Hall *et al.*, *Policing the Crisis*, Chapters 8, 9, and 10.

76   For a discussion of the general tendency of late capitalist states to 'deliver the goods' and the ensuing political contradictions see: A. Melucci, 'The new social movements: a theoretical approach', *Social Science Information*, vol. 19, no. 2 (1980).

77   This accusation was made by Margaret Thatcher in the build-up to the 1979 election when she said: 'In their muddled but different ways the vandals on the picket lines and the muggers in our streets have got the same confused message – "we want our demands met or else" and "get out of our way, give us your handbag or else" '. Speech in Birmingham, 19 April 1979.

78   F. Burton and P. Carlen, *Official Discourse: On Discourse Analysis, Government Publications, Ideology and the State* (Routledge and Kegan Paul 1979), p. 138.

79 It is important to note however that the terms of the debate have not remained constant since the 1979 election, and that the process of the criminalization of black youth has progressed much further now.

80 In this sense the argument of Burton and Carlen quoted above is too narrow. What should be looked at is not really *official discourse* but *social discourse*. The latter term is more amenable to the study of how ideologies change over time.

81 A. Sherman, 'Britain's urge to self-destruction', *The Daily Telegraph*, 9 September 1979.

82 Hall, 'Race, articulation and societies structured in dominance', p. 339.

83 In fact the relationship between 'problems' and 'solutions' is not as discrete as we have made it sound. For example the implementation of policies through state agencies often results in the articulation of new problems, or at least new aspects of old issues. This is because the actual mechanisms and manner in which specific policies are implemented feeds back into the definition of what issues policy-makers should concentrate upon. This is why in much of contemporary neo-conservative thinking we find a simple reversal of the Keynesian formula: the state is now the cause of capitalism's problems and not its saviour. The reasons why such views develop do not concern us here, but it is important to emphasize that these notions are not abstract ideological shifts but outcomes of material practices which question whether the state can actually solve the problems which it aims to do. Such a 'suspicion' of the state has very wide implications, which have hardly begun to be considered.

84 This formulation of articulation owes much to the discussion in: Hall, 'Race, articulation and societies structured in dominance'.

85 An example of this was his speech reported in the *Guardian* on 24 January 1980 under the headline 'Joseph blames decline on immigrants'.

86 A wider discussion of the role of the media as definer of specific discourses about race, and particularly black youth, can be found in Chapter 2.

87 K. Middlemas, 'Unemployment: the past and future of a political problem', in B. Crick (ed.), *Unemployment* (Macmillan 1981), p. 151. This line of thinking is close to some strands of 'wet' or 'traditional' Conservative thinking, and Middlemas himself is a reputable historian of the British state and its development in the twentieth century. Moreover he is in the intellectual vanguard of attempts to reconnect the Conservative Government to its 'roots', by which is meant the idea of an all-class alliance. Although it is by no means a popular view in terms of current Conservative policies it is by no means out of order to think that it may become more popular at a future moment of failure.

88 *House of Commons Debates (Hansard)*, 4 June 1981, Column 1180, Mr Ivor Stanbrook. He goes on to refute the charge that the Bill is racist by arguing that it is simply an accident of history that it affects black people: 'Most people in Britain happen to be white-skinned. Most of those who would like to become British citizens happen to be black-skinned'.

89 The issue of 'identity' in this sense was a clear theme in the various debates on the 1981 Nationality Bill: *House of Commons Debates (Hansard)*, 3 June 1981, Columns 931–90. The interventions by Enoch Powell and the reply

by John Tilley are particularly interesting. See also: R. Behrens and J. Edmonds, 'Kippers, kittens and kipper boxes: Conservative populists and race relations', *The Political Quarterly*, no. 52 (1981), pp. 342-7.

90   A. Sherman, 'Britain is not Asia's fiancée', *Daily Telegraph*, 9 November 1979.

91   The classic studies by Paul Foot are still a good starting-point for situating this issue: *Immigration and Race in British Politics* (Penguin 1965); *The Rise of Enoch Powell* (Penguin 1969). More generally see: G. Ben-Tovim and J. Gabriel, 'The politics of race in Britain; 1962 to 1979', *Sage Race Relations Abstracts*, vol. 4, no. 4 (1979), pp. 1–56.

92   M. Crawford, 'Sir Geoffrey's great gamble', *The Sunday Times*, 30 March 1980.

93   The extension of forms of control at the territorial level has been a common theme in many working-class communities (see Cohen, 'Policing the working class city'), but the racialization of these forms of control has also been extensive over the sixties and seventies. See: Institute of Race Relations, *Police Against Black People* (IRR 1979); for the early developments see: D. Humphrey, *Police Power and Black People* (Panther 1972).

94   The case of Lambeth has been one which has been most extensively studied. See for example: London Borough of Lambeth, *Final Report of the Working Party into Police/Community Relations in Lambeth* (London Borough of Lambeth 1981). But we try to show in this book the pattern is both much more extensive and deeper than is generally appreciated.

95   This is clear for example in the way in which policies aimed at 'helping' black youth have been formulated. See for example: Commission for Racial Equality, *Ethnic Minority Youth Unemployment* (CRE 1980). L. Wood, 'Where work is a black white issue', *Financial Times*, 23 March 1981. But the exact fixing of the various determinants will be discussed later when we consider the development of specific policy alternatives.

96   The usage of 'race' in explanations of the 'riots' should not be seen in isolation from the wider usage of racially based common-sense ideas about why the crisis of the seventies took specific forms. Even when discussion of the riots has been limited to local cases the national issues have fed into these debates. See for example the coverage of the Brixton riots in the *South London Press* from 14 April to 16 April 1981.

97   *House of Commons Debates (Hansard)*, 6 July 1981, Column 26. In this debate Powell's views received strong support from a number of back-bench Conservative MPs although they were generally dismissed by the Cabinet, who adopted a mixture of a social problems approach with assurances of strong support for the police. In his speech in this same debate for example Whitelaw expressed both a call to study the 'social reasons' for the violence and the need to act firmly against 'mindless violence in our society'.

98   This is not a book which aims to provide a specific account of the 'riots' since the Bristol events of 1980, but we have attempted to look at some of the connections between these events and the issues which concern us. Nevertheless a specific analytical account of the themes developed in the media would be a useful example of how the articulation between 'race' and 'crisis' is transformed when political legitimacy is questioned and forms of

resistance grow on the streets. This theme will be discussed in detail by Bob Findlay in his Ph. D thesis on 'Race and the media: a redefinition of the problematic'.

99   *The Financial Times*, 11 July 1981.

100 The history of the various right-wing movements and their attempts to link up the themes of race with repatriation is summarized in: M. Billing and A. Bell, 'Fascist parties in post-war Britain', *Sage Race Relations Abstracts*, vol. 5, no. 1 (1980), pp. 1–30. The various right-wing movements are also analysed on a regular basis in the anti-Fascist magazine *Searchlight*. But the resonance of the repatriation theme has a much wider resonance than the right-wing movements, as is shown in: P. Gilroy, 'Managing the "underclass": a further note on the sociology of race relations in Britain', *Race and Class*, vol. 22, no. 1 (1980), pp. 47–62.

101 This division parallels the wider policy divisions within the Conservative Party about the orientation it should take to counter the dangers of 'greater state control' and 'lawlessness': contradictory divisions whose ideological roots have a long and complex history.

102 The inadequacy of pure control theories which ignore the historical basis of contradictions has been demonstrated in: G. Stedman Jones, 'Class expression versus social control? A critique of recent trends in the social history of "Leisure" ', *History Workshop Journal*, no. 4 (1977), pp. 162–70.

103 Some of these contradictions are analysed in: G. John, *In the Service of Black Youth*, National Association of Youth Clubs (NAYC 1981).

104 *House of Commons Debates (Hansard)*, 16 July 1981, Column 1414. The exact phrase which Powell used in the Debate on Civil Disturbances was: 'Inner London becoming ungovernable or violence which could only effectually be described as civil war'. He saw this as the inevitable result of the growth of the black population in the inner-city areas.

105 *House of Commons Debates (Hansard)*, 16 July 1981, Column 1416.

196 In the area of youth unemployment, for example, the ameliorative actions of the state have to some extent taken precedence in the immediate response of the state. But at the everyday level the role of the police remains strong and there is a clear attempt to strengthen the technical forms available to the police.

107 See two clear reports about the Brixton events and the July 'riots' which summarize and critically situate the development of police practices: 'Brixton: new facts emerge', *State Research Bulletin*, no. 24 (June–July 1981); 'The July riots', *State Research Bulletin*, no. 25 (August–September 1981); 'Riot control: a new direction?', *State Research Bulletin*, no. 25 (August–September 1981).

108 This is already clear in the aftermath of the massive rise in unemployment from 1979 to 1981 and the cuts in social expenditure which have been put into practice. The attempt to control the 'social problems' aspect of these policies is one which will take a number of forms, including a reconstruction of the possible options of resistance which are open to oppositional groups. For an elaboration of this theme from a theoretical perspective see: C. Offe, 'The separation of form and content in liberal democratic politics.

109 We would emphasize in this context that the question is not one which can

be thought of in narrow class terms, with race added on as an extra dimension to unchanged fixed concepts. Rather it is important (a) to rethink the basis and unity of the concepts themselves and (b) to conceptualize the politics organized around black communities in their own autonomy. This is also a debate which goes beyond race as such, since it has implications for how we think through the history of working-class movements in general, and their complex articulation at all levels of society. For discussions of these issues see: A. Prezworski, 'Proletariat into a class: the process of class formation from Karl Kautsky's *The Class Struggle* to recent controversies', *Politics and Society*, vol. 7, no. 4 (1977), pp. 343–402; S. Bowles and H. Gintis, 'The Marxian theory of value and heterogeneous labour: a critique and reformulation', *Cambridge Journal of Economics*, vol. 1, no. 2 (1977).

110   S. Hall, 'Summer in the city', *New Socialist*, no. 1 (September–October 1981), p. 7.

111   As quoted in: B. Brick and M. Postone, 'Friedrich Pollock and the "primacy of the political": a critical re-examination', *International Journal of Politics* (Fall 1976), p. 7.

2 Just plain common sense: the 'roots' of racism

Errol Lawrence

I've learnt something that I've known all along, that black people and white people can get on very well as individuals. It's when they get into groups, when they become afraid, when the herd instinct takes over, that trouble starts.

LORD SCARMAN

[Ideologies] work most effectively when we are not aware that how we formulate and construct a statement about the world is underpinned by ideological premises; when our formulations seem to be simply descriptive statements about how things are (i.e. must be), or of what we can 'take-for-granted'.

STUART HALL

Introduction

This chapter deals with the racist ideologies that form the cement of that structural configuration we have referred to as the 'new racism'. We have indicated that we do not agree with the school of thinking which views racism as 'prejudice', and 'prejudice' as the inevitable outcome of something which is mythically conceived of as 'human nature'. Neither do we believe that racist ideas are the mere 'relics' of a distant imperial past, which are out of place in a 'modern industrial society'. Racist ideologies, as we have argued in the preceding chapter, are an organic component of attempts to make sense of the present crisis. The fear that society is falling apart at the seams has prompted the elaboration of theories about race which turn on particular notions of culture. The 'alien' cultures of the blacks are seen as either the cause or else the most visible symptom of the destruction of the 'British way of life'.

Common-sense images of the 'family' play a crucial role here since the 'family' is seen as the fundamental unit of society; it reproduces culture. Just how deeply the rot is thought to have set in is revealed in the renewed concern with its functions and with the responsibilities and duties of parents. For this reason we preface discussion of common-sense *racist* imagery with an exploration of the more generalized common-sense images of the 'family'. In the third section of this chapter, we go on to look in more detail at the specific images of the black 'family', where we have been concerned in particular to examine the ways in which the 'problems' that black people are thought to pose for white society and indeed for themselves, are situated within the organization of black households.

Our concern to note what is specific about racism in the present, though, does not mean that we consider Britain's imperialist past to be irrelevant. On the contrary, we feel that, among other things, it provides important clues as to how racist ideologies have come to be such a tenacious feature of the common-sense thinking of the white working (and other) class(es). The past is alive, even if transformed, in the present. Accordingly, in the second section of the chapter, we explore the historical 'roots' of racist ideologies. This has, hopefully, prevented us from falling into the kinds of reductionist argument which see these ideologies as a ploy perpetrated by the ruling power bloc in order to divide the working class. In our view the more developed racist ideologies *are popular* precisely because they succeed in reorganizing the common-sense racist ideologies of the white working class, around the themes of 'the British nation', 'the British people' and 'British culture' – themes which explicitly exclude black people. Certainly, this has had the effect of strengthening the mechanisms whereby the working class is reproduced as a racially structured and divided working class,[1] but to view this process simply in terms of the machinations of the ruling bloc is to be blind to popular politics and struggles. This is why we have decided to begin our discussions with common-sense racist and other ideas and to leave our discussion of how the more organized racist ideologies intersect common sense, until last.

Finally, although we know that some of our readers will already be familiar with the way we are using the term 'common sense' here, others will not be. What follows immediately is a short detour explaining somewhat crudely how our understanding of the term differs from popular usage. We hope that those who are familiar with the arguments will bear with us.

Common sense

The term 'common sense' is generally used to denote a down-to-earth 'good sense'. It is thought to represent the distilled truths of centuries of practical experience; so much so that to say of an idea or practice that it is only common sense, is to appeal over the logic and argumentation of intellectuals to what all reasonable people know in their 'heart of hearts' to be right and proper. Such an appeal can act at one and the same time to foreclose any discussion about certain ideas and practices and to legitimate them.

Common sense has not always occupied such a pre-eminent position, neither has it always been so easily equated with good sense. In his *Prison Notebooks*, Gramsci traced its development as a concept from a term particularly favoured by 'the 17th and 18th century empiricist philosophers battling against theology, to its subsequent usage as a confirmation of accepted opinion rather than its subversion'.[2] He characterized common sense thinking as 'eclectic and unsystematic' in the way in which it accumulated contradictory knowledges within itself. Common sense, he argued,

is strangely composite: it contains elements from the Stone Age and principles of a more advanced science, prejudices from all past phases of history at the local level and intuitions of a future philosophy which will be that of the human race united the world over.[3]

The contradictory nature of common sense means that it should not be thought of as constituting a unified body of knowledge. It does not have *a* theory underlying or 'hidden beneath' it,[4] but is perhaps best seen as a 'storehouse of knowledges' which has·been gathered together, historically, through struggle.[5]

As a way of thinking and in its immediacy, common sense is appropriate to 'the practical struggle of everyday life of the popular masses'. It is one of the contradictory outcomes of the division between mental and manual labour under capitalism. Yet, while common sense embodies the practical experience and solutions to the everyday problems encountered by the 'popular masses' throughout their history, 'it is also shot through with elements and beliefs derived from earlier or other more developed ideologies which have *sedimented* into it'.[6] The practical struggle of everyday life refers not simply to that 'perennial struggle against nature' but to class struggle - the struggle for the power to decide, in the present conjuncture, for example, where the social costs of economic recession are to be borne. The new restrictions on organized labour, the deliberate creation of unemployment and the other attempts by the present Government to reorganize the production process, are not policies that can be pursued willy-nilly. Consent for them has to be continually won. It is within this process of winning consent and in the decomposition and recomposition of alliances between the ruling bloc and 'sub-altern classes',[7] by the granting of economic concessions to those classes (which do not however touch the essential interests of the ruling bloc), that the subordination of the 'popular masses' is ideologically and practically secured. The securing of 'hegemony' by the ruling bloc, though, is not a once and for all victory. The situation is rather a 'negotiated truce' between hegemonic cultures of the ruling bloc and the 'corporate' cultures of the subordinate classes;[8] while the general ideas of the society are defined within the hegemonic cultures and form the horizon of thought about the world, this does not mean that the thought of the subordinate classes is wholly given over to ideas derived from elsewhere. Common sense also contains 'more contextualised or *situated* judgements' which are the product of their daily lives. The sometimes oppositional and always contradictory nature of this thought is captured quite neatly by Stuart Hall *et al.* when they point out that

it seems perfectly 'logical' for some workers to agree that 'the nation is paying itself too much' (general) but be only too willing to go on strike for higher wages (situated).[9]

The class struggle, as is indicated by these contradictions, is fought out on one level within common sense. In order that it may remain in the position of command, the ruling bloc needs to ensure that the 'good sense' of the subordinated classes – those situated judgements – does not become elaborated into a coherent, alternative and *generalized* set of ideas and practices. Of importance here is the continuing success of the ruling bloc in gaining acceptance for the equation between an essentialist view of human nature and the social relations generated historically under capitalism.[10] This equation operates so as to 'effectively discount the possibility of change and to "naturalise" the social order',[11] by obscuring the historical struggles that have produced the present configuration of social forces. Through the mechanism of this 'naturalization process' the *social* construction of, for example, gender roles is collapsed into the biological differences between the sexes. In common-sense terms, historically and culturally specific images of femininity and masculinity are presented as the 'natural' attributes of females and males. Whilst we should not forget that these dominant definitions are contested, we must also remember that they are embodied within the dominant institutional order and are inscribed within the social relations of everyday life. This 'massive presence' has the effect on the one hand of disciplining the subordinate classes in *practice* and on the other hand of giving these common-sense ideologies their 'taken-for-granted' character.

Keep it in the family

The family is a crucial site in the construction of common-sense ideologies and has a particular relevance to our concerns here. Within common sense, it is portrayed as the crucial site for the reproduction of those correct social mores, attitudes and behaviours that are thought to be essential to maintaining a 'civilized' society. The family is after all the place where 'primary socialization' takes place and where 'culture' is reproduced. It is in the domain of the family that children are supposed to learn 'right from wrong', the basic dos and don'ts that will inform their future behaviour. It is here also where girls first learn the duties and functions associated with womanhood and motherhood and where boys learn the responsibilities and privileges accruing to the 'man of the house'. The family then is seen as the site in which self-discipline and self-control are 'knocked into' childrens' heads and in which relations of authority and power are internalized. It is important to recognize that the common-sense image of the *kind* of family which is to fulfil these crucial tasks is that of the nuclear family, where father goes out to 'work' while mother remains at home to attend to her household 'duties' and rear their 2.2 children. Obviously then mother's role is a vital one, since apart from looking to hubby's 'needs' in order that he may be mentally and physically prepared to win their daily bread, she must also see to it that the 'kids are brought up properly'. Within common sense women do not exist as women, they exist only as actual or potential wives and mothers. These are their 'natural' roles. And it is the 'good homes' provided by the ideal wife/mother that produces the well-adjusted children who will become the model citizens of tomorrow.

The family here is seen as the 'natural' outcome of the biological differences between the sexes; men and women were quite literally 'made for each other'.

Monogamous marriage as encapsulated in the familiar movie image of primeval man
and his mate, is similarly seen as arising out of these natural differences as indeed
are the familial roles of mothering and fathering. This view of the family's natural
structure and role has a particular place in the assessment of both individual and
group behaviour. Where the 'normal' family will generate the correct 'moral social
compulsions' and 'inner controls', 'criminal' or 'immoral' behaviour will be seen
as the outcome of an inadequate upbringing or even in some cases as the result of
an *abnormal* family life.[12] But of course these images are not naturally given. There
is a history to their development which is obscured by the 'naturalization process'.
As Michèle Barrett has recently pointed out, people have not always thought about
the family in this way. The particular form of household arrangement which the
common-sense images refer to arose at a particular time and under specific circumstances and represents the 'specific *historical* achievement of the bourgeoisie'. The
fact that this view of family life is popularly accepted as the 'natural form of
household organization' attests to the bourgeoisie's success at securing at an
ideolological level

a hegemonic definition of family life: as 'naturally' based on close kinship, as
properly organized through a male breadwinner with financially dependent wife
and children, and as a haven of privacy beyond the public realm of commerce and
industry.[13]

The sedimentation of this piece of ideology into common sense has probably, as
Barrett argues, been of benefit to capital by providing a 'motivation for male wage
labour and the "family wage" demand'. It has undoubtedly also provided further
legitimation for male demands in the household. Nevertheless it seems to be
reasonably clear that although working-class households may approximate the ideal
arrangement, they are organized differently and according to their own needs.

Where the working class adopted, as it has increasingly in the twentieth century, a
similar form, it is much more as an adaptation to its own particular circumstances
(the organisation of work patterns, the move towards consumerism, the lowering
of the birth rate) rather than as a simple acceptance of the bourgeois model.[14]

As we have already argued, it is consistent with common-sense thinking for working
women to subscribe to its image of the family and yet acknowledge that their
households are not arranged in this way. It is likely, for example, that they go *out*
to work though at the same time feel guilty about not being at home with the
children. The idea that 'a woman's place is in the home' has of course generated a
particular concern for the fate of 'latch-key' children. At another level it has
proved to be a fertile area of research within the sociology of education, yielding an
abundant crop of theories about the inadequacies of working-class home life and
culture, which seek to explain the 'failure' of working-class children at school.[15]
Here, the common-sense 'logic' which expects that failings in home background

will be reproduced in the academic failures of the children is given a 'scientific' validity and once again it is the role of the mother that is thought to be particularly significant.

The family, though, has also been a favoured site for the construction of conservative ideologies. In this instance the common-sense logics have been transformed and extended to include not just a concern with the connection between 'falling standards' within the family and the evident moral degeneration of the nation's youth, but the more general 'threat to law and order' as well. During the battles between black and white youth and the police in July 1981, this vexed question was posed with an urgency and insistence that bordered on panic. Merseyside's Chief Constable Kenneth Oxford appears to have set the ball rolling when he asked with seeming incredulity,

What in the name of goodness are these young people doing on the streets indulging in this behaviour at that time of night? Is there no discipline that can be brought to bear on these young people? Are the parents not interested in the future of these young people? [16]

Home Secretary Willie Whitelaw, in Liverpool on a flying visit to survey the debris, concurred with these sentiments and stressed the 'considerable responsibility on parents to keep their children off the streets in these difficult circumstances'.[17] Fleet Street obviously felt that Oxford and Whitelaw had got to the 'heart of the matter'. The floodgates opened. 'And after the problem children looting in Liverpool', the *Daily Mail* (8 July 1981) asked in outraged voice, 'the question is DON'T THEIR PARENTS CARE?' This was followed by a front-page story which dismissed unemployment and 'racial tension' as possible contributory factors, preferring a scenario in which questions 'about our sanity in letting *them* become a nightmare' could be raised. The improbable scenes of parents in the courtroom seeming 'no more concerned than parents waiting to see the maths master [*sic*] on Speech Day', and the 'authentic' voices of the working-class parents of 'ten to 14' year-olds ('Well, you've got to let them have their play, haven't you? There's only the streets.' 'We were out ourselves, having a jar, so how the hell could we know what he was up to?'), form the telling backdrop of parental 'irresponsibility' to the reporter's regurgitated homilies. Even 'yobbism', it appears, 'has its fashions', and 'these past nights (in Toxteth) have been more about criminal greed' than anything else.[18]

The following day amid the general clamour for Whitelaw to 'READ THE RIOT ACT' and following Prime Minister Thatcher's televised broadcast reminding us that 'a free society will only survive if we, its citizens, obey the law and teach our children to do so',[19] the *Daily Express* ran a special double-page feature. 'Are the young really protesting', it asked, 'or are they sowing the first seeds of anarchy?' The *Express* then produced a 'cross-section of the people who might have some sort of answer' – answers which, however, were all conveniently alike. We heard again of the 'copy-cat' violence; that 'parents must take a firmer hand'; and were given a

picture of the 'sad' top policeman who informed us that the police force would
'never be the same again'. Jill Knight, Tory MP for Edgbaston and infamous
amongst the black community for her proposal to ban West Indian house parties,[20]
put her finger on the pulse of this apparently generalized feeling. Good parents,
she intoned,

teach discipline and restraint. Bad ones . . . find it easier to give a child what he
[*sic*] wants rather than face the battle of wills.[21]

'Bad parents' produce 'delinquent children' who are responsible for the rising
'crime rate'. As a solution, Knight proposes that parents be encouraged to relearn
their 'natural' roles and in this connection she suggests that 'the mothers of very
young children' be offered 'tax incentives and bonus benefits' in order to persuade
them to stay at home. Similar proposals have been made before by the present
Government's ministers and would appear to be part of a 'package' of mooted state
interventions in this area. The *Guardian*, for example, had informed us some time
ago that,

The Government is considering amending the law to give the courts greater and
clearer powers to bring *home* to parents their responsibility for their children's
behaviour.[22] (our emphasis)

The youth of today
The events which followed this article must have made such considerations appear
particularly relevant. The large-scale confrontations in Bristol, Brixton and then
'nationwide' indicated the heightened tempo of political struggle and in the process
raised the anxieties about 'youth' to a new level of visibility. Ever since *The Times*
coverage of the 1958 race riots in Nottingham and Notting Hill, the media had
shown a distinct tendency to 'map' social unrest involving young people – particularly where racial conflict was evident – 'directly into hooliganism, teenage violence,
lawlessness and anarchy'.[23] This undoubtedly made it easier to locate the genesis
of 'mob violence' within the ailing institution of the family, but still left a problem
of how society was going to deal with the new situation.

Whitelaw's 'short, sharp shock' treatment was one way devised to contain this
new breed of 'young criminal', though it was not designed to meet the challenge
of large-scale disorder. Like the 'gun-courts' which followed the police offensive
against the 'passive' Asian residents of Southall (1978), and the 'stiffer sentences'
handed out to 'muggers' throughout the seventies, it was more an indication of
the desire for revenge than a long-term solution. The police, on whom the main
burden of maintaining 'law and order' fell, could in the case of the black communities continue and even intensify their already brutal and intensive 'saturation
policing' methods, though not without harvesting the bitter fruits of their efforts.[24]
More recent events have shown that the contestation of such methods by black
youth has reached a new pitch of purpose and effectiveness as they have learned

the lessons of the past; while the extension of 'tough policing' to include growing sections of the white working-class poor will provoke a similar combative response. In the aftermath of July's insurrections, the police may well get the full 'riot gear' for which they have been clamouring so long; but as they continue to remind us, this is likely to undermine even further their already tarnished helpful 'British bobby' image.

In this context, the idea that bad 'parenting' *causes* 'riots' performs a number of different but related ideological tasks quite apart from its dubious explanatory power. It legitimates repressive 'counter-measures' being taken by the police, for as Chief Constable Oxford put it,

If the parents are not going to pick up their responsibility and apply a discipline, it means that I have got to do it to protect the community at large.[25]

It also suggests possible solutions of which Jill Knight's is only one. Here the anticipated beneficial effects of 'strengthening the family' square nicely with making the official unemployment statistics look a little healthier. On the other hand, badgering the parents to resume their 'rightful duties' would, if they comply, involve them also in the arduous task of policing their own offspring. From the other end, the 'youthful' end, we should consider whether the Government's deliberations about 'making punishment fit the parent' are not indicative of an attempt to reconquer the semi-autonomous space which successive generations of youth have marked out as their own. The age at which parental responsibility ceases is certainly not made clear at this stage of the Government's considerations, but the interventions that have already been made in this area (the raising of the school leaving age, the MSC's youth opportunities programmes) are perhaps illustrative of a more general trend towards an increased supervision of young people. None of these shifts and proposals is without its attendant problems, however, as the rejection of YOPs by large sections of youth reveals. There are growing indications as well that women will not allow themselves to be quietly 'sent back home', while it is by no means obvious that working parents' ideas of 'discipline' equate simply with those of Thatcher or Oxford.

Not in front of the children
It is precisely at this point that common-sense notions require to be, and often are, ruptured. The common-sense assumptions about 'childhood' and 'youth', particularly the age at which young people can be accepted as having 'minds of their own', suffused most accounts of the July upheavals. When Whitelaw asked, from the pages of the *Daily Telegraph*, 'What were these children doing in riot [*sic*]?', no one was expected to suggest that he might be begging the question – except perhaps for the 'Trotskyites', 'feminist extremists' and other assorted 'left-wing loonies' whom the *Telegraph* regularly singles out for gratuitous abuse.

'Childhood' and 'adulthood' tend to be viewed in our society as inflexible, universal categories, with the idea of 'youth' referring to that area of transition

between these two apparently fixed states. However, while this area may be defined
with the greatest clarity in law, it appears consistently hazy in practice. The varying
ages at which young people may legitimately begin to work, vote, marry, or engage
in sexual intercourse demonstrate this confusion and the difficulty of implementing
these general rules is visible in 'youth's' connotations of rebellion and conflict. The
idea of 'youth', though, like that of 'retirement' is not simply a reference to some
objective natural state of being, it is a social construction which has its origins in
the capitalist division of labour. For this reason, workers and their employers have
predictably tended to have very different ideas about the age at which it is desirable
for young people to begin to sell their labour power in exchange for wages. In
Britain this issue was at the centre of long and bitter struggles which have only been
resolved relatively recently, and the campaign to restrict child labour is not easily
separated from a whole complex of working struggles in the eighteenth and
nineteenth centuries. It dovetails not just with the struggle for popular education
but also with the battle for a shorter working day which was initially focused around
the hours worked by children. Their health, and the safety hazards they were subject
to, are exemplified in the plight of the chimney sweep's climbing boys. Children
were, it seems, considered cleaner and more efficient than the mechanical
alternatives.

We need to recognize then that the very rules which today prevent children
from working before they are 'old enough', acknowledge at the same time their
potential capability as workers. We must remember also that the processes of
transition from girl to woman, boy to man, pocket money to wage packet,
immaturity to maturity have changed, developed and appeared differently through
history as a result of economic and political shifts. In the present period our view of
child labour is restricted to the representations of Third World countries where
pre-capitalist relations of production persist, or where children may learn a family
trade under an older relative's guidance.[26] Indeed such images are explicitly defined
against the ideas about how things ought to be in a 'modern, civilized' country like
Britain and underpin the sense of moral outrage about parental irresponsibility. In
our society, children are expected to act 'like children', that is, 'childishly'. They
are viewed as thoroughly dependent upon adults and in constant need of supervision and discipline. 'Give them an inch and they'll take a mile.'

The image of youth, on the other hand, is that of a carefree, irresponsible state
prior to the ravages of 'adult' concerns. It is a period in which the 'child' meta-
morphoses into the fully-fledged 'adult' and a time of life thought to be
characterized by the existence of 'highly-charged emotions', psychological
instability and idealistic *naïveté*. Precisely because it occurs within a period of
transition, juvenile gaiety is held to be easily transformed into an equally 'youthful' violence and disregard of the adult world. This dual picture has been at the
heart of 'youth' since the generation gap was first invented, and the threat of
violence, the role of music in youth subcultures and the carefree, happy-go-lucky
connotation invite comparison with the common-sense racist images of 'the West
Indian'.[27]

The distinction between 'childhood' and 'youth' played an important part in the reporting of the July confrontations. The consternation of the *Daily Mail*'s reporter was directed towards the presence of 'ten to 14' year-olds in and around the skirmishes, rather than at the older 'yobs' from whom he evidently expected nothing else. The *Daily Telegraph* (and most other dailies) thoughtfully averaged out, at 14 years, the ages of the '24 juveniles' arrested in Toxteth on 7 July, while Whitelaw demanded to know why children in the 'age group 9 to 16' were in the 'riot'. Clearly if you were around 14 – or is it 16, or older? – you had no right being in a 'riot area', though by implication if you were older than this then presumably you did! Obviously, readers were meant to think that these children were 'too young' to understand. They were after all only *children*. To be sure there may well have been people at the scenes who were not fully aware of the signifi- cance of their actions or who were merely taking advantage of the situation; but it is by no means clear that the 'children' necessarily fell into this category. Never- theless, the strategy of dwelling on the presence of the 'children' no doubt made it easier to 'report' on the events and to concentrate the mind on what was at issue; the apparently imminent collapse of our 'free society' under the onslaught of these 'problem children', 'yobs' and 'criminals'. It also worked to add another layer of illegitimacy to violent resistance and pushed to one side any concerns, other than those focused on the state of the family, with the underlying social conditions which produced such a response.

Common-sense racist ideologies

The linkages that are made between the 'inadequate family', 'criminal youth' and the 'cultures of deprivation' that are thought to sustain them, form an important element in the common-sense images of black people. In this case, however, the ideas combine with a common-sense racist imagery which encompasses all blacks. Where the common-sense images of the white family and white youth are naturalized through reference to the gender-specific 'natural' roles, attributes and characteristics of women and men, the images of black families and black youth are the outcome of a kind of *double* naturalization. Blacks are pathologized once via their association with the 'cultures of deprivation' of the decaying 'inner cities' and again as the bearers of specifically *black* cultures. This is not just a matter of 'ethnocentric' English commentators misunderstanding black cultures and misinterpreting black family life. The hegemonic definition of family life that has been secured by the bourgeoisie was not, we suspect, organized simply around themes that were 'internal' to England, but was like other notions about what it means to be English, 'forged in relation to the superiority of the English over all other nations on the face of the globe'.[28] The common-sense notion of the family, and its place within bourgeois ideology as the 'cornerstone' of all societies, may indeed be 'ethnocentric'; more important though is the idea that the family is the 'corner- stone of *our* (British) society'. We can get a hint of how this universal yet exclusive definition of family life may have been shaped by racist ideologies from,

for example, what the eighteenth-century historian Edward Long had to say about
the likely social effects of the continued importation of blacks.

We must agree with those who declare, that the public good of this Kingdom
requires that some restraint should be laid on the unnatural increase of blacks
imported into it. . . . The lower class of women in England, are remarkably fond
of the blacks, for reasons too brutal to mention; they would connect themselves
with horses and asses if the laws permitted them. By these ladies they generally
have numerous brood. Thus, in the course of a few generations more, the English
blood will become so contaminated with this mixture, . . . as even to reach the
middle, and then the higher orders of the people. . . . This is a venomous and
dangerous ulcer, that threatens to disperse its malignancy far and wide, until every
family catches infection from it.[29]

The threat to the English 'race' comes across clearly in this onerous passage. In
Long's view the 'nature' of female sexuality is such that they cannot be expected
to contain themselves. They must be restrained, disciplined by law and no doubt by
other unspoken means. One can detect as well the vestigial remains of racist ideas
directed against the 'lower class of women' but despite his obvious disdain for
them he still implicitly distinguishes them from black women. They can, indeed
must, be 'saved'; if not in order to 'breed' for the 'race', then to prevent its
degeneration. Black 'blood' is the 'infection' which the 'lasciviousness' of these
women 'threatens to disperse'. It is not simply the 'numerous broods' that are the
result of their liaison with the equally lascivious black man, that is the issue. The
more important point for Long is that this 'mixture' will 'contaminate' the 'race'
with the blood of blacks, who are 'by nature inferior'. What is more, no family
could escape infection, not even those of the 'higher orders'. The 'race' would
disappear and with it 'our society' and 'civilisation as we have known it'.

When dipping into the bowels of history like this it is tempting to view racist
ideologies as having been constructed only by the Edward Longs of the past, solely
for the purposes of rationalizing slavery, indenture and colonialism. Clearly there
is something in this. Long and others did put forward arguments in support of
these relations of production and domination, stating quite categorically that this
was the 'natural' state of affairs. Long, for example, wrote of these historical
relations in terms of the

Three ranks of men [*sic*] (white, mulatto and black), dependent on each other,
and rising in a proper climax of subordination, in which the whites hold the
highest place.[30]

But the racist ideas that are being drawn on and reworked here have a history which
goes back beyond the period of English imperialism. Some of these ideas had been
associated with earlier relations of production throughout Europe. Others were
romanticized, mythical and in some cases ancient ideas associated with those
'far off' places and peoples of Africa and Asia – tales of great riches; of powerful

and exotic Queens and Emperors; tales of bizarre animals and even stranger customs. It would be a mammoth task to attempt to trace these ideas back to their historical 'roots' and then to reconstruct the subsequent histories of their gradual elaboration – paying attention to their complex articulations within specific historical social formulations – into the anti-black racist ideologies we are familiar with today. Needless to say, we have not attempted such a task here. What we have thought it useful to do though is to explore some aspects of this history, tracing particularly the gradual sedimentation of these ideas into common-sense thinking.

In deepest Babylon

In an article which explores the beginnings of capitalist development, Cedric Robinson[31] raises some issues which are pertinent to the present discussion. He argues that there was a radical discontinuity between the bourgeoisies of the sixteenth century and the earlier 'bourgeoisies' associated with the merchant towns of the Middle Ages. The 'new' bourgeoisies were, he says, 'implicated in structures, institutions and organisations which were substantively undeveloped in the Middle Ages'; and he criticizes the idea of 'evolution', suggested by the phrase 'the rise of the middle class', as being an illusory image 'unsupported by [the] historical evidence'. In his view, one of the outcomes of the economic decline of Medieval Europe, 'marked in a final and visible way by social disorders (peasant rebellions) much more profound than the territorial wars', was the shifting of the focus of trade from the Mediterranean to the Atlantic.

The city, the point of departure for the earlier bourgeoisies and their networks of long-distance travel and productive organisation proved incapable of sustaining the economic recovery of those bourgeoisies. . . . The absolutist state, under the hegemony of Western European aristocracies, brought forth a new bourgeoisie.[32]

The nub of Robinson's argument, as we see it, is that the economies within which capitalism begins to develop were not 'national' economies but rather political economies bounded by 'absolutist' states. While this structural feature cannot be said to have *determined* capitalist social relations, it did nevertheless shape them in profound ways, and ideologies associated with earlier feudal relations were preserved and transformed in the new situation. The transformations of 'racist' ideologies directed against the 'lower orders' are a case in point. Robinson recalls that

In the Middle Ages and later the nobility, as a rule, considered themselves of better blood than the common people, whom they utterly despised. The peasants were supposed to be descended from Ham, who, for lack of filial piety, was known to have been condemned by Noah to slavery.[33]

These ideas, like the racist ideologies that were to be constructed out of them in a later period, were grounded in notions about the significance of difference. The European nobility were, quite often, not drawn from the same 'ethnic' and cultural groups as the 'common people'. Robinson notes that the practice of drawing army volunteers 'from the least "national", most nondescript types, the dregs of the poorest classes', was not something that was peculiar to the organization of standing armies. This is merely the 'best documented form of a more generalised pattern of structural formation and social integration', which in later periods would be extended to include the new industries, shipping and agriculture.[34] Sections of the bourgeoisie and the emerging proletariat were drawn as much from other lands as from parts of the particular state, and as we know the slave labour force would be brought from 'entirely different worlds'. Robinson maintains though that the significance of 'immigrant' labour in the developing capitalist economies has remained largely unanalysed, partly because of the uncritical use of the 'nation' as a unit of analysis. However, the nation as such did not yet exist and the ideologies of the nation which were to attempt to bind the disparate groups and classes together, were not elaborated until after the capitalist mode of production had already begun to produce. Initially, at least,

The tendency of European civilisation through capitalism was thus not to homo-genise but to differentiate – to exaggerate regional, subcultural, dialectical differences into 'racial' ones.[35]

The enslaving of Africans and Asians, the use of Asians as indentured labour, and the particular forms of racist ideologies that were constructed to rationalize such activities, were not peculiar to capitalism but rather would appear to have their 'roots' firmly embedded in earlier forms of organization of labour within European societies.[36]

Of course, Robinson's account presents its own problems not least of which is his tendency to equate capitalism with trading activity. This has the effect of pre-cluding any discussion of what is specific about capitalism, namely its 'mode of production', and in terms of his concerns prevents him from examining in similar detail the class struggles that created the necessary conditions for capitalism, by 'freeing' labour in order that relative surplus value could be extracted from the efforts of the labourer.[37] Nevertheless, he does point to a potentially fruitful area of enquiry, which if made more specific to the English case should shed considerable light on the 'peculiarities of the English', and guard against the temptations of 'economic reductionism'.

Although Robinson's arguments are suggestive of the longevity and depth of ideological racist mechanisms in European cultures, it seems clear that other elements have been worked in during later historical periods, to produce speci-fically 'anti-black' racist ideologies. Winthrop D. Jordan for example, argues that the literary evidence from the Medieval period and after shows a clearly delineated 'colour symbolism'.

Black was an emotionally partisan color, the handmaid and symbol of baseness and evil, a sign of danger and repulsion.[38]

The opposition between Black (evil) and White (good) was not merely a poetic device but, suggests Jordan, was actually an integral part of their view of themselves, though it is not clear in his account how far this was a common theme outside of those involved in the production and reproduction of the literate culture.[39] Again from the journals that have been left by those literate people involved in the first excursions to the west coast of Africa, it was the fact of blackness that was the salient feature of Africans and it was the idea of *black* Africa that filtered back to and became established in England. It was an image though that carried with it decidedly negative overtones in an English setting. According to a pre-sixteenth-century version of the *Oxford English Dictionary*, to be 'black' was to be

Deeply stained with dirt; soiled, dirty, foul . . . . Having dark or deadly purposes, malignant, etc.[40]

The thought that some of the world's people could have 'black' skin was, apparently, disconcerting enough to generate a long and convoluted debate about the possible origins of such a condition. One writer in 1578 argued that

the most probable cause to my judgement is, that this blacknesse proceedeth of some naturall infection of the first inhabitants of that Countrey and so all the whole progenie of them descended, are still polluted with the same blot of infection.[41]

The writer speculated that the cause of this original infection was Ham's disobedience to his father Noah. This explanation, as we have seen, had been used in a slightly different way in earlier times. In the eighteenth century, the question was still being hotly debated. A certain John Atkins, writing in 1735, confessed to being 'persuaded [that] the black and white race have, *ab origine*, sprung from different-coloured first parents'. He conceded though that his argument was 'a little Heterodox' at the time.[42]

   This preoccupation with the colour of the African's skin does not mean, of course, that racism is an unfortunate accident of history – the outcome of a meeting between people with a 'black' skin and a 'fair'-skinned people with an already developed and largely negative body of ideas about blackness. The cap had to be made to fit before the Africans could wear it. Jordan notes that many travellers were well aware of the range of skin complexions, amongst Africans, which were later to be included under the single rubric of blackness; but perhaps more telling is the way in which the term 'black' comes to include Indians, Arabs and other non-white peoples. By the eighteenth century, according to Wylie Sypher, the British were in the 'habit of calling yellow, brown, or red people "black"'. The 'noble African' was not distinguished, even by anti-slavery writers, from the 'noble

Indian'.[43] This practice of almost literally 'tarring' all non-whites with the same brush, is indicative of the fact that racist ideologies have not simply been organized around differences in skin 'colour'. Of equal importance was the European view of the religious and cultural practices of those peoples.

The early European travellers, explorers and intrepid entrepreneurs did not stumble upon the docile and ignorant 'tribal' peoples so beloved by film-makers. They were confronted instead by the powerful and complexly organized social, political and economic systems of the Hindu and Islamic states. If they wanted to do business, then they would have to pay a no doubt grudging respect to the existing structures of power.[44] But this did not generate anything so 'tolerant' as a notion of 'cultural relativity'; rather the religious, legal, political and cultural practices of these societies were viewed more or less uniformly as 'heathen'. This characterization should be seen in the context of a Europe in which the Christian Church was even then busy trying to eradicate all alternative 'pagan' forms of worship. The fact that, in their view, such practices were the norm elsewhere, 'proved' to the Europeans and particularly the English that these people were 'barbarians' despite the apparent sophistication of their societies. God was definitely not on their side. The 'Saracen infidels' who had in an earlier period occupied the 'Holy Land' and defeated the English and other European powers in many a bloody 'crusade', had ensured that the Islamic religions would be familiar enough. In the case of Africa, however, even though the Islamic Empires of the west coast were an obvious political and military fact, it was the other indigenous non-Islamic, non-Christian religious practices that came to be associated most clearly with the continent. Indeed many commentators argued that what the Africans practised could not be regarded as religion at all.[45] The dominant image of the African was that of the primitive 'savage' rather than the 'heathen barbarian'. One outcome of this was the image of the 'noble savage', close to 'nature' and free of the cares and responsibilities thrust upon one by 'civilization'. This image of innocence coexisted with its opposite, the 'violent savage'; ungodly, depraved, subhuman, almost 'like a wild animal' – a being who is the antithesis of 'civilization'. Indeed within Christian cosmology this being was transformed into a 'devil' whose black skin on the outside was merely a visible sign of a greater darkness within. As one eighteenth-century 'scholar' put it,

[Africans] in colour so in condition are little other than Devils incarnate . . . the Devil . . . has infused prodigious Idolatry into their hearts, enough to relish his pallat and aggrandize their tortures when he gets power to fry their souls, as the raging sun has already scorcht their cole-black carcasses.[46]

This was not simply the ravings of a lone racist lunatic, or even of a small 'lunatic fringe'. Jordan, for example, has argued that the linkages that we can see being made here, between evil blackness, 'disobedience' (to God) as a reason for the 'curse' of blackness, and 'carnal copulation' as evidence of a fall from grace, represented a projection onto the African of the bourgeoisie's own anxieties about their role as entrepreneurs in the burgeoning capitalist developments that threatened to disrupt their social order.

It was the case with English confrontation with Negroes then, that a society in a state of rapid flux, undergoing important changes in religious values, and comprised of men who were energetically on the make and acutely and often uncomfortably self-conscious of being so, came upon a people less technologically advanced, markedly different in appearance and culture. From the first, Englishmen tended to set Negroes over against themselves, to stress what they conceived to be radically contrasting qualities of color, religion, and style of life, as well as animality and a peculiarly potent sexuality.[47]

Doubtless there was pressure of this sort on the bourgeoisies, to 'make sense' of their exploitative activities, but it is equally clear that the ideas they drew on for these purposes did not spring unbidden into their heads. The cultures of the ruling bloc had long since become infused with racist images, but as we have already pointed out, what is not so clear is the extent to which these images were also shared by the subordinate classes.

The kinds of detailed histories which have chronicled the shifts and transformations in the racist ideologies and practices of the ruling blocs have not been undertaken in the case of the subordinated classes, and it is perhaps for this reason that the 'race riots' in 1919, in which massed groups of whites attacked the black communities in Liverpool, Cardiff, London and elsewhere in Britain, appear as such 'unique' events at that point in British history.[48] In fact though, given the context in which they occurred, such events were hardly surprising. The immediate post-war years were a period of intense insurrectionary and revolutionary struggles, with their different histories, but which must have gained some encouragement from the successful October 1917 revolution in the USSR. Certainly, several commentators in England at the time of the 'race riots' were quick to spot the connections. An editorial in the Liverpool *Daily Post*, for example, warned that

Careful and commonsense handling of the colour disturbances is necessary if . . . [they are] . . . not to turn into an Imperial problem. There would be unfortunate possibilities of mischief if any idea gained ground in India and Africa that the attitudes of the [rioters] reflected British attitudes.[49]

This fear of rebellion in the colonies, however, had as much to do with the already visible signs of resistance to colonialism as it did with possible reactions to the riots. Bomb blasts in Egypt in March 1919 signalled the existence of an insurrectionary movement there, while in June of that year uprisings were reported in Kurdistan. In India throughout the summer, 'constitutional agitation was followed by a massive strike (involving 200,000 workers) in the Bombay cotton mills'. 'Riots' were also reported in Belize, Trinidad, Guyana, and Sierra Leone, while further 'disturbances' took place in the Belgian Congo, Panama, and Costa

Rica. This was also the year in which black people in South Africa began a campaign of 'passive resistance' to the Pass Laws and of course, closer to home, the continuing struggle for Irish independence was a constant reminder to the ruling bloc of the difficulties involved in maintaining control over the Empire.

In Britain too, the natives were in restive mood. The temporary war 'boom', which had proved a lifeline to many British industries hitherto wallowing in the pre-war economic stagnation, was now at an end. The few blacks who had been lucky enough to find work in the munitions and allied industries during the war years were dismissed, and in this industries were aided and abetted by white workers who refused to work with blacks and trade unions which insisted that whites should be employed first. The Liverpool *Courier*, 11 June 1919, estimated that 120 black workers in Liverpool had been dismissed because of the refusal of white workers to work alongside them and reported the case of an Indian, who having served four years in the Navy, was fired with 24 hours notice from his job on a Mersey river-hopper and told, 'you were quite efficient but there are 11,000 demobilised soldiers to be reinstated and they must have first chance'.[50] Needless to say with British industry 'contracting at an alarming rate' these and many other demobbed soldiers were destined to remain unemployed for some considerable time. This did not stop the Labour Party though from supporting such racist practices, in Parliamentary debate. Apparently they were 'guided in that direction by the amazing belief that the working class was necessarily white'.[51] The response of whole sections of the white working class to economic and social crisis was not to assail the citadels of power, but armed with a decidedly racist interpretation of the causes, they rounded on people who were suffering even more than they were – the black communities in their midst.

One element of the common-sense racist ideologies of this period, which was linked to the seemingly perennial argument that blacks 'take white jobs', was the idea that blacks had benefited by not taking part in the war. Of course, nothing could have been further from the truth. Blacks were recruited in their thousands from the colonies, even though they were required to fight in specially created separate black units. At the same time the 2500 'black British' volunteers were barred from combat duty and consigned to their 'age-old role of being beasts of burden for their white masters'.[52] Indeed in 1918 at Taranto in Italy, black soldiers of the West India Regiment

violently revolted against racist restrictions promulgated by the British War Office. . . . Eight battalions – some eight thousand troops – were disarmed; from fifty to sixty were arrested, charged with mutiny and sentenced.[53]

The mutiny lasted several days during which time 180 black sergeants of the Ninth Battalion sent a petition to the Secretary of State for the Colonies protesting against military racist practices. But the dominant ideological element and the reason most often quoted as the 'cause' of the riots was white 'resentment' about relationships between white women and black men. The image of the African as sexuality personified is an ancient one and as both Walvin and Jordan note, has been current in English thought at least since the fifteenth century. Obviously for many of the early adventurers and gold-hunters who were members of a culture within which the human body signified the temptations of lust, the sight of scantily clad Africans must have conjured up all of the Catholic horrors of sin and depravity, hell and damnation. In any case it seems to have been but a short step from these original visions to a view of Africans as akin to animals in terms of their sexuality. The very fact that they appeared to be unashamed of their nudity would merely have served to reinforce that view. We have already noted the equation between 'blackness' and 'sin' and have seen a sample of Edward Long's views on miscegenation. The racist ideologies of the late nineteenth and early twentieth centuries, while drawing on these earlier images of 'blackness' and the attendant threat to English nationhood, also broaden them out to include the threat to Empire and white superiority. One 'serious publication' in 1889 railed against the apparently common practice of exhibiting African men at Earl's Court. The images here were of 'raw, hulking and untamed man-animals' who were being 'corrupted by unseemly attention from white girls'.[54] An article in a 1917 edition of *Titbits*, however went further.

Some years ago we used to have large bodies of natives sent from Africa on military service or in some travelling show, and it was a revelation of horror and disgust to behold the manner in which English women would flock to see these men, whilst to watch them fawning upon these black creatures and fondling them and embracing them, as I have seen dozens of times, was a scandal and a disgrace to English womanhood. How then is it possible to maintain as the one stern creed in the policy of the Empire the eternal supremacy of the white over black?[55]

These images manage to convey, at one and the same time, the idea of the docility yet bestial sexuality of the 'untamed man-animals', but it is the seemingly rampant sexuality of English womanhood that threatens to undermine white manhood and the Empire at a stroke. For the white working class, on the other hand, even though such scribblings may have touched a raw nerve in their feelings, the 'problem' was of a different order. It was black men who were 'rampant'. To be sure a white woman seen 'stepping out' with a black man was likely to be verbally and physically assaulted but it was black men who were fundamentally to blame. Not only were they 'taking our jobs', they were 'stealing our women as well'. The newspapers and magazines may have reinforced public opinion, but they certainly did not manufacture it.[56]

   The common-sense racist imagery of the white working class which we have illustrated here was shaped by their involvement in Britain's imperialist expansion. Without wishing to prejudge the issue, there are a number of areas where we feel that further research might yield valuable information on this history. Certainly those periods in which race becomes a salient feature of British politics require further investigation. (We are thinking here, for example, of Elizabeth I's 1596 communiqué telling her Lord Mayors to send 'blacks forth of the Land' and the repatriation of some blacks to Sierra Leone in 1787.) Similarly, the various histories of the working class that have been written, have been written largely without reference to black people. At the moment, then, it is not clear whether white workers merely colluded in racist practices at work, or whether they actively instigated them. As we have seen white workers were, by the beginning of this century, quite prepared to organize against blacks; but how were they implicated in the order of 'The Lord Mayor and Court of Aldermen' of London (October 1731),[57] which stated that 'no Negroes shall be bound Apprentices to any Trades-man or Artificer of this City'? What was their reaction to this piece of news?

The contradictory outcomes of the eighteenth- and nineteenth-century struggles for popular education must also have a bearing here. Obviously, the mere fact that the expansion of 'schooling' was carried out under bourgeois rather than proletarian hegemony, would not of itself explain the prevalence of racist ideas amongst the working class. Nevertheless 'schooling' is *an* important site in which relations of dominance and subordination are reproduced,[58] and as such would be one more place where racist ideologies coming 'down from the top' could become embedded in working-class common-sense. How many generations of little white children, for example, have been encouraged to pity or despise the 'poor little black children' at the other end of the Empire? and what would they have made of the 'little black Sambo' stories with which they were entertained?

The 'end of Empire'

Traces of the ideas we have been exploring are to be found today at the centre of the common-sense imagery of black peoples and black cultures. Some of these have almost certainly sedimented into common sense from the earlier, more devel-oped racist ideologies; others have undoubtedly been created within imperialist social relations, by the subordinate classes themselves. Although such images, whatever their source, are cross-cut by other contradictory images about the essential equality of all people, for example, they nevertheless tend to pull popular opinion towards racist interpretations and understandings. Black cultures are still likely to be viewed as 'primitive' in comparison to British 'civilization', though this does not mean that black cultures are necessarily viewed as being the same. Asian cultures are at least thought to exhibit a degree of development and cohesion which is not generally associated with African cultures. Indeed, Africans are often thought not to have possessed cultures as such, that is not until the British came along and 'civilized' them. Within common-sense thinking Africans are viewed as having been in a state of childlike 'innocence', while Asians might at best be credited with having emerged into a state of adolescence. The relative 'underdevelopment' and poverty of many 'Third World' countries is of course not viewed as the outcome of centuries of imperialism and colonial domination, but rather is thought to be expressive of a *natural state of affairs*, in which blacks are seen as genetically and/or culturally inferior. The naturalization of the differences between these cultures and

English culture helps to 'explain' why Asians adhere to 'backward' religions and 'barbaric' customs, it also helps to 'explain' the 'superstitious' and 'primitive' beliefs and customs of Africans.

There is an important sense as well though, in which such 'distinctions' as are made are only the icing on top of the racist cake. Whether they are called blacks, browns, coloureds, darkies, nig-nogs, or Pakis makes little real difference, since in one essential – their apparent alienness – they are 'all the same'. In popular discourse they can, and frequently do, double for each other. The 'slave-figure', for example, 'is by no means limited to films and programmes *about* slavery. Some "Injuns" and many Asians have come onto the screen in this disguise'.[59]

Racist ideologies in the post-war period, however, are not simply a rehash of old ideas. The two core images of colonial peoples, as children needing protection or as the equally immature 'brutal savage', gain new meanings and inflexions in the period of decolonization. Harold MacMillan, for example, referred to decolonization as 'the development of the nations to which we already stand in the relationship of parents' and maintained that 'like all parents, we would like to see our children take after us.[61] This was not a view that was confined to the 'right' of British politics; on the contrary, it held a position of central importance in the attitudes of both major political parties. Both parties were adamant in their opinion that their own political and cultural system was superior to all others, that they had a civilizing mission, and that what was British was best. This not only influenced their attitudes to the colonies but also their attitudes to independence. Challenges to British rule were interpreted as challenges to 'civilization'. Independence or 'self-government' was something to be bestowed; it was presented as a *gift* that could only be given after a period of preparation, after the conditions had been created for a 'stable' and 'responsible' government. The whole debate about the 'end of Empire' was suffused with this general attitude of paternal superiority; the talk was all of 'trusteeship', 'standards', 'conditions', 'building up', 'guidance', 'responsibility' and 'granting', and is aptly summed up in a statement by Arthur Creech Jones, Labour Colonial Secretary in 1948.

The central purpose of British colonial policy is simple. It is to *guide* the colonial territories to *responsible* self-government.[61]

This statement was to become a basis of future policy for both Labour and Tory politicians. But while Labour and Tory politicians shared certain common assumptions about independence, there were also real differences. Sections of the Tory Party went along with notions of the innate inferiority of colonial people in a way that Labour politicians, because of the democratic and egalitarian strands of Labour Party philosophy, did not.

In the event, and despite the consensus in British politics about the necessity of a 'long period of preparation', the pace was set by the various nationalist movements within the colonies. The first batch of countries to gain self-government were the Asian colonies, India, Ceylon and Burma. With India there had indeed been a long period of preparation, although Churchill's query about Powell – 'who was that young madman who has been telling me how many divisions I will need to reconquer India'[62] – illustrates how difficult it would have been for a war-torn Britain to hold onto India in the face of a strong and determined nationalist movement. John Strachey summed up the problems the British faced in Asia:

If the British had been unyielding and had not gradually introduced parliamentary institutions into India during the last forty years of British rule, the nationalist movement must have organised itself in a revolutionary form; it must have become a nationalist junta, like Kuomintang in China, or more probably in contemporary conditions, a communist party.[63]

It was against this background that India was *granted* self-government, but shortly after Mountbatten – with 'Divide and quit' as the slogan – had 'guided' the country to independence, it erupted into violence. This must have provided additional fuel for those who were arguing that 'self-government leads to anarchy'. Malaya though was the trickiest problem for Britain as she tried to extricate herself from the Asian portion of her Empire. Britain's stake in Malaya's lucrative rubber plantations clearly needed to be defended but Britain's projected vision of independence was hotly contested by Malaya's large and active Communist Party. In this struggle we begin to see the elaboration of a 'communism equals barbarity' image – the beginnings of the new cold/hot war psychology – which is underpinned by the wartime/post-war representations of the Japanese. The boost given to the African nationalist movements by Indian independence raised the tempo of independence struggles in the African colonies. The British looked on in shocked surprise as each successive nationalist movement, at some stage or another, became involved in violent confrontations with their erstwhile 'masters'. These struggles, particularly in the areas of white settlement in Central and East Africa, gave rise in Britain to new images of savagery and barbarism, with the Mau Mau movement in Kenya being taken as the perfect example of what would happen when the 'children finally left home'. As Fanon has pointed out, Mau Mau was characterized by a refusal to compromise with conciliatory blacks; hence most of its 'victims' were black, not white. However, Fanon maintained that it was this refusal to compromise which really terrified the Europeans.[64] *The Economist*, 17 January 1953, put its finger on Britain's anxiety when it argued that, 'the whole incident underlines how baffling and intractable is the political future of colonies with several races, especially where the dominant race is in a tiny minority'. This statement should be viewed alongside the Tory arguments against the 1948 Nationalities Act, where in support of their kith and kin in Africa they argued that 'Africans were Africans whether they are black or white'. We should also remember that in 1948, despite Britain's labour shortages, West Indians were being discouraged from entering Britain by Tory and Labour MPs alike. In its issue of 21 March 1953 *The Economist* again returned to the theme of Mau Mau.

Mr Blundell's explanation is that the Kikuyu have been compelled to try to assimilate 2,000 years of Western ideas of progress in 50 years, and that their minds have suddenly rebelled. The Mau Mau, he feels, is sheer atavism. If he should be right, it points to a disturbing conclusion for other parts of Africa.

The attitudes and language which surround the 'Suez crisis' are further illustration of the depth of British anxiety over Africa. Nasser is reputed to have said to the British, 'May you choke to death on your fury'. Morrison responded to Nasser's actions and speeches by claiming that 'it is not a *civilised* . . . way of conducting business'. Sir Robert Boothby's statement though was more revealing.

the rabid nationalism which is now developing is reactionary and atavistic – a revolt against the demands of the modern world and of life itself. . . . [Nasser's language] is the language of Hitler and the rule of the jungle; and if we were to allow him to get away with it, it would be a most damaging blow to the whole conception of international law.[65]

Britain of course lost this particular battle and found herself isolated in the international community with the USA, the USSR, and the UN opposing her actions. The idea, though, that struggles for independence were threats to 'civilization' and the arguments by means of which struggles against domination could be represented as their opposite – namely as struggles to dominate in 'Hitler-like' fashion – lived on to find renewed expression in the 1960s and 1970s. As Hall puts it,

Primitivism, savagery, guile and unreliability – all 'just below the surface' – can still be identified in the faces of black political leaders around the world, cunningly plotting the overthrow of 'civilization'.[66]

Of course it was precisely in this moment of decolonization that, because of labour shortages in England, immigration from the colonies and ex-colonies gained momentum. The way that the notion of race differences is posed in the present period owes a great deal to attitudes engendered throughout Britain's imperial past and to the way nationalist movements are portrayed in the period of decolonization. The imperial past in no way determines the shape of contemporary racism, but the attitudes of superior/inferior, responsible/irresponsible, mother/children, barbarism/civilization, etc. provide a reserve of images upon which racists and racism can play. It helps explain the specific way racist ideas are formed in the British (as opposed to the American) context.

The image held of those black people already settled in England in the late forties is of interest here. On 2 July 1949, for example, *The Picture Post* enquired 'Is there a BRITISH COLOUR BAR?' and found to their evident surprise that indeed there was. Probing the possible consequences of this, *The Picture Post* informed its readers that because all colonial coloured people, of whatsoever origin or class, have been brought up to think of Britain as 'The Mother Country', they would not only resent the 'British colour bar' but 'a deep emotional illusion (would be) shattered for them as well'. With an argument that was later to become the bedrock upon which the future edifice of 'race relations' was constructed, the article went on to say that for West Indians in particular the disillusion would be most severe. This was because,

the West Indians . . . no longer have the tribal associations and native language which can still provide some fundamental security for the disillusioned African. The West Indian disillusioned with Britain is deprived of all sense of security. He [*sic*] becomes, quite understandably, the most sensitive and neurotic member of the coloured community, and may be inclined to drift into bad ways.

The article also raised fleetingly the spectre of communism which as we know is already being linked in this period to barbarism. What is interesting about this argument is not so much the view that 'many coloured people look to Communism to release them from their social humiliation', but that in the case of 'coloured' people, this represented a 'strange emotional leap'. This image of black political activity as 'emotional' rather than considered clearly parallels the characterizations of the various nationalist movements. As we shall see, it is also a hint about the dominant way in which black struggles in Britain throughout the sixites and seventies were to be conceptualized.

It seems necessary here to consider working-class attitudes to the 'end of Empire'. We have argued that there is by this time a bundle of racist images about blacks which have sedimented into working-class common sense, or else have been generated by the working class in its experience of imperialism. Undoubtedly though, in situations of conflict there is a sharpening of the racist imagery. The recruitment of working-class people into the armies that fought the initial 'imperial wars', the two world wars and which went to put down the 'restless natives' in the period of decolonization, must have had effects upon their consciousness of the differences between themselves and their various enemies.

Knowledge of the Empire was therefore necessarily partial and incomplete. George Orwell, for example, in *England Your England*, commented as part of a different argument that, 'in the working class this hypocrisy takes the form of not knowing the Empire exists'.[67] After World War II there was certainly a general disinterest in colonial affairs amongst a fairly large section of British society. Hugh Dalton remarked in 1947, at the time of Indian independence,

I don't believe that one person in a hundred thousand in this country cares tuppence about [India] so long as British people are not being mauled about out there.[68]

Dalton would appear to be speaking for most people here for according to the Government's Social Survey Unit investigations, in 1948 51 per cent and in 1951

59 per cent of the population could not name a single British colony.[69] As if to illustrate the point one reader of *The Picture Post* responded thus:

How does a negro come to have an old English name like Smith? Has he not adopted it for the sole purpose of gate crashing? [70]

In post-war Britain, then, it seems that there was very little chance of creating strong feelings in favour of maintaining an Empire. While the jingoism of the Boer War may have shown itself again in the jingoism of World War I, the attitudes of World War II about the fight for 'freedom' and 'democracy', which were so important in generating nationalism in Asia and Africa, seem to lead to a general attitude in Britain of 'give them their independence if that's what they want'. This does not imply that the racism of the colonial period is not carried over into the new period. Certainly there is in this attitude the air of resignation of parents who know that their child is 'too young' to leave home but who compromise with a 'well we won't stand in your way, but don't come running to us when things go wrong'. More generally, we need to separate out two strands of thought: on the one hand there is an agreement to end colonial rule, but on the other there is a residual set of attitudes accumulated during the imperial period around the idea of child/savage. These attitudes were reinforced in the period of decolonization.

The period immediately after decolonization is also important, for it is at this moment that 'not knowing the Empire exists' becomes 'official'. From the late fifties onwards the question of 'race' is viewed as an essentially 'external' problem, 'foisted on English society from outside'. Hall has already identified this response to the 'end of Empire'[71] and the consequent refusal to acknowledge the imperial past. Politicians of the left and the right have persistently debated the question of 'race' as though the 'problem' *began* with the black immigration of the fifties and sixties. This 'profound historical forgetfulness' provides exactly that space within which the racist ideas from the imperial past can be elaborated anew. Their starting-point is with the idea that 'they (the blacks) have no right to be here' and since this is the case we need only *allow* 'a few to come in'. Another letter in response to *The Picture Post*'s 'colour bar' article indicates the direction in which racist ideologies were to develop. After arguing that 'colour mixing' would be 'distasteful to the average person', the writer went on to offer a solution:

I believe the best solution is to prevent any large number of coloured people taking up permanent residence in this country. Why import a social problem where one did not previously exist? [72]

Winds of change?

Of course the images of the primitive, childlike savages who might 'turn nasty', at any moment and who in any case have no place in a 'civilized' society, are not the only images to have been carried over and reworked. Images of black sexuality are also still massively present. Think of the way, for example, in which the supposedly impartial TV cameras unerringly find their way to those 'quaint' and 'exotic' ceremonials where they can get their close-up of the naked bosoms of African women. Think as well about the 'slave-girl' in James Bond type movies, who even more than her white counterpart is rarely anything but sexually available. Of course this view of Africans and their Caribbean and American sisters and brothers has reached its fullest and most vicious expression in the USA, where the rape by slave owners of their female slaves has prompted the elaboration of the myth of African women as always ready and willing to satisfy the carnal longings of men. The attentive reader will have noticed that the arguments and feelings about mis- cegenation, discussed earlier, were aimed at preventing white women from sleeping with black men. Nothing was said about the rape of enslaved black women even though it was a regular occurrence in the colonies at that time. Indeed even such amicable relationships as were entered into freely by black women and white men were not thought worthy of a mention. One popular explanation for this (more popular in the USA than here) is that white men viewed white women as *their* property and that their image of their own masculinity was somehow bound up with this 'ownership'. Since both black women and black men were quite literally his property and in any case considered inferior, he could use them as he wished – which of course he did. Black women were used sexually and, along with black men, as 'beasts of burden'. In this scenario then, sexual advances towards white women by black men would be viewed as attempted theft of white mens' 'property', masculinity and indeed, as we saw with Long, of their 'race'. The argu- ment is then extended to include the 'free' black man. Here, black men aware of the damage they can do to the 'master' have developed a peculiar lust for white womanhood. We would not wish to argue for or against this view at the present time but we note that in its extension to include the consciousness of black men it assumes too readily that black men have necessarily internalized the white man's view of things. Indeed it suggests that the racists have got a point. Black men are after 'white flesh' after all!

Another way of explaining the apoplexy generated by the thought of sexual relations between white women and black men, which would avoid some of the above pitfalls, would be to examine more closely ideas about the role of women as the reproducers of the 'race' and seventeenth/eighteenth-century beliefs about paternity. Long's comments, for example, expressed a desire not just to control the sexuality of white women but also to control their *fertility*. In his view they should 'breed for the race', that is produce white children. White women who bear 'mulatto' children have 'failed in their duty' and have also 'polluted' the race by introducing into it 'inferior blood'. But there is something else going on here as well. If we think for example of the plight of the European woman, in numerous Western movies, who is taken off by the 'injuns', it is clear that the woman herself is regarded as 'polluted' by sexual contact with them. She will never be 'the same again' and in the eyes of the cowboys who have so gallantly 'rescued' her she is viewed with evident distaste. Such a woman is regarded as 'worse than a whore' and therefore, no longer sexually available. Furthermore, she is certainly not of the right 'stock' any longer, for breeding fine upstanding members of the 'race'. Her whole child-bearing potential then is 'lost' to it.

The rape by the slave master of his female slaves though is interpreted in quite a different manner. While any offspring will still be considered 'half-breeds', 'half-castes', 'mulattos' or whatever, they were never, in any case, potential members of 'the race', since their mother was black. Further no shame of 'pollution' attaches itself to the white man in the way that it does to the white woman, presumably because he can 'cleanse' himself in a way that a woman – in the passive 'feminine' position as a 'receptacle' – cannot. Indeed there is a sense in which the white man can congratulate himself on introducing some 'superior blood' into the 'inferior' black race. The experience of John Griffin, a white reporter who, in the early sixties, travelled through the southern USA posing as a black man, serves to illustrate the point:

He told me how all of the white men in the region craved coloured girls. He said he hired a lot of them both for housework and in his business. 'And I guarantee you, I've had it in every one of them before they got on the payroll.' . . .
'What do you think of that?'
'Surely some refuse?' I suggested cautiously.
'Not if they want to eat – or feed their kids,' he snorted, 'If they don't put out, they don't get the job. . . . We figure we're doing you people a favour to get some white blood in your kids.'[73]

We have not as yet worked these ideas through fully and our comments on this matter are provisional. Nevertheless, we do feel justified in suggesting that these ideas, or ideas like them, are a part of today's common-sense racist beliefs. As Folarin Shyllon commented,

in Britain today, the question is never: Would you allow your son to marry a black girl? It is always: Would you allow your daughter to marry a black man?[74]

Although there is a definite connection between the elaboration of these ideas and the enslaving of African people, this does not mean that these are applicable only to people of African descent. On the contrary they are applied to all black people regardless of their origins. To be sure, there are differences between the common-sense views of African and Asian sexuality; for example, Asian humanity is not called into question in the same way. The common-sense view of the sexuality of Asian women is at first sight contradictory: it would be strange if no associations were made between Asian women and the idea of the 'exotic' sexual practices contained in such works as the *Kama Sutra*, but this appears to cut across the deeply held view of the 'passive' Asian woman walking three steps behind her domineering and sometimes brutal 'lord and master'. Here the idea of Asian women as having 'secret knowledge' about sex is combined with a suspicion that she is not sexually available to men other than her husband. Her very 'passivity' is thought to be a reflection of her upbringing, geared to her learning to accommodate and please her future husband. This notion, working in conjunction with the abso-lute power of the male to elicit her compliance and mediated through the image of the lithe and sinewy gyrations of the 'belly-dancer', works so as to produce a composite image of a smouldering sexuality – 'full of Eastern promise' – waiting only to be fanned into flames by the most potent masculinity.

Of course in the 'real world' such power does not reside exclusively with the Asian male and in later chapters we will be considering the ways in which these views of black women generally as 'erotica', of Asian women as passive and of Afro-Caribbean women as well suited to laborious tasks, structure their experience of work in England at the present time.[75] We will content ourselves for the moment with a brief look at some of the other common-sense racist images which are important today in the elaboration of racist ideologies. We mentioned earlier that Asian humanity is not questioned in the same way as is the humanity of Africans and their descendants. Yet of the black communities settled in England it is Asians who tend to be viewed as the most alien. Doubtless this has something to do with the idea that Afro-Caribbean people have been 'given' English culture, even if their 'innate inferiority' has caused them to debase it. The full weight of Asian 'alienness', though, comes out in ideas about food – not just in the way in which food is prepared and cooked but also what is (thought to be) eaten. The stories from white neighbours about the 'constant smell of curry' emanating from next door are well known, as is the peculiarly British distaste for the smell of garlic. But it is the association in the popular mind between the Indian (and Chinese) restaurants and the disappearance of the neighbourhood cats that prompts particular feelings of horror.

Language, however, is a key element in lending coherence to the various other images. While it has taken the English a long time to recognize that Afro-Caribbeans speak a different language and not merely a form of 'bad English', no such tardiness was possible with regard to the Asian communities. The important point is not that Asians speak languages that are dissimilar to English, but the fact that this is perceived as evidence of inferiority. Common sense tends to make a leap from the recognition that English is not their first language to the feeling that they are incapable of speaking English. This is brought out quite clearly in the popular practice of speaking to 'foreigners' in a way that suggests that they are children or imbeciles or both; as though speaking to them in pidgin English somehow aids understanding! Indeed the stand-up comic only has to affect an Asian or 'West Indian' accent to raise a laugh, and of course language in particular and 'race' in general have become popular themes in situation comedies. It is frequently argued that these jokes normalize the presence of blacks in British society, and that they demonstrate a certain degree of acceptance. However, it is difficult to know how racist (and sexist) jokes can be funny unless you share the underlying assumptions. As Hall has already argued, the same old categories of racially-defined characteristics and qualities, and the same relations of superior and inferior, provide the pivots on which the jokes actually turn, the tension-points which move and motivate the situations in situation comedies. The comic register in which they are set, however, protects and defends viewers from acknowledging their incipient racism. It creates disavowal.[76]

We should also consider the way in which the successful presence of black people in sport and entertainment is handled. Within common sense, such roles are only fitting for blacks, since these roles provide an outlet for the expression of their 'natural' rhythmic and athletic qualities. A study of the representations of black sports personalities would be most revealing. Consider for example Frank McGhee's description of Thomas Hearns (former WBA welterweight champion). After giving us the comments of Hearns's physician that Hearns 'knows only how to fight' and 'he is a physical freak', McGhee goes on to tell us that

He has enormously muscled arms, so long he could almost *scratch* his knees without bending.[77] (our emphasis)

We have little doubt that McGhee would disavow any racist intent here but the question remains of why is it *this* description rather than another which springs into his mind? This is not an isolated incident; in the same edition of the *Daily Mirror*, we are treated to the spectacle of (Vivian) 'Richards the Killer' . . . 'assaulting Warwickshire's attack'. It is not enough to argue that these writers do not have racist intentions; as Hall says in relation to the 'joke tellers', the circumstances in which such descriptions are produced and read are 'conditions of continuing racism' over which the writers have little control.

Common sense and the black family

Before we go on to discuss in more detail the elaboration of neo-conservative racist ideologies during the seventies, it seems appropriate to examine some of the more novel features of common-sense imagery about blacks and particularly how they have been represented in the media in this period. We aim to emphasize the way in which black cultures and more specifically black households have been constructed as 'problem categories' posing difficulties for themselves and for society at large. It is especially important to recall the 'collective amnesia' of the British people which underpins current thinking about 'race' and which supports the notion that the problems have been 'imported' by blacks themselves. The *Sun* in a feature article about 'Black Britain', for example, situated the problems in this way:

Many of the black people who have chosen to build their future in Britain accept bad housing, poor education, unemployment and insults. They regard it as the price they pay for coming here. Some of them are even grateful. But young blacks are not. They did not choose to be born in Britain.[78]

The theme of 'youth' which we discussed earlier is clearly *one* reason for the present position of the 'family' as a crucial site of the 'class struggle in ideology', but if 'youth-in-general' have raised anxieties about the strength of the social fabric, black youth – particularly of the 'alienated' kind – have been seen as specifically prone to indulge in crime, violence and other subversive activities. Such common-sense racist ideologies that have been elaborated to 'explain' the struggles of young blacks, in school and elsewhere, are a clear instance of where common-sense images of blacks are secured via that double naturalization process we spoke of earlier. First they are 'young', with all that that means, but second they are young *blacks*, ensnared in the 'deprivations' of their home/cultural background.

To begin with there is the 'fact' that black families tend to be larger than the *average* white family. This is considered the 'natural' consequence of the Afro-Caribbean's sexuality and the power that Asian men wield over Asian women. There is the further notion here that neither group bothers to use contraception, either because 'they don't understand' or because religious strictures and taboos forbid such practices.[79] This view is summed up in that popular slogan, 'they breed like rabbits!' For the Asian communities, this is thought to be compounded by their extended family/kinship system – 'overcrowding' is seen as a direct product of their predilection for being together. The real problem of poor and inadequate housing – a consequence of racist practices – is therefore something they have brought on themselves.

It is not these practices in themselves that are thought to constitute the main problem for British society, but the fact that such practices are being continued 'here in Britain'. This view turns in part on the notion that British culture is inherently superior to all others. Thus the 'meeting' of the cultures on British soil is felt to put undue 'pressure on the [black] family' and to undermine their 'traditional ways'. The children are viewed as the agents of change in this process. They go to school with white English children, imbibe certain aspects of British culture and are said to be influenced by the greater 'freedom' of their white peers. Naturally enough, so the argument runs, they would like to enjoy such 'freedoms' as well, but this introduces tensions and stress into their home life and may even bring them into conflict with their 'traditionalist' parents. Asian parents are thought to face 'the gentle revolt of their children' against Asian cultural practices. Arranged marriages are presented as a specific site of conflict, particularly for Asian girls who apparently yearn to adopt the 'permissive' customs of the English. They 'want to uncover their legs and wed boys they choose, not partners arranged for them by their families'.[80] The 'freedom' to marry the partner of your choice is of course one of those cherished British freedoms which marks out British culture as 'superior'. From this point of view, the institution of arranged marriage, in which it is assumed that the girl has no say in who she marries, is indicative of the inherent 'barbarity' of Asian cultures. At the same time, it fits in with the common-sense image of the Asian household as being hierarchically organized with a despotic male at the apex, who rigidly circumscribes the activities of the children – especially the females. Numerous TV documentaries and newspaper articles have taken up the theme of the 'inevitable casualties' produced by the conflict between tyrannical Asian parents with archaic ideas and their Anglicized offspring who 'only want to do what any normal British girl does'. Thanks partly but not solely to their efforts, the girl who is hustled into a premature arranged marriage with someone 'twice her age' whom she had never met; the girl who commits suicide because her parents wouldn't allow her to marry 'the boy she loved'; and the girl who is bundled back to the Asian subcontinent at the first sign that she is 'going British', are all commonplace images of the plight of Asian girls. Such imagery adds further layers of respectability to Whitelaw's claim to 'have had many letters' and serves to underpin the view that, on the Asian fiancé issue, the present Government is on the side of the girls against their religious and tyrannical parents. It also assumes that white English girls have complete freedom of choice in whom they marry, conveniently glossing over possible class-based determinations and even the frequently obstructive role of the parents. Similarly, the complex negotiations involved in arranging a marriage and the differing ways different communities and parents have of going about it, remain unrecognized within the common-sense view.

For Asian girls, the amount of choice they have over who they marry varies a lot from one Asian community to another, and from one Asian family to another. Some parents are more strict than others, just like some White English parents exercise more control over their children than others.[81]

We should emphasize at this point that these common-sense notions, like common-sense ideologies generally, are not just carried around in peoples' heads. They are embedded within actual material practices. In schools, for example, Asian girls are often 'automatically excluded from whole areas of extra curricular activities' on the grounds that 'their parents will object to their daughters mixing with boys'. In a similar way careers advice for Asian girls is frequently structured around notions about the ways in which their future lives will be circumscribed. They are not, for example, advised about further education because it is assumed that their parents have something else – namely arranged marriage – in mind for them.[82]

In the case of Afro-Caribbean families, the problem is posed in a similar but slightly different way and revolves around the way in which the parents 'discipline' their children. Apparently 'West Indian families . . . have to adapt to permissiveness in Britain. Traditionally West Indian parents are much stricter with their children.'[83] Here, the tensions arise not because these children want to 'adopt Western dress' and marriage customs, but because they want to be allowed to stay out late like 'the white children they meet'. Furthermore, they 'fail' at school because they are unused to the 'permissive' regime of British schools which supposedly runs counter to the strict discipline of the home. Predictably, in this view, the children react violently. They 'throw off' the 'strict traditional upbringing' and 'run wild'. We are not surprised then when the *Sun* tells us that Afro-Caribbean parents want 'stricter discipline for their children in school and at home'. The *Sun*'s case is strengthened by the way it uses the remarks of blacks themselves – especially community leaders – to state the case. The idea that Afro-Caribbean youth are throwing off their 'strict traditional upbringing' is attributed to Courtney Laws as is the argument that 'they do not respect the black leadership. We cannot control them'.[84] We should reiterate here a point made earlier in connection with equating working-class ideas of discipline too straightforwardly with the views of the police or Tory Party politicians. Statements made by black people in the context of black struggles against racism in schools and outside do not necessarily have the same meanings as they do in the context of bourgeois ideology.[85] Of course we are not saying that Laws doesn't mean what he says; rather we are arguing that the context in which the *Sun* chooses to place his quote alters its meaning. Perhaps we can illustrate this point better by looking in more detail at what happened when another 'community leader' attempted to talk through the media about these issues. Barbados-born Mr Jeff Crawford, senior community relations officer for Haringey, was reported in the *Daily Express* (22 April 1981) as telling 'his people' to 'get your kids under control'. Crawford's remarks, repeated that night on BBC's *Nationwide*, were in response to the confrontation the previous Bank Holiday Monday night between black youths and the police at Finsbury Park. He was keen to distinguish between the earlier events in Brixton and what he called the 'mindless violence', perpetrated by 'a gang of lawless black youths just off their heads', on his patch. Whatever the validity of such a distinction, it is clear that his comments about the Afro-Caribbean family's contribution to those events was meant to apply more generally. In an apparently 'angry' manner he told the *Express* reporter that:

When the West Indians first came to Britain social workers and some left wingers described black parents as too Victorian, too disciplinarian and as a result of this they lost confidence and lost the battle for their children's minds.

These remarks were meant to point to the common-sense racist assumptions which lay behind social work and other institutional practices, but it would appear that the *Express* was more intrigued by the link that he established between lack of familial control and gangs of 'lawless black youths'. Crawford's argument that the racist criticisms and practices of social workers, 'some left wingers' and teachers had undermined black parental authority, was eclipsed behind the more familiar common-sense image of the clash between two cultures. It was this 'understanding' (whereby the authority of black parents is undermined by contact with the more permissive English cultural mores, and where the resulting mix produces the preternatural black youth bent on violence) which the *Express* emphasized. Using Crawford's own words the *Express* headlined the story in order to reveal the threat.

These social workers and teachers helped to make a handful of black Frankensteins and now white society is afraid of them.

Crawford's intervention and the handling of it by the *Daily Express* would appear to furnish both an interesting case study on how not to present an anti-racist argument and an indication that common sense can be made to cut both ways. In his account, lack of black parental authority is the result of earlier racist interventions by social workers etc., and this at least provides a counter to the argument that Afro-Caribbean children 'run wild' because their minds can't cope with the 'permissive' regime of British schools. However, it is precisely because Crawford's arguments rest upon common-sense assumptions about the family and the link between the family and the activities of 'youth', that the *Express* is able to appropriate his anti-racist remarks for its own racist purposes. Of course the fact that his remarks suggest that racism is the outcome of individual actions also fits in nicely with the *Express*'s own views on the harm caused by 'do-gooders' and 'left-wing agitators'.

Much of the concern about Afro-Caribbean 'youth' is in reality a concern about the activities of the male children. The *Sun*'s middle-page feature, which we examined above, does however make Afro-Caribbean 'girls' visible even if in this case visibility is not to their benefit. Predictably the *Sun* chose to focus upon the incidence of unmarried mothers within the Afro-Caribbean community. This image may be thought to contradict the image of a 'strict traditional upbringing' and therefore undermine the common-sense characterization of the Afro-Caribbean family. The *Sun* though manages to resolve these contradictions by reference to common-sense images of black women's sexuality: the parents remain unconcerned when their daughters become pregnant because 'traditionally a West Indian girl proved her womanhood in this way'. Given the centrality of the mother in common-sense images of the family, it is not difficult to see how this image can act as another means of 'explaining' the behaviour of young Afro-Caribbeans. Not only does the absence of a 'father-figure' suggest a lack of discipline in the home but, more importantly, Afro-Caribbean mothers will presumably pass on such 'cultural traditions' to their offspring. Similarly, the fact that many Afro-Caribbean mothers have to go out to work in order for their families to survive, easily gets translated into the argument that they are neglecting their children. The resultant 'maternal deprivation' then 'explains' the 'violence' of the children.

The common-sense image of the Asian mother is similar. She is portrayed as isolated from the beneficial effects of English culture because her movements are circumscribed by custom, and she therefore invariably fails to learn English. She is viewed as particularly prone to superstitious beliefs and, being more traditional than the other members of her family, is also more 'neurotic' in her new urban setting. We will discuss this imagery in more detail in Chapter 7, but it is is worth noting here how the Asian mother is presented within such imagery as the main barrier to the integration of her children into the 'wider British society'.

Finally, we ought to consider the connections that are continually drawn between blacks and crime. Belated recognition of the scale of Fascist violence and a reluctance to concede the extent of police malpractice, when it comes to policing the blacks, form part of the context in which black resistance comes to be viewed as criminal activity. As one reporter said of black peoples' combative response to

Fascist activity in their communities, 'stone-throwing Asians and West Indians hardly improve race relations' and in any case, he adds, 'stone-throwing' is quite simply 'illegal' regardless of the circumstances.[86] In much the same way as the earlier nationalist movements were viewed as the aggressors attacking 'civilization', black people here are viewed as the aggressors standing in the way of an improvement in 'race relations' by 'over-reacting' to the 'power crazed Nazis' who parade through their communities. They are expected, of course, to leave their protection to the police!

The idea that blacks are 'too sensitive' and walk around with a 'chip on their shoulder' is popular enough. Underlying it is the view of blacks as inherently 'emotional' and liable to react with violence at the slightest provocation. As we have seen the Afro-Caribbean family is viewed as being unable to contain the wilder impulses of its children, particularly since their parents' efforts at control have been undermined by British permissiveness. In this view the fact that Afro-Caribbeans are unused to such laxity produces children who are undisciplined, with little respect for authority and particularly prone to extreme violent emotions and behaviour. This, and the popular image created by the media of these youths as 'muggers', serves to legitimate police repression of the Afro-Caribbean community in the public mind. Asian crime is seen as being much more internal to the community, either in the form of violence in the family – a product of the male's tyrannical power – or else in the harbouring of 'illegal immigrants' within the extended family/kinship network. All Asians are therefore 'suspect', a view which sanctions 'fishing raids' into their communities and places of work. Asians are viewed as the 'passive' members of the black communities but *young* Asians, particularly the boys, are thought to be just as prone to violent outbursts as their Afro-Caribbean 'cousins'. Thus the contradictions between the view that Asians are 'passive', yet also, like all 'natives', inherently violent, and the knowledge that they are more than prepared to defend themselves and their communities against Fascists and the police alike, is partially resolved in common-sense thinking in two ways: first, by the notion that Asians keep themselves and their 'violence' to themselves, and second, by attributing any 'violence' outside of their communities to 'young hotheads', thereby mapping it into the more general problem of 'youth'.

The common-sense images and ideas about 'blacks', 'youth' and 'the family' that we have been examining and attempting to draw together do not, of course, exist in anything like so coherent a fashion in 'reality'. Common sense is unsystematized, inconsistent and contradictory. Although sections of the media do take up these themes, rework them and re-present them to 'the public', this is a selective and 'patchy' process and serves more to 'revamp' and 'up-date' common sense than to organize it. Such activities provide common-sense legitimations for repressive measures directed against blacks (the 'mugging' scare for example) and the 'recycling' of common sense in which they are involved provides fertile terrain for the cultivation of more 'theoretical' racist ideologies that seek to bring coherence to common sense. In the final section of this chapter we trace the contours of such ideologies in the present conjuncture, pointing as we go to the connections with and intersections of common sense.

Racist ideologies

This section will not deal with the racist ideologies of the organized Fascist movements. This is not because we believe that they are a 'lunatic fringe' with little support in the country. On the contrary, their ideas on 'race' do have a popular appeal and they have succeeded to some extent in defining the terms of the debate about immigration and 'race relations'. However, their strategy on race is an alternative to rather than an extension of the bipartisan strategy of the state. For the time being, popular racist opinion has been appeased by the speed and severity of the state's initiatives on the 'race issue', which have been carried through regardless of who was 'in power'. Furthermore the Conservative Party itself has provided an organized forum for the expression of racist ideas. Indeed in recent years, and as an organic component of its strategy for dealing with crisis conditions, it has provided the platform for the elaboration of a racist ideology which is probably more credible than the more 'instrumental' and conspiratorial Fascist alternative.[87] It is this ideology that we aim to examine here.

There is a link between the development of this racist ideology and the post-war forgetfulness which obscured the historical connections between England and her colonial Empire. As Hall puts it,

The very definition of 'what it is to be British' – the centrepiece of that culture now to be preserved from racial dilution – has been articulated around this absent/present centre.[88]

At another level the impetus for its elaboration can be found at the point where the Butler/Gaitskell consensus cracks to reveal not 'one nation' working together so as to expand the 'economic resource-pie', with everyone getting a larger share, but an increasing chasm between rich and poor.[89] Martin Barker explains:

The Tory party has had to sell its ideology of limitless human wants and the need for economic growth. But when the crucial prop of that One Nation stance was kicked away by recession, the liberal Tory ideology went into crisis.[90]

A question of culture

The form of Conservatism that emerged out of this crisis contains, as one leading element, a particular view of 'race' which is articulated around the differences between English culture and the cultures of black people. Its novelty lies not so much in the 'newness' of the ideas as in where the emphasis is placed. The current crop of racist ideologues are concerned to distance themselves from any notions that blacks might be inferior, though they do not always find this easy, as we shall see. Alfred Sherman, for example, who as the *Daily Telegraph* explains, 'sees mass immigration as a symptom of the national death wish', argues that even while 'at considerable cost' Britain was trying to cater for her own 'disadvantaged',

it simultaneously imports masses of poor, unskilled, uneducated, *primitive* and under-urbanised people into the stress areas of this country where they are bound to compete with the existing urban poor for scarce resources.[91] (our emphasis)

A little later he tells us that 'immigration was bound to *import* problems'[92] (our emphasis). Sherman is one of the more hard-nosed of the ideologues and his disdain for black people shows through. What is more important, however, is the suggestion that the blacks brought the 'problems' with them. His argument is not that they came into the most run-down areas and worst-paid jobs, but that because of their cultures they are not able to surmount these initial 'difficulties'. Indeed their cultural practices actually generate more problems.

We can understand this shift in emphasis better if we go back to one of Enoch Powell's early speeches. As far as he was concerned, the problem was neither the alleged 'harassment' of whites by their black neighbours – of which he gave vivid examples – nor the high black birth-rate. These things were merely symptomatic. The real problem was the growth within English society of *alien* communities with *alien cultures*.

To suppose that the habits of the mass of immigrants, living in their own communities, speaking their own languages and maintaining their native customs, will change appreciably in the next two or three decades is a supposition so grotesque that only those could make it who are determined not to admit what they know to be or not to see what they fear.[93]

According to Powell, the 'rivers of blood' will flow not because the immigrants are black; not because British society is racist; but because however 'tolerant' the British might be, they can only 'digest' so much alienness. This rather cannibalistic metaphor is instructive for (at least) two reasons. First, it fits in well with the assumptions of assimilation. If blacks could be 'digested' then they would disappear into the mainstream of British society. They would no longer be visible or different, and therefore no longer a problem. On the other hand there is also the inference – given the context in which such language crops up – that this alien food will not agree with a British stomach used to less 'exotic' fare. Consequently we can expect the violent ejection; the 'vomiting' up and out of 'all those ethnic lumps of Empire which Mother England agreed to bring home and swallow'.[94] This idea, that the black cultures are not just different but so very foreign as to cause much discomfort in 'mother England's' digestive tract, is one point at which this racist ideology intersects with common-sense racism. Blacks are alien, aren't they? and because they are alien it is simply *common sense* that Britain can only assimilate a small number.

We said earlier that the current racist ideologues are concerned to distance themselves from notions of racial superiority, which, though implied, are seldom explicit in their arguments. At one level this is because such talk is not necessary. Once the argument has been couched in terms of 'alien cultures', common-sense racism can be relied upon to provide the missing inflexions. At the more 'abstract' level, however, the ideology is not at all secure at this point. It needs other ingredients. Ivor Stanbrook MP gives us a clue:

Let there be no beating about the bush. The average coloured immigrant has a different culture, a different religion and a different language. This is what *creates* the problem. It is not *just* because of race.[95] (our emphasis)

Most of this is familiar by now, but while it may not be 'just because of race' it seems clear that 'race' does have something to do with it. A little later Stanbrook lets the cat out of the bag.

I believe that a preference for one's own race is as *natural* as a preference for one's own family.[96] (our emphasis)

'It's only natural'

In the section on 'common sense' we argued that the idea of 'human nature' held an important place in common-sense thinking generally, and in particular we pointed to the bourgeoisie's success in securing, ideologically, the notion of the nuclear family as the only 'natural' unit of household organization. We also suggested that these ideas and ideas about 'race' were linked only tendentially within common sense, since this mode of thinking is inherently eclectic, unsystematic and contradictory.

The new conservative ideology 'rediscovers' these ideas about human nature – the 'natural' family and so on – and represents them as the key to a resolution of 'the nation's' problems. Here, what are only tendential links within common sense are presented as though necessarily connected. They form an organic unity. Barker's work is useful in this respect. He argues that while the 'New Toryism' is strongly individualistic in that it 'demands a new contract between the individual and the nation', we must be wary of equating it simplistically with liberalism. Liberal individualism and the new Tory individualism are not the same thing. He explains thus:

To be strictly accurate, it is not individualism. It is 'familyism'. Commitment to the family is essential to social cohesion, it is regularly said, for the family is seen as the transmitter and regenerator of traditions, it is the source of order and the sense of responsibility, it is the focus of loyalties below the nation; and all these are 'natural' and the embodiment of Toryism's primary values.[97]

He goes on to point out how these ideas have been harnessed to underpin the present Government's monetarist solutions.

Thatcher herself blamed the decline in just about all standards one could name on 'our having stripped the family, the *fundamental unit of society*, of so many of its rights and duties'.[98]

It is possible to see connections between this view and the current redefinitions of sexuality (for example, in the anti-abortion movement)[99] and morality (for example, Mary Whitehouse's 'moral crusade'). It is also possible, needless to say, to see connections between these developments and the elaboration of a 'new' racist ideology.

The family is seen to transmit traditions and generate loyalties (amongst other things), at least within the immediate family. It is the family's role in reproducing a certain sort of culture, a certain 'way of life', that makes it 'the fundamental unit of society'. Not only is the 'family' structure of the black communities seen to be different; it also, as Powell and others tell us, reproduces different cultures. Blacks are different and recognized as such not just (or even) because they have different features and/or complexions, but primarily because they have different cultures, different 'ways of life'. R. Page tells us what this means:

It is from a recognition of racial differences that a desire develops in most groups to be among their own kind; and this leads to distrust and hostility when new-comers come in.[100]

Groups, then, develop a racial consciousness based upon their racial similarity (defined as shared 'way of life') which is akin to a 'herd instinct'. What is more, through the family, this racial consciousness generates loyalty to the herd and distrust of and hostility towards other 'herds'. The important point to note here is that this 'herd instinct' is presented, as we saw in Ivor Stanbrook's speech above, as a 'natural' evolutionary development. Thus far we have been furnished with reasons for initial antagonisms between groups, but we may even at this late stage want to argue that surely it's only a matter of time before familiarity leads to 'understanding' of each other's cultures and the peaceful coexistence of the different cultures in a 'multicultural' society. Looking through the various writings and speeches of the ideologies, though, it does seem that they have seen this argument coming. What gives this ideology its particularly nasty twist is the yoking of the cart of biological culturalism to the rogue horses of the 'nation' and 'nationhood'.

The 'alien wedge'

The links that have been made between 'human nature', the family, culture and the nation have not been forged without a great deal of 'ideological work' that, as Barker puts it, 'requires some re-writing of history'. It also requires that class and gender divisions are obscured. Thus Norman St John-Stevas argues for a thousand-

year continuous and uninterrupted development of the 'dominant culture';[101]
a notion which erases the history of myriad peoples who have invaded or migrated
to Britain at the same time as it ignores class exploitation and the subordination of
women. Powell appears to be equally ignorant:

The Commonwealth immigrant [he argues] came to Britain as a full citizen, to a
country which *knew no discrimination* between one citizen and another.[102] (our
emphasis)

The importance of the ideological construction of a homogenous nation and
national culture, is made clear by Sherman whom, given current events, not even
Powell can match for sheer audacity.

The United Kingdom is the national home of the English, Scots, Welsh, Ulstermen
(and those of the Southern Irish who *retained British Identity* after their fellow-
Irish eventually rejected it).[103] (our emphasis)

Here, England's domination and suppression of neighbouring peoples is transformed
into something that approximates a family quarrel. Whatever one may think of the
methods of struggle adopted variously by the Scottish Nationalists, Plaid Cymru,
the IRA (or earlier, the 'Southern Irish') it does not appear convincing to describe
these struggles for a measure of independence as exercises in retaining or rejecting
'British identity'. Nevertheless it does give us a clue to the particular form of
nationalism being propounded by these ideologues. Sherman says it best. He
argues that 'nationhood . . . remains together with family and religion man's main
focus of identity, his roots'. At this point the 'herd instinct' of the group becomes
a national consciousness and produces a particular 'national character',

reflected in the way of life, political culture and political institutions no less than
in culture. The difference between the social and political institutions in this
country and those in the Indian sub-continent, the Caribbean or Africa – or for
that matter Russia or China – reflect this national character among other things.[104]

'National consciousness' forms the basis of an 'unconditional loyalty' to and
'personal identification with the national community'.[105]
    The blacks are 'alien', they have a different 'national character' and it follows
from this that they can never attain the crucial element of a British national
consciousness. Their loyalty to Britain is suspect and this makes them a threat.
To the bona fide British, as Sherman defines them, Britain's

History, institutions, landmarks are an *essential* part of their *personal identity*.[106]
(our emphasis)

and it is this umbilical cord that makes Britain not just a 'geographical expression'
that can be wished away, but 'the national home and birthright of its indigenous

peoples'.[107] The territory of Britain is as much a part of the British as their culture; indeed their culture appears as a kind of dialectical relationship between the 'herd' and its territory. Their defence of this space is in this scheme of things only 'natural'. It is in this context that we can begin to understand the metaphors of warfare that riddle much of the writings of the ideologues. Powell, for example, argues that the black communities are not merely 'numbers' of people but

detachments of communities in the West Indies, or India and Pakistan encamped in certain areas of England.[108]

These military metaphors, as with the metaphors of consumption we looked at earlier, suggest their own solution - repatriation - but the ideologues do not stop here. They go on to give reasons as to *why* this is the only tenable solution. On the one hand, if the British have this peculiar relationship to their territory then it follows that the blacks must have a similar relationship with their 'natural environment'.[109] It would then be in *their* interests to send them back. On the other hand their presence is experienced as an attack upon the very person of the British, an attack upon their 'national identity'. That is why they have 'genuine fears'[110] about their culture, their 'British character [which] has done so much for democracy, for law, and done so much throughout the world',[117] being 'swamped' by people with alien cultures. Should these 'genuine fears' not be assuaged, then the 'Dunkirk spirit' of the 'herd' will reassert itself with disastrous consequences.

National consciousness like any other major human drive - all of which are bound up with the instinct for self-perpetuation - is a major constructive force provided legitimate channels; thwarted and frustrated, it becomes explosive.[112]

This gives the 'peculiarities of the English' a distinctly new and gruesome twist. More to the point repatriation is the 'natural' solution to a 'natural' problem. We should point out here that this argument contains a particular, not to say peculiar, idea about citizenship as well. As Sherman tells us, 'residential qualifications' by themselves do not confer 'membership of the nation' any more than they give the recipient 'a sense of responsibility towards it'. This is because, according to him, national identity depends upon race. It is not so much a matter of where you were born as it is a matter of the culture into which you were born. This means that Asian and Afro-Caribbean migrants have an identity with and 'loyalty' to somewhere other than Britain. In 'many cases' they apparently 'bring with them anti-British attitudes'.[113] These different 'identities', 'loyalties' and 'anti-British attitudes' are then reproduced, through their cultures, in their children - even if they were born here. Since 'citizenship' in this view is 'designed to reflect membership of a nation', all those blacks who are at present 'British citizens' can quite easily lose that status overnight. To paraphrase Sherman, 'the Law giveth and the Law taketh away'.[114]

The 'self-destructive urge'

We have tried throughout this section to indicate specific points at which the new racist ideology intersects with common sense. We have also stressed its connections with other aspects of a new conservative philosophy. We would like to conclude by pointing to one final 'site' where it intersects with common sense and where its implications are broader than its immediate threat to the black communities.

The specific 'site' we are referring to is the relationship of dominance and subordination between the ruling bloc and the working class. The 'anti-intellectualism' within working-class common sense which, Hall *et al.* argue, is a recognition of that relationship, is represented in the new racism as

the conflict between the instincts of the people and the intellectual fashions of the establishment where British Nationhood is concerned.[115]

The idealogues do not seek to shatter the relationship of dominance and subordination for all their appeal to the 'people' and their common sense. Rather they aim to harness that common sense and win popular support for their particular political project. Sherman, for example, wants to single out those intellectuals who have 'studied the pseudo-sciences of sociology and economics, mainly stemming from America' rather than 'classical and European history and languages'.[116] This needs to be set next to Powell's earlier prognostications. He was concerned more with the location of the 'problem intellectuals, than with their intellectual origins. They were, he said:

a tiny minority, with almost a monopoly hold upon the channels of communication, who seem determined not to know the facts and not to face the realities and who will resort to any device or extremity to blind both themselves and others.[117]

The ground has shifted considerably since Powell's remarks. It is now necessary to be a little less woolly about who this tiny minority are and why they appear to be so 'wilfully blind'. Again it is Sherman who provides the crucial motivation behind the actions of the 'immigrationists' as he calls them.

I can see no other answer than the self-destructive urge identified so scathingly by Orwell, three decades back, when he lumped together Russophilia, 'transposed colour feeling', inverted snobbery, a craving for the *primitive*, and anti-patriotism on the part of the intellectuals, as expression of disaffection, alienation and self-hate.[118] (our emphasis)

The assertion that those whites who oppose racism have been unduly influenced by an *alien* system of ideas together with the extreme biologism of the new racism, prepares the ground for dealing with 'this tiny minority'. They are going against the instincts of the 'herd'. According to the racist ideologues, it is only 'natural' that the British should be racist; obviously those British people who are anti-racist (and it should be said those who support feminism) must 'logically' be *unnatural*. Something has gone wrong, they do not have the correct (natural) 'national identity'; they are filled with 'self-hate'.

The 'crime' that this 'tiny minority' have committed is of course to allow blacks into the country. In this connection, it is worth noting once again the changes that have taken place between Powell's earlier utterances and those of Sherman and others more recently. Powell argued that black immigration was a consequence of foolhardiness. The 'visible menace' which he sighted way back in 1966[119] was due largely to 'the legal fiction of commonwealth citizenship' which allowed an 'alien element' to be introduced into Britain. By 1976, Sherman is talking of 'Britain's urge to self-destruction',[120] the implications of which are far more sinister.

By 1979 he is talking of 'jet-age migrants' for whom Britain is 'simply a haven of convenience where they acquire rights without national obligations', and where they are '*encouraged* to see immigration restrictions as something to be circum-vented'.[121] In Sherman's hands immigration becomes a deliberate invasion. The 'barbarians' are no longer 'at the gates', they are within the city itself! The 'tiny minority' of pseudoscientists are to blame for this. It is no longer enough to blame a few 'blind' politicians. The 'genuine fears' of the people have been raised but the 'tiny minority' refuses to listen. Indeed they will not listen because they have an 'evil intent'; they are subversive. Barker indicates the consequences of this line of argument.

The logical outcome of this failure of the nation to protect itself is that the minority who press for these self-destructive actions must be purged. If they do not see the error of their ways, they put the pack at risk. How exactly they are to be dealt with is of course open to doubt. But the theory, with its semi-biological orientation, would make easy space for the idea that those who support immigration, those who attack the family, and so on, are biological failures.[122]

The common-sense racist ideologies and their theoretical counterparts which we have been examining are an important part of the context within which our dis-cussion – in Chapter 3 – of 'race-relations' sociology takes place. We have emphasized the connections between common sense and the right-wing theories of 'race' with the purpose of demonstrating how it is that they are able to command popular support. We are not saying that common-sense racist ideologies are synonymous with the more theoretical racist ideology or that they necessarily lead to the same conclusions. It is clear that there are important disagreements even within the Tory party about 'race' and that what appear as logical solutions to the hard-nosed right wingers would seem to many 'wets' to be 'rather extreme'. As one irritated right winger put it

They (the wets) don't seem to realise that the barbarians are at the gates . . . and that if the Tory party don't do the job and legitimate the instincts of the people, within ten years it'll be a choice between the National Front and the extreme Left.[123]

Nevertheless, the new racist ideology which has been forged in the white heat of the crisis can, because in its own terms it is coherent and puts forward a cogent strategy, be expected to dry out the liberalism of the 'wets'. Furthermore the Labour Party, despite its wish for egalitarian solutions to the race-relations 'problem', also finds itself unable to counter the arguments of this racist ideology, partly at least because Labour politicians share many of its common-sense assumptions.[124] Lastly, it is not difficult to see how this new racist ideology follows similar contours to the racist ideologies of the organised Fascist parties. The Tory 'hards' may not at the moment be prepared to openly share the same bed as the Fascists but they are not above stealing their sheets and indeed, 'sewing, washing and ironing them'.

Acknowledgements

This chapter and Chapter 3 were originally going to be one, but in the end there was so much that needed to be said about common-sense racist ideologies (there's a lot more still to be said) that it became increasingly easy for the thread of the argument to get lost in the welter of detail. Splitting the chapter into two seemed to be one way of making the relevant points and keeping the overall argument reasonably clear. The debts I acknowledge here then go, for the most part, for Chapter 3 as well. Obviously the work presented here is the outcome of months of discussion with the Race & Politics Group as a whole, but Pratibha Parmar and Paul Gilroy have been particularly helpful. Also, the section on 'youth' owes a lot to the work that Paul had already done for an Open University course unit and the section on the end of Empire draws on some work that was done for the group by Robin Doughty. Outside of the group, Gilly Saxon helped me to think through some of the themes in this chapter and, along with Rajinder Bhagal, did a lot of the typing, particularly for the earlier drafts. I also had some useful discussions with Sue MacIntosh and Richard Johnson and benefited from a different kind of dialogue with the work of Martin Barker and Stuart Hall. If I've missed anyone else, then I thank you as well.

Notes and references

1   See: S. Hall 'Race and "moral panics" in post-war Britain', BSA public lecture (2 May 1978), also reprinted as 'Racism and reaction', in Commission for Racial Equality, *Five Views of Multi-Racial Britain* (CRE 1978).

2   S. Hall, B. Lumley and G. McLennan, 'Politics and ideology: Gramsci', in CCCS, *On Ideology* (Hutchinson 1978), p. 49.

3   A. Gramsci, *Prison Notebooks* (Lawrence and Wishart 1971), p. 324; quoted in Hall, Lumley and McLennan, p. 50.

4   M. Barker, 'Racism – the new inheritors' (an early draft for his book *The New*

Racism), *Radical Philosophy* (Winter 1978). On p. 3 he argues that:

> If it were not for the presence of a theory behind the racist 'common-sense', the obvious lacunae and untested assumptions of its approach would not so easily escape scrutiny.

We would argue that is is precisely because racist ideologies have been elaborated from 'common-sense' assumptions, which are already 'taken for granted', that they gain popular support and acceptance.

5   Hall, Lumley and McLennan, p. 49.

6   S. Hall, C. Critcher, T. Jefferson, J. Clarke and B. Roberts, *Policing the Crisis: Mugging, the State and Law and Order* (Macmillan 1978), p. 154.

7   See: Gramsci, *Prison Notebooks*, on 'the war of manoeuvre and the war of position'.

8   Hall, Critcher, Jefferson, Clarke and Roberts, p. 155.

9   ibid., p. 155.

10 In this connection it is worth remembering Marx's remarks about the nature of bourgeois ideology:

> In this society of free competition the individual appears free from the bonds of nature, etc., which in former epochs of history made him [*sic*] part of a definite, limited human conglomeration. To the prophets of the eighteenth century . . . this . . . individual, constituting the joint product of the feudal form of society, of the new forces of production . . . appears as an *ideal whose existence belongs to the past*; not as a result of history, but as its starting point. Since that individual appeared to be in conformity with nature and correspond to their conception of human nature, he [*sic*] was regarded not as developing historically, but as posited by nature.

General Introduction to the Grundrisse, in D. McLennan (ed.), *Karl Marx: Selected Writings* (Oxford University Press 1977), p. 346.

11 Hall, Lumley, McLennan, p. 50.

12 See, for example, Chapter 5 of *Policing the Crisis*, especially samples of the abusive letters sent to one of the mothers of the three youths given twenty-year jail sentences for 'mugging'.

13 M. Barrett, *Women's Oppression Today: Some Problems in Marxist/Feminist Analysis* (New Left Books 1980), p. 256.

14 J. Weeks, 'Capitalism and the organisation of sex', in Gay Left Collective (ed.), *Homosexuality – Power and Politics* (1980). See also: Barrett, Chapter 6; and J. Donzelot, *The Policing of Families* (Hutchinson 1980), for a history of the changing nature of working-class households in France.

15 For a useful critique of this aspect of the sociology of education, see: Education Group, CCCS, *Unpopular Education: Schooling and Social Democracy in England since 1944* (Hutchinson 1981), Chapter 6.

16 *Guardian*, 8 July 1981.

17 *Daily Telegraph*, 8 July 1981.

18 B. James, *Daily Mail*, 8 July 1981.

19 Party Political Broadcast, 8 July 1981, reported in the *Daily Express* etc., 9 July 1981.

20 This was in response to an 'eleven day non-stop party' which was alleged to have taken place in Birmingham between Christmas 1980 and the New Year 1981. See: *Birmingham Evening Mail*, 2 January 1981.

21   Jill Knight, MP, *Daily Mail*, 9 July 1981.

22   *Guardian*, 'Making punishment fit the parent', 21 June 1980.

23   Hall, 'Race and "moral panics"'. See also *The Times* editorial, 5 September 1958.

24   See our Chapter 4.

25   *Guardian*, 8 July 1981.

26   It is interesting to set our 'enlightened' picture of the 'less developed' countries alongside the more complex reality. The ILO, for example, estimated that in 1978 there were 327,000 child labourers in the USA. This number had fallen from 800,000 in 1971 when children comprised 25 per cent of the paid farm labour force.

27   Such a comparison would not be purely arbitrary. It has proved relatively easy to demonstrate that the forms and styles of post-war white male working class youth subcultures relate directly to black cultural forms in a number of ways. See, for example: D. Hebdige, *Subculture: The Meaning of Style* (Methuen 1979). See also though: A. McRobbie and J. Garber, 'Girls and subcultures; an exploration', in S. Hall and T. Jefferson (eds.), *Resistance Through Rituals* (Hutchinson 1976); and A. McRobbie, 'Settling accounts with sub-cultures', *Screen Education* (Spring 1980).

28   Hall *et al.*, *Policing the Crisis*, pp. 146–7.

29   E. Long, *Candid Reflections . . .* (London 1772), pp. 46–9. Quoted in F. Shyllon, *Black People in Britain 1555–1833* (Oxford University Press 1977), pp. 104–5.

30   E. Long, *History of Jamaica: or, General Survey of the Ancient and Modern State of that Island* (London 1774). Quoted in S. Hall, 'The whites of their eyes: racist ideologies and the media', in C. Bridges and R. Brunt (eds.), *Silver Linings: Some Strategies for the Eighties* (Lawrence and Wishart 1981), p. 38.

31   C. Robinson, 'The emergence and limitations of European radicalism', *Race and Class*, vol. XXI, no. 2 (Institute of Race Relations 1979).

32   ibid., pp. 155–7.

33   ibid., p. 158.

34   ibid., p. 160.

35   ibid., p. 162.

36   Slavery was also of course, a feature of some African and South East Asian states. See: J. Watson (ed.), *Asian and African Systems of Slavery* (Basil Blackwell 1980).

37   For a useful discussion of these points see: R. Brenner, 'The origins of capitalist development: a critique of neo-Smithian Marxism', *New Left Review*, no. 104 (July–August 1977).

38   W. D. Jordan, *White over Black: American Attitudes Toward the Negro 1550–1812* (Penguin 1969), p. 7.

39   Jordan refers to the fact that whiteness

> carried a special significance for Elizabethan Englishmen; it was particularly when complemented by red, the color of perfect human beauty, especially female beauty.

and also remarks upon the practice of whitening the skin still further at the 'cosmetic table', p. 8. However, his examples are drawn from middle English and Elizabethan literature and since we know that the rate of illiteracy was high at that time, it makes it difficult to know how much these were merely the ideas of an educated elite and how much they were the ideas of the English people in general.

40   Jordan.

41   J. Walvin, *The Black Presence: A Documentary History of the Negro in England 1555–1860* (Orbach and Chambers 1971).

42   ibid.

43   W. Sypher, *Guinea's Captive Kings* (Chapel Hill 1942), p. 106. Quoted in F. Shyllon, p. 122.

44   See W. Rodney, *How Europe Underdeveloped Africa* (Bogle-L'Ouverture 1972).

45   Jordan.

46   Sir Thomas Herbert. Essay reprinted in Walvin.

47   Jordan, p. 43.

48   R. May and R. Cohen, 'The Liverpool race riots', *Race and Class*, vol. XVI, no. 2 (IRR 1974). N. Evans, 'The South Wales race riots of 1919', *The Journal of the Society for the Study of Welsh Labour History*, 1980. J. Walvin, *Black and White: a Study of the Negro in English Society 1555–1945* (Orbach and Chambers 1973).

49   May and Cohen, p. 121.

50   ibid., p. 119.

51   Walvin, *Black and White*.

52   ibid.

53   A. X. Cambridge, 'Marxism and black nationalism', *Black Liberator*, vol. 2, no. 1 (July–September 1973).

54   F. Henriques, *Children of Conflict: A Study of Interracial Sex and Marriage* (E. P. Dutton 1975), p. 140.

55   R. Blathwayt, *Titbits*, 21 July 1917. Quoted in Henriques, p. 141.

56   As Walvin puts it, when *The Times* deplored 'the familiar association between white women and negroes [sic] which is a provocative cause' and argued that 'his chief failing is his fondness for white women', it came close to sharing the views of the rioters (Walvin, *Black and White*).

57   Shyllon, p. 84.

58   See: Education Group, CCCS, Chapter 2.

59   Hall, 'The whites of their eyes', pp. 39–40.

60   D. Horowitz, 'Attitudes of British Conservatives towards decolonization in Africa', *African Affairs*, vol. LXIX, no. 274 (January 1980).

61   D. Goldsworthy, *Colonial Issues in British Politics 1945–1961, From 'Colonial Development' to 'Wind of Change'* (Clarendon Press 1971), p. 17.

62   T. E. Utley, *Enoch Powell* (William Kimber 1968), p. 60. Quoted by Paul Foot, *The Rise of Enoch Powell* (Penguin 1969), p. 19.

63   J. Strachey, *The End of Empire* (Victor Gollancz 1959), p. 132.

64   F. Fanon, *The Wretched on the Earth* (MacGibbon and Kee 1965).

65   R. Skidelsky, 'Lessons of Suez', in V. Bogdanor and R. Skidelsky (eds.), *The Age of Affluence 1951–1964* (Macmillan 1970), p. 175.

66   Hall, 'The whites of their eyes', p. 41.

67   G. Orwell, *England Your England* (Secker and Warburg 1953), p. 17.

68   Quoted in J. Higgins, 'Partition of India', in M. Sissons and P. French (eds.), *Age of Austerity, 1945–51* (Hodder and Stoughton 1963).
69   Goldsworthy, p. 399.
70   *The Picture Post*, 16 July 1949, p. 9.
71   Hall, 'Race and "Moral panics"', pp. 1–2.
72   *The Picture Post*.
73   J. H. Griffin, *Black Like Me* (Hamilton and Co. 1962), pp. 121–2. Quoted in Shyllon, p. 108. See also Henriques on this point. He cites a piece of legislation enacted in Virginia in 1662, which 'laid down that if an Englishman indulged in fornication with a black woman any offspring inherited the status of the mother – that is, automatically became a slave' (p. 59).
74   Shyllon, p. 106.
75   See Chapters 6 and 7.
76   Hall, 'The whites of their eyes', p. 43.
77   *Daily Mirror*, 14 September 1981
78   *Sun*, 11 November 1980.
79   Brent Community Health Council, *Black People and the Health Service* (BCHC April 1981), for clear examples of how these common-sense racist images shape the 'service' provided to black women by the NHS. See particularly Section 4, 'Towards new forms of control', pp. 19–26.
80   *Sun*.
81   V. Amos and P. Parmar, 'Resistances and responses: black girls in Britain', in A. McRobbie and T. McCabe (eds.), *An Adventure Story for Girls: Feminist Perspectives on Young Women* (Routledge and Kegan Paul 1981).
82   P. Parmar, 'Young Asian women: a critique of the pathological approach', in *Multiracial Education*, vol. 9, no. 3 (NAME Summer 1981), p. 27.
83   *Sun*.
84   ibid.
85   Hall, Critcher, Jefferson, Clarke and Roberts, pp. 139–50, contains a useful argument on how working-class understandings of 'respectability', 'work', 'discipline', etc. differ from yet can be articulated to the dominant 'traditionalist' consensus.
86   *Telegraph and Argus*, 15 July 1978.
87   D. Edgar, 'Racism, Fascism and the politics of the National Front', *Race and Class*, vol. XIX, no. 2 (IRR 1977).
88   Hall, 'Race and "moral panics"', p. 2.
89   See: Barker, *The New Racism*, Chapter 4, for a good discussion of the ideology of 'Butskellism'.
90   ibid.
91   A. Sherman, 'Britain's urge to self-destruction', *Daily Telegraph*, 9 September 1976.
92   ibid.
93   E. Powell, *Freedom and Reality* (Paperfront 1969), p. 307.
94   G. Brook-Shepherd, 'Where the blame for Brixton lies', *Sunday Telegraph*, 19 April 1981.
95   I. Stanbrook, *Hansard*, p. 1409. Quoted in Barker.
96   Barker.
97   ibid.

98   ibid.

99   ibid.

100 R. Page, 'To nature, race is not a dirty word', *Daily Telegraph*, 3 February 1977. Quoted in Barker.

101 N. St John-Stevas, BBC 1, 2 March 1978 (Barker). As Barker observes:

> This idea of a 1,000-year continuous development is either sheer fiction, or it is so all-embracing that there is no reason why it shouldn't continue developing happily even if blacks became 75% of the population overnight.

Of course Barker is right but its worth recalling here the work of Walvin and Jordan on the early presence of blacks in Britain.

102 Powell, p. 285. Powell is indeed ignorant of British history. He argues, for example, that Guyana was a 'fragment of the large and miscellaneous spoils of the Napoleonic wars' (p. 246), acquired almost by accident and nothing to do with Britain's imperialist expansion. But see: Tom Nairn, *The Break-Up of Britain* (New Left Books 1977), on this point.

103 A. Sherman, 'Britain is not Asia's fiancée', *Daily Telegraph*, 9 November 1979.

104 A. Sherman, 'Why Britain can't be washed away', *Daily Telegraph*, 8 September 1976.

105 Sherman, 'Britain is not Asia's fiancée'.

106 ibid.

107 ibid.

108 Powell, p. 311.

109 See: Barker.

110 ibid. Barker argues that the evocation of 'genuine fears' is an important mechanism here.

111 M. Thatcher, front page, *Daily Mail*, 31 January 1978. Quoted in Barker.

112 Sherman, 'Britain's urge'.

113 Sherman, 'Britain is not Asia's fiancée'.

114 Sherman, 'Why Britain can't be washed away'.

115 Sherman, 'Britain is not Asia's fiancée'.

116 ibid. Obviously no-one has told him of the European origins of those 'pseudo-sciences'!

117 Powell, p. 300.

118 Sherman, 'Britain's urge'.

119 Powell, pp. 246–52. A reproduction of his speech at Camborne, 14 January 1966, on the 'myth' of the Commonwealth.

120 Sherman, 'Britain's urge'.

121 Sherman, 'Britain is not Asia's fiancée'.

122 Barker. He argues that there is a 'conceptual connection' between the new racism, its 'theory' i.e. socio-biology) and the 'idea of a strong state and a nation founded on organic blood-relationships' (Fascism). His section on 'The new philosophy of racism' dealing with socio-biology, makes these connections more explicit. See also: Barbara Chasin, 'Sociobiology: a sexist synthesis' (May–June 1977); Freda Salzman, 'Are sex roles biologically determined?' (July–August 1977); and Richard Lewentin, 'Biological determinism as an ideological weapon' (November–December 1977). All in editions

of *Science for the People* (Ann Arbor & Boston, USA), for how socio-biology has been taken up in USA.

123　Quoted in: Barker.

124　See, for example: R. Jenkins' speech, *Hansard*, 5 July 1976, pp. 973-4; and R. Hattersley's opinion quoted in: Deakin and Rose, *Colour and Citizenship*, that 'without integration limitation is inexcusable: without limitation, integration is impossible'.

3   In the abundance of water the fool is thirsty: sociology and black 'pathology'

Errol Lawrence

They got so much things to say right now,
so much things to say (they labberin' all the time),
so much things to say . . . (rumour about)
they got the rumour without humour
they don't know what the're doin', yeah.

BOB MARLEY and THE WAILERS

A 'fakelore of black pathology' easily becomes translated to a 'folklore of white supremacy'. Within such a translation process, *different* behaviour (black) becomes *deviant* behaviour (black), and as everyone knows, *'deviant'* behaviour is *pathological*, worse than *inferior:illegitimate*! As such, 'deviant' behaviour needs to be 'normalized' (white is right) and its 'causes' eradicated.

THOMAS KOCHMAN

In Chapter 2, we were concerned to highlight the existence of common-sense racist ideologies and to give an account of their historical development. We also attempted to demonstrate how some elements of common sense are even now being taken up and systematically reorganized in order to construct a more coherent, more comprehensive racist ideology. One could perhaps be forgiven for hoping that the latter process would have been disrupted by the interventions of the sociologists of 'race relations' and 'ethnicity studies', who claim to be writing in order to promote a 'better understanding' between blacks and whites. Unfortunately this has not happened. One reason for this is that these sociologists have failed to question all but the most obvious common-sense racist assumptions. Indeed in many ways it is precisely these sorts of images and assumptions which have been theorized. In this chapter, we aim to explore the convergence between racist ideologies and the theories of 'race/ethnic-relations' sociology. As in Chapter 2, we have again found it necessary to explore the past, only this time we have looked to the neglected side of the imperialist coin; to black peoples' experiences of colonialism, slavery and indenture. In particular we have been concerned with how this experience has been 'made sense of' within the sociologies of 'race/ethnic relations', where a picture of 'pathological' black households has been produced which fits in only too well with common-sense racist imagery.

In the present situation, where 'race' has come to signify the crisis; where popular racist ideologies underpin and legitimate the institutionalized racist

Source: R. C. Edwards *et al.*, *The Capitalist System* (Prentice-Hall 1972)
Reproduced by permission of Prentice-Hall, Inc.

practices of the state; and where 'induced repatriation' is placed on the political agenda as the 'British solution to the "race-relations" problem',[1] it becomes necessary to challenge the orthodoxies of 'race/ethnic-relations' sociology. It is necessary not simply because it might contribute to academic debate, nor even because this field of enquiry provides a theoretical cover for racist ideas. Of more importance is the fact that their 'theories' about black people help to shape public policy at every level, from the exalted heights of the Home Office to the humbler ranks of the school staff-room. We have illustrated our argument throughout with references from some of the more recent contributions to this field.[2] Readers who are familiar with these works will notice, as we have done, that despite the differing theoretical approaches that each researcher adopts, all roads appear to lead to Rome!

Racist connections

From our discussions in Chapter 2, it is clear that the tendency within common-sense racist ideologies is to recognize but not to emphasize the differences between the Asian and Afro-Caribbean communities. Within the 'new' racist ideology, this tendency is even more marked. Much of Sherman's work, for example, even though it is constructed largely around the Asian presence, is not solely about Asian people. Rather his arguments are aimed at demonstrating what the black communities have *in common* – that is, their cultural 'alienness'. The prevailing ethos amongst 'race/ethnic-relations' researchers, on the other hand, runs in the opposite direction. The tendency here has been to concentrate upon either the Asian or the Afro-Caribbean communities and often to concentrate upon a single community (e.g. Sikhs, Pakistanis, Jamaicans etc.) within the broader categories. In this particular, at least, the sociologists could claim to be presenting an alternative to the gross over-generalizations of the racist ideologues.

Recently, however, the sense that the different communities pose different problems for the state and for 'British society', has begun to find expression within racist discourse. After the first sequence of confrontations between black (and white) youth and the police in Brixton (April 1981), the late Sir Ronald Bell – member of Parliament and leading member of the Monday Club – appeared on BBC's *Nationwide* to explain that Afro-Caribbean youth's 'rootlessness' was the principal cause of the 'riots'.[3] Bell argued that this 'rootlessness' could be linked in a straightforward way to the fact that these youths had been raised on what was to them 'alien soil'; but in the pages of the *Sunday Telegraph* a few days later (19 April 1981), Gordon Brook-Shepherd proposed a more elaborate version of this argument. He contrasted the Afro-Caribbeans' apparent failure to be 'digested' by 'mother England' with the Asians' apparent success. They had integrated better he argued, 'for the paradoxical reason that they had stayed foreign'.

Their religion and language have stayed different . . . and this, alongside their *whole* culture, has bound them tightly together both as communities and as families – this family bond being something, incidentally, which many white as well as black parents would envy. (our emphasis)

According to him, the trouble with Afro-Caribbeans is that they do not appear to realize that they are foreign, and this he suggests is connected with their supposed lack of a 'whole' culture.

They came to us from the oldest part of the Empire with the same religion and a colourful variant of the same language. They expected to find a ready made niche in what they thought would be a familiar society.

Thus, even though they made an effort to 'fit in', becoming 'as indispensable on the trains and buses' as were 'the Asians on the high street', they were not able to provide the same cohesive cultural ties and family bonds. The consequence of this apparent failure is that their children 'slipped completely from' their control. For Brook-Shepherd, it is not simply that this has enabled 'left-wing aggro groups' to exploit the 'natural frustrations' of Afro-Caribbean youth. What is more important is that this lack of control has had the effect of undermining the natural order of things. Through the improbable use of cricket as a social metaphor, he hints at his anxiety:

For a while cricket preserved the illusion that only the pitch had been moved, and that this was still the plantation relationship under more equitable conditions.

With scarcely concealed nostalgia for those good old days when blacks knew their place, he reminds us of 'that day in June 1963' when a broken-armed Cowdrey 'saved England from defeat' at the hands of 'one of those legendary West Indian teams'. He contrasts those halcyon days with the 'politics-ridden' 1981 tour of the West Indies,[4] but what is more revealing – not to say bizarre – is his juxta-position of his cricketing memories with the events that took place at Brixton:

In the streets of South Lambeth they have been playing a new and gruesome version of the game, with bricks for balls and plastic police shields for bats.

To say that for Brook-Shepherd 'this is just not cricket' would be to understate the case; it shatters his vision of a continuing 'plantation relationship'. The only people who can replace 'the missing element in the Brixton equation' and thus restore the relationship to its mythical harmony, are the 'black parents of Brixton'. In his view the other actors in this drama (government ministers, the police, even the 'left-wing aggro groups' and 'the loony Labour Council of Lambeth') are merely trying to cope with and/or exploit a situation for which the parents are ultimately responsible.

This argument was made more specific in the aftermath of July's nationwide 'riots', when Richard West wrote two feature articles on the Caribbean for the

Daily Telegraph. West tells us that Britain doesn't have a black problem, or even a West Indian problem. We should, he argues, be talking about a 'Jamaican problem' and a 'small minority of Jamaicans' at that. In his view the adherents of Rastafari constitute the real 'problem', for it is they

who set the tone for the unacceptable face of Britain's West Indian community: the rebellious, resentful and violent criminal fringe and who have been at the forefront of recent riots and looting.[5]

For West, the 'problem' is not of the English home-grown variety, it has been *imported* by the Jamaicans themselves. In a sense he succeeds in completing the circle which first Bell and then Brook-Shepherd had begun to draw, combining their attempts at a fuller explanation with the conviction of Sherman and Powell that the 'problem' was essentially an alien one. He states that there has always been a strain of rebelliousness in Jamaican society and acknowledges the link between the maroons, through Marcus Garvey, to Rastafari. However, as far as he is concerned this tradition of rebellion and resistance is a purely psychological inheritance, which has little relation to social conditions. He identifies this tradition as the 'back to Africa' movement and characterizes its ideology as 'escapist' and racially 'prejudiced'. It is this psychological inheritance, he suggests, which lies at the heart of the 'political violence' which has afflicted Jamaican society in recent years, and, oblivious to the fact that the Rastafarians have always been implacably opposed to such activities, he suggests that they were the chief protagonists. He then draws the apparently obvious parallel between Kingston where 'it is risky to walk . . . even by day', and 'muggings' and 'riots' in Brixton. He leaves us in little doubt that violence is an endemic feature of Jamaican society and in a concluding paragraph gives a summary of the reasons for this.

Jamaica and Brixton have many problems in common, like dope, Rastafarianism and violent crime. But there are other social problems affecting all British West Indian countries beside Jamaica: single parent families, harsh corporal punishment at home yet lack of discipline at the school and, *at a deeper level, the psychological wounds going back to slavery.*[6] (our emphasis)

This is a novel development in the elaboration of racist ideologies but it is not altogether a surprising one. The invocation of a contrast between the 'strong' Asian cultures on the one hand, and the 'weak' Afro-Caribbean cultures on the other, is commonplace for those working in and around 'race relations', as is the tracing of the 'weakness' of Afro-Caribbean cultures back to the 'psychological wounds' inflicted by slavery. Within the more academic frame of reference, as well, these assumptions tend to be taken for granted; although here the movement to- wards specialization, which we noted earlier, means that one rarely finds the differences between Asian and Afro-Caribbean cultures consciously articulated.[7] Only Rex and Tomlinson, of the researchers we will be referring to, have attempted to cross the cultural divide and to make such explicit comparisons a part of their overall argument.

Culture: the Afro-Caribbean case

Unlike the common-sense perceptions of the 'race-relations industry', the sociologists of 'race relations' who have specialized in studies of the Afro-Caribbean communities do provide us with a theory which purports to explain the 'weakness' of Afro-Caribbean cultures. The key term here is *acculturation*, which refers to the 'culture stripping' or 'cultural castration' which African slaves supposedly underwent during slavery. Pryce claims that this process entailed the loss, by the slaves, of their 'languages, religions and family/kinship systems', leaving them with no alternative but to 'learn his [sic] master's language and to ape his values and institutions'.[8] Thus, as Rex and Tomlinson argue, they were 'forced into accepting British Culture along with their servitude'.[9] Ideas derived from this initial starting-point inform the accounts of Rex and Tomlinson, Cashmore, Troyna and Garrison, but it is Pryce who gives the clearest exposition of what 'acculturation' has meant for Afro-Caribbean people. He succeeds in reinforcing the common-sense notion that Afro-Caribbean children 'fail' at school because they have a 'negative self-image'; and at the same time he deflects the arguments (his own included) which suggest that the racist structures and practices of the British education system in particular, and of British society more generally, may have something to do with this. In his view, the 'identity of West Indians' had – before they set foot in England – already been formed in a negative mode, under the 'punishing conditions of slavery' and colonialism. They had, he argues, internalized a culture which is fundamentally at odds with the 'Negro [sic] – African elements in their backgrounds'.

Because it was the early formative stage of slavery which defined the initial circumstances of cultural *accommodation*, there is within the [creole culture] complex a scandalously strong 'white bias'. . . . In keeping with this bias, things European have the greatest value and prestige, while everything black or African, . . . is downgraded, devalued and considered inferior.[10] (our emphasis)

Pryce recognizes that there is a difference between the 'European orientated value system of the elite classes' and that of the 'peasantry', but he appears not to notice the importance of African elements in either component of the 'creole culture complex'. Even his brief mention of the early use of 'drums, trances, spirit possession and obeah' in the spiritual life of the masses, is important only in so far as it illustrates the functional devices which enabled them to

interpret and develop in matters of the soul whatever *trickled down* to them from their masters, and to satisfy the deep spiritual needs of communities *starved of glamour and denied creative outlets in public life.*[11] (our emphasis)

His characterization, in a footnote, of obeah as simply 'Jamaican black magic'[12] Europeanizes this phenomenon at the same time as it prevents him from exploring its origins in a more rigorous manner. This is in keeping with his wish to establish that the period of slavery represented a complete break with the slaves' African past. For Pryce, Afro-Caribbean cultures are derivatives of European cultures and it is partly for this reason that he views them as being weak. They are 'weak' because they cannot give Afro-Caribbeans a sense of their 'true' identity; these cultures reproduce 'anomic' personalities.

This is a dominant strand of thinking within 'race-relations' research about Afro-Caribbeans but it is not the only one. Foner, for example, appears to draw different conclusions from her knowledge of Jamaican history. She does not argue that the experience of slavery has led to the creation of a weak culture amongst the 'peasant folk'. Where she does agree with Pryce and others, however, is on the question of 'white bias' in Jamaican society. Pryce's use of the concept of 'acculturation' enables him to discount differences between the two class-based components of Jamaica's 'creole culture complex', by attributing a 'white bias' to both. Foner, on the other hand, does not talk about the internalization of a European culture as such. Instead she grounds her account of 'white bias' in the historical formation of a 'three-tiered color–class system', which has its roots in 'slave society'.[13] In a sense she simply ignores the different cultures within Jamaican society and talks about *the* 'traditional value-system' in which

since the days of slavery it came to be expected, although never exactly realised, that 'white persons should belong to the upper class, coloured to the middle, and black to the lowest class'.[14]

In her view colour came to be *symbolically* associated with status attributes. Because whites were, by and large, wealthy and powerful, 'white' came to be associated with 'wealth and power'. Similarly 'brown' came to be associated with 'middle-class privilege' and 'black with poverty'.[15] Despite their different formulations, Foner and Pryce end up in the same place. According to Foner, 'lower-class Jamaicans' have a 'negative image . . . of their blackness', which is illustrated by their apparent preference for European features. This is why 'Jamaican black women' straighten their hair and use 'lotions to whiten their skin'.[16] The fact that hair straightening is one among a range of ways that Afro-Caribbean women have of dressing their hair and the fact that 'lotions for whitening the skin' are not the only items in their cosmetic repertoire, appears to be lost on Foner. Len Garrison argues in a similar vein to Foner, but goes a step further to argue that the 'self-hate' of Afro-Caribbean women who become mothers constitutes a handicap for their sons and daughters.[17]

These accounts of 'white bias' betray a startling ignorance about the 'day-to-day' resistances of the slaves and their descendants through which the dominant, white definitions of themselves were continually contested. Foner, for example, argues that those black Jamaicans who have attained positions of prestige and power and

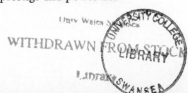

who have acquired the 'cultural characteristics associated with English whites' are 'thought of "as if" they were white'. In support of her argument she quotes an incident mentioned by David Lowenthal, in which 'a black Jamaican maid identified as "white" a pitch black but elegantly dressed visitor'. Lowenthal apparently goes on to say that 'when a lady is elegant and a man is a professor in Jamaican eyes they are not black'.[18] However, such an identification cannot be taken in this straightforward manner to indicate respect for the 'elegant black lady' or the 'black professor'. It can just as easily signal disrespect for someone who 'puts on airs and graces', or indicate the utmost contempt for someone who has 'sold out' and 'gone over to the other side'.

The problem here rests upon some fundamental misconceptions about Caribbean societies and cultures. These societies are viewed as having been 'manufactured' rather than 'organically grown', but this dichotomy obscures the fact that all societies are in a sense 'made' by human beings, even if it may appear that they 'jes grew'. Of course the dichotomy does refer to the very real historical activity in which African people were forcibly taken from Africa and shipped to the Caribbean; and the analogy with manufacturing does suggest the 'newness' of the conditions under which the slaves were forced to live and the 'rebuilding' which had to be done. However, the analogy also has its problems. First, there is just a hint of biological determinism in the juxtaposition between 'manufactured' and 'organic', since it suggests that African cultures are somehow 'natural' outgrowths of the *place* Africa, rather than creations of African people. Second, the analogy suggests that Caribbean societies, including the people themselves, have been artificially created by Europeans and 'in their own image'. This has led many researchers to ignore the slaves' active participation in the creation of Caribbean societies and cultures. The 'masters' may have been the dominant group, but they were not Gods; and the slaves although dispossessed in a material sense did not arrive in the Caribbean as 'zombies', with nothing other than the husks of their bodies, waiting conveniently to be filled up with European culture. In order to redress the balance and come to a more adequate understanding of the dynamics of Afro-Caribbean cultures, we need to thoroughly reappraise much of the existing commentary about 'slavery times'. The section which follows attempts to suggest some points at which such a reappraisal might usefully begin.

Do you remember the days of slavery?

The importance of the period of slavery for an understanding of the present has been more recognizable, for obvious reasons, in the United States than it has in Britain. As an area of historical research and debate it forms an almost unbroken chain with the earlier ideological struggles between pro- and anti-abolitionists and has generated a welter of argument and information that is not paralleled in British circles. The recent success of black people in Britain in raising the issue of 'culture' to the forefront of their struggles against racism, and the state's response to that cultural offensive, have forced the British researchers in the race/ethnic-relations field out of their 'host/immigrant', 'assimilationist' perspective, through a 'social deprivation' problematic, and into a concern with 'cultural pluralism' and 'integration'. This was a necessary shift if their research was to be relevant to current policy initiatives.[19] However, the relative dearth of material on Afro-Caribbean cultures in British work necessitated the reaching out to the American material and to work done in the Caribbean (which itself had been shaped in a dialogue with similar work in the USA). Had the recent appropriation of this material approx- imated to the objective and impartial canons of the sociological disciplines, we might now be engaged in a somewhat different kind of argument. As it is this appropria- tion has been rather partial, in that it has drawn on only one side (the arguments about acculturation) of the American/Caribbean debate. There is another more pressing reason why we feel that other aspects of that debate should be given more space than they have thus far received. The same movement from a 'social depri- vation' model to a concern with the cultural 'poverty' of black people has already taken place in the USA. This trend, initiated in the *Moynihan Report*[20] – as it came to be called – was also aimed at informing government policy, and Afro-Americans have had to suffer the consequences of it.

We will come back to this report a little later but for the moment we intend to take a step backwards and look at a piece of work which Ernest Cashmore, at any rate, feels is worth examining; that is, the theory of slave personality con- tained in the classic work on slavery by Stanley Elkins.[21] As Eugene Genovese remarks, this work

Despite the hostile reception given (to it) by historians . . . has established itself as one of the most influential essays of our generation.[22]

Stated briefly, Elkins argued that there was a reality behind the common-sense racist image of the 'sambo' slave personality. The typical slave, he argued, was indeed 'docile', 'lazy', 'irresponsible' and 'childish' as well as being given to 'lying and stealing'. Where Elkins differed from the racists was in arguing that these were not the innate characteristics of African people but rather were the inevitable consequences of the institution of slavery as practised specifically in the Southern United States. According to Elkins, slavery in the feudal Latin American societies was less harsh than the plantation South's slave system. He argues that the exis- tence of laws which recognized the slaves' humanity, the existence of well-travelled paths to manumission, and the power of the European monarchy and churches to intervene and shape the practices of the slave masters, all contributed to a tempering of Latin American slave systems. Within these systems slaves were, for example, allowed to marry and raise families – a fact which was of some importance in Elkins's view, since the 'adult' responsibilities entailed militated against the development of childish, dependent, 'slavish' personalities amongst the slaves. In the plantation South on the other hand the 'master' enjoyed more or less absolute power over the slaves. Elkins borrows a number of concepts from psychology[23] in order to argue that, because the 'master' was the only 'significant other' in the slaves' world and because there were only a limited number of roles available to them, they came to identify their interests with those of their master. Thus these slaves were psychically and physically dependent upon their master. Elkins illustrates his arguments by drawing an analogy between the slave system of the plantation South and the Nazi concentration camps of World War II. These two 'institutions' were similar, he suggests, both in terms of the 'closed' nature of their systems and the 'powerlessness' of the inmates and also in terms of the 'shock of detachment' which was 'so complete that little trace of prior (and thus alternative) cultural sanctions for behaviour and personality remained'.[24] This allowed him to argue that for those slaves born into slavery, the system represented 'normality'. Furthermore, the concentration camps provide him with 'evidence' that even first-generation 'fresh slaves' would have made a more or less total adjustment to the slave system. The way in which he secures this part of his argument is interesting in itself.

We do not know how generally a full adjustment was made by the first generation of fresh slaves from Africa. But we do know – from a modern experience – that such an adjustment is possible, not only within the same generation but within two or three years. This proved possible for people in a full state of *complex civilization*, for men and women who were not black and *not savages.*[25] (our emphasis)

Genovese criticizes Elkins on a number of points. He argues first that the construction of a 'sambo-like' image was not peculiar to the plantation South, because it existed both in earlier slave systems and in those slave systems that were contemporary with slavery in the United States. As Genovese put it, 'Negroes, if we believe the French planters (in Haiti), were childlike, docile, helpless creatures up until the very moment they rose and slaughtered the whites'.[26] Genovese has also suggested that the 'sambo' image begins to be constructed in the USA around the time of the slaves' revolt led by Nat Turner.[27] Second, Genovese suggests that *in practice*, slavery in the plantation South was not so very different from that in Latin America. Elkins's concentration upon the *formal* institutions of slavery (legal codes etc.) has led him to overemphasize their efficacy and to overlook the fact that Latin American slave masters could and did simply ignore the legal sanctions and the monarch's wishes. Further, Genovese argues that there is sufficient evidence to suggest that both the crown's agents and the church personnel in the colonies were also, more often than not, implicated in the slave systems themselves.[28] Similarly, Elkins overlooked the existence in the South of other 'significant others' who could intercede to influence the actions of slave owners. This, Genovese feels, together with the sheer weight of social conventions, militated against the worst excesses of slavery on the Southern plantations.[29] Genovese goes further; he suggests that both Elkins's concentration camp analogy, and the models he draws from psychology, are inappropriate to an understanding of how the slaves accommodated themselves to slavery. Here he hints at an important element that is neglected in Elkins's account – namely the activities of the slaves themselves, which tempered 'the authority of the master', and their creation of their own cultural institutions, which provided a source of alternative sets of values and practices, alternative understandings of their situation and an alternative locus of authority.

Elkins and many other sociologists, historians and anthropologists both before and after him, have assumed that because slaves were not a part of 'society at large' (i.e. white·society), they therefore had no society at all. The more access slaves had to society outside the plantation the more they were thought to be leaving a cultural void and entering into a more fully 'human' world. For this reason, the activities of the slaves have only been seen as significant where they have been 'legitimized and protected *outside* the plantation'.[30] The constant 'acts of stealing' which many writers on slavery have commented upon, have tended to be looked upon as childish, amoral acts which took place with the amused acknowledgement of the 'master'. Indeed for Elkins, this dependence on the 'master's' pleasure effectively guaranteed the 'infantilism' of the slaves. For the slaves, however, these were not merely playful acts of childishness but a necessary means of supplementing a meagre diet. Kenneth Stampp, for example, notes the difference between the 'slave's code' and the 'master's code' on the subject of 'stealing', although he seems not to realize its significance. For the slaves, 'stealing' from the 'master' was not stealing at all but 'taking'; 'taking his (the master's) meat out of one tub, and putting it in another'; whereas 'stealing . . . meant appropriating something that belonged to another slave, and this was an offense which slaves did not condone'.[31]

Mina Davis Caulfield points to the numerous 'slave narratives', which emphasize the importance of 'taking' and 'illegal' hunting for sustaining the social role of 'family provider' amongst the slaves.[32] These activities were sanctioned by the slave community and carried out independently of the 'master's' wishes. She draws attention also to the ease with which successive researchers have conferred leadership status, posthumously, upon the house servants. In their view, the house servants' proximity to the 'seat of power' and their adoption of white standards and manners, made them seem to be 'natural' candidates for leadership of the slave communities.[33] In fact, the field hands were just as likely to despise 'the "fugle̜ men" who "put on airs" in imitation of the whites', as they were to follow their lead. Often, indeed, the real leaders of the 'slave quarters' were people chosen independently of white patronage. Often as well they were not regarded with favour by the 'master'.

Each community of slaves contained one or two members whom the others looked to for leadership because of their physical strength, practical wisdom, or mystical powers. It was a 'notorious' fact, according to one master, 'that on almost every large plantation of Negroes, there is one among them who holds a kind of magical sway over the minds and opinions of the rest; to him [*sic*] they look as their oracle. . . . The influence of such a Negro, often a preacher, on a quarter is incalculable'.[34] (our emphasis)

This appears to be a suitable point at which to make some mention of the importance of 'religion' in the slave community and in their development of alternative
cultural forms. Here, we can see that the ideas we have been reviewing about
'acculturation' have led researchers in the USA to take up positions similar to those
adopted by Pryce, Rex and Tomlinson and others in England. The slave, argue
Kardiner and Ovesey, was 'obliged to learn a new language' and to 'adopt a new
religion'. Furthermore, this religion did not 'evolve out of his [*sic*] old cultural
conditions' but was 'foisted on him as a new credo'.[35] There is, however, ample
evidence – some of it quoted by these people themselves – to suggest that the
slaves did indeed retain elements of their 'old cultural conditions' and that these
formed the basis for the re-creation of their culture. The prevalence of *secret*
'praise meetings' all over the South and *before* the missionary efforts of the
Baptists and Methodists, is testimony to this. These meetings in which knowledge
of voodoo, insurrection and 'the underground railway' were shared, were feared
by some of the 'masters' and repeatedly outlawed by the authorities. It was in these
meetings that plans for revolt and escape were hatched and the slaves went to great
lengths to avoid detection, meeting in out of the way places, posting lookouts and
turning 'the kettle down outside the door, raised so that the sound can get out
under there and you couldn't hear them'.[36] The slaves drew a distinction too,
between their 'praise meetings' and the white churches, and were in little doubt
about which was the most valuable to them.

The coloured folks had their code of religion, not nearly so complicated as the
white man's religion, but *more closely observed*. . . . When we had our meetings of
this kind, we held them *in our own way* and were not interfered with by the white
folks.[37] (our emphasis)

The Baptists and Methodists who were later to achieve some success in 'converting'
the slaves to Christianity, were successful precisely because of the 'large degrees
of local autonomy granted to slave congregations'.[38] Indeed it has even been argued
that instead of converting the slaves to Christianity, the Methodist revival movement
ended up by 'converting itself to an African ritual'.[39] We would not necessarily
want to 'bend the stick' that far, but there is an important point here that needs
to be emphasized. Where the slaves adopted elements of European cultures, they
did so on their own terms, in the light of their own concerns and circumstances.
This process was also mediated by the elements of African cultures which had
been retained and reworked in the initial period of slavery. The resultant transformation did indeed lead to the creation of something 'new'. It was not 'European', nor yet was it 'African' in any pure sense, but it was nevertheless rooted in
African cultural forms and developed into a distinctive Afro-American, *black*
culture.

There are other elements to this 'culture building' process which we do not have
the space to go into here but which have an important bearing on this discussion.
It would be worth considering, for example, the *form* of worship that is peculiar to

Afro-Americans. It would be worth considering as well the role of song and 'story-telling' within those communities, by means of which the ideologies and 'knowledges' of those communities are transmitted. Important too, particularly in 'slavery times', is the socialization of the children. Who were their 'significant others'? Caulfield suggests that the 'masters' were not usually interested in children 'below the age of useful labour', and that young children were left in the care of 'an older child, a superannuated slave woman, or the cook'.

> In the critical years for the internalization of values . . . slave children appear to have been for the most part *neglected* by the white system, regarded as only potentially valuable property, and left to absorb the prevailing standards and values of the slave quarters.[40] (our emphasis)

We have taken the Afro-American experience of slavery as our 'limit case', partly because American accounts of slavery have been influential in British circles. Also, it might be thought – using the crude yardstick of 'size of population to be acculturated' – that 'acculturated negroes' would be found in abundance in the USA. In our view the historical and current evidence suggests that this is not so. We can still find echoes of Africa in their religions and in their modes of worship. The behaviour and language of Afro-Americans, long thought to be an aberrant version of white behaviour and language, has been shown to be *culturally distinctive* rather than imitative.[41] More surprising has been the relative silence about their music. What marks out the blues, ragtime, jazz, be-bop, soul, funk and gospel music as distinctive is precisely the fact that the theme of 'Africa' is constantly played out – rhythmically and melodically – within their tunes. This music has been dismissed as 'escapist' or as merely the sound of 'suffering'; sometimes it has been recognized as being expressive of their opposition to subordination and racism; but only rarely has the fact that the music is based in African themes and rhythms been noted. Needless to say the continuing inspiration provided by current African, Caribbean and Asian music has gone more or less unnoticed.[42] It seems to us that what we should be talking about then, at most, is *degrees* of 'acculturation' rather than a total 'acculturation'. Indeed we would wonder whether the concept is at all useful for understanding how the slaves made sense of, challenged and rebelled against slavery.

No one remembers . . .

The ideas about 'loss of culture' and 'acculturation' which were developed to 'explain' the Afro-American experience of slavery have been adopted and adapted to speak of the Afro-Caribbean case as well. Here, however, the argument is even weaker; indeed, a much stronger case can be made for the 'survival' of elements of African culture in the cultures of Afro-Caribbean people.[43] But rather than repeat the arguments we have already made, this time using Caribbean material about 'plantation slavery' instead of the American material, we feel that it is necessary to raise another issue concerning 'slavery times' which has not received the attention its importance warrants. We refer, of course, to the fact that a not infrequent response to slavery was flight or *marronage*.

The extent of escapes from the slave plantations, and the frequency with which maroon communities were established in the Americas, should cause us to think again about the plantation-bound interpretation of slavery which is all too familiar. Maroon communities sprang up continuously from the first moment of slavery up until the various moments of 'emancipation', and although many of them tended to be short-lived, their existence indicated a continuing resistance to slavery.

Throughout Afro-America, such communities stood out as an heroic challenge to white authority, and as a living proof of the existence of a slave consciousness that refused to be limited by the white's conception or manipulation of it.[44]

For the Europeans these communities constituted a 'chronic plague', but for the slaves who remained upon the plantations they represented the possibility of freedom and underlined their own acts of 'day-to-day' resistance. In turn the 'plantation slaves' actively aided and abetted the maroons, providing them with items of food, clothing and weaponry and passing on crucial bits of 'intelligence' information. Throughout the Americas, in Brazil, Colombia, Cuba, Ecuador, Mexico and Surinam, the colonial regimes were forced to 'sue their former slaves for peace'. As we know, in Haiti the slaves rose up in rebellion and drove their erstwhile 'masters' into the sea. In Jamaica as well, the two principal communities were never defeated militarily and their influence upon the 'plantation slaves' – encouraging further escapes and rebellions – was considerable. Indeed, Orlando Patterson suggests that at the very point at which they struck their peace bargain with the British, their alliance with the 'plantation slaves' was strong enough to present an opportunity – unfortunately never realized – to break the imperialist grip on the island.[45]

It is not our intention to go into the military strategies and tactics developed by the maroons in their campaigns against the colonialists, even though this is an important corrective to the dominant view of the 'docile' slave. Contrary to the eighteenth-century image of the maroons as 'sons and daughters of Africa perfectly adapted 'to the harsh natural environments' of the Americas, we need to recognize that life for the maroons – initially in any case – was a continual struggle not just against the pursuing troops, but with their environment as well. It is necessary to think then about the economic adaptations that were developed by the maroons and which allowed them to 'carry on the business of daily life'.

Swidden horticulture was the mainstay of most maroon economies with a similar list of cultigens appearing in reports from almost all areas – manioc, yams, sweet potatoes, and other root crops, bananas and plantains, dry rice, maize, groundnuts, squash, beans, chile, sugar cane, assorted other vegetables, and tobacco and cotton. These seem to have been planted in a similar pattern of intercropping – for example, vegetables scattered in a field of rice – from one end of the hemisphere to the other.[46]

Maroons also learned to utilize their environment so as to provide themselves with many other and varied useful items,[47] particularly their own medicines and poisons. It is not clear how much 'maroon technology' owed to the knowledges that African slaves brought with them from Africa. Richard Price suggests that much of this technology may have been learned initially from the American 'Indians', although in Jamaica, for example, the indigenous Arawak 'Indians' had already been exterminated by the Spanish before the British took over and began shipping slaves to the island. What is reasonably clear is that the techniques which the maroons subsequently refined had been developed by the slaves on the plantations during the early period of slavery.[48] This was forced upon them by the 'master's' unwillingness to provide anything but the minimum requirements. In this situation the slaves' 'gardens' and the other methods devised for utilizing the environment were crucial additions to the 'master's' meagre fare.[49]

Of course people do not live by bread alone and in this context the social organization of the maroons needs to be taken into account as well. The importance of their religious beliefs and practices is worthy of mention here, for these were the source of the ideologies which sustained them in their harsh environment and which 'spelled the ultimate difference between victory and defeat' in their constant battles with the European troops. Religious leadership was, as we remarked earlier, important in the lives of slaves generally; but for the maroons the knowledge, wisdom and skills of the obeah men and women was crucial. Price recalls a story still told today by the Saramakas in Surinam, about the original

band of runaways who, after months of wandering . . .were unable to drink the water because it was filled with tiny worms. It was only after performing major rituals . . . that they were able finally to purify the river and settle by its banks.[50]

The importance of obeah men and women did not necessarily give them political power in the maroon communities. This depended upon other factors. In Jamaica, for example, Cudjoe's authority meant that the obeah men and women were important but minor figures amongst the Leeward maroons. Here the military organization, forged in the early days to combat the British troops, was the dominant political force. Amongst the Windward maroons, on the other hand, it was obeah *women* such as Nanny who wielded effective power. Nanny is reputed to have refused the peace settlement offered by the British to the headman Quao, because 'she did not trust the whites to keep their part of the bargain'.[51] While Nanny's renown is concretely enshrined in the two maroon towns named after her, the fact that two other towns in the 'Nanny town complex' – Molly and Diana towns – are also named after women, suggests that the political importance of obeah women was well established in those communities. Barbara Kopytoff argues that because of their child-bearing and child-rearing roles, women were unable to run away with the same frequency as the men. This led to a 'shortage' of women in the maroon communities and meant that women were regarded as an important 'resource' particularly in terms of the continuation of these communities. However, while her descriptions of the ways in which the relationships, between men and women, were organized differently by the Leeward and Windward maroons is interesting in itself, it tells us little about how much the women participated in this process.[52] Certainly it does not explain the political pre-eminence of obeah women amongst the Windward maroons; this may have been grounded in their military prowess. It is noticeable that the stories about Nanny's 'supernatural feats' which are still recounted by the descendants of the early maroons, place her uncompromisingly upon the field of battle. It is said, for example, that she 'was able to attract and catch bullets between her buttocks, where they were rendered harmless'.[53] Similarly, the report of an unnamed obeah woman – who may or may not have been Nanny – describes her as having 'a girdle round her waste, with (I speak within compass) nine or ten different knives hanging in sheaths to it'.[54] These snippets are clearly not enough to make a whole story, but given that we know that women are consistently written out of history and given that we know that the military organization of women was not an uncommon phenomenon in Africa, they are perhaps enough to suggest that women were heavily involved in the military organization at least of the Windward maroons.[55]

Like voodoo which, as C. L. R. James has pointed out, served as the slaves' political ideology during the Haitian revolution, the beliefs and practices of maroon communities represented the coming together and transformation of African religions drawn from differing 'ethnic' groups.[56] This 'ethnic diversity', it has sometimes been argued, actively aided the process of acculturation, since this very diversity made the relevant European culture the only thing that slaves shared in common apart from their common experience of slavery. Price argues, however, that

the remarkably rapid formation by maroon groups of whole cultures and societies *was made possible . . . by the previous existence throughout the hemisphere of rather mature local slave cultures* combined with a widely shared ideological commitment to things African.[57] (our emphasis)

He suggests further that not only did these local slave cultures represent distinctive 'Afro-American ways of dealing with life', but that the 'geographical range' and mutual compatibility of 'particular cultural principles' in Africa actually made the process of 'culture building' all the more easy. Indeed when one reflects on the way in which slaves and maroons borrowed cultural forms from the 'Indians', one begins to wonder about just how much of a barrier 'ethnic diversity' would have been. Maya Deren in her work on Haitian voodoo furnishes an interesting example here for she suggests that not only do the voodoo Gods bear striking similarities to figures in indigenous African religions, but that the religious ideas of the Haitian 'Indians' were also incorporated into voodoo under the 'hegemony' of African religious forms.[58]

We would argue then that the view of Afro-Caribbeans as 'acculturated' is an erroneous view at odds with the available evidence. Far from wallowing in a sea of anxiety somewhere between Africa and Europe, Afro-Caribbean people have, like their Afro-American sisters and brothers, developed distinctive cultures and have their own distinctive political and ideological traditions.[59] The theorists of 'acculturation' have mistaken the 'master's' *wish* to stamp out any hint of Africanness for the deed. The 'masters' at least recognized something that the theorists appear not to have noticed – whenever the Afro-Caribbean people reached into and began to emphasize their own traditions, this was the prelude to rebellion. It is no accident either that the recent resurgence of popular culture in Jamaica, and the reorganization of the peoples' *good sense* which Rastafari represents, should have begun in St Thomas, an area of *maroon* settlement.[60] We have concentrated on the historical period of slavery partly because much of the available evidence remains unread and unacknowledged and partly as a counterweight to the distorted view of the Afro-Caribbean experience that 'acculturation' theories represent. It should be reasonably obvious that Afro-Caribbean people in Britain today are a 'cultured' people in the fullest rather than elitist sense of the term. We would draw the reader's attention for example, to the Afro-Caribbean language, where recent researchers have argued that there are substantial links between them and West African languages and suggested that while 'the words may be European, the syntax is African'.[61]

The fact that Afro-Caribbean people did not merely 'adopt' the English language but actively transformed and 'blackened' it appears to have confused some sociologists. Like Brook-Shepherd they believe that the languages Afro-Caribbean people speak are 'colourful variants' of the English language. This notion is the residue of the decidedly more racist idea, that Afro-Caribbean people are *unable* to cope with the subtleties of 'standard English'. In schools this idea has traditionally taken the form of deriding 'patois' as 'bad English' (or even worse as 'monkey talk') and its speakers as ESN. Obviously Afro-Caribbeans are perfectly capable of speaking 'standard English' but historically many have *preferred* not to,[62] a tradition carried on consciously and determinedly by many of the 'second generation' of Afro-Caribbean youth in the 'mother country'.

We will be looking later at the ways in which their family/kinship systems, sex/gender systems and political ideologies have been characterized and where we disagree with those accounts,[63] but anyone interested in doing some leisurely and enjoyable 'empirical' research could do worse than compare reggae with the 'ju-ju' music currently popular in West Africa.

The 'absent' Raj

When we turn to consider the view of the Asian communities we find that the preferred modes of explanation are similar to, but not the same as, those adopted to speak about Afro-Caribbean people. As we have said, the existence of 'strong' Asian cultures is not in doubt here. They are not seen as having undergone the traumatic process of acculturation and their languages, religious and social institutions and family/kinship systems are, consequently, viewed as having remained more or less intact. However, the implicit contrast that is made between the historical experiences of Asians and Afro-Caribbeans should not be thought of as representing a simple symmetrical opposition. The accounts about Asian people and Asian cultures reveal important absences – absences that parallel those we have already witnessed in respect to accounts about Afro-Caribbeans. The most striking feature about what 'race relations'/'ethnicity studies' sociologists have had to say about the experiences of Asian people, is their failure to comment upon the impact of British imperialism in that part of the world. What is implied if this is not taken into account is that the Asian subcontinent has enjoyed an uninterrupted historical development. Such an omission is, to say the least, misleading and can only serve to fuel the commonly held belief – paraded weekly on our TV screens – that the poverty and hardships of these 'underdeveloped' regions are the result primarily of their 'backward' and 'rigid' social and cultural institutions.

Verity Khan, a prolific contributor to our 'knowledge' of Asian people, is obviously aware of this danger. In a recent contribution she informs us that

Village life in the Indian subcontinent is neither isolated nor static. The gradual adaptation in past decades indicates the strength of traditional institutions rather that the absence of outside influence.[64]

Unfortunately, the 'outside influence' that she has in mind here is not the historical 'influence' of indenture, colonialism and neo-colonial dependence; rather, she is concerned to let us know that these villages have benefited from Western-style progress and that 'all but the remotest areas' now enjoy 'communications, transportation, electricity, consumer items and a cash economy'. Even here the only 'outside influence' Khan will deal with is the remittances sent back to the villages by migrants. This she argues is the main source of the 'influx of capital and investment' which undermines 'the traditional power structure' and which because it is unevenly distributed 'causes tensions and jealousies between individuals, families and villagers'.[65] At one point she refers to the building of Mangla Dam in Mirpur during the 1960s, but the effects of this event, which apparently led to the 'displacement' of 100,000 people, are viewed by her only in terms of providing an impetus for some to try their luck in Britain. She provides no information that would enable us to understand why it was built – whether it was part of a larger development project or who made available the funds for such a large undertaking. Presumably it was not paid for by remittances! There is nothing in her account, either, which makes migration to Britain a necessary response to 'displacement', except for her comment that 'there has always been a tradition of migration from Mirpur'.[66] Khan notes that 'the political instability of Azad Kashmir has also affected its economic development and future prospects', but says nothing about the source of that political instability or about the cause of the 'general unemployment' in the country. Indeed she only seems to mention these things because of her feeling that they will discourage people from returning 'from life in the west'.[67]

The failure to make connections at a structural level between Azad Kashmir and the rest of Pakistan – let alone the wider 'world economy' – is not Khan's failure alone, but a failure of the cultural pluralist problematic generally. Here, 'culture' is seen as an autonomous realm which merely 'interacts' with other social processes. The effect of this is to produce a static and idealized vision of Asian cultures which cannot really take account of class, caste or regional differences and which cannot help us to understand how or why those 'cultures' have changed over time. To do this would require an attention to historical circumstances and conditions which was more comprehensive than the foreshortened historical vision which appears to be fashionable in 'ethnicity studies' circles. A couple of examples from the Indian experience of colonization may serve to illustrate our point. In the early centuries of trade between Europe, Asia and Africa, Indian cloth was much preferred to the English variety; so much so that 'Europeans relied heavily on Indian cloth for resale in Africa, and they also purchased cloth on several parts of the West African coast for sale elsewhere'.[68] However, two important factors eventually tipped the balance in Europe's favour. First, shipping as a trading activity was more fully developed in Europe than in Asia and Africa. This enabled Europeans to more or less control the sea trade routes. Second, the capitalist mode of production – the outcome of class struggles – enabled the British cloth industry in particular to 'copy fashionable Indian and African patterns' in large enough quantities to swamp the Indian and African markets with their own (European) cloth. The effect of these two (and other) factors was initially to retard and eventually to destroy the emerging Indian and African cloth industries.

India is the classic example where the British used every means at their disposal to kill the cloth industry, so that British cloth could be marketed everywhere, including inside India itself.[69]

During the colonial period, the 'legal and institutional changes in land and revenue systems' that were introduced by the British had the effect of transferring land from the 'rural magnates (tuluqdars) and small landholders to urban trading and money-lending castes'. This introduced changes in land use which 'dispossessed' the peasantry in much the same way as the earlier destruction of the cloth industry had 'displaced' the weaver.

We can draw certain lessons from these examples which should influence the ways in which we think about 'culture'. Under the pre-colonial mode of production, weaving was carried on largely by women. Women also held land in their own right, which would have given them a certain degree of power within their communities and a degree of autonomy from their men. The destruction of India's cloth industry and the changes in land and revenue systems would not only have 'displaced' them as weavers but, to the extent that they lost their land holdings, would also have weakened generally their bargaining position. We need to think then about the ways in which these ruptures and the introduction by the British of work – designated 'men's work' – in the urban centres, may have served to strengthen the position of men and certain aspects of the patriarchal structures of Indian society. At a different level, Iftikhar Ahmed has argued that the land and revenue changes precipitated the 1857 rebellion which seriously threatened 'the continuation of British rule in India'. This eventuality evoked a change in British policies towards India, whereby

The intensive penetration of traditional society was replaced by cautious preservation of the pre-existing social order. It seemed more sensible to take Indian society as it was, to concentrate on administration and control, and to shore up the landed aristocrats, who came to be viewed as the 'natural leaders best suited to the 'oriental mind'.[70]

Again certain structures of the Indian social formation were strengthened at the expense of others. We should stress at this point that we are not putting forward the idea that Asian cultures (as well as Afro-Caribbean cultures) were undermined during British rule. Indeed we would argue that an adequate analysis would need to progress beyond these small beginnings and enquire into both the resistances and struggles of Asian people against imperialist domination and the ways in which Asian people reached into their cultures and traditions, transforming them at the same time as they *used* them to inform their struggles. What we are saying is that accounts which neglect these histories are at best only telling half the story. We return to some of these themes in Chapter 7, but for the moment we intend to look at the arguments which suggest that Asian cultures, as strong as they are, nevertheless cause 'problems' for British society and for Asian people themselves.

  For the 'ethnicity studies' researchers, the relationship between the 'ethnic minorities' and the 'majority society' is viewed exclusively in cultural terms. They are concerned with the differences between the respective cultures and how these differences interfere with effective communication. This in turn directs their attention to the ideas, attitudes and knowledge that each group has about the other. On the one hand, they argue, members of the 'majority society' rarely know about and do not understand the cultural 'preferences' and practices of the 'ethnic minorities'; on the other hand members of the 'ethnic minority' communities are bewildered by and suspicious of the cultural practices and social institutions of the 'majority society'. The seemingly inevitable outcome of any interaction between these groups, then, is a series of obstructive 'mutual misunderstandings'. Thus while the re-establishment in Britain of Asian 'village kin systems' is a source of support for those communities,

To the 'outsider' English neighbour in the same area the apparent segregation of the population is perceived as a deliberate statement of not wanting to mix or adapt.[71]

Similarly Khan argues that Asian people often fail to take up the 'services' provided by the statutory agencies either because they are 'unskilled in informal, matter-of-fact, distance-maintaining interaction typical of urban and Western life-styles' [72] or because custom dictates that they utilize their own, communal networks and institutions. Where they do seek 'official' help, their 'linguistic difficulties' and lack of appropriate 'social skills' combine with the lack of knowledge amongst practitioners – whose attitudes and responses reflect 'the dominant values in British society' – to give a further twist to the tangle of 'mutual misunderstandings'.

The question of *power* which, one would have thought, would be crucial to an analysis of the relationship between the 'ethnic minorities' and the 'majority society', is mentioned but never explored in these accounts. Instead we are treated to explanations of the 'ethnic relations equation'. This requires the notion that 'all members of the society are subject to the *same* political and economic troubles', in order that blame can be apportioned to both sides and the equation be made to balance. Khan seems oblivious even to class inequalities and determinations let alone those secured by gender and racial differences.

Uneven distribution of power and resources [she intones] combine with linguistic and cultural differences to hinder direct communication and equal opportunity to participate fully in society. Whether they choose to do so when there is the opportunity is a question of attitudes, preferences and prejudices on both sides of the question. [73]

This is a familiar argument in 'ethnicity studies' circles. Brooks and Singh, for example, argue that while racism placed blacks in specific occupations to begin with, 'their own distinctive traditions and their ethnic identities . . . in turn influenced their occupational and industrial distribution'. [74] (Such ideas have even found expression in the work of Rex and Tomlinson who claim to be antithetical to the culturalism of the 'ethnicity studies' school. In their view 'immigrants' are to be found in 'jobs requiring the lower grades of skill' because 'manufacturing employment' is a new experience for them. At another point in their argument Rex and Tomlinson further suggest that unemployment amongst Asian people may be linked to their 'linguistic difficulties'. [75])

Khan is clearly chiding the 'ethnic minorities' for not taking up the 'opportunity' when offered, although what the opportunities were and when they were offered, is not made clear. Neither is it clear what she means by the 'uneven distribution of power'. If power is an attribute as she seems to imply, how does one acquire it? More importantly, how did the particular 'distribution of power' she speaks of come about? Wouldn't this process, in itself, have important consequences for the 'ethnic minorities'? The Asian – like the Afro-Caribbean – communities live in, and their cultures operate under, conditions that are not of their own making. It is not just that 'institutional racism' *restricts* their access to the various markets and services:

the different structures *work together* so as to reproduce the class relations of the whole society in a specific form on an extended scale; and . . . race, as a structural feature of each sector in this complex process of social reproduction, serves to 'reproduce' that working class in a racially stratified and internally antagonistic form.[76] (emphasis in original)

It seems to us that there are *power relations* in operation here which limit the range of choices black people can make. They do not 'choose' to live in inadequate housing any more than they 'choose' to do 'shit-work'. Given the frequency, for example, of violent physical attacks upon them, and the reluctance of the police to investigate these attacks, it makes a good deal of sense to remain within a community where support, protection and mutual defence can be relied on. This cannot be characterized simply as a 'cultural preference' interacting with 'external determinants'.[77]

The 'pathological' black family

The shift from a 'social deprivation' to a 'culturalist' problematic has entailed a closer scrutiny of the family/kinship systems, household organization, marital arrangements and child-rearing practices of the black communities. The 'family' is important not only because it is here that culture is reproduced but also because it is the principal site where black people are recognized as having a degree of autonomy. This makes it possible to argue that the cultural 'obstructions' to 'fuller participation' in society are reproduced within black families by black people themselves and that like 'original sin' these 'problems' descend from the 'immigrants' to their children, their children's children and to all who came after them. As we said earlier these kinds of arguments and shifts in emphasis have already taken place in the United States. Daniel Moynihan, using statistics – which were apparently 'rigged'[78] – to support his case, argued that the experience and deprivations of slavery had 'forced' the Afro-American community into a 'matriarchal structure'. Basically his argument was that black women were too dominant, were more likely to be able to find work, and were therefore too independent. The outcome of this was the 'emasculation' of the black male. This, he felt, retarded the progress of the community as a whole, since it was contrary to the family structure of the rest of 'American society'. He went on to say:

Obviously not every instance of social pathology afflicting the Negro community can be traced to weaknesses of family structure . . . [but] once or twice removed, it will be found to be the principal source of most of the aberrant, inadequate, or anti-social behaviour that did not establish, but now serves to perpetuate the cycle of poverty and deprivation.[79]

The sixties were years during which black people initially pressed their claims for 'civil rights'; then took direct action on the streets against, among other things, police brutality; and then took up arms against the state. Moynihan's report, coming out as it did in the mid-sixties, meant that he was well placed to influence policy initiatives, and the economic and political climate at the time made 'throwing money at the problem' a viable option. The policies derived from this report had the effect of increasing the prospects and opportunities for some black men at the expense of black women. In particular, those black families with a female head of household were neglected, and indeed became poorer. Michele Wallace argues that the already low income of black women 'increased only slightly' during this period (1965–76).

Jobs for black men did not translate into more financially secure black families with male heads. . . . The black males who were given access to employment and educational opportunities did not, for various reasons, automatically connect such opportunities with the imperative of family building.[80]

Although Britain in the seventies and eighties is not comparable to America in the sixties, it is worth bearing the Afro-American experience in mind.[81] The present Government clearly has no intention of 'throwing money' at their 'problems' and it is not clear, given the depth of the current recession, that such a policy could be pursued in any case. Furthermore while the images about the Afro-Caribbean 'family' are similar to Moynihan's ideas about Afro-American 'matriarchal structures', the images of Asian family/kinship systems are decidedly different. Nevertheless the pathological approach to black family life which characterizes Moynihan's report is evident in British research on black people. The view of the 'traditional' Asian family/kinship systems suggests that Asian households provide the structured and cohesive atmosphere wherein all members of the household are made aware of their roles, rights and obligations towards other members of the household and members of the wider kinship group. This arrangement promotes a 'certain stability and psychological health in all individuals'.[82] The view of the Afro-Caribbean household presents a stark contrast to this. Pryce argues that the family in Jamaica with its proliferation of common-law unions and high rates of illegitimacy among the 'lower class folk' is an inherently unstable institution, and locates the 'peculiarities of family life in the West Indies' as stemming 'directly from the institution of slavery, which was responsible for the total destruction of *conventional* family life among slaves'.[83] We will come back to what he means by 'conventional' in a moment but for the time being it is worth noting that according to Pryce, these 'peculiarities' are only part of a 'complex of causes responsible for his [*sic*] inability to establish a firm, rooted sense of identity'. These 'other causes' include an 'excessive individualism' which though a part of the Afro-Caribbean's European heritage, is exacerbated by their economic position. Thus the kinship system has to remain fluid in order to 'permit individuals to *abandon* family obligations and migrate at short notice to take advantage of economic opportunities overseas'.[84] Needless to say the 'white bias' and 'negative self-image', which we heard tell of before, adds to the Afro-Caribbean's sense of 'self-doubt'. The weakness of the family and culture can do nothing to overcome this 'self-doubt', but more importantly the family fails to instil a sense of fatherly responsibility in the Afro-Caribbean male and fails also to control its members. It is from this perspective that Ernest Cashmore is able to argue that the involvement of Afro-Caribbeean youth with the British police and the 'emergence (among them) of subterranean values as dominant motivating vectors of social action', has to do with 'the lack of social control exerted by the West Indian family, due historically to the fragmentation of family structure in slavery'.[85] Thus far the Asian household appears to have fared quite well in comparison to that of the Afro-Caribbean community, but we should not be complacent.

Again, the very strength of Asian culture is seen to be a source of both actual and potential weaknesses. It is not clear how much this has to do with the failure of students of ethnicity to erase their own ethnocentrism and how much it has to do with their pluralist perspective, which as we have said tends to obscure relationships of power and to treat the topic as a question of a meeting of cultures on equal terms. In any case Khan argues that the hierarchical structure of Asian households promotes 'stress-ridden relationships' particularly between sisters-in-law; and suggests that the underlying 'jealousies' and 'hostilities' are exacerbated by life in England, causing irreconcilable rifts between family members. Furthermore, while the family/kinship system promotes a healthy psyche, it does not 'prepare the members for change beyond that of the *natural* development cycle of the family'. The strength of 'traditional relationships' is thought to determine 'the skills and *handicaps* the migrant brings to his [*sic*] new situation in Britain', one of these no doubt being the way in which the 'severe reprimand or control' of deviant members of the community is exercised in the maintenance of group *izzat*.[86] It is for this reason too that Asian women, whom Khan invariably talks about as simply wives and mothers, are 'fettered' by traditional customs and remain tied to the house. In this view Asian women are particularly unlikely to have the opportunity to learn English, and the resultant 'linguistic difficulties' not only put them at a 'disadvantage' in terms of obtaining health and social services but also mean that they are unable to 'make contact' with their white neighbours. They 'fail' therefore to partake of the progressive and beneficial effects of English culture and in their 'isolation' cling all the more to their more 'traditional' views of the world. This in turn causes problems for their more 'modern' – because partially 'Anglicized' – children. For Asian women apparently even the English *climate* is hostile.

The new climate, the lack of sunshine and limited outdoor activity can be detrimental to health, particularly for women restricted by custom and necessity to the house. The higher incidence of osteomalacia, rickets and anaemia found among some Asian populations in Britain is partly due to the unsuitability of a diet well suited to a different life style and climate.[87]

Vitamin D deficiency, the cause of rickets, used to be a problem of white families as well until governments applied the simple remedy of adding vitamin D to margarine. Asian people do not use margarine, and have campaigned repeatedly for vitamin D to be added to chapati flour and other foodstuffs which *are* a part of their diet. The state's response has been 'let them eat margarine'. For all her supposed knowledge about the Asian communities, Khan remains woefully ignorant about their campaigns on this matter and merely reproduces the racist explanations of the DHSS. As the Brent Community Health Council argues:

Asian children, adolescents and pregnant women get rickets because of (state) racism, but what all the advice on diet, often beautifully produced in Gujarati, does is to imply that it is Asian mothers who are to blame.[88]

Given our scholars' propensity to discover and tackle any 'problem', except the burning problem of racism, it should not come as any surprise to find that the 'migration process is a major source of stress in itself', although what the stress is and who suffers it is subject to a degree of variation. For Pryce, who is seeking to establish a basis for the 'teenybopper' problem which he wants to deal with later, it is the children left behind in the Caribbean who experience the 'stress'. Since family obligations are 'devoid of any formal or binding significance', the child is open to neglect or else finds it 'easy to evade the discipline of guardians'. Furthermore,

The absence of a viable supportive culture that is independent and capable of tightening family relations to help the West Indian poor carry the burden of their deprivation and impoverishment.[89]

is a cause of the psychic and cultural confusion that the youngsters experience when united with their parents. At the same time, the 'mutilating colonial heritage' and 'inferior educational upbringing and colonial origin' mean that the Afro-Caribbean child is unable to cope with the 'demands made on him [*sic*] by the British school system'.[90] Khan on the other hand sees the greatest source of 'stress' as being on the male Mirpuri 'migrant'. Here the familiar notion that Afro-Caribbeans came to England because England was the 'mother country' is trans-formed into the Mirpuri villager's supposed perception of England as 'a land of promise and a way to solve all one's problems.' The stresses here turn on the movement from a 'backward' rural to an advanced industrial urban setting and his separation from and obligation to his family back in the village.[91]

These arguments concede ground to the new racism. Pryce absolves the racist structures of the English education system by defining the Afro-Caribbean child's struggle against its racism as 'maladjusted behaviour'. He then locates this 'mal-adjustment' in the Caribbean household structures which he sees as pathologically reproducing 'failure'. Khan performs similar operations upon the Asian community and goes on to highlight the '*many* migrants' who 'obtain false documents' and arrive 'illegally' in Britain, without saying anything about the ways in which the Immigration Acts have *broadened* the definition of illegality so that *no* member of *any* black community - even those born here - can now feel secure in thier continued citizenship. She says nothing either about the restrictive practices of immigration officials on the Asian subcontinent; the racist practices of immigration officers in Britain; the sexual harassment of Asian women under the guise of so-called 'virginity testing'; the suspension of habeas corpus in cases of suspected illegal entry; or the 'fishing raids' and general thuggery which the British police force practise upon the black communities.[92] She lends support as well to the present Government's intended restrictions on the entry of Asian fiancés, by suggesting that the woman's greater familiarity with English life will conflict 'with the established pattern of public male authority and knowledge of the outside world'.[93]

The idea that slavery produced a weak, unstable, 'matriarchal structure' in Afro-Caribbean communities is, like the arguments about Afro-Caribbean culture generally, the result of a one-sided reading of history. As in every other sphere of their lives, so in their familial relations, slaves resisted the debilitating effects of slavery. Indeed the very experience of slavery made 'family life' highly valued.

For the black man and woman family life was their only daily refuge. It offered them companionship, some modicum of comfort, a positive and reinforcing view of themselves and a future. Gutman describes the slaves as having been considerably pre-occupied not only with their husbands and wives and children but with their cousins, nieces, and nephews, aunts and uncles and grandparents. Whenever it was possible they maintained family ties across generations.[94]

Numerous accounts testify to the strength and resilience of Afro-Caribbean and Afro-American family life,[95] and Foner, if not Pryce, was clearly impressed by the warmth and stability of familial relationships amongst Jamaica's present rural population. However, there is more at issue here than the recovery of historical information and the simple 'rehabilitation' of the pathological view of the Afro-Caribbean household. We noted earlier that Pryce measured the Afro-Caribbean family against 'conventional family life' and saw it as having certain 'peculiarities' which blocked its proper functioning. What he means by *conventional* here, is obviously the common-sense image of the English family with father, mother and 2.2 children, where father is the breadwinner and mother nurtures the children. As we have already seen, this is not the 'natural' form of household organization but rather the specific achievement of the European bourgeoisies. Further, its universal applicability is more a 'fact' of a certain 'familial ideology' than a fact of life. The particular household organization of certain sections of the Afro-Caribbean peoples can only be viewed as inherently 'unstable' if one holds to the view of a 'father figure' as an absolute necessity and if one holds the sexist view that women are not capable of rearing children without a male presence. Such a view though posits women as given quantities with certain natural attributes and capacities and fails to take into account their ability, individually and collectively, to manipulate their environment. Since Pryce recognizes that this is what has actually happened in his (mistaken) characterization of the family of the subordinate Jamaican classes as 'matriarchal', it can only be his uncritical acceptance of an ideological conception of the family that leads him to see this family system as necessarily unstable and pathological. Cashmore also fails to question the patriarchal ideology that sees the fatherless households as a problem. For him the creation of a matrifocal family and its reliance on women has led Rastafarians to usurp motherhood, assert a 'new male identity' and 'create for themselves a father-image and God in Haile Selassie'.[96]

Gayle Rubin, in her illuminating discussion about sex/gender systems and their corresponding empirically observable manifestations in differing kinship systems, provides useful guidance here. She defines a sex/gender system as

a set of arrangements by which the biological raw material of human sex and pro-creation is shaped by human, social intervention and satisfied in a conventional manner, no matter how bizarre some of the conventions may be.[97]

and argues that the social construction of sexuality and gender informs both the type of kinship system and the position of women, often though not necessarily subordinate, within that system. Important here is her awareness that sex/gender systems are culturally and historically specific. To use a model drawn from one sex/gender system to talk about or measure another will produce a distorted picture but hardly aid understanding.

A second point we would make here derives in part from our first. We agree with the 'race-relations' sociologists that Afro-Caribbean societies' sex/gender systems are *different* but cannot agree that this difference is pathological. We need to remember here that their view of the family is not simply the ideological view of the white bourgeoisie, it is also a view forged historically within a white patriar-chal society. It is only from this position that 'race-relations' sociologists have been able to launch their attacks upon what they see as either a 'black matriarchy' or the black 'matrifocal' family. Hence, too, Rex and Tomlinson's view of the Afro-Caribbean as having been 'culturally *castrated*'. We must be equally on guard here against the kind of 'cultural imperialism' that simply seeks to tint the argument another shade of white by first accepting that black households are organized differently but then arguing that they are *more* patriarchal than their white counterparts. The assumption that liberation for black women consists in acting like white women is particularly visible in the images of the house-bound 'passive' Asian women, who wouldn't, apparently, say 'boo to a goose'. It is visible also in the idea, fashionable on the left these days, that Asian women only learned to struggle when they came to England. Like their Afro-Caribbean sisters, Asian women do not meekly submit to their men and have a history of struggle as distinguished as anyone's.[98] Gail Omvedt's recent work reveals quite clearly that their very awareness of the sexual division of labour through which they are exploited at work and the sexism that oppresses them in their homes and villages, has propelled them to the forefront of their people's struggles.

'Women were the most militant' they said. It was not only these particular leaders of the local Lal Nishan (Red Flag) party who said it, but other organisers also. . . . 'Women are the most ready to fight, the first to break through police lines, the last to go home'.[99]

It would be wrong to make a too easy correspondence between the Indian women who Gail Omvedt speaks to and Verity Khan's Mirpuri women, but it does seem necessary to reiterate the point that these women are not given quantities. Khan comes to the rather dubious conclusion that Asian women don't identify 'freedom with self-assertion'.[100] Yet, given the 'self-assertion' of Asian women in India, Pakistan and Bangladesh in their various liberation and revolutionary struggles and the 'self-assertion' of Asian women under our very noses at Grunwicks and Chix, it is not at all clear why Mirpuri women in Bradford should not be equally capable of organization and 'self-assertion'.

Youth: between two cultures

The arguments about the 'problems' caused by the 'cultural preferences' of Asians and the 'negative self-image' and 'weak' family structures of Afro-Caribbeans, form the backdrop against which discussions of Asian and Afro-Caribbean youth take place. The themes here are organized around the 'one and a half' or even 'two' generation gap which is thought to afflict the Afro-Caribbean community and the 'cultural conflict' between Asian parents and their children, who are 'caught between two cultures'.[101] The reasons put forward for this vary from author to author, although they all boil down more or less to the view that the different experiences and backgrounds of parents and youth lead to differing responses to and expectations of life in Britain, which in turn provide the occasion for conflict between parents and their children.

The Community Relations Commission, which had always been concerned to promote a better understanding of the 'ethnic minorities' and their cultures, was quick to adopt the 'cultural pluralist' approach and the ideas about 'cultural conflict' and 'identity-crisis' that went with it. The Commission for Racial Equality inherited this baggage along with many other of the CRC's bad habits, and in its recent publication *The Fire Next Time* has continued popularizing the notions about black youths' apparent cultural and psychological 'handicaps', which the CRC had begun in its *Between Two Cultures*. The first murmurings of this approach to black youth were visible in Thompson's *The Second Generation . . . Punjabi or English?* (1974). The murmurings grew louder in the years that followed with the publication of Taylor's *The Half-Way Generation* (1976), Ballard's *Culture Conflict and Young Asians in Britain* (1976) and Meadows's *In Search of Identity* (1976). The CRC echoed this theme in the title of its own publication and outlined its starting-point by proclaiming:

The children of Asian parents born or brought up in Britain are a generation caught between two cultures. They live in a culture of their parents at home, and are taught a different one at school, the neighbourhood and at work . . . parents cannot fully understand their children, children rarely fully understand their parents.[102]

Presaging the *Sun*'s article which we referred to in Chapter 2 and which completed the circuit in the reproduction of racist common sense, the CRC argued that Asian children's exposure to British values, norms and attitudes undermined their parents' traditional authority and caused the youth to question certain aspects of their parents' culture. For the girls in particular this revolved around the issue of arranged marriage, while Asian youth's militant response to Gurdip Singh Chaggar's murder was seen to further exacerbate generational conflict.

Time has apparently not dulled the necessity to repeat these ideas. John Rex in a recent pronouncement warns us of the 'problems' that Asian children face on entering school. The 'problems' are not the problems of racism in schools or the possibilities of Fascist violence. In his view the chief 'problem' is that Asian children have to step outside of the 'well-integrated culture' of their homes and perform well in the 'secular, utilitarian and instrumental' discipline of 'middle class school culture' which, with its emphasis upon individualism, threatens to undermine the children's commitment to their 'family culture and values'.[103] Surprisingly, for Rex at least, many Asian children do manage to perform well at school despite the 'tensions' created for them by the opposing pressures of the Asian communities' expectations of 'altruistic solidarity' and the schools' demand for 'egoistic' competitiveness. This presumably fuels Rex's rather quaint expectation – though it is none the less racist for all its quaintness – that Asian people 'face a Jewish future' and will follow them into the middle class.[104] Rex explains the children's successful attempts to negotiate the conflicting pressures, partly by reference to the strength of Asian culture and partly by telling us that there is no necessary contradiction for those children who are able to increase 'the family's honour through individual success'.[105] However, Rex is convinced that things can't possibly run so smoothly and that somewhere there must be 'cases of breakdown', but rather than look for such 'breakdowns' in the racist practices of the education system, for example, he looks for evidence of cultural conflict. Not surprisingly he finds it! He achieves this turnaround in two ways. First, unlike the cultural pluralists of the 'ethnicity studies' school, Rex does at least recognize class distinctions if not class determinations.[106] This allows him to argue that the threat to Asian 'family culture and values' comes not from one but from '*two* sources', the other one being

the ecstatic working class youth culture [which] appears doubly alien and dangerous. It is corrupting of family values and damaging to any prospects of instrumental success in the culture to which the immigrant has necessarily and seriously to adjust.[107]

It is significant that Rex chooses to illustrate his scenario by reference to the 'plight' of Asian girls who he sees as being 'required to accept considerable limitations on their freedom of movement and, *above all*, arranged marriages' (our emphasis). Digging in the soil of common sense, Rex goes on to inform us that 'boys may be required to give their wages to their fathers' and that girls may get married while still at school; although he is keen to concede that arranged marriages may hold the possibility of some 'rewards' too. However, against the 'restrictions' imposed on girls by Asian cultures the apparent 'permissiveness' and 'freedom' of the 'ecstatic working class culture' holds out the promise of 'greener pastures' on the other side, if not of liberation by St George on his white charger.

There must be few Indian girls who have not been tempted by these possibilities, particularly as they are presented in popular music. Thus being a good Indian and also being a successful middle-class student at the same time, are by no means easy goals to attain. There is *bound* to be breakdown.[108] (our emphasis)

For West Indian youth, on the other hand, who had always been noted for their 'aggressive behaviour', the problem has been to explain their 'failure' at school and their increasing penchant for taking on the 'boys in blue'. John Brown's *Shades of Grey*, redolent with the common-sense rationalizations of the Handsworth police and his own colonial memories, located the problem much as Pryce was later to do in the family life and inadequate schooling in the Caribbean. This 'bad start' he saw as merely having been exacerbated by the higher standards of English schools, which led to a subsequent failure to find a job and the inevitable drift into crime.

Deprived and disadvantaged, they see themselves as victims of white racist society, and attracted by values and life style of alienated Dreadlock groups, drift into lives of idleness and crime, justifying themselves with half-digested gobbets of Rastafarian philosophy.[109]

Brown's formulations which purported to show a split between the law-abiding West Indian community and the religious Rastas on the one hand and the 'criminalised dreadlock sub-culture' on the other, managed to set the parameters of future race-relations research even though some of the academic contributors protested that he had given all Rastas a bad name. It is not clear whether it is their sympathy for Rasta which prompted these protests or their need to keep the West Indian community 'open' as an object of study.[110] In any case having kicked Brown down the front steps they invariably 'sneak him in through the conceptual backdoor a few pages later'.[111]

Len Garrison argues that because the majority of West Indian parents come from rural backgrounds characterized by low living standards, lack of education, limited employment prospects and therefore low expectations of the future, they were prepared to make sacrifices in order to establish themselves in Britain. Their children, however, either born or largely reared in Britain in an urban and secular environment, exhibited a 'new defiant attitude' in their rejection of both racism and their parents' religious 'humility'. The generational conflict, then, revolves around the differences between parent/rural culture and youth/secular culture.[112] Cashmore on the other hand in his attempt to approach an understanding of Rastafari through a mobilization of some concepts borrowed from the 'sociology of religion', suggests that the conflict really has to do with differing religious perspectives. Where the parents because of their 'limited cultural resources' had attempted to transcend the harsh realities of life in Britain by a headlong flight into Pentecostalism, thereby 'opting out of the race for conventional rewards', their sons and daughters having been educated along with whites saw themselves as equals and insisted upon equal treatment.[113] The expectation that the children, through the medium of education, would be able to enter into and participate in the mainstream of British society, and the apprehension that these expectations 'were not going to be met', adds further to family tensions as the parents begin to blame the children for failure.[114] If this were not enough, the shattering of certain illusions about British 'fair-mindedness' and associations of whiteness with 'wealth and prestige',[115] only adds fuel to the fire and plunges West Indian youth into an 'identity crisis'.

Garrison links this to the way in which the child's experience of school undermines a confidence which is already low, since they are members of a minority that has a 'less well defined culture'. As we saw earlier, in his view their parents' negative self-image adds to this, representing 'part of the complex problem the black child will have to overcome in order to arrive at his [*sic*] own *essential* personality'[116] (our emphasis). West Indian youth are, he claims, suffering from 'personality dislocation'; while for Cashmore these conditions precipitate the need for 'discrepancy reduction' and for Pryce they lead to a 'psychic disorientation'. John Rex and Sally Tomlinson present their own particular variation on this theme, for they seek to locate the reasons for the supposed differences in performance between the two communities in their respective personalities.

If the West Indian is plagued by self-doubt induced by white education, and seeks a culture which will give him [*sic*] a sense of identity, the Asians have religions and cultures and languages of which they are proud and which may prove surprisingly adaptive and suited to the demands of a modern industrial society.[117]

It is no doubt the 'Jewish future' they see for Asians, and the 'Irish route' they see West Indians taking, that fuels some recognition of Asian cultural and political traditions while at the same time denying those same traditions of West Indians. Nevertheless, they are not averse to suggesting that Asian youth are caught 'between two cultures' and that they suffer – along with West Indian youth – 'considerable uncertainty about ethnic identification'.[118]

One step forward . . . two steps back

The interesting thing here is that while the 'ethnicity' studies school initially promoted these themes, they have both in their unfortunately titled *Between Two Cultures* and their latest *Minority Families in Britain* tried to challenge the way in which their earlier work was taken up. Catherine Ballard, in her recent contribution, argues that the talk about 'culture conflict' merely serves to reinforce the common-sense perceptions of practitioners and 'sets young Asians apart as a "problem" category'.

More seriously, it assumes that cultural values are

fixed and static and that there is no possibility of adaptation, flexibility or accommodation between one set of values and another.[119]

Having thus argued, however, she then persists in trying to explain 'the strange half-British half-Asian behaviour of the children'; illustrating 'the kinds of inter-generational conflicts which may occur'; and assessing the 'usefulness of the popular concept of *culture conflict*' which she has just argued is a damaging and erroneous concept (our emphasis). She tramples across the same dreary terrain of the *inevitable* 'gulf' between generations which 'sharpen' as the children get older, and dredges up the idea that they have never experienced their culture 'in the totality of its original context', in support of what is basically a 'between two cultures' argument. This can, perhaps, be explained by her 'professional' interest. But in the pursuance of that interest, she first of all falls back upon the fact of the parents' 'linguistic handicaps' and then begins to explicate the 'extreme case'. This is odd since she had only just criticized the 'sensationalist media' for the same thing.[120] Even here in one of the 'extreme' cases she cites she erases the possibly obstructive role of the practitioners involved, who 'could not understand what her parents' position might be', by arguing that the girl is to blame.

Finally it became clear that their involvement was worsening the situation by making it possible for the girl to sustain and exaggerate her problems, and particularly the Asian aspects of those problems, while continually passing the responsibility for solving them to outsiders.[121]

Unable to find any conclusive evidence to suggest that conflict within the Asian family is any more likely than in any other family, Ballard proposes the notion of 'reactive ethnicity', whereby Asian youth's response to racism is to close ethnic ranks and maintain 'contact with the sub-continent and familiarity with Asian social and cultural norms'. This is to be their 'ultimate security'. Somehow we do not feel that the Asian youth who have organized so as to make sure that racist attacks upon their community do not go uncontested, would agree with her designation of their activities as an exercise in 'reactive ethnicity'.

The Bengalis who sat down in Brick Lane and refused to move in 1977 were not indulging in an Asian or peasant tradition as a means of recreation on a Sunday morning. They were bringing an Asian cultural form of *resistance* to bear on their British fight against racism: the fascists should not sell their wares in the community, the Bengalis would be terrorised no longer.[122]

Ballard's colleague Peter Weinreich, on the other hand, has been concerned to replace 'the loose and ambiguous term "identity conflict" with the concept of "conflict in identification with another"'. The latter term he feels can be made more concrete since it refers us to 'specific "identification conflicts" with particular others', which can be measured empirically through the modified application of 'Kelly's theory of personal constructs'.[123] The assumption of his paper is that the process of identity development is something which is common to all adolescents and in this connection an 'individual's conflicts in identification with others' are regarded as 'an important psychological impetus for personal change'.[124] This allows him to argue that such conflicts are more often a *resource* than a liability, an argument which undercuts the view held by the other theorists we have been looking at and is supported by his results which 'demonstrate that ethnic identity conflicts do not generally imply self-hatred'.[125]

Unfortunately the study itself is not as unproblematic as Weinreich implies. Quite apart from the considerable violence he does to his respondents' 'specific value connotations',[126] his assumption that their 'contra-value systems' can be read off simply from their 'positive-value systems' is in itself misleading. The reader will remember that in the earlier arguments about common-sense thinking, we suggested that even though the dominant ideology formed the parameters for common sense, it did not necessarily involve 'conflict' for people to hold contradictory ideas (general *vis-à-vis* situated judgements). Weinreich's 'bipolar constructs' do not enable him to recognize this. For him 'believes in law and order' must necessarily contrast with 'each man for himself'; although it is by no means clear why the individual should not mobilize 'law and order' in furtherance of an individualistic objective. This points to a fundamental weakness in Weinreich's concepts. They can deal only with individuals who as he says have already been 'socialised', but they cannot grasp the social context within which the individual's 'identifications' - conflicted or otherwise - have been formed and have meaning. This has the effect of stripping those 'identifications' of their pertinence and effectivity, a point which comes out quite clearly in his uncritical acceptance of the conclusions of Parker and Kleiner. They had argued that ambivalence in identification patterns is 'realistic and adaptive for the Negro', and that 'it is the polarisation of racial identification or reference group behaviour that is *psychopathogenic*'[127] (our emphasis). It is as well to remember here that when Parker and Kleiner were making their study, Afro-Americans were engaged in yet another struggle against the racist structures and oppressions which have been grinding them down for centuries. In this context Weinreich's preference for those males who, seeing themselves as 'black British', 'will be *realistic* about colour prejudice', and 'their female counterparts [who] are likely to proceed towards potent conceptions of themselves as black British',[128] is slightly suspect. Especially so when those with a 'consciously defined ethnic conception' who identify with Africa or the Caribbean must by inference be a associated with their 'psychopathogenic' sisters and brothers in America! (our emphasis)

This goes together with the rather dubious notion that it will be the retention, by Asian youth, of their 'ethnic distinctiveness' which will cause them to 'remain apart from native whites and, in this sense, not assimilate to them'.[129] Both formulations betray Weinreich's concern that blacks should not go too far in their struggles to transform the capitalist racist structures of British society. His view of a 'multi-ethnic' society is one in which the 'self-concepts' of blacks are 'interactive with the values of the broader community',[130] rather than one in which the structures and practices that subordinate blacks have been overturned.

The 'identity crisis' and criminality

The point at which the 'race-relations' sociologists discover Afro-Caribbean youths' 'identity crisis' (or if you prefer 'conflict in identification' with others) is also the point at which Brown's ideas about the 'criminalised dreadlock sub-culture' resurface. In a sense this is linked to the idea that there has always been a 'criminalised sub-culture' in the Afro-Caribbean community. Rex, for example, grounding his account in Pryce's categories of the 'stable law-abiding (life) orientation' and the 'expressive-disreputable orientation', argues that the existence of 'old time religion' in the Afro-Caribbean community necessarily 'presupposes its opposite'. He draws our attention to the 'small minority of West Indians' who having been forced into unemployment or else refused 'shit-work', turn away from thoughts of respectability and *choose* to

live with an eye on the mainchance and, not being bound by the constraints which the Pentecostalist 'saints' impose upon themselves, they find that the mainchances which come their way carry a load of erotic satisfactions. They live by pimping, by cheating and thieving, and by peddling ganga, and some few live well in this way.[131]

The 'problem' in the Afro-Caribbean community, however, apparently goes much deeper than this rift between the 'rough' and 'respectable' elements of the working class, which has traditionally been 'discovered' by politicians, the police and others concerned with 'public affairs'. For here that rift is compounded by a split along generational lines. Cashmore tells us that during the sixties young blacks at odds with an English culture that degrades their blackness, drifted into a 'rude boy' gang structure where: 'Flitting between the white squares of [their] parents' background and the black of his gang enterprise'[132] they derived 'gratification from non-instrumental violence'. This formation of gangs was in the first place facilitated by 'familial fragmentation', for as Rex remarks, 'the link between a young West Indian male and his parents is relatively weak'.[133] In this situation the peer group became the major socializing agent and it is here that the 'subterranean values' we heard tell of before led him and her into an involvement with the police. Garrison agrees:

Failure in the education system, poor employment prospects, homelessness, bring many youths into contact with the police.[134]

And so does Pryce:

Now divorced from the security and protection of the parental home, the would-be teenybopper, finds it difficult to go straight and remain law abiding. After the loss of his first one or two jobs, the drift into a life of petty crime and homelessness becomes steadier and steadier as his unemployability militates against a conventional life style.[135]

Cashmore goes on to argue that these gang structures were 'inherited' by younger blacks (in the seventies) where they acted as *'breeding* grounds of Rastafarian themes'.[136] The effect that Rastafari (and reggae) are seen to have had on Afro-Caribbean youth is crucial here. Although it may be viewed as providing a 'new and independent channel of expression' (Garrison) or 'new conceptual maps' (Cashmore), it is also seen as the cause of further conflict between youths and their parents. Colin Lago and Barry Troyna, for example, argue that

The recent adoption of Rastafarian *regalia* by an increasing number of black youths in Britain has added new dimensions to the intergenerational conflict amongst West Indian families in this country.[137]

The relatively recent recognition that Afro-Caribbean people do have a 'culture', which has been thrust upon the 'race-relations' sociologists by the activities of the youth, has prompted the elaboration of ideas about Rastafari which are similar to those about Asian cultures. Rastafari is invariably characterized as a 'withdrawal' from society and as such is presented as the obstacle to 'integration'. Its philosophy is seen to contain a 'separatist ideology' or even in Pryce's view a 'racist ideology' which contrasts sharply with the, apparently, 'predominantly integrationist aspirations of the first generation'.[138] Lago and Troyna maintain that the parents' opposition and hostility to Rastafari is 'symbolically represented' in their insistence on 'English being spoken rather than patois' and in their 'rejection of the "heavier" forms of Reggae'.[139] Indeed Troyna insists that the politics of the Afro-Caribbean community generally, and of the youth in particular, can be read off from the music they listen to.[140] However, while there are disagreements within the Afro-Caribbean communities it is not so clear that these constitute the rigid divisions that Troyna and others suggest. For example, the extensive use of 'patois' amongst young Afro-Caribbeans when in their own company indicates a level of agreement which is 'taken for granted' and which forms the context within which their continuing discussions take place. The 'overstandings' transmitted via 'patois' cannot be reproduced adequately on the printed page, where the reader can neither see nor hear the respondent and has to rely on the knowledge, selection and interpretation of the 'reporter'. The following piece of conversation illustrates this. One of Troyna's respondents, James, criticized Rastas because

They believe that Haile Selassie is God, but if he was he wouldn't have died before them. Haile Selassie is Man and Man can't make Man.[141]

Without more knowledge about James, we cannot know whether, for example, the word 'before' is being used in its familiar English sense to indicate the passage of time (i.e. 'he wouldn't have died before they did'), or in the familiar Afro-Caribbean sense to mean 'in front of [their very eyes]'. If James does habitually use 'patois' when in the company of his friends, this would also indicate an area of agreement with the Rastas he is apparently criticizing.

Another youth, Calvin – although speaking to Troyna in 'standard English' – indicates his areas of agreement and disagreement with some Rastas thus:

Prejudice; it's no good wanting to go back there to the West Indies. You've got to stand up and fight here. *Like Bob Marley says.*[142] (our emphasis)

Other examples can be drawn even from the work of Troyna, Cashmore and Pryce, which suggest that what we are dealing with here are not individualized polar oppositions but *collective processes* of argument and counter-argument which are not yet at an end.

Throughout his articles Troyna is keen to push the idea that there are 'real Rastas' and others who just 'follow fashion'. Although Troyna himself doesn't pursue this point, others 'discover' Brown's 'criminalized dreadlocks' precisely amongst the followers of fashion. Garrison argues, for example that Rastafari is a vehicle which is being 'exploited by some black youngsters who use it as a fashionable outlet for their frustration and aggression';[143] but while researchers protest that the 'real Rastas' are peaceful people, the distinction between them and the 'dreads' proves difficult to maintain. Cashmore, for example, who criticizes Brown's spurious formulations, ends up by making similar claims. Rasta beliefs and symbols are, he feels, being used as a 'sanction for criminal behaviour' and he goes on to imply that this has something to do with Rastafari itself, which he argues is a 'Pandora's box' of ideas.[144] The fear that Rastafari constitutes an incipient threat to the 'wider society' is visible in his idea that the absence of a 'locus of final authority' introduces the problem of *controlling* the youth and in the equation he draws between the early Rasta communes and Charles Manson's cult.[145] We should also consider the metaphors of disease and psychological instability which he employs to speak about Rasta. He describes Rastafari as a 'millenarian cult' which has produced a 'bizarre', 'exotic' and 'fantastic synthesis' and can only understand why the youth have embraced it in such numbers by referring us to their supposed 'identity crisis' which initially made them 'suggestible' and therefore susceptible to such ideas.[146] The youths' take-up of Rasta themes is described by him as a 'contagion' and he states that their 'drift' towards Rastafari involves them in cultivating an 'idiosyncratic mode of thought' and indulging in 'increasingly eccentric' behaviour.[147] Within this context it is hardly surprising when Cashmore portrays their involvement with the police as more or less inevitable.

Rex and Tomlinson, on the other hand, were not going to deal with the relations between black youth and the police and only decided to do so because the youth who graced their sample emphasized its importance. In their commitment to objectivity Rex and Tomlinson actually went to check the police side of the story, 'a picture so chilling in its absurdity that it is only matched by their verification of the number of unemployed West Indian youths by a visit to the local Careers Office'.[148] They accept uncritically the police's view that Rastafarian symbols are in themselves signs of possible 'trouble', yet ignore the police's own admission that there are racists in their midst and therefore fail to associate them with the problem. Like the other theorists Rex and Tomlinson appear to believe that the racial conflicts between black youth and the police are the 'natural' consequence of non-racial phenomena – youth unemployment and the 'absence of a "feeling" of legitimacy in police authority'.[149] More recently Rex has come to accept the police argument that if the youth stay off the streets then they won't be harassed. With an engaging simplicity he argues that,

Young Rastafarians gather on street corners. Young thieves gather on street corners. Some marginalised men gather on street corners. Some Rastas are thieves and marginalised men. Some marginalised men become thieves and Rastas or both. Some young Rastas are simply lawfully and peacefully going about their business. But the police, in the task of preventing crime . . . stop, question and harass the most visible of those on street corners, the Rastas.[150]

Presumably it would make just as much sense if the police harassed the street corners!

'Race relations' and 'ethnicity studies' sociologists have not yet associated Asian youth – or the Asian communities generally – with 'crime', in the same way or to the same extent as they have done with Afro-Caribbeans. The police do, however, have their own views on this subject; and it is worth noting that Rex's closer contacts with the Home Office appear to have involved him in 'a certain degree of movement between perspectives and hence a move along the road to objectivity', which now requires him to embrace their rationalizations.

Police *claim* that, whereas West Indian boys get into trouble because they are out of control, the problems presented by the Indian community are often those arising from violence in the enforcement of discipline or fighting for the control of institutions. From the point of view of Indian youth, what this means is that any possibility of deviance on their part will bring down the most *violent oppression* on them.[151] (our emphasis)

The CRE seems to be travelling on a similar path. In the report to which we referred earlier, they provide us with an account of Afro-Caribbean youth which is heavily influenced by Pryce's work and go on to stress the potentially 'extremist and destructive' direction that political organization among these 'hard-core alienated' youth may take. They warn, however, that Asian youth too are implicated in the process of 'alienation'. Following the academics, they argue that the essential dynamic of this 'alienation' lies within the black communities. It is merely 'exacerbated by practices of racial discrimination, unemployment and problems with the police'.[152] The CRE suggests the shape of things to come by pointing to the 'noticeable degree of militancy among Asian youth' in Southall and East London; and in a slightly different context Rex echoes their concerns by telling us that the severity of 'social control' in the Asian community will be enough to generate 'a small group of (moral) outcasts'.[153] It is too soon to tell whether we are witnessing the beginnings of the criminalization of Asian youth, although the 'conspiracy charges' brought against the Bradford 12 suggest that Asian youth are fast losing the image of docility with which they have hitherto been saddled.[154]

Conclusion

The ideas about 'identity crisis', 'culture conflict' and 'intergenerational conflict' which power the accounts of 'race/ethnic relations' sociologists have been constructed in large part without reference to the struggles that the parents have been involved in before and since coming to Britain. They have been characterized as the passive, acquiescent victims of racism wanting only to 'integrate'; as recalcitrant 'traditionalists', suspicious and bewildered by white society, who 'withdraw' wilfully into their own 'ethnic' or 'religious' enclaves; or as a combination of both. Theorists have, for example, highlighted the parents who supposedly refuse to allow 'patois' to be spoken in their homes, but say nothing about the parents who don't act in that way. This is surprising given the recent concern of schools and other 'professional researchers' that the language spoken in Afro-Caribbean homes 'interferes' with the children's ability to use 'standard English'.[155] (This view paints an equally pathological picture of Afro-Caribbean home life but at least recognizes Afro-Caribbean cultures.) The idea that the struggles of black youth, against police harassment, Fascist attacks and racism in schools and at work, are 'new' phenomena is hardly borne out by the facts. Who were the objects of the police's 'nigger hunting' expeditions in the fifties and early sixties when many of today's youth weren't even a glimmer in their parents' eyes? Who fought the Fascists and Teddy Boys in Nottingham and Notting Hill in 1958? Who are the people who fought trade union racism up and down the country for the last thirty years and more? Who initiated the campaigns against ESN placements and 'sin-bins'? The fact that the youths have brought new understandings and different modes of struggle to bear on their communities' struggles, does not mean that they are not still following in their parents' footsteps or that they don't stand firmly *side by side* their parents in opposition to racism.[156]

The theorists, however, have chosen arbitrarily to divide the communities along generational lines and to ground their accounts in pseudo-psychology. In our view these theorists have mislocated the 'identity crises' in the black communities; indeed it is because black youth know very well who they are that the heavy hand of the state has come down with such force upon them. Years ago in his book *Black Skins: White Masks*, Franz Fanon correctly located the 'identity crises' within the black petty bourgeoisie, the 'comprador' class. A close reading of Pryce's work and the work of Foner lends support to his view. Foner tells us that

While all (the villagers) were *sensitive* to the slightest gradations of skin color . . . the dark-skinned white collar workers (teachers, nurses, clerks, and so on) were *most concerned* with the prestige-conferring functions of light·skin.[157] (our emphasis)

It is understandable that members of this class, concerned to put much distance between themselves and the black masses, should suffer from a crisis of identity and this perhaps goes some way towards explaining why Pryce and Garrison are so attached to such ideas. They recognize themselves in them, but then proceed to generalize the ideas across the whole community. In a sense as well this is their way of exacting a vengeance upon those *black* youths who have no such problems and who, in standing firm, threaten and challenge the black petty bourgeoisie's sensibilities. Listen to Pryce:

The more respectable you are the more likely you are to be shocked. The Rasta is usually a *lower-class* black man [*sic*]. In appearance, his [*sic*] most distinguishing feature is his [*sic*] hair. He [*sic*] *grows it long, never washes it, and allows it to become thick and matted* so that it hangs down in numerous spiky strands.[158] (our emphasis)

His genteel disgust of the Rastas underscores his equally genteel view of reggae, which he considers to be 'no more than the distillation of visceral images of sex, violence and protest'.[159] The 'identity crisis' of the black petty bourgeoisie is not without its possibilities of resolution. As Amilcar Cabral once said, the best thing that they can do for black people is to commit 'class suicide'. Nevertheless we need to recognize that this is doubly difficult for those members of this class who have been schooled in the race-relations subdisciplines of white sociology, even if their own experience of the subtler forms of racism prompts them to attempt to give it a 'radical' edge.

We use the term 'white sociology' quite deliberately. This is not simply to register the fact that sociology generally and 'race/ethnic-relations' sociology too, are top-heavy with white personnel. Rather it is in recognition of the historical conditions and circumstances within which the various 'fields' of sociology have developed. We have merely hinted at this history in our attempt to locate the 'theories' about black people within the context of slavery, colonialism, indenture, racism and black peoples' resistance to and struggles against those forms of domination. In our view, if there is anything within 'race/ethnic-relations' sociology that is worth rescuing, then this is where such a rescue operation ought to begin. We have remarked elsewhere about the tendency of white sociologists to obscure the question of their relationship to the black people they study; a relationship which is structured by racism.[160] We do not want to repeat those arguments here but we do feel that it is necessary to emphasize the *patriarchal* nature of 'white sociology'. We have already seen how the pathologies of black family life are grounded in patriarchal notions about what the 'family' is or ought to be. We have mentioned too the common-sense images of femininity which inform accounts both of the 'passive' Asian woman and the 'masculinized' but always 'sexually available' Afro-Caribbean woman who, as Rex puts it,

Far from being oppressed by her menfolk . . . may taunt and even bully them. But it is the ultimate fact of maternity which *defines* her condition.[161] (our emphasis)

Where young Asian women have become visible it has only been because of the 'problems' they are thought to present. Young Afro-Caribbean women, on the other hand, rarely get noticed by sociologists apparently besotted with the males' conflicts with the police, the schools, their families etc. It is not enough merely to note such 'absences' as though such an omission has no consequences for one's theories;[162] neither is it enough to try to compensate for them by deflecting possible criticism back onto black people themselves with the argument that the 'cultures we have been discussing are themselves "sexist" '.[163] We do not deny that the patriarchal structures of these communities, and the patriarchal practices and attitudes of black men, actively oppress black women. We would argue, however, that patriarchy here does not always correspond simply to 'white' patriarchy, and that it is necessary to consider also the gender-specific characteristics of racism, which oppresses and exploits black women as *black* women.[164] Needless to say the least satisfactory response of all is to simply ignore these questions.

Lastly we would stress that we have presented this 'critique' of 'race-relations' sociology and 'ethnicity studies' not simply because we happen to disagree with their 'theories'. Their common-sense imagery is 'to be found at the base of a new popular politics tailored by crisis conditions'.[165] Where the sociologists are not merely repeating the common-sense rationalizations of the state, their arguments lend themselves to being incorporated into existing state ideologies. We have been accused of depicting these researches as 'mere instruments of the dominant institutional order',[166] but in fact we don't actually believe this. We are fully aware of the 'relative autonomy' of their profession, indeed as we have argued the 'problem' resides in part within the very structures and traditions of that profession. In a situation where *state racism* has intensified, it is disingenuous for policy-oriented researchers to expect that their racist and patriarchal conceptualizations of black people will not be of interest to the state institutions which oppress black people. In the next chapter we consider in detail just such a convergence between the sociologists' view and the views of the police; and in Chapter 5 we will see a similar dovetailing of explanations with those of the professional educationalists. It is clear too that these ideas are shared by local government, the health service, the youth service and the social services[167] and that they even go into the formulation of the CRE's recommendations. Whenever policies are being formulated to *deal* with black people and black youth, the 'race-relations' and 'ethnicity studies' sociologists are there in the background, where they are not actually there in person.

Notes and references

1 P. Gilroy, 'Managing the"underclass": a further note on the sociology of race relations in Britain', *Race and Class*, vol. XXII, no. 1 (IRR 1980), pp. 47–8. See also: A. Sivanandan, *From Immigration Control to 'Induced Repatriation'*, *Race and Class* Pamphlet no. 5.

2 The 'basic' texts we have used are: J. Rex and S. Tomlinson, *Colonial Immigrants in a British City: A Class Analysis* (Routledge and Kegan Paul 1979); V. Khan (ed.), *Minority Families in Britain: Support and Stress* (Macmillan Press Ltd 1979); K. Pryce, *Endless Pressure* (Penguin 1979); E. Cashmore, *Rastaman* (Allen and Unwin 1979); N. Foner, *Jamaica Farewell: Jamaican Migrants in London* (Routledge and Kegan Paul 1979).

3 *Nationwide*, BBC, 15 April 1981.

4 Brook-Shepherd is referring to Guyana's decision to expel Robin Jackman from the country, after his cricketing links with South Africa had been exposed. See: *West Indian World*, 6 March 1981, and of course the reaction of the national daily and Sunday newspapers, during the week 23 February to 1 March 1981.

5 R. West, 'Yearning for the grass of home (a Caribbean tour, part 1)', *Daily Telegraph*, 10 August 1981. West is a regular contributor to *The Spectator*. See, for example: his article 'Sex, race and Grunwick', 23 July 1977.

6 R. West, 'Jamaica versus the rest (a Caribbean tour, part 2)', *Daily Telegraph*, 11 August 1981.

7 'Ethnicity studies', in particular, promotes such specialization. They prefer the category 'ethnic minorities' on the grounds that it allows specific attention to be paid to particular groups of people. However, this category contains its own problems. It refers us too quickly to the realm of 'culture' and once there it becomes difficult to descend to more mundane levels. This is because 'ethnicity' is defined in cultural and/or religious terms and once we take 'ethnic identity' rather than gender, age, class, caste, etc., as our fundamental unit of analysis, we are in danger of sliding into a kind of 'cultural pluralism' which is incapable of recognizing that these 'determinations' act in concert rather than subsequently 'interacting' with each other. It says nothing about the relations of power which bind the various 'ethnic minorities' together and by means of which some groups are subordinated to others. This means in turn that the gains which are made by, quite rightly, recognizing the different 'cultures', are made at the expense of other equally crucial elements. We can make this point more clearly by thinking about who the 'ethnic minorities' are. In Britain, we have Sikhs, Jamaicans, Italians, Punjabis, Guyanese, Bangladeshis, Antiguans, Greek Cypriots, Turkish Cypriots, Hindus, Nigerians, Montserattians, Pakistanis, Trinidadians, Sri-Lankans, Ghanaians, Grenadians, Hungarians, Australians, and other who have migrated to these shores. But it would be purely arbitary to stop there. What about the Irish, Scottish, Welsh

Cornish and Manx peoples? What about the people of Wessex? Further, are the 'Scousers' an 'ethnic minority'? and the 'Geordies'? and the 'Cockneys'? What do all these people have in common apart from the fact that like all human beings they possess cultures? More significantly, on what grounds – apart from the odd study on Cypriots and Italians – have the 'ethnicity studies' researchers singled out only the darker-skinned 'ethnic minorities' as fitting objects of study?

8   Pryce, p. 3.
9   Rex and Tomlinson, p. 291.
10   Pryce, pp. 5–6.
11   ibid., p. 16.
12   ibid., p. 16.
13   Foner, p. 28.
14   ibid., p. 27. She is quoting: P. Mason, *Patterns of Dominance* (Oxford University Press 1970), p. 301.
15   ibid., p. 33.
16   ibid., p. 34.
17   L. Garrison, *Black Youth, Rastafarianism and the identity-crisis in Britain* (ACER 1980), pp. 10–11. When reading these comments about 'negative self-image' etc., we are tempted to speculate as to whether the practices among white women of curling their hair, and the practice amongst white people generally of going to such extraordinary lengths to get a 'suntan', should also be seen as evidence of a 'negative self-image' amongst the white population.
18   Foner, p. 34, quoting D. Lowenthal, *West Indian Societies* (Oxford University Press 1972), p. 99.
19   For an excellent review of the historical development of 'race-relations' sociology see: J. Bourne and A. Sivanandan, 'Cheerleaders and ombudsmen; the sociology of race relations in Britain', *Race and Class*, vol. XXI, no. 4.
20   D. P. Moynihan, *The Negro Family: The Case for National Action* (Office Planning and Research, US Department of Labour 1965).
21   S. M. Elkins, *Slavery. A Problem in American Institutional and Intellectual Life* (University of Chicago Press 1959).
22   E. D. Genovese, *In Red and Black: Marxian Explorations in Afro-American History* (Baton Rouge 1971), p. 73.
23   See: 'Three theories of personality' in Elkins, pp. 115–39.
24   ibid., pp. 86–9.
25   ibid., p. 89.
26   Genovese, p. 75.
27   ibid.
28   ibid., pp. 85–6.
29   ibid., p. 90.
30   Elkins, p. 136, quoted in: M. D. Caulfield, 'Slavery and the origins of black culture', in P. I. Rose (ed.), *Slavery and its Aftermath* (Atherton Press 1970).
31   K. Stampp, *The Peculiar Institution: Slavery in the Ante-Bellum South* (A. A. Knopf 1956), p. 125. This is not simply a case of honour among thieves. The slaves reasoned that since they and the food belonged to the master, their taking of this food could not be stealing. How could one piece of

the master's property steal another piece of his property?

32   Caulfield, pp. 180–2.

33   ibid.

34   Stampp, pp. 335–6; quoted in: Caulfield, p. 183.

35   A. Kardiner and L. Ovesey, *The Mark of Oppression: Explorations in the Personality of the American Negro* (Meridian Books 1951), p. 44. Kardiner and Ovesey follow more in the sociological tradition of Gunnar Myrdal than the anthropological/historical tradition of Elkins, although there is clearly some overlap. In terms of their theoretical framework, Rex and Tomlinson are also closer to Myrdal than Elkins, although once again they don't mind borrowing his ideas.

36   ibid., p. 184. See also: Social Science Institute, *Unwritten History of Slavery* (Fisk University Press 1945).

37   E. Franklin Frazier, *The Negro Church in America* (Schocken Books 1963), p. 16.

38   ibid.

39   LeRoi Jones, *Blues People: The Negro Experience in America and the Music that Developed from it* (Morrow 1963), p. 42. Jones is quoting Ernest Borneman 'another student of (black) music'.

40   ibid.

41   See, for example, the 'ethnographies' in T. Kochman (ed.), *Rappin' n' Stylin' Out: Communication in Urban Black America* (University of Illinois Press 1972), and E. A. Folb, *Runnin' down some lines: the Language and Culture of Black Teenagers* (Harvard University Press, London, 1980).

42   See: F. Kofsky, *Black Nationalism and The Revolution in Music* (Pathfinder Press 1970).

43   See, for example: R. Hart, *Black Jamaican's Struggle against Slavery* (Institute of Jamaica 1977); G. Beckford, 'Plantation society: toward a general theory of Caribbean society', in *Savacon*, no. 5 (June 1971). Also: E. Braithewaite, *The Development of Creole Society in Jamaica* (Clarendon Press 1971).

44   R. Price (ed.), Introduction to *Maroon Societies* (Anchor Books 1973), p. 2.

45   O. Patterson, 'Slavery and slave revolts: a sociohistorical analysis of the First Maroon War, 1665–1740', in Price.

46   Price, p. 10.

47   ibid., p. 11.

48   ibid., p. 12: but see: E. Genovese, 'The negro laborer in Africa and the slave South' – a reprint of pp. 78–84 of his *The Political Economy of Slavery* (Pantheon 1965) – in Rose, pp. 71–81.

49   See, for example: B. A. Botkin (ed.), *Lay my Burden Down: A Folk History of Slavery* (University of Chicago Press 1945).

50   Price, p. 6.

51   B. Kopytoff, 'The early political development of Jamaican maroon societies', in *William and Mary Quarterly*, no. XXXV (2 March 1979), p. 300.

52   Kopytoff's account is framed in terms of how the men arranged their 'system of rights in women'.

53   Price, p. 10.

54   P. Thicknesse, *Memoirs and Anecdotes of Philip Thicknesse: 1* (London 1788). Quoted in: Kopytoff, p. 300.

55   Carey Robinson, *The Fighting Maroons of Jamaica* (Collins and Sangster, Jamaica, 3rd impression, 1974). Robinson has taken a lot of trouble to track down information about Juan de Bolas, Cudjoe and Quao, but he is content to leave Nanny as a purely legendary figure.

> Latter-day Windward Maroons treasure the *legends* of Nanny and acclaim her as their greatest leader; but the only *real* leader of the Windward Maroons who is *mentioned with authority* during the period is Quao. (p. 54) (our emphasis)

See Chapter 6 for a discussion of the specifically female traditions that were 'carried over' from Africa.

56   Price, pp. 23–7, and C. L. R. James, *The Black Jacobins: Toussaint L'Ouverture and the Haitian Revolution* (Allison and Busby 1980).

57   Price, p. 27.

58   M. Deren, *The Voodoo Gods* (Paladin 1975).

59   C. J. Robinson, 'Coming to terms: the third World and the dialectic of imperialism', *Race and Class*, vol. XXII , no. 4. We also develop this theme in Chapter 8.

60   See: R. Hill's introduction to *The Complete Rastafarian Bible* (Walter Rodney Books 1982).

61   M. Dalphinis, 'Approaches to the study of Creole languages – the case for West African language influences', *The Black Liberator* (December 1978); also: D. Dalby, 'Ashanti survivals in the language and traditions of the Windward maroons of Jamaica', *African Language Studies*, XII (SOAS 1971).

62   Price points to the swift development of these languages, which took place despite the 'linguistic diversity' and in opposition to the acquisition of 'standard English'.

63   See Chapters 6, 7, and 8.

64   V. Khan, 'Migration and social stress: Mirpuris in Bradford', in Khan, *Support and Stress*, pp. 40–1.

65   ibid., pp. 39–42.

66   ibid.

67   ibid.

68   W. Rodney, *How Europe Underdeveloped Africa* (Bogle L'Ouverture 1972), p. 133.

69   ibid.

70   I. Ahmed, 'Pakistan: class and state formation', *Race and Class*, vol XXII, no. 3 (1981), p. 243.

71   Khan, Introduction to *Support and Stress*, p. 8.

72   Khan, 'Migration and social stress', p. 44.

73   ibid., p. 5.

74   D. Brooks and K. Singh, 'Pivots and presents', in S. Wallman (ed.), *Ethnicity at Work* (Macmillan 1979). Wallman makes a similar argument in her introduction to this volume. See: Bourne, pp. 343–4.

75   Rex and Tomlinson, p. 80, where they argue that

> For many immigrants, manufacturing employment is a new experience and they have, on the whole, gone into jobs requiring the lowest grades of skill.

See also p. 291, where they suggest that Afro-Caribbeans are 'better equipped to obtain employment as individuals than Asians' because they speak English. This is one benefit apparently of 'acculturation'!

76 S. Hall, C. Critcher, T. Jefferson, J. Clarke and B. Roberts, *Policing The Crisis; Mugging, the State, and Law and Order* (Macmillan 1978), p. 346.
77 Khan argues this in: 'The Pakistanis: Mirpuri villagers at home and in Bradford', in J. Watson (ed.), *Between Two Cultures* (Blackwell 1977); quoted in: Bourne, p. 343.
78 See: L. Carper, 'The negro family and the Moynihan Report', in Rose.
79 Moynihan.
80 M. Wallace, *Black Macho and the Myth of the Superwoman* (Platform Books 1979), p. 109–16.
81 See: L. Kushnick, 'Parameters of British and North American racism', *Race and Class Special Issue*, vol. XXIII, nos 2-3 (1980-1).
82 Khan, 'Migration and social stress', p. 44.
83 Pryce, p. 16.
84 ibid., pp. 108–9.
85 Cashmore, p. 139.
86 Khan, 'Migration and social stress', pp. 42–6.
87 ibid., p. 52.
88 Brent Community Health Council, *Black People and the Health Service* (BCHC London, April 1981), p. 16.
89 Pryce, p. 112.
90 ibid., p. 120
91 Khan, 'Migration and social stress', p. 46.
92 See, for example: R. Moore and T. Wallace, *Slamming the Door* (Martin Robertson 1975); and A. Sivanandan.
93 Khan, 'Migration and social stress', pp. 49–51.
94 Wallace, p. 140.
95 See, for example: O. S. Egypt, J. Masouka and S. Johnson, 'Unwritten history of slavery: autobiographical accounts of ex-slaves', in S. Lerner (ed.), *Black Women in White America* (Pantheon 1972); E. Genovese, *Roll Jordan Roll: The World the Slaves Made* (Pantheon 1974); H. Gutman, *The Black Family in Slavery and Freedom* (Random House 1977); also E. P. Martin and J. M. Martin, *The Black Extended Family* (University of Chicago Press, Chicago and London, 1978).
96 Cashmore, p. 78.
97 G. Rubin, 'The traffic in women: notes on the "political economy" of sex', in R. Reiter (ed.), *Towards an Anthropology of Women* (Monthly Review Press 1975), pp. 165–9.
98 See Chapters 6 and 7
99 G. Omvedt, *We Will Smash This Prison: Indian Women in Struggle* (Zed Press 1980), p. 2.
100 Khan, 'Purdah in the British situation', in D. L. Barker and S. Allen (eds.), *Dependence and Exploitation in Work and Marriage* (Longman 1976).
101 These ideas are propounded most clearly in: Commission for Racial Equality, *Youth in a Multi-Racial Society: The Urgent Need for New Policies: 'The Fire Next Time'* (CRE 1979).
102 Community Relations Commission, *Between Two Cultures: A Study of*

Relationships between Generations in the Asian Community in Britain (CRC 1970).

103   J. Rex, 'West Indian and Asian youth in Britain – some research perspectives', in E. Cashmore and B. Troyna (eds.), *Black Kids* (Allen and Unwin 1982).
104   ibid.
105   ibid.
106   Rex employs a stratification model of society which 'relegates classes to the *distributive* sphere'. See Gilroy. On this point as well see: S. Hall, 'Race, articulation and societies structured in dominance', in *Sociological Theories: Race and Colonialism* (UNESCO 1980); and A. Green, *The Political Economy of Black Labour*, CCCS stencil paper no. 62, 1980. On Rex's 'methodological individualist' problematic see: R. Wilson, unpublished paper for Race and Politics Group, CCCS, 1979. Also, for an overview of the 'sociology of knowledge', see: S. Hall, 'The hinterland of science: ideology and the "Sociology of Knowledge"', in *On Ideology* (Hutchinson 1978).
107   Rex.
108   ibid.
109   J. Brown, *Shades of Grey: Police/West Indian Relations in Handsworth* (Cranfield Police Studies 1977), p. 8.
110   For example, Cashmore records the renewed suspicions about his work after the publication of *Shades of Grey*.
111   V. Amos, P. Gilroy and E. Lawrence, *White Sociology: Black Struggle*, paper presented to the BSA Conference on 'Inequality', April 1981, p. 26.
112   Garrison.
113   Cashmore, pp. 39–42.
114   ibid., p. 85.
115   ibid., see Chapter 5.
116   Garrison, p. 11.
117   Rex and Tomlinson, p. 237.
118   ibid., p. 228.
119   C. Ballard, 'Conflict, continuity and change: second-generation South Asians', in Khan, *Support and Stress*, p. 109.
120   The media, she says, 'sensationalise only the casualties among them; those who run away from home, who have attempted suicide etc.', ibid., p. 109. But see p. 119 where, after talking about one father who had been 'verbally abusing his family' and resorting to 'sporadic outbreaks of great violence', she remarks that 'such cases are *rare*'.
121   ibid., p. 121.
122   Bourne and Sivanandan, p. 345.
123   P. Weinreich, 'Ethnicity and adolescent identity conflicts', in Khan, *Support and Stress*, pp. 90–3.
124   ibid., p. 89.
125   ibid., p. 89.
126   ibid., pp. 93–4. Weinreich tells us that,

Their constructs were elicited during semi-structured probing interviews which ranged across various areas of life experience. . . . Notes were made of all significant others mentioned.

But it is by no means clear, just *who* thinks the 'others' are significant.

Certainly it appears as though the constructs are made up of 'others' who Weinreich feels are (or should be) significant.

127 ibid., pp. 98–9.
128 ibid., p. 104.
129 ibid., p. 101.
130 ibid., p. 105.
131 Rex.
132 Cashmore, p. 198.
133 Rex.
134 Garrison, p. 13.
135 Pryce, p. 133.
136 Cashmore, p. 56.
137 C. Lago and B. Troyna, 'Black and bitter', *Youth in Society*, no. 29 (June 1978), p. 17. According to the blurb on the cover, *Youth in Society* is 'The bi-monthly inter-professional journal for everyone concerned with young people and youth affairs'.
138 ibid., p. 17; and see: Pryce, p. 148.
139 Lago and Troyna.
140 See particularly: B. Troyna, 'Differential commitment to ethnic identity by black youths in Britain', *New Community*, vol. 7, no. 3 (Winter 1979).
141 B. Troyna, 'Angry youngsters: a response to racism in Britain', *Youth in Society*, no. 26 (December 1977), p. 15.
142 ibid., p. 15.
143 Garrison.
144 Cashmore, p. 143.
145 ibid. See his opening two chapters.
146 ibid.
147 ibid., p. 57.
148 Gilroy, p. 53.
149 ibid.
150 Rex.
151 ibid. See also: *Home Office Research Bulletin*, no. 8 (1979), in which The Home Office Research Unit director explains that:

While the Home Office is interested in policy-oriented research, it is of course far from being the principal executant or initiator of such research. The largest single body of recent published academic research on ethnic relations which bears on issues of social policy is that undertaken by the SSRC ethnic relations unit, the directorship of which has just passed from Professor Michael Banton at Bristol to Professor John Rex.

A few pages on Rex added that the Unit's work 'will also form an essential and complementary background to the work carried on for immediate policy and political purposes by the Home Office'. Quoted in: Gilroy, 'Managing the "Underclass"', pp. 58–61. It is also worth noting that some of the ethnicity studies' researchers were members of the Unit when Professor Banton held the directorship.

152 CRE, *The Fire Next Time*, pp. 14–18.
153 Rex.
154 Eleven of the youths were arrested in raids on Bradford's black community on 30–31 July. A twelfth was arrested some time later. The charges were

conspiracy, 'to damage or destroy by fire or explosion, property belonging to others' and conspiracy to 'cause grievous bodily harm'. No petrol bombs or other explosives were found. All of the youths pleaded not guilty. At time of writing ten have been released on bail.

155   See, for example: V. Edwards, *The West Indian Language Issue in British Schools* (Routledge and Kegan Paul 1979).

156   See: A. Sivanandan, 'From resistance to rebellion: Asian and Afro-Caribbean struggles in Britain', *Race and Class*, special issue, for an excellent and concise history of these struggles.

157   Foner, p. 70; also: F. Fanon, *Black Skin White Mask* (Paladin 1970).

158   Pryce, p. 147.

159   ibid., p. 151.

160   Amos *et al.*, partly reproduced in *Multiracial Education*, vol. 9, no. 3 (1981), pp. 7–10.

161   Rex.

162   As Lago and Troyna do in *Black and Bitter*, p. 19.

163   As Rex does in 'Some research perspectives'.

164   See Chapters 6 and 7.

165   Amos *et al.*, p. 20.

166   E. Cashmore and B. Troyna, 'Just for the white boys? Elitism, racism and research', *Multiracial Education*, vol. 9, no. 4 (1981).

167   See, for example, critical articles by: M. Cross and G. John in 'Black kids, white kids, what hope?', papers presented at two symposia organized by the Regional Training Consultative Unit at Brunel University (M. Day and D. Marsland, eds.), National Youth Bureau (December 1978); A. Jansari, 'Social work with ethnic minorities: a review of literature', *Multi Racial Social Work*, no. 1 (1980).

4 Police and thieves

Paul Gilroy

The greatest problem I will have in my commissionership, and that my successor and probably his successor will have, is getting on with the ethnic minorities in this great city.

SIR DAVID MCNEE, Radio 4, 2 July 1981

Fire fe de Babylon law
Away wid de Babylon law . . .
Babylon law is a flaw
It deal with partiality, and thats no mentality.

DILLINGER

The uprisings of July 1981 and subsequent discussion of police tactics and orientation have focused critical attention on the relationship between police and the communities in which they are standard bearers for the law. Police malpractice has fuelled intense debates, particularly in Liverpool and Manchester, over the status of police committees and their powers under Section 4 of the 1964 Police Act. These developments have shifted the issue of police/black relations nearer to the centre of the stage on which the drama of civil liberties unfolds. Conflict between black people and the police, however, predates these recent eruptions, and it is regrettable that civil liberties campaigning betrays real ignorance of the history of this difficult relationship. Few of those who recoiled in horror as petrol bombs flew in Brixton can have been familiar with the saga of local 'community relations' in which these 'riots' were only the latest episode. Joseph Hunte's 1965 report to the West Indian Standing Conference, published as 'Nigger hunting in England', opens a vast catalogue of police malpractice in their dealings with black people which is concluded by Lambeth Council's own report.[1] Allegations of police racism are consistent throughout the sixteen years which separate these publications.

Limited insight into the place of racism in the *professional* ideology of police officers has also been provided by the press. Supt Dick Holland of the West Yorkshire CID, for example, having cited young West Indian 'muggers' as his illustration, recently told a Police Federation seminar in Oxford, 'Police must be prejudiced if they are to do their job properly'.[2] An unnamed inspector stationed at Brixton explained to the *Daily Mail*[3] that the operational vocabulary of his men had been extended during the riots from the words 'Coon, Sooty or Spade, which

"If I'd not been told this wasn't a race riot but only their way of getting rid of frustration, I would be really worried."

Source: *Police*, May 1981
Reproduced by permission of *Police*

like other four-lettered words in industrial language [*sic*] are something blokes
working together will say without meaning a thing' to include habitual use of
'words like Nigger'. Yet these examples of a racism which Maureen Cain has argued
is a key component of the policeman's occupational culture[4] are not our object
here. Just as Sir Robert Mark's admission, that police present racist attitudes and
preconceptions in proportion to those found in the rest of society, is only a small
part of any overall explanation of police racism, of greater interest is the more
systematic and 'theoretical' racism imparted in police training and disclosed by
official pronouncements and analyses. In a 'law and order society', ideologies of
illegality have a special pertinence, particularly when the legitimacy of police practice becomes more difficult to secure. Ideas of black criminality appear in the
struggle for legitimation, intersect with racist common sense and, in that process,
provide a wealth of justifications for illegitimate, discriminatory and of course
illegal police practices at the grass roots level. Official police thought on race and
black crime transforms both the 'common sense' and the sociology we looked at in
the preceding chapters. It moulds these around a framework of police concerns
dictated by the exigencies of 'policing the blacks', which has become a paradigm
for maintaining the 'rule of law' in crisis conditions. The struggles it conceals under
the bulk of legal ideology are experienced from the other side as battles for black
civil rights and liberties. They cannot be explained away by the cavalcade of lawless
images - of stowaways, drifters, pimps, and drug dealers - whose procession extends
into the present in the forms of muggers, illegal immigrants, black extremists and
criminal Rastafarians (dreads). The black folk-devil has acquired greater power
with each subsequent permutation.

Police theorizations of 'alien blackness' as black criminality show where the
filaments of racist ideology disappear into the material institutions of the capitalist
state. This chapter presents a fragment of their recent history which is generally
relevant for the precision with which it exemplifies the transformation of those
institutions in the direction of authoritarianism. This is visible in the changing
forms, methods and aims of policing under crisis conditions. The related extension
of social control functions into the agencies and institutions of the welfare state
provides a second illustration of the same process which is nowhere more obvious
than in the manipulation of categories and rights of citizenship[5] which has affected
black exclusion as a step towards repatriation. Both examples are details from a
larger mozaic of state racism[6] which, as part of the struggle for ethico-political
hegemony, provides the *popular* underpinning of an otherwise unattractive
authoritarianism.

We want to look at the problems 'race' raises for the left's understanding of the
relation of politics to 'crime'. We will trace something of the history of police
thinking about black crime and, finally, assess 'community policing', which is an
increasing popular strategy for containing the effects of crisis - not without
support on the left. Our aims are to demonstrate the differential intensity at which
blacks engage the law and its officers, and second, to establish the centrality of
'race' to struggles for civil liberties.

In focusing on the problems blacks face at the hands of the police, we confront the role of law in marking out the shrinking arena of legitimate politics. This is important not only because black struggles have frequently been deprived of the appearance of legitimacy, particularly when they have reached beyond the factory gates into the streets; studying this process provides insights into the British state at a particular stage in its development. In decline more than ever,

Physical violence and consent do not exist side by side like two calculable homogeneous magnitudes, related in such a way that more consent corresponds to less violence. Violence-terror always occupies a determining place – and not merely because it remains in reserve, coming into the open only in critical situations. State monopolised physical violence permanently underlies the techniques of power and the mechanisms of consent: it is inscribed in the web of disciplinary and ideological devices; and even when not directly exercised, it shapes the materiality of the social body on which it is brought to bear.[7]

If, as Sivanandan has suggested, the politics of the reproduction of black labour can, like a barium meal, reveal the whole organism of the state, our intention here is to explore the components of the body politic illuminated by Sir David McNee's remarkable admission:

Policing a multi-racial society is putting the fabric of our policing philosophy under greater stress than at any time since the years immediately after the Metropolitan Police was established in 1829. (*Guardian*, 25 September 1979)

His statement identifies the black communities as a problem for the police and, through the historical reference, for the whole nation. This association of blacks and criminality has attained popular status during the post-war period. We must place the view of these communities, in terms of the alien, criminal threat they embody, in its historical context, and examine the police's own role in its dissem - ination and reproduction. They have elevated it to sociological credibility, even analytic status, and mobilized it not only in the struggle to police the blacks themselves, but also as part of securing the consent of white citizens to police practices which they might otherwise find unacceptable. We challenge the categorization of crimes according to the skin colour of their perpetrators, but we must go deeper still and face the question of whether black crimes and criminality are distinct and separable in any other sense. This will not be resolved by empiricist haggling over official crime statistics even if they are the product of class struggle.[8] Neither are popular images of black crime discredited, exposed or stripped of their cultural force merely by being revealed to occur in a political and ideological struggle for state authority and legitimacy. What is at issue here[9] is not therefore whether there are 'illegal immigrants', 'muggers' or 'criminally inclined Rastafarians' in 'tea-cosy hats', but the universality with which the authorities apply these terms to all black people, while ignoring the level of 'criminal' violence against blacks themselves.

These images, and the conceptualizations of black cultures which power them, have been established at the heart of police practice. Their effects are felt by whole communities rather than a minority of aberrant individuals who fall directly foul of the law. The well-known instance of the 'sus' law[10] was but a single example of a generalized process in which any Afro-Caribbean youth is assumed to be criminally inclined and anyone of Asian appearance is adjudged an 'illegal immigrant' until they can produce acceptable documentation to the contrary. These racialized portraits of criminality derive a new power from the way the law has reconstituted the politico-social field in crisis conditions. We have already argued that popular racism has a privileged political place amidst novel circumstances for class struggle: economic decline, structural unemployment, microprocessor technology,[11] and the mass impact of feminist ideas.

The left, critical criminology and black crimes

What Poulantzas has identified as 'the redeployment of the police/legal network' has provided a severe test for radical and neo-Marxist approaches to law, police and 'crime'. The additional perspective afforded by considering 'race' confirms that these approaches continue to be dogged by the inability to maintain what is *specific* to the study of these objects, which are either collapsed into general analysis of the capitalist state[12] or confounded by the ideological mode of the category of 'crime'. Political and ideological struggles over the meaning of 'crime', and its discursive appropriation, remain to disrupt the discussion.

E. P. Thompson's valuable surveys of law as an aspect of developing 'statism'[13] provide an example of this problem particularly where they disregard his own earlier warnings against simply taking over 'the definitions of those who own property, control the state, and pass laws which "name" what shall be crimes'.[14] His work also typifies the left's widespread inability to make the experience of black Britons relevant in its own right. Blacks are not acknowledged to be part of the English working class, either historically or contemporarily where their sufferings become a moral issue under the general heading of 'Race Relations'. It is therefore consistent that Thompson's solution to the problem of encroaching statism, in an appeal to English constitutionalism, wilfully excludes any consideration of the race/crime nexus which might disrupt this all too simplistic response:

where a suggestion is made that a jury which acquitted a man who appears to have been guilty of flagrant racial incitement must itself have been racialist . . . my own speculation would lead to a different conclusion. British juries have, for hundreds of years, shown a recurrent dislike of finding against accused for their opinions. It is consonant with that tradition to suppose that a jury, some of whose members genuinely abhored racialism, would nevertheless acquit an accused, simply because it disliked punishing opinions even more than it disliked the opinions in question . . . it is too easy to categorise this very complex reaction as 'racialist'.[15]

Thompson appears ignorant of the extent to which the ideology of the 'freeborn Englishman' was itself a product of struggle to differentiate slave from slave-holder.[16] It should not be necessary to emphasize that this same constitutional tradition has yet to demonstrate its inclusion of Britain's black subjects. Even when 'Englishness' was cultural and political rather than 'racial', 'lesser breeds without the law' were the counterpart to Thompson's Briton.[17] The century of legal argument over the chattel status of blacks[18] which preceded Lord Mansfield's celebrated decision in the Somerset case[19] forces the conclusion that the law of habeas corpus for example, afforded greater protection against the ravages of racism in 1772 than it does today. In over 1000 actions up to the case of Zamir in July 1980, only five applications related to the 1971 Immigration Act have been successful.[20] The common law which was a battleground for black rights as early[21] as 1670 remains powerless to defend the interests of black people today. Indeed, modern immigration laws are remarkable for the extent of their fortification against their 'constitutional rights'. Though 'illegal entry' is a criminal act under the 1971 legislation, and the police are intimately involved in locating and processing 'offenders' and 'suspects', incarceration pending removal or appeal is classified as 'administrative' rather than criminal procedure. This means that bail arrangements do not apply, and the discretionary power to release prisoners is not exercised. This classification and procedure has the additional effect of placing the burden of proof on the accused rather than the accusers. Restriction of rights of appeal,[22] retroactive operation of the 1971 Act[23] and increasingly narrow definitions of 'illegal entry' 'settlement' and 'ordinary residence' are further examples of 'constitutional' violation. Despite his concern with their activities in other spheres, the role of special branches in these procedures has evaded Thompson. Of the 382 commonwealth citizens arrested as 'illegal entrants' in 1979[24] a total of 144 are accounted for by the activities of the five special branches to which reference was made in their chief constables' reports: [25]

Cleveland	2	illegals arrested
Manchester	92	illegals arrested
Lancashire	38	illegals arrested
Strathclyde	15	illegals arrested
Avon and Somerset	7	illegals arrested

As there are 52 forces in the UK it would not be unreasonable to assume that the activities of the other 47 forces could account for the balance of 238 blacks.

It will be interesting to see whether Thompson's affection for the plight of the 'freeborn Englishman' will be stimulated by the renewed assault, represented by the latest nationality legislation, on the rights and liberties of the black population. So far he has been silent as to whether the 'Englishman' in question is of patrial or non-patrial status; although the nationalist character of his rhetoric invites unlibertarian conclusions:

The freeborn Briton has been bred out of the strain and the stillborn Britsperson has been bred in. . . . An operation has been done on our culture and the guts have been taken out.[26]

There can be little doubt that blacks (even patrials) are familiar with the legacy of British 'bloody mindedness' in which he takes great pride. From where they stand it is easier to see that its present-day cornerstones are racism and nationalism; its foundations slavery and imperialism. It is yet more troubling that Mr Thompson's genuine concern over the murder of Blair Peach did not require him to take note of the histories of racial conflict, and black political struggle which contributed to the context in which such a death became acceptable.[27] Whilst on this point, we wonder whether he views the arrest of some 342 people in Southall on 23 April 1979, as another unfortunate instance of 'the actual increment' in criminal offences which he has asserted, presumably having taken crime statistics at their face value?[28] Those who are unwilling or unable to note that the political character of the law is visible elsewhere than in conspiracy trials and official secrets cases, construct a racially exclusive conception of civil rights to all our cost.

Like many on the left, Thompson not only fails to challenge the contemporary conception of 'crime', but also endorses the dominant view of a relation between race and crime. He cites the example of an increase in sexual assault with the implication that this has been precipitated by black settlement in 'parts of our cities where women are afraid to walk alone'.[29] It is odd that this example appears in the context of comments on racism, law, crisis and the gap between popular perception and a supposedly 'objective record of suffering, loss and fear'[30] which Thompson appeals to the police to rectify. Perhaps it is because he is unable to concede the achievement of feminist struggle in placing the problem of male violence higher on his own agenda, that he asserts rather than demonstrates the historical novelty of this state of affairs.

It is ironic that the well-documented sufferings, losses and fears of black men and women at the hands of the police have been unable to enter Thompson's concerns.[31] I hope to show that the growth of crime that he invokes is a far more evasive phenomenon than he allows. We must recognize the wisdom of his instruction that

we should be on our guard against accepting moralistic categories which offer a facile apologia for criminality.[32]

Yet we must also be alert to those moralistic categories which offer a facile apologia for the processes of criminalization which have been directed at black people as part of an inducement to leave these shores. This chapter should illuminate the extent to which for blacks, the police are part of the problem rather than its solution. In this regard we would draw Mr Thompson's attention to the views of a policeman at the scene of the Brixton riots who confided in a passing reporter that:

We (the police) are here to give our coloured brethren all the help we can – all they need to go somewhere else.[33]

The hardy seeds of this latter moralism have settled far beyond the patrician lawns of Wick Episcopi. Their peculiar blooms currently appear wherever 'left' criminologists address the vexed issue of 'street crime'. Jock Young,[34] rather than account for the ideological power of 'mugging' or confront its racial connotations with precision or honesty, argues that it is 'qualitatively different' from other forms of 'crime' because:

street crime is the only form of serious crime in which the victim is in the same social category [*sic*] as the offender.[35]

We are forced to enquire where domestic violence and murder fit into Young's schema as well as to query the meaning of the word 'serious' in his formulation. We are unable to accept his assertion that 'all sections of the population . . . are united in their opposition to street crime'. The very popularity of images of black criminality, particularly around the 'street crime' theme, demands historical accounts of where, how and why this has come about. Although explicitly opposed to the views of Young and his colleagues, Paul Hirst's influential opinions on 'Criminality' present similar problems.

Hirst conjures away the relation between criminalization and repression and argues that:

Criminality is an individualised response by backward and pauperised sections of the working class, not a political response by its vanguard.[36]

We reject the notion of a 'vanguard' which balances this equation. The simple counterposition of 'criminality' against real politics is not only essentialist but unhelpful. 'Criminality' is once again taken at face value as meaningful from an analytic rather than common-sense point of view. Hirst does not present his analysis of the Tolpuddle martyrs, the Shrewsbury three or the Bradford twelve, nor of the criminal offences of blasphemy and conspiracy. He obscures the fact that under certain conditions the struggle to define crimes and criminals not only acquires a political character, but becomes central to the process of class formation. This occurs most often where 'criminality' is at its least individualized; indeed, 'individualization' can be an *effect* of the legal process, as for example when 'ringleaders' are 'snatched' from a 'rioting' crowd and made responsible for its actions. Hirst's retreat from analysis of criminal law is therefore partly explained by the fact that a *political* requirement that certain actions are designated purely and simply criminal, can represent a response by the state to collective political action which it does not wish to legitimate.[37]

Hall *et al.*'s view[38] of the progression from proto-political to 'organized' forms of class struggle is a considerable advance on Hirst and bypasses the moralism of

Young and Thompson. Yet they too encounter problems around the conception of 'criminality' which is not subjected to the rigorous interrogation they accord its specific representation as 'mugging'. They obscure the complex relation between behaviour designated criminal and political consciousness, by conceding the reality of 'false appropriations of oppression through crime'.[39] This opens the door to conceptions of black culture and political traditions generating criminality. Their idea of criminal acts negotiating oppression is dangerous[40] because it ignores the fact that ideologies which rationalize or politicize 'criminal' acts do not necessarily cause them. Politically conscious people may reluctantly engage in acts by which they know they risk breaking the law, the most persistent street criminals may be aware that their actions are not the basis of strategies for socialist transformation and so on.

Policing the Crisis does, however, have the considerable virtue of initiating discussion of the forms of political activity and organization which are adequate to the task of contextualizing criminal income opportunities and identifying their political limits. All these accounts share a problem in the confusion between 'criminality' as a descriptive behavioural term and as a gauge of the end products of the political processes which constitute criminals. The former presents real difficulties for the social analyst regardless of political affiliations, when asked to explain for example how standing on a street corner becomes the criminal act of 'attempt to steal'.

The followers of E. P. Thompson may be disturbed to find out that his model of policing, which assumes its capacity for 'rational deterrence',[41] and in which the 'increase in crime' is accepted as a simple empirical fact, is being progressively abandoned by the police services in favour of a new political model in which

People who *feel* well policed are well policed.[42]

This perspective accommodates what Thompson dismisses as a 'marvellously abstract notion',[43] namely that the increase in crime may indeed have a 'fictional character'. Certainly police are increasingly aware that their own practices may generate and transform 'crimes' through the ways they are 'discovered', recorded and defined. Evelyn Schaffer whose 'understanding and no-nonsense approach to the problems and pressures of modern policing continually impress' Sir David McNee, who wrote the preface to her book *Community Policing*,[44] is refreshingly candid on this point:

The important influence of the divisional commander is borne out by a study of juvenile offending in a Scottish City division over a ten year period. The pattern of offences showed regular changes – with a differing peak offence tending to go in cycles. It was possible to date almost exactly the changes in divisional command by these 'crime waves'. . . . One commander was very tough on group disorder, another on football in the street, another on weapon carrying and so on. Whatever offence was regarded as one to be dealt with became the immediate concern of all patrols in the area.[45]

Schaffer's research relates exclusively to Scotland, and therefore she is spared the implications of the likely effect on criminal statistics of a divisional commander preoccupied with the problem of rooting out 'muggings'. Her revelations are sufficient to raise some specific doubts about the nature and extent of 'street crimes' in the Handsworth area, particularly when coupled with the statistical profile of the Handsworth subdivision which even John Brown's *Shades of Grey* (see below p. 160) admits 'is unremarkable amongst the 12 divisions of the force'.[46] We will return to this question in the discussion of police effectiveness which follows. It is important to understand how the variable visibility of crime she outlines, supports a view of law, policing and criminalization as elements in a political and ideological struggle, in which the question of 'immigrant crime' has a twofold effect. First, it acts as a popular signifier for the threat of social instability and change to which 'law and order' is the only antidote. Second, it rationalizes new forms of control over the black communities at a time when their political traditions and the additional burdens of racial oppression mean that they are the first fractions of the working class to give spontaneous opposition to the pressures of the crisis. We focus on criminalization as an instance of this struggle, but it must not be viewed as its entirety.

Police failure to acknowledge that violence against blacks is racially motivated, let alone accord it the 'criminal' character one might anticipate, is a second significant element in black encounters with the law:

If a stone thrown at no. 324 breaks the window, it may be a racial incident because people there are Asians. If it goes next door, then that's not a racial incident because the occupier may be white. . . . whether or not its a racial matter is often *purely conjecture.*[47]

This view is apparently representative of opinion in the force. It is important because it prepares the way for blaming blacks themselves for the violence they suffer: *their difference* generates 'natural' hostility, *their cultures* create myriad possibilities for misunderstanding. The radio programme from which the above quote was taken went on to explain that 'immigrants'' accusations of police indifference were a result of their inability to speak English.

Processes of definition and selection are intrinsic to police methods. They elucidate the particular efficacy of the law – creating and recreating consent whilst simultaneously organizing repression. Their intensity is an index of the climate in which repatriation is no longer merely facilitated, but increasingly seen to be practised.[48] With this in mind we will not be drawn to debate the extent and character of 'ethnic' crime.[49] We have chosen instead to examine policing practice and the laws and criminalization process which attend it. The basis of this choice and the view of certain criminal acts as political struggle which it implies has been presented by Colin Sumner:

Law lies in the cradle of political practice and is therefore subject to the pressures and imperatives of politics. . . . as an instance in the social formation, law is a politico-ideological phenomenon produced in a form of political practice [struggle]. That practice is geared to the creation, definition and maintenance of power relations. As such it is only one weapon within a whole armoury.[50]

Police views of black criminality

In the summer of 1967 a Home Office circular to chief constables on the race issue explained that:

There is little doubt that the most likely cause of friction between police and the immigrant community is the lack of knowledge and the misunderstanding of each other.[51]

This was the era in which officialdom understood blacks seriously if paternalistically in terms of 'the problems of the coloured school leaver', outside the syntax of 'mugging', and without reference to racial conflict in American cities. The gulf which separates these sentiments from the discourse of crime, conflict and stress to which Sir David McNee gave expression twelve years later, marks Britain's apprehension and acceptance of organic crisis. The painful awareness of this chronic ailment brought images of the alien threat posed by blacks into the forefront of a bitter struggle to secure and rebuild popular consent:

In many cases migrants bring with them anti-British attitudes. They are encouraged to take all benefits for granted and blame all shortcomings on discrimination. They are also encouraged to see immigration restrictions as something to be circumvented. Marriage is one simple way. Virtually all Asians belong to an extended family system with a much larger branch in the Indian sub-continent.[52]

As the state has faced the crisis and the discourse of 'the nation' has been introduced as an answer to the blacks' refusal of racial oppression, this threat has been presented politically in criminal terms. Not only are hordes of unseen illegal immigrants about to swamp true Britons, but *all* immigrants have been tainted by illegality.

Margaret Thatcher's 1979 election campaign synthesized these political and criminal themes and served up the result in an implicitly racist appeal:

In their muddled but different ways the vandals on the picket lines and the muggers in our streets have got the same confused message 'we want our demands met or else', 'get out of the way give us your handbag or else'.[53]

The common-sense images of black criminality from both communities have been related to the supposed national cultures of the 'immigrant groups' involved. Here again we discover precisely the same pathological conceptions of black life we examined in the preceding chapters. We must return to these ideas and images, this time in their role as motor for the authoritarian response to the black problem they define. They have been established as the *operational* analysis for the state's institutions of social control and occupy a key place in the struggle to legitimate new police tactics and methods for containment of social disorder. Poulantzas has pointed to the deficiencies of analysis in which

the role of violence in the grounding of power is still underestimated, and all that is ever mentioned are the reasons for consent.[54]

We have attempted to rectify this by looking closely at the controlled and targeted violence which has been a feature of the black communities' conflict with the law.

The authors of *Policing the Crisis* point to 'the new tempo and character of the black response to casual police harassment'[55] after 1973, and to the problems posed for a straightforward social control response by internal contradictions in environmentalist theories of crime. Both observations are important signs of the movement towards 'the synchronisation of race and class aspects of the crisis'.[56] They require grounding in a more detailed presentation of the relation of policing theory both to the dynamics of black resistance, and the political facts of long-term crisis.

Environmentalist approaches to black crime were built on the bedrock of John Lambert's 1970 *Crime, Police and Race Relations*[57] which significantly contained no distinctive conceptualization of black crimes and criminality. Though Lambert gestures at a pathological conception of immigrant cultures[58] this precedes rather than produces their conflict with the police. Gus John's influential *Race and the Inner City* provides the earliest suggestion that conflict between police and blacks may be explained by reference to police practices and behaviour. It is worth noting that at least five years before the popularization of Rastafari, and long before 'dreads' entered official discourse, Thornhill Road police station in Handsworth was being referred to as 'Babylon house'.[59] Both John and Lambert describe conflict on a qualitatively different scale from its post-1973 level.

Conflict in Notting Hill and Handsworth during the summer of 1970 was the ominous background to Supt G. J. Dear's *Coloured Immigrant Communities and the Police*[60] which presented the first substantive account of black settlement from a policing point of view. 'Street crime' is not discussed by Dear, and even when he cautiously associates West Indians with prostitution and Asians with fraud and drug smuggling, he is quick to warn that 'it is too easy . . . to create a dangerous and false stereotype of a criminally prone class'. He is adamant that 'crime among coloured communities tends to be low'. The pathology of alien cultures, which he discovers not surprisingly in their family life, is not related to the crimes which aliens commit once they arrive in the 'mother country' but refers solely to the expectations and preconceptions about the police which they have imported:

So it is that the West Indian immigrant may well expect police brutality and harassment together with fabrication of evidence since these are frequent occurrences in his own country. . . . Similarly the Asian immigrant well used to graft and corruption on a very wide scale amongst police and public officials in India or Pakistan, will frequently display a tendency not to speak the truth when questioned by the Police.

He argues that the social problems facing immigrants congeal around housing rather than any alien impulse to crime:

whatever the country of origin of the immigrant, his primary and continuing problem will be that of housing, and this particular problem does not concern the police directly.

Given the attitudes of those who have followed in his wake, Dear is remarkably well disposed towards the West Indian:

If the general image of the Asian is one of a peaceable yet negative character, that of the West Indian must essentially be of a positive individual.

His piece is more significant for its predictions of the crisis and its status as a founding text of police professional interest in academic research[61] than for its views of black crime. It is important to understand that the race issue was considered to span both academic and managerial aspects of the courses on offer at Bramshill.[62] This is further illustrated by the treatment of the subject in several contributions to *The Police We Deserve* volume[63] which was the public confirmation of a new approach to police work with the policeman firmly established:

in the front line of change and social disintegration . . . (where) the many problems associated with immigrant communities, industrial disputes, urban renewal, youth and drugs depend heavily on police resources for their containment if not their solution.[64]

However, the winds of change must have blown slowly in the direction of the Home Office because their December 1973 White Paper on police/immigrant relations[65] which commented on the earlier Select Committee report, endorsed the view that 'immigrants are not in themselves a problem for the police'. The paper differentiated between the 'law-abiding, hard-working' sections of the black community and the new home-grown problem embodied in

a small minority of young coloured people . . . apparently anxious to imitate behaviour amongst the black community in the United States.

This was achieved along straightforward generational lines. There was extensive reference to the problems encountered in policing their white peers, propounding the theory that these black British youth were doing little more than claim their subcultural birthright to disrupt seaside resorts on bank holiday afternoons:

It is worth remembering that the police have over the years had difficulties with different groups of young people – who have been easily identifiable by dress or appearance and whose collective behaviour has given cause for offence to the public at large.

While John Biggs-Davidson's warning to the Royal United Services Institute – 'If we lose in Belfast we may have to fight in Brixton or Birmingham[66] – was still ringing in the ears of senior policemen, the need for a more sophisticated understanding of the black problem was confirmed. First by Dr Stanislaus Pullé's research into police/community relations in Ealing[67] which required detailed refutation, and second on the streets of Brixton where a confrontation with the police developed after a firework display in Brockwell Park, and the whole community closed ranks against the police, joining the fray regardless of age. Deterrent sentences on individual muggers were simply not adequate to the task of allaying the fear of collective violence, which had increasingly an explicit political dimension. The Wailers performed for the first time in London during the summer; the police waited outside for the inevitable confrontation.

If the Home Secretary's speech of 1 November 1973 set out the philosophical co-ordinates of the official rejoinder to Pullé,[68] its direction and velocity were determined by the first of John Brown's important interventions in this field. The 1974 *Theory of Police/Immigrant Relations*[69] which appears to have been a text book for the courses at Bramshill, takes the decisive step of relating the cultural practices of 'immigrants' to specific patterns of criminal behaviour, transcending environmentalist wisdom on the causality of *black* crime.

The crime patterns of first generation immigrants derive much more directly from background cultures and circumstance. Just as West Indians tend to find themselves in unskilled or semi-skilled jobs, so their criminal minority tend to take to unskilled or semi-skilled crime–robbery; theft from the person; breaking and entering; driving unlicensed vehicles; poncing, etc. – much of it casual and physical by nature, born rather of impulse than of deliberation: in essence, disorganised crime. Characteristically, the West Indian may tend to drift into crime, as like as not by accident as by design. He shacks up with a white girl, for instance; likes to live at ease, playing dominoes with the boys, taking a drink or two; finds it easier to let the girl work, what way better is the life, eh? [*sic*] By contrast the Asian attitude to poncing tends to be premeditated, organised, impersonal, directly commercial. Most policemen say that West Indians give them most trouble. They prefer the compliant evasion of the Asians to the thick skinned aggression of the West Indians. This attitude is understandable, though it may be somewhat misleading, for West Indian crime is so much more on the surface, so much more visible than Asian crime. As the West Indian looks outward to our society, so his crime tends to involve us too. As the Asian tends to look inward so his crime tends to be internal, within his community, covert. . . . Thus Asian crime in this country has several main characteristics. Firstly it rarely crosses racial frontiers. . . . Secondly it tends to be more cerebral, sophisticated and organised than West Indian crime, characteristically concerned in areas such as fraud, tax evasion, conspiracy, bribery and other aspects of financial malpractice and corruption. Thirdly it is largely underground, only glimpses showing to police eyes, as in the area of illegal immigration.

Brown linked this argument to a pessimistic forecast of social strife in which 'the pressures of economic and social forces acting against good police-immigrant relations have grown more intense' and, borrowing some of Sir Robert Mark's ideological garb, made a detailed case for a 'more rational system of social organisation in areas of community stress'. This system would provide police with 'a greater voice in society and . . . greater involvement in matters of social policy and practice'. His pamphlet is notable both for its identification of black grievances as the raw material for exploitation by black and white extremist groups, and its extended attack on the sociological research of Pullé and John. This sociology, Brown writes, is 'among the most potent and capricious factors affecting police-immigrant relations'. But Brown's piece is most important for the invocation of 'community' which it has become the burden of the police to reconstruct in the face of crisis and social disintegration. It is unclear from the text whether Brown believed that 'community' actually existed in the form he implies, but the process of *constructing* it is presented as invaluable in the furtherence of the police role, not least because it familiarizes the police with the anatomy of the communities they have to control amidst 'rapid change and growing instability':

. . . a police (community) leader has to know a great deal about his community. In order to have some measure of control over them, he is led willy nilly into ever greater community involvement.

Brown is quick to add that

the problems of policing immigrant areas are finally in no way different from the problems of policing in contemporary society. Wherever tension is caused by minority activities as occurs ever more frequently in our ever less stable society, similar problems of control confront the police, and similar methods of approach are needed to solve them. In areas of industrial strike action, for example, understandings worked out in detail between police and trades unions enable the police both to enforce the law of picketing with confidence and to isolate and deter those who seek to use the occasion for disruptive and destructive purposes.

The prescription of 'community involvement' and a 'rationalised' social control operation, through an orchestrated local state, is his general strategy for the crisis. It has been developed out of the problems posed by policing 'immigrant communities', which in this period came to represent *the paradigmatic model of urban policing in crisis conditions* (recognized euphemistically as a 'society in which the only permanence is change'[70]).

All these themes were taken up by the contributors to the Cranfield conference on 'Police and society' in September 1974 and were published the following year under the title *The Police and the Community*. [71] This volume was said to contain 'senior policemen thinking aloud and often in highly revealing fashion about the current shape and direction of their work'.[72] It is shot through with the fear of imminent social instability, as well as the belief that 'it is within our own organisation (the police) that the key lies to the successful handling of society's problems'. The price paid for this diagnosis and the preferred treatment is, as in Brown's earlier work, that the concept of 'community' is entirely inappropriate to the complexities and conflicts of urban life. Brown and Commander Peter Marshall, sometime head of the Metropolitan Police Community Relations Branch, argued that the 'retrieving and refashioning of the community itself' is required in policing 'urban twilight areas with high immigrant populations',[73] and Brown extended his claim that 'in general society has much to gain from consulting the police more fully on matters of social policy'[74] untroubled by the contradiction with Marshall's more plausible view that 'the underlying causes (of street crime) are not of the police's making, nor amenable to policy solutions'.[75]

Though the elections, Shrewsbury pickets, Red Lion Square, disorder at Essex University, and the IRA bombing campaign temporarily relegated the blacks to secondary status in popular ideological struggle, the rising tide of police–black confrontations visible in a number of well publicized court cases of the period[76] had important effects on the rank-and-file police officers. The racial threat was a central theme of the 'law and order campaign' launched by the Police Federation in November 1975[77] with the following aims.

1. Concern about the growing volume of crime.
2. Anxiety about violence.
3. Concern about the effectiveness of existing criminal legislation.
4. The attitudes of courts at all levels towards the punishment of offenders.
5. The need for changes in the criminal justice administrative procedures.
6. The attitude of some people and some bodies in public life towards the rule of law, instancing the sympathy shown to law breakers whose crimes have allegedly 'political' overtones.
7. The need for the silent majority to assert itself in order that politicians and judges fully understand the feelings of the public.
8. The need for public support of the police to be more positive.[78]

Fuelled by the 'Spaghetti House Seige'[79] and the bonfire night confrontation in Chapeltown as well as the arrival of East African Asians, the images of the black street criminal and the illegal immigrant once again proved powerful signifiers of a hidden threat. This campaign took the Federation into public territory which Sir Robert Mark had opened up in his elaborate personal crusade for acceptance of a police role in the 'moulding of public opinion and legislation'[80] and which had politicized the platform his office provided in an unprecedented manner. They responded to the accusation of meddling in politics with the disarmingly simple question 'what is political about crime?'[81]

The militancy and intensity of confrontations in East and South London, Liverpool and Birmingham[82] confirmed that the limits of 'indirect control' of black communities[83] were being rapidly reached. The environmentalist/social problems analysis of black crime which maintained this approach, understanding police/black conflict by reference to 'youth' and solving it by means of more 'ethnic minority' policemen, community-relations training, and multi-cultural complaints procedures, was on the way out. Its death rattle can be detected in the failure of the Metropolitan Police Commissioner's well-publicized bid to recruit black officers. Although the posters bore the question 'Is Racism Keeping You Out Of The Met?',[84] they managed to generate a paltry 135 new enquiries from potential black bobbies in the months before March 1976. In a total force of some 21,000 officers there were only 39 blacks.[85]

Despite friction between them', the rank-and-file police and their senior officers were increasingly in agreement over the diagnosis of society's ills, and the requisite remedy – a large dose of 'law and order' which might prove difficult to swallow. This alternative, 'direct control', also emphasized the political struggle to legitimate police responses to black resistance. These would now proceed unimpeded by the idea of social responsibility for crime which was an unwanted residue of the waning environmentalist theories. Under crisis conditions, it threatened to provide partial justification for the now criminal violence which Lambert and John in particular had presented as the inevitable fruit of real black grievance. If the most disruptive section of the West Indian community was its youth fresh from their encounter with Rastafari, and standing firm outside the social and cultural institutions in which their politics was refined, then the direct control which social disintegration invited required that they be identified as criminals *in their particularity*, that is in a racially specific mode, but one which was still consistent with the law's interest in *formal legal rationality*.[86] The ideology of the solitary 'dark figure' was less and less appropriate to the reality of large-scale confrontations, and the racial connotations of 'mugging' would have to be qualified by the growth of 'white' street crime. The Met's evidence to the Commons Select Committee in March 1976 makes clear the rising scale of problems which police faced on the immediate technical/ control level. It presents their understanding of racial politics, assembled from the academic research of Brown, Marshall, Dear and Alderson. A section entirely devoted to confrontations explained:

There has been a growth in the tendency for members of London's West Indian communities to combine against the police by interfering with police officers who are affecting the arrest of a black person or who are in some other way enforcing the law in situations which involve black people. In the last twelve months forty such incidents have been recorded; each carries the potential for *large scale disorder*. . . . experience indicates that they are more likely to occur during the summer months and that conflict *invariably* is with young West Indians. (my emphasis)

Further on, a section entitled 'The dilemma of public debate' pointed to the newly perceived specificity of the race field. It too was marked by the poles of extremism and moderation, and consolidated by generational conflict:

(the) continuing attempt by the few to 'politicise' the criminal actions of a minority of young blacks, has its effects on more moderate and constructive community spokesmen. Wherever they speak for public consumption they cannot be unaware of these negative extremists waiting in the wings to deride any constructive black approach as uncle Tomism.

The comprehensive analysis presented in the evidence received dramatic confirmation during the months which followed. In Wood Green and outside Winson Green prison, the grievances of black youth intersected with those of white 'demonstrators' and 'extremists'. The popular protest against the murder of Gurdip Singh Chaggar in Southall announced the 'arrival' of equally home-grown and troublesome Asian youth on the front pages. John Brown's insistence that[87] the long-term effects of 'reactive' deterrent, police operations by the SPG or equivalent, were counterproductive, and more trouble than they were worth for the local police forces in the areas involved, would seem a lot more persuasive after the carnival battle in which black youth established that they were more than a match for the Met's finest on their own territory.[88] John's work, memories of the Storey case, and local anxiety that Handsworth would host the next eruption made it entirely fitting that Brown should return to Handsworth to furnish an academic, rational but nonetheless partisan account of police/black conflicts. This would provide legitimation in the broader contest between police and public, as well as the final impetus for an experiment in urban policing which, if successful, would supply a paradigm for the eighties – once again derived from the experience of policing black areas.

The terms, parameters and concepts of all subsequent discussion of the relation of police to blacks have been determined by Brown's report *Shades of Grey* and the award-winning BBC film of the same name which provided its audio-visual counterpart. The report, which was intermittently Powellite in language and argument,[89] gave a vivid and most importantly *collective* form to the race problem no longer adequately referenced by the mugger's lone figure.

... the couple of hundred 'hard-core' Dreadlocks who now form a criminalised subculture in the area live in squats. Almost all are unemployed. And apart from the specific crimes for which they are responsible, they constantly threaten the peace of individual citizens black, brown and white.[90]

Brown's resonant picture of alienated hard-core criminal dreads accommodated the political change in the black communities by relating crime to black political organization. The issue of police harassment had passed the point at which it could be dismissed out of hand, and Brown returned to the earlier theme of

reckless youth in a new permutation to pull equivalence over the power relations
which separated the young blacks and the police:

The truth, I believe, is to be seen in human rather than political terms. The blues –
plain clothed or uniformed – with whom these blacks have the most contact
resemble them in that they too are young people under intense, often frightening
pressures. On the one side, the young Dreads, brimful of unused energies, fear and
resentment, aggression and ideological ardour, some with the violence aching to
be out of them: a short fuse for any police sparks. On the other, the young coppers,
understaffed, overworked. Some on overtime (the young men with young families
are those under the greatest economic stress, and thus the most likely to take it on),
their noses constantly rubbed in the shit of human experience, the sufferings of
Dreadlock victims, abuse, obstruction, lies: tense with the expectation of meeting
violence.[91]

It is hard to know whether Brown anticipated the impact[92] of the images he
mobilized. Copies of his report were received unsolicited by community workers
and activists, and its tone recalled an earlier report about Rastas in the *Reading
Evening Post* which had some of the characteristics of a planned 'disinformation'
exercise:

Scotland Yard has alerted police forces in England and Wales about the infiltration
threat by a West Indian mafia organisation called Rastafarians. It is an international
crime ring specialising in drugs, prostitution, extortion, protection, subversion and
blackmail. Inroads have been made in coloured communities in London, Leeds,
Bradford and Birmingham, and Scotland Yard has warned forces about their
activities. The syndicate's home base is Jamaica but they are spreading their
operation world-wide. They are known as 'Red Devils' or 'Red Dreads' and have
been in existence for decades. They favour red, high-powered cars, wear their hair
in long rats tails under multi-coloured woollen caps and walk about with 'prayer
sticks'– trimmed pick axe handles. They are known to police and intelligence organisations on both sides of the Atlantic as being active in organising industrial unrest.[93]

The source of the *Post*'s report was never disclosed, and Scotland Yard denied ever
having issued the warning.

Brown's principal achievement was the transposition of the debate about black
crime and politics into the key of black culture, indexed by the 'pathetic West
Indian family'.[94] Here, the parents were incapable of exercising authority correctly
and this caused family breakdown, impelling the offspring – already caught
between two cultures – into gender-specific identity crises; the boys lapsed into
criminality, whilst the girls whose cultural bastardy was confirmed by their unfeminine predisposition to violence, produced unplanned children and the cycle
started anew.

the girls are often more vicious, stirring the boys to violence and viciousness
themselves.

Brown's tentative theory of the black identity crisis producing a backlash among white youth[95] which inclines them to Fascism, has been taken a little further by Major General Richard Clutterbuck who tells us that:

In some of these (borstals) the West Indian boys are well organised in the intensely racist Rastafari movement, and establish 'no-go' areas for themselves – the best washrooms and toilets etc. – 'Rastas Only', 'White Trash Keep Out'. There is not much doubt where the white boys will turn when they get home.[96]

Sir Robert Mark gave *Shades of Grey* more publicity and his own seal of approval.[97] The report's influence was discernable in a wide variety of national and local press coverage. Both 'popular' and 'respectable' press reproduced its trademarks without crediting their source:

Handsworth not long ago a racial hell hole, where the community was terrorised a few years ago by 200 Dreadlocks, rootless squatting pseudo-Rastafarian young thugs.[98]

West Indian families have to adapt to permissiveness in Britain, traditionally West Indian parents are much stricter with their children.[99]

The Police Federation magazine delved into the Rasta discourse which Brown had made part of their vocabulary and traced the culture of criminality back to the West Indies, casting doubts on the barrier of respectability he had erected between generations.

To a large majority of the underemployable population of Jamaica – an overwhelming majority – the police are Babylon, a word used in their jargon to mean 'evil, the sinful, the hated'. All Babylon are to be killed. That is the rule of the enormous slum areas of Jamaica's towns, and it applies equally here in the sons and grandsons of the criminal element that poured unchecked into the U.K. in the 1950s when immigration was at its height. Decent, hard-working Jamaicans both here and in Jamaica, were aghast that so many criminals, prostitutes, etc. were allowed to come to the U.K. It was a standing joke that the most hardened criminals were given their tickets to the U.K. as they left the general penitentiary.[100]

The report's most enduring theme was the separation of the real, spiritually inclined Rastafarian, from the criminal imposters who were able to assume the appearance of the former. This is an old theme in literature on the movement[101] and Brown's version once again drew the line of respectability at the door of the Ethiopian Orthodox Church which was tangential to the development of popular Rastafarianism in this country. This division is significantly endorsed by Lord Scarman's report into the April 1981 disturbances in Brixton and reveals something of its common-sense power in reporting of the 1980 riots in Bristol. Once the trigger events had been isolated, the inauthentic criminal 'Rasta' was discovered at their centre:

It was then that all the aggravation started. The crowd was jeering and shouting and two or three youths *dressed in the Rastafarian style* began throwing stones and planks of wood.[102]

Coverage of the sporadic conflict which marred a march in protest over the handling of police investigations into a fire in which thirteen black youngsters had died reveals a similar pattern:

A television crew with commentator David McCormick were surrounded by blacks *with Rastafarian haircuts* and threatened.[103]

Neither report actually states that the youths described were Rastafarians, but both pieces connote criminality precisely in the way that the protagonists were able to appear true religious devotees whilst remaining affiliates of the 'criminalised dread-lock subcult'.

Any professed independence from the imperatives of the police service has been abandoned in Brown's more recent writings in *Police Review* and *Police Studies*.[104] His influence over the criminalization process, broadly conceived, is also visible in the way that, during the inquest into the fire mentioned in the last paragraph, the council for the Metropolitan Police inquired whether 'Rastafarian skanking' had taken place at a party as part of his attempt to establish its disreputable character.[105] The case of fifty-one year old Alfred Rose, found not guilty of assaulting two policemen who claimed he had abused them in 'Rastafarian slang',[106] is a further small illustration of the way in which the association with Rastafarianism can become a ticket to conviction even for people who are a very long way from 'criminal subculture'. The extent to which Brown's ideas guided police practice in Birmingham is revealed in a paper prepared by the former commander of the Handsworth subdivision:

[The] unfortunate break-up of family association has been formation [*sic*] of substantial groups of young blacks leaving home and banding together in numerous squats and communes. Unemployed and completely disillusioned with society, most of them have donned the mantle of Rastafarianism, or more precisely the criminal sub-cult of the dreadlock fraternity. . . . we have the unfortunate spectacle of young West Indians in many parts of Britain, Jamaica and the U.S. wearing dreadlock hair styles festooned with Ethiopian national colours on their tea cosy hats and scarves, trousers at half mast, no socks and open sandals on their feet, the universal uniform of the Rasta man.[107]

He continues: 'stabilising the home surroundings and drying up the flow of young-sters moving towards the squats and Rastafarianism is of paramount social importance.

Brown's status as an authority on the problem of police–black relations was bolstered by his role in media discussion of the Brixton 'riots'.[108] Long after

Shades of Grey had faded from public view, a series of leader articles in the *Daily Telegraph* were testament to his enduring influence over the way Rastafarianism and West Indian culture are defined:

Jamaica and Brixton have many problems in common, like dope, Rastafarianism and violent crime. But there are other social problems . . . single parent families, harsh corporal punishment . . . and . . . psychological wounds going back to slavery.[109]

Brown's primary importance is as an ideologue internal to the police service.[110] He is a well-known advocate of 'proactive' or community policing as the solution to the law and order problems encapsulated by the experience of policing black youth in the inner cities. His report was the immediate stimulus to the institution of the Lozells Community Policing project, which has apparently solved the crime problems in that area.[111] The ideology and the practice of community policing are points at which the specific history of police–black relations articulates with the more general history of the crisis.

From counter-insurgency to community policing

Maureen Cain[112] and Simon Holdaway[113] have outlined the professionalization of British policing which followed the 1962 Royal Commission on the Police.[114] This is where we must situate the definition of the black problem proposed by Geoffrey Dear, Peter Marshall, John Brown, John Alderson and others. The relevance of sociological analysis of race, community and crime to the 'managerial-professional' approach[115] to police work, had been anticipated by the 1969 Report of the Working Party on Police Training.

all members of the police service must be able to show by their actions and their attitudes that they are aware of the major sociological forces which influence our way of life; that they are alert to the changing patterns of community living, the merging of social classes, and the broad effects of immigration particularly by coloured peoples.

It is easy to demonstrate that race has implications for each of Holdaway's definitive principles of police professionalism.[116] We have already examined their body of academic knowledge on the subject, and Superintendent Lawrence Roach of the Met's Community Relations Branch has revealed how the information of specialist units interlocks with patterns of black struggle and the apprehension of racial conflict.[117] The first community relations officer was appointed to Scotland Yard in the aftermath of the 1958 riots with the responsibility of 'coordinating and developing police activity in the field of race relations',[118] and the first community relations branch was established there ten years later, significantly in the wake of Powell's 'rivers of blood' speech. An indication of the extent to which

community relations is synonymous with race relations is provided by the fact
that the first seven functions of the department, as outlined by Roach, are all
specifically concerned with blacks. A second is provided by the Home Office's
recent admission[119] that 'in forces with major communities of ethnic minorities
. . . the race relations aspect of the work tends to dominate'. Their hasty qualification that 'in areas where there are no large settlements of ethnic minorities the
emphasis tends to be on juveniles and other aspects of community work' illuminates
the unique double position of race in the professional approach of the urban
policeman, whose attempt to kill the two birds of 'the blacks' and 'the youth' with
the single stone of community relations has all too often resulted in killing the
first bird twice under the different headings of 'the blacks' and 'the young blacks'.
The application of computer technology to the pursuit of 'illegal immigrants' is a
simple illustration of the role of race in the technological principle, while the
writings of Brown and Dear[120] demonstrate the application of 'informed dis-
cretion'[121] to the specific circumstances of policing black communities.

Despite the strengths of his model, Holdaway fails to address the place of race
in the occupational culture of the rank-and-file policeman. One would have thought
that the definition of blacks as criminal, disreputable and violent would have made
them a prime object of the 'action and hedonism' orientation he has confirmed
following Cain. The distance squad cars have been alleged to travel in pursuit of the
opportunity to conflict with blacks is further evidence of this. The main point,
though, is that contrary to his view of the professional approach 'quietening' the
'action and hedonism orientation',[122] race relations are one area in which these two
trends are in a considerable degree of harmony, drawn together by the cultural
pathology of black criminality which unites common sense and managerial
perspectives. If professionalism is the immediate context of concern with race in
police thought, the wider dynamic is supplied by demands for crisis management to
which police professionalization was itself a response. The specialist community
relations policemen were not being nostalgic for environmentalist theories of crime
when they began to admit that the problem of black crime reflected

a situation not primarily of our making and outside our compass to resolve.[123]

and that

The major forces which determine the socio-economic condition of our society are
not under the control of the police . . . [and] community relations activity is
therefore limited by the political and economic decisions which take into account
considerations wider than merely [sic] those of social harmony.[124]

These views are tacit acknowledgements of a new role for law and law enforcement
in conditions of long-term crisis. On this new terrain, 'the paramount need is that
the police should retain public support during a period of what may be intensifying
social crisis'[125] and 'unless the underlying social factors are tackled . . . we (the

police) must look for more conflict rather than less'.[126] These themes are an important backdrop to the consideration of community policing which follows. With these observations in mind, as well as the awareness that 'state power is a complex social relation that reflects the changing balance of forces in a determinate conjuncture',[127] we must examine the appearance of senior policemen in popular politics, as perhaps a 'morbid symptom' of the crisis of political representation so vividly described by Gramsci:

When such crises occur, the immediate situation becomes delicate and dangerous, because the field is open for violent solutions, for the activities of unknown forces, represented by charismatic men of destiny.[128]

The activist approach to 'the moulding of public opinion and legislation', and the mobilization of the 'communal will' through press and media, is traceable to Sir Robert Mark's regime at Scotland Yard.[129] Whilst Mark's influence should not be underestimated, it is important to locate him at the end of a sequence of popular police politics, which in the most recent phase dates back to the appointment of a press and information officer to the Met in 1945, charged with the task of 'improving the image of the police'.[130] E. P. Thompson is therefore correct to insist that:

There is nothing new about Sir Robert Mark's or Sir David McNee's illiberal and impatient notions. What is new is the very powerful public relations exercise which disseminates these notions as an authorised consensual view.[131]

Mark's achievement was in part the *personalization* of his office and platform. Recent fruits of this can be detected in the way that the law and order debate has been structured around the apparent counterposition of police personalities, each with his own distinctive cure for the national malaise. Mr James Anderton, Chief Constable of Greater Manchester and outspoken moralist, has come to typify the 'fire-brigade' or reactive mode[132] while the mild-mannered but nonetheless fervent Mr John Alderson, Chief Constable of Devon and Cornwall, personifies the 'preventive' or 'community' alternative. We shall see in a moment how policing Handsworth's blacks with a model derived from the writings of Brown and Alderson himself has become the acid test of the applicability of Alderson's methods of policing the crisis; as *The Times* reflected:

The question is whether such an approach could be used in a comprehensive way in a run-down city area.[133]

Discussion of the political and ideological importance of community policing in Handsworth requires that we linger a moment over Alderson's philosophical and political positions in their own right, not least because he warns that the polarization of do-gooders and 'hard liners' from which he has suffered – being labelled a 'softie'[134] – 'obscures more than it reveals'.[135] Alderson's distinguished career does not appear to have suffered through his being revealed to be the pioneer of links between the Police college at Bramshill where he was commandant, and the Institute for the Study of Conflict.[136] In June 1972 he wrote to Peter Janke, research officer at the ISC, that the students and staff at Bramshill took 'a great interest in the work being done by your institute'.[137] The reading list of 'Paget, Thompson, Kitson, Arendt, Crozier, Luttwak and Moss' which Alderson cites confirms police interest in counter-insurgency, though the nature of their interest is conveyed more precisely by the forms of conflict he lists as subject headings in their library catalogue:

> Government resistance to guerrillas
> Military aid to civil power
> Military intervention in politics
> Revolutions
> Student revolt
> Terrorism
> Algeria
> Malaya
> Cuba
> Ireland

Mr Janke's report of his visit to Bramshill is one of several indications that Mr Alderson's contemporary commitment to 'democratic communal policing' may be rather more strategic than principled.

Mr Alderson was clearly aware that the whole topic of police concern with subversion was a delicate one and that the Home Office felt particularly strongly about this. Mr Maudling when in office, had suggested that it would not be a good idea to invite Brigadier Kitson to lecture at Bramshill. Despite the extreme wariness of the Home Office, Mr Alderson felt that the Police College and even the Police itself *had a certain autonomy* derived from daily decision taking and that small steps along new paths could in fact be made without prior consultation. He was anxious that the public should be made aware that law and order depended upon the attitude of the population itself and not on that of the police, and that although, in his opinion, the public's confidence in the police was probably greater in this country than in an any other European countries, it might be beneficial to advertise the police in a low-level campaign. The denigration of the police came from small subversive groups and it was important, he thought, to nip these in the bud.[138]

Alderson's March address to the Royal United Services Institute, published in their journal for December 1973, referred to

The reality of the malevolent activities of a society of extremist groups . . . marxists of every brand, anarchists, nihilists and at least some elements of the various nationalist movements, all these have a determined interest in subverting existing British society.[139]

The relevance of Alderson's observation that totalitarian police organizations are able to flourish, is in the way he stresses the need for public support:

rightly or wrongly, broad sections of the community identify with them and think that for all their ruthlessness they are doing a necessary and unpleasant job.[140]

This is connected to his realization that:

The high status of the British Police is a priceless asset which might enable the system to maintain adequate order even in the severely regimented society envisaged by Toynbee.[141]

These remarks are a long way from the war against crime which has been histor-ically identified as the proper police role. At a time when crime control is a decreasing aspect of the police function and:

a large proportion of police time is devoted to matters unrelated to crime, or marginally related to crime fighting objectives.[142]

community policing has spearheaded the separation of the ideological struggle for consent and legitimation from the 'technical' aspects of police practice. It can be said to comprise the reconciliation of several related but distinct strategic tenden-cies, each in its own way stamped by the anticipation of crisis euphemistically recognized as 'social and economic stress':

1   The open acknowledgement of political and ideological dimensions to the practice of social control, crystallized in the statement that those who feel well policed are well policed.
2   A commitment to the importance of criminal intelligence, obtained in the practice of 'penetrating the community in all its aspects'.[143]
3   Assertion of police hegemony over the centralization and extension of control functions into a broad range of institutions and apparatuses of the 'welfare state' disguised in the proactive policeman's credo 'Policing is too important to be left to the police alone.[146]
4   A tactical conception of force which departs formally from the doctrine of minimum force.

The experiences of people whose communities have furnished the discrete laboratories in which these experiments in control have been tested, supply the best vantage point from which we may examine each strand in turn. Community policing is the proof that the peculiarly British tradition of policing by consent[145] is no longer restrained by the illusion that such consent is guaranteed in the ideology of the 'British bobby'. The reality of police/public relations dictates that support must be fought for. This struggle lays bare the contradictory relation between the police's legitimation requirements, and their increasingly vocal concern to allay not crime itself, but *the fear of crime* which though 'only marginally related to the objective risk of becoming a victim'[146] can be easily stimulated to amplify demand for greater law and order.

the popular image of the police battling it out with an almost intractable crime problem is arguably the main source of people's fear of crime – a fear justified by neither the risks nor the nature of the vast bulk of crime.[147]

The rational deterrent model of police work which continues to structure the boundaries of popular ideologies of policing is built around two core assumptions, that social control is reduceable to crime control, which thus constitutes the primary object of the police, and that police work is primarily crime oriented. However, important and underpublicized work by the Home Office Research Unit has argued that

A moment's reflection will show that the model is a quite inadequate description of the totality of Police work, which comprises a multiplicity of tasks both related and unrelated to crime. . . . the rational deterrent model of policing is a transparently inadequate description of police work.[148]

The police ideologue's new interest in the *fear* of crime signifies more than their making a virtue of necessity now that this model has been discredited with the rigged studies that established it in the first place.[149] It manifests their intellectual commitment to a popular law and order politics which is an increasingly important part of the way they operate in crisis conditions. It should be clear from Brown's influence and the way that 'the mugger' continues to reappear, that racial symbols are particularly pertinent in this new political campaign. Research on police effectiveness has forced police officers to realize that

The crime prevention value of a police force rests less on precisely what it does than on the symbolic effect of its presence and a public belief in its effectiveness.[150]

and though 'community policing' may have trouble accommodating the deterrent expectations of the Police Federation[151] as well as action/hedonism orientation of the lower ranks, its clever manipulation of symbols – 'the village in the city', 'the copper in the classroom' – has made an extraordinarily broad bid for public support.

The commitment to intelligence gathering in modern police work is not the sole prerogative of the theorists of community policing, but it should be obvious that their venture into the veins of communities offers both unique and acceptable methods by which criminal intelligence may be gathered and 'key offenders' identified.

Thus, the permanent beat officers appointed to Handsworth in the wake[152] of *Shades of Grey* have had a key role in the development of the West Midlands Police's new command and control computer system. This includes: a street index which would list by beat all streets contained within the West Midlands Police area, some 27,000 streets'.[153] The aim of this street index was to reintroduce 'local knowledge into the control room', and it is clear that the intelligence gathering exercise is complementary to the activities of the community police, not only in Handsworth but also in Castle Vale, Wood End and Wolverhampton.[154] It will organize their data for strategic operational use in the future.[155]

The synchronization of social services, education, probation and social policy is a feature of both theoretical and practical models of this style of policing. It is never clear why the resultant synthesis requires police leadership rather than simply police participation. Poulantzas begins to clarify this relationship by pointing out that:

It is impossible to overemphasise the fact that the various 'social' measures taken by the welfare state with respect to the reproduction of labour power and the field of collective consumption are at the same time geared to police/political management and control of labour power.[156]

It may simply be that any movement towards the coercive pole renders these connections more explicit than before. The progression from ideologies which stress the isolated and individual action of the mugger to those which can account for the collective, politicized proto-insurrectional protest of whole black communities in 'cultural' terms,[157] illuminates the way in which these connections are exposed.

control is shifted from the criminal act to the crime inducing situation, from the pathological case, to the pathogenic surroundings, in such a way that each [black] citizen becomes as it were an a priori suspect or a potential criminal.[158]

Recent events in Liverpool provide the clearest[159] example of how the police claim to deploy minimum force has been qualified and even nullified in practice. It is, however, important in the light of renewed criticism of 'reactive' and 'technical/military' responses to public order situations, to emphasize that the benevolent 'home beat' police man at the heart of community policing is no refuge. Mr David Brooke's experience at the hands of his local 'community police' in Exeter – the capital city of the Alderson regime – presents an insight into the workings of *flexible* force:

A Devon builder is waiting for an apology by the police after being interrogated for five hours as a suspected terrorist, because a car jack he had been holding was mistaken for a sten gun. Mr David Brooke and three friends were leaving London after a Cup-Final visit when an ex-army officer mistook the jack for a machine pistol. He thought their Devon accents were Irish brogue and alerted the police to a possible IRA attack. The warning triggered off a major anti-terrorist operation, when Mr Brooke aged 38 arrived back in Devon. As he drove out of an Exeter garage with his wife and son, their car was surrounded by over 30 armed police. A helicopter hovered overhead as he was dragged from the driving seat at gunpoint. Armed detectives wearing flak-jackets then raided his home in Blackthorn Crescent, Exeter. *They put a gun to a neighbour's head and handcuffed him to the steering wheel of his car.* A detective thrust a handgun into another friend's stomach when he opened the front door. After searching the house Mr Brooke and his friends were questioned for nearly five hours before police accepted they had made a big mistake.[160]

Police writings on community policing make extensive reference to the northern Ireland situation.[161] *Police Review* told its readers:

Community involvement includes 'blue lamp discos' (a straight pinch from the RUC).[162]

and ex-Supt Webb confided:

Many will, however, find a parallel with the Northern Ireland tragedy, particularly when they examine the aspirations and difficulties encountered by Ulster catholics, and our own Black West Indian population. The friction between these people and their police forces is not just a co-incidence, and must surely give food for thought.[163]

The fact that these parallels are constantly drawn should not be taken to signify that the six counties supply another laboratory from which control techniques can be transplanted. This has a conspiratorial ring and could obscure the obvious differences between police operations there and on the mainland. Yet there are many similarities, and the explanation may reside in the influence of counter-insurgency thought on the theory and practice of policing. This goes far beyond Alderson's historic ties with the ISC, and can be pinpointed in 'community policing'. Phillip Schlesinger has argued that crisis conditions have their own determinacy on the shape and scope of counter-insurgency thought.[164] He provides a framework for situating 'community policing' within the tradition of counter-insurgency theory:

Counter-insurgency thinkers may be regarded as intellectuals working within and/or for the repressive apparatus of the state. Their function is to produce ideas of a strategic and tactical kind for use by that apparatus.[165]

Alderson formally disputes the applicability of Kitson's *Low Intensity Operations*[166] to the contemporary British situation,[167] but it is clear that both Kitson's definition of subversion (which includes 'political and economic pressure, strikes, protest marches and propaganda[168]) and his notion of a preparatory non-violent phase, in which the rule of law has a key *tactical* role – 'just another weapon in the government's arsenal'[169] – invite the application of his theories and models to present circumstances. The ideological offensive of Alderson and Brown must be understood in relation to Kitson's stress on psychological struggle.[170] Their attempt to *construct* a community bounded by the flexible barriers of law is an adaptation of his instruction to isolate the 'extremists' and 'criminals' (key offenders) who will eventually threaten the social fabric of the nation. Kitson also sets great store by the integration of social control and civil functions in the management of crisis ridden areas.[171] This point is also apparently emphasized in the Army Land Operations Manual[172] and it is worth remembering that:

In Northern Ireland, the Army (under the direction of Kitson) initiated a system of community liaison officers – 'Mr Fixit' – to improve relations with the community.[173]

An editorial in *Army Quarterly* reveals the double pertinence of the race issue to this particular intellectual tendency:[174] not only do black grievances comprise a law and order problem in their own right, but also provide the raw material on which communist and subversive elements are able to thrive.

We hope to have demonstrated that the complexity of 'community policing' cannot be reduced to the activities of benevolent individual officers, nor taken as a step in the democratic transformation of the police force. A senior West Midlands officer noted for his interest in 'race relations' voices our own anxieties:

We are not always the nice guys. . . . These are good sound operational PCs in uniform doing an operational PC's job, but they are doing it a little more effectively. . . . We're not trying to create a force of social workers, its very much policing.[175]

In practice, policing can never operate in a *purely* preventive mode, and the ideological dimensions which mask its totality should not be conceded by analytical approaches to it. We shall let former Supt Webb have the last word:

The fundamental police priority is therefore, to bring the reactive and preventive roles of the police service into a balance appropriate to long-term aims and objectives.[176]

Community policing was never intended to appear in the ideal typical form of policing only by consent. Mr Alderson admitted this in a candid interview with *The Times*:

Of course we're mercenaries. . . . I know that policing is ultimately about being licensed to use violence. I know that. And I would shoot a man, if I had to. That kind of question doesn't particularly trouble me.[177]

Yet the success of his intervention can be gauged by both his 'blatant and contrived upstaging of the Met's own evidence [to Lord Scarman's enquiry]'[178] and by the phenomenal amount of press coverage his opinions received in post-riot public debate.[179] More fundamentally, it is significant that overt criticism of his strategies has come almost exclusively from inside the police force. Outside, large sections of right and left alike agree that 'community policing' is an excellent idea. The internal campaign against Alderson has been marshalled by the Police Feder-ation. The October 1981 issue of their journal *Police* demanded – echoing September's *Spearhead* – 'whose side is he on?'. Surprisingly, the fundamental point of Alderson's popular enterprise has evaded many of his critics. Barry Pain, Chief Constable of Kent, demonstrated this when he protested:

I've been employing community policing for years. The difference between me and John Alderson is that I don't go around shouting it from the rooftops.[180]

Alderson's response to this would presumably be to ask Mr Pain; 'Why not?'. If the task of police is to 'reduce fear and hurt in society' as he insists, such an exercise in public relations could only increase their contribution to the public's sense of security. The July conflict provided him with a unique opportunity to establish community policing as a *popular* alternative to confrontation.

Having watched even the Liberal Party assembly vote to abolish the Special Patrol Groups and establish community policing immediately, it is tempting to conclude that the Police Federation and the Tory rank and file are the sole remaining voices of dissent. 'Putting the bobby back on the beat' is supported by a remarkable range of contradictory opinion. Alderson's *Sun* article[181] went so far as to present community policing as the means to regain traditional British values swamped by the pressures of modern urban life and diluted by the 'wild-bunch culture'. He has been borne along on the wave of concern provoked by the sheer scale of the July 'riots' and their obvious roots in real deprivation. This same swell submerged Mrs Thatcher's April view that ameliorative measures were useless:

Sometimes too much money does not help to solve problems. It causes more trouble ... money cannot buy either trust or racial harmony.[182]

The resurgence of environmentalism may have taken the indiscrete edge off overt police militarization – hence Mr Anderton's embarrassment at the purchase of machine guns – but there is no reason to suppose that it will actually halt this process. In these conditions, Alderson's philosophy of law and order appears to be a real alternative. We hope to have demonstrated that this is not the case. He trumpets, 'the authoritarian society is dead', only to whisper, 'long live the authoritarian society'.

Conclusion

This chapter has attempted to draw out the racist ideologies of black crime and criminality which inform police operations, and the ways in which the law – mediated by police – marks out new terrain for popular politics in the face of crisis. In this movement blacks have been identified as the 'dangerous classes' whose criminal culture erupts periodically, infecting the healthy Britishness of the working-class communities they once invaded. The popular conceptions of their criminality embodied in the mugger, the Rasta and, latterly, the rioter have been defined and amplified by the police. They ground common-sense knowledge of alienness in authoritarian legality. The lesser breeds are once again outside the law. Any response to this version of national decline requires detailed attention to the mechanisms of criminalization which merge the crisis and the black problem, but it would be misleading to reduce the relevance of race in a law and order society to this alone. The labelling of a generation of young blacks as a priori criminals is one measure of profound and complex changes which involve as much non-decision making as decision making[183] and as much non-intervention as action. It is no more the result of conspiracy than the transformation of Britain's inner cities into slums for the workless, and it is no less a question of class struggle. The summer of 1981 demonstrated that these young people are not on the margins of political struggle but at its centre.

We must also account for the situation in which the forces of law are able to deny a specifically *racial* dimension to the rising volume of attacks on black people. The problem of relating this analytically to the other police/legal processes discussed here remains; though an important part of the solution is to be found in the racist construction of Asian passivity. The militancy of these black communities has been unable to destroy this image which has provided the counterpart to the wild and lawless West Indian.

However, locating the point at which it enters the discourse on black criminality enables us to perceive how patterns of criminalization interlock with ignoring the crimes perpetrated on blacks and treating black victims of crime as if they were themselves criminals. There has been no moral panic about racist violence. Common-sense dictates that immigrant interlopers bring this on themselves; it is a consequence of their difference: their blackness and their illegality. This returns us to the theme of repatriation and the variety of inducements to leave these shores which has been multiplied by the progress of popular authoritarianism. The transformation of the welfare state in the direction of control is being accomplished under the guise of measures designed to safeguard its benefits from foreign abuse. Meanwhile the Special Branch caters for the problems posed by 'illegal immigrants'[184] and subversives alike. The 'community policing' of inner-city areas with high crime rates and high conflict potential offers another window on the changing practices of a range of state institutions united under 'police leadership'.[185] The popular representation of these developments betrays the more open struggle for legitimacy specified by crisis conditions in which skin colour is more vivid and important. Even here, the policed must give their consent and this is secured by images of coppers in the classroom and bobbies on the beat through riot-torn twilight zones. This same popular statism invokes race and nation yet again in the continuing debate over black rights to citizenship and subjecthood which recruits the law into politics and police work in a different but complementary manner. The blacks are within the city gates, and controlling them has gone beyond the internal aspects of the 1971 Immigration Act. The openly racist distinction of 'patriality' is being progressively incorporated into a broad range of welfare legislation.[186] As the institutions of the welfare state, which were built on black labour, become implicated in processes of domination and control,[187] the *de jure* racism of new rules and procedures aligns with the 'theoretical' but *de facto* racist mobilization of the law which is the central feature of criminalization. Together they reproduce and consolidate the differential legal status of blacks who become political and legal subjects of the nation[188] in a racially specific mode. This is the final inducement to go 'home'. Legal attacks on black people have become, at the ideological level, a condition of existence for a climate in which repatriation has become the preferred solution to the problems of an alien black presence and therefore to the crisis itself. In the era of structural unemployment, the family-centred, cultural and legislative racism which structures this response provides the rationale for expelling settler labour which is both unproductive and disruptive.

Acknowlegements

Outside our group I wish to thank Stuart Hall, Richard Johnson, Kathy Bor, Vron Ware, A. Sivanandan, Beryl Gilroy and especially Lee Bridges for their comments and criticism of earlier drafts. Kelly was a great source of support during rewriting.

Notes and references

1 London Borough of Lambeth, *Final Report of Working Party into Community Police Relations in Lambeth* (London Borough of Lambeth 1980).

2 *Guardian*, 14 September 1981. The full text is reprinted in *Police* (October 1981).

3 *Daily Mail*, 20 July 1981.

4 Maureen Cain, *Society and the Policeman's Role* (Routledge and Kegan Paul 1973).

5 Steve Cohen, 'The thin end of the white wedge: the new nationality laws – second class citizenship and the welfare state', Manchester Law Centre Immigration Handbook no. 5 (1981).

6 Dominique Lecourt has argued in 'On Marxism as a critique of sociological theories', in *Sociological Theories: Race and Colonialism* (UNESCO 1980) that the legal basis of the liberal democratic state *requires* the structural exclusion of certain groups:

> to enable humanist ideology to hold, to be able to persist in asserting that all human beings are born 'equal before the law', just at a time when equality is no longer safe-guarded by existing positive law, some characteristic has to be found in the 'nature' of human beings who are thus disbarred from universal equality to set them apart in some way from the community of mankind. (p. 284)

See also; Winthrop D. Jordan, *White Over Black* (Penguin 1971), pp. 321–5, Stanley B. Greenberg, *Race and State in Capitalist Development* (Yale University Press 1980), pp. 385–91, and ' "Remember the ladies": Abigail Adams vs. John Adams, selected letters from the Adams family correspondence', in

Alice S. Rossi (ed.), *The Feminist Papers* (Bantam 1974).

7   Nicos Poulantzas, *State, Power, Socialism* (New Left Books 1978), p. 81.

8   Jock Young, 'Left idealism, reformism and beyond: from new criminology to Marxism', in National Deviancy Conference/Conference of Socialist Economists (eds.), *Capitalism and the Rule of Law* (Hutchinson 1979).

9   E. P. Thompson, *Whigs and Hunters* (Penguin 1977), p. 194.

10 Clare Demuth, *'Sus'*, *a Report on the Vagrancy Act 1824* (Runnymede Trust 1978).

11 The Clayton Report, *The Application of Semi-Conductor Technology* (HMSO 1978).

12 Richard Quinney, *Class, State and Crime*, 2nd edn (Longman 1980), p. 39.

13 E. P. Thompson, 'The state of the nation', reprinted in *Writing by Candlelight* (Merlin 1980).

14 Thompson, *Whigs and Hunters*, p. 194.

15 E. P. Thompson, Introduction to *State Research's Review of Security and the State* (J. Friedmann 1978). This offensive passage relates to the trial of John Kingsley Reid, leader of the British National Party. In a speech, Reid had greeted the news of Gurdip Singh Chaggar's murder in Southall with the phrase 'one down a million to go'. To Thompson's credit, he omitted this passage from the reprinted version of this essay.

16 Jordan, pp. 49–52.

17 Gelly v. Cleve (1694) and Butts v. Penny (1677). A brief account of these cases is provided by F. O. Shyllon in *Black Slaves in Britain* (Oxford University Press 1974), pp. 24–5.

18 ibid.

19 James Walvin, *Black and White* (Penguin 1973).

20 Penny Smith, 'Immigration law and internal control', unpublished paper, University College, Cardiff, 1981.

21 Walvin, pp. 106–7.

22 Suthendran v. Immigration Appeals Tribunal (1976).

23 *Ex Parte Azam*, 1974, AC 18; see also J. A. Griffith, *The Politics of the Judiciary* (Fontana 1977), pp. 93–7.

24 *Control of Immigration Statistics*, Cmnd 7875 (HMSO 1979).

25 I am extremely grateful to Tony Bunyan for pointing this out.

26 Thompson, *Writing by Candlelight*, p. 255.

27 Campaign Against Racism and Fascism, *Southall – the Birth of a Black Community* (Institute of Race Relations 1981).

28 This is a complex and difficult issue. Key texts in the debate, which demands a high degree of numeracy, are: Brian J. Hilton, 'Can sense be made of crime statistics?', in D. W. Pope and N. L. Weiner (eds.), *Modern Policing* (Croom Helm 1981), and K. Bottomley and C. Coleman, *Understanding Crime Rates* (Gower 1981).

29 Thompson, *Writing by Candlelight*, p. 173.

30 ibid.

31 Among the most reputable studies, I have in mind: Derek Humphry, *Police Power and Black People* (Panther 1972), Gus John, *Race and the Inner City* (Runnymede Trust 1970), Institute of Race Relations, 'Police against black people', *Race and Class* pamphlet no. 6 (1979), and London Borough of

Lambeth.
32 Thompson, *Whigs and Hunters*, p. 194.
33 *Newsweek*, 27 April 1981, p. 24.
34 Young.
35 ibid., p. 20.
36 Paul Q. Hirst, *On Law and Ideology* (Macmillan 1979), p. 144.
37 The criminalization of radical meetings in Trafalgar Square in 1886 is an excellent example. See Gareth Stedman-Jones, *Outcast London* (Penguin 1978), Victor Bailey (ed.), *Policing and Punishment in Nineteenth Century Britain* (Croom Helm 1981), and L. A. Tilly and C. Tilly (eds.), *Class Conflict and Collective Action* (Sage 1981).
38 S. Hall *et al., Policing the Crisis* (Macmillan 1978).
39 ibid., p. 397.
40 See for example the way in which some of the positions of *Policing the Crisis* and earlier CCCS work on this subject have been taken up by Scotland Yard's Dr Michael Pratt in his *Mugging as a Social Problem* (Routledge and Kegan Paul 1980). Pratt presents mugging as a machismo cultural solution to the real difficulties of being a young urban unemployed black, etc.
41 R. V. G. Clarke and J. M. Hough (eds.), *The Effectiveness of Policing* (Gower 1980), pp. 1–16 (Editors' introduction).
42 Devon and Cornwall Constabulary, *Chief Constable's Report* (DCC 1980), p. 4.
43 Thompson, *Writing by Candlelight*, p. 173.
44 Evelyn B. Schaffer, *Community Policing* (Croom Helm 1980).
45 ibid., p. 17; see also K. Bottomley and C. Coleman, 'Criminal statistics: the police role in the discovery and detection of crime', *International Journal of Criminology and Penology*, vol. 4 (1976), pp. 33–58.
46 John Brown, *Shades of Grey* (Cranfield Institute of Technology 1977), p. 3. See also *Chief Constable's Annual Reports* (West Midlands Police 1977), p. 63; (1978), p. 64; (1979), p. 63; Even if reported crime did fall in Handsworth after the PBO scheme started, in itself that would not be sufficient to establish a causal relation and an effective police deterrence; see Bottomley and Coleman, 'Criminal statistics', and their chapter, 'Police effectiveness and the public: the limitations of official crime rates', in Clarke and Hough.
47 Chief Superintendent John Alleyne (Tower Hamlets), quoted on BBC Radio 4, 'File on Four', 25 and 26 February 1981.
48 As I write, the cases of Cynthia Gordon and Nasira Begum are reaching their conclusions. These are only the most visible examples.
49 Because 'Asian crime' is generally thought to be low, it has become the subject of a meandering criminological debate. The two key texts are: R. I. Mawby and I. D. Batta, *Asians and Crime* (NAAY 1980), and P. Stevens and C. Willis, 'Race, crime and arrests', *Home Office Research Study* no. 58 (1979). Of course, since police rely heavily on intelligence from outside their own ranks to catch criminals or even to detect their crimes, and Asian people have every reason to steer clear of a force which assumes them to be illegally resident rather than take their grievances seriously, there may be some much simpler reason for the low rates of reported crime.
50 Colin Sumner, *Reading Ideologies* (Academic Press 1979), p. 268.

51　Cited by Superintendent (now Assistant Commissioner in charge of training at Scotland Yard) G. J. Dear, 'Coloured immigrant communities and the police', *Police Journal*, vol. 45, no. 2 (April–June 1972).

52　Alfred Sherman, *Daily Telegraph*, 9 November 1979.

53　Margaret Thatcher's speech in Birmingham, 19 April 1979.

54　Poulantzas, p. 79.

55　Hall *et al.*, p. 331.

56　ibid., p. 332..

57　John Lambert, *Crime, Police and Race Relations* (Oxford University Press/Institute of Race Relations 1970).

58　ibid., p. 244.

59　John, p. 14.

60　See note 51 above. Dear wrote his article as part of the Senior Command Course at Bramshill.

61　Michael Banton, 'Crime prevention in the context of criminal policy', *Police Studies* (June 1978).

62　P. J. Stead, 'The idea of a police college', in J. C. Alderson and P. J. Stead (eds.), *The Police We Deserve* (Wolf 1973), p. 130.

63　See contributions of T. A. Critchley, p. 35, J. C. Alderson, p. 47, and P. C. Neivens, pp. 135–44 *passim*.

64　J. C. Alderson, 'The principles and practice of the British police', in Alderson and Stead, p. 46; please note the order of the symptoms of disintegration which he has listed.

65　*Police/Immigrant Relations*, Cmnd 5438 (HMSO 1973).

66　J. Biggs-Davison, 'The role of the armed forces in peacekeeping in the 1970s', RUSI Seminar, 4 April 1973.

67　Dr S. Pullé, *Report on Police/Community Relations in Ealing* (Ealing CRC/Runnymede Trust 1973).

68　Robert Carr, *Hansard*, 1 November 1973, cols. 325–43; also *The Times*, 2 November 1973.

69　John Brown, *A Theory of Police/Immigrant Relations* (Cranfield Institute of Technology 1974).

70　J. C. Alderson, 'People, government and the police', in J. Brown and G. Howes (eds.), *The Police and the Community* (Saxon House 1975), p. 11.

71　ibid.

72　Brown and Howes, p. 1 (Editors' introduction).

73　ibid., p. 3.

74　J. Brown, 'The social compact of the police service', in Brown and Howes (eds.), p. 103.

75　Peter Marshall, 'Urban stress and policing', in Brown and Howe (eds.), p. 25.

76　Cliff Macdaniel case: Clapton Park four, Swan disco seven, Carib Club twelve, Stockwell ten. See *Race Today* for the period.

77　This campaign climaxed with their full-page advertisements in the popular press prior to the 1979 election. Uncannily prefiguring the Conservative election manifesto which was published a few days later: CARF no. 9 (1979).

78　Robert Reiner, *The Blue Coated Worker* (Cambridge University Press 1978), p. 46; see also *Police* (November 1975).

79　Sir Robert Mark, *In the Office of Constable* (Fontana 1978), pp. 197–205.

80 Sir Robert Mark's introduction to T. A. Critchley's *A History of the Police in England and Wales*, 2nd edn (Constable 1978), p. xiii.

81 Reiner, p. 47.

82 *Race Today* (August 1975).

83 Lee Bridges, 'The ministry of internal security: British urban social policy 1968–1974', *Race and Class*, vol. 16, no. 4 (1975). See also: John Lea, 'The contradictions of the 60s race relations legislation', in NDC (ed.), *Permissiveness and Control* (Macmillan 1980), and Ira Katznelson, *Black Men White Cities* (Oxford University Press/Institute of Race Relations 1973).

84 The ad. in question is reproduced in between pages 120 and 121 of Syd Bidwell's *Red, White and Black* (Gordon and Cremonesi 1976).

85 Metropolitan Police evidence to Select Committee on race relations and immigration, 25 March 1976, p. 186.

86 Isaac Balbus, *The Dialectics of Legal Repression* (Russell Sage Foundation 1974), and K. Boyle, T. Hadden and P. Hillyard, *Ten Years On in Northern Ireland* (Cobden Trust 1980).

87 Brown, *A Theory*, Brown, 'The social compact', and John Brown, 'Police-immigrant relations', *New Community*, vol. 4, no. 1 (1974–5).

88 Cecil Gutzmore, 'Carnival, the state and the black masses in the United Kingdom', *The Black Liberator* (December 1978).

89 In particular his use of a letter (p. 21), the words 'wide eyed' (as in picca-ninnies) crop us from time to time, and Brown's fascination with sexual themes (pp. 10, 16 and 18) and excrement (p. 28) is at odds with the scientific status of the work.

90 Brown, *Shades of Grey*, p. 8.

91 ibid., p. 28.

92 Large sections of *Shades of Grey* were reproduced in *Police Review* (17 March 1978).

93 The original has been removed from Reading's local library but reference to it can be found in *West Indian World*, no. 259 (9–15 July 1976), and in J. Plummer, *Movement of Jah People* (Press Gang 1979), p. 6.

94 Brown, *Shades of Grey*, p. 11.

95 ibid., p. 22.

96 Richard Clutterbuck, *Britain in Agony* (Penguin 1980), p. 254 and footnote on p. 343.

97 Mark, *In the Office*, p. 237.

98 Blake Baker, *Daily Telegraph*, 9 May 1980.

99 *Sun*, 11 November 1980.

100 Ivy Reid, 'The roots of Babylon', *Police* (April 1979).

101 M. G. Smith, R. Augier and R. Nettleford, *The Rastafari Movement in Kingston Jamaica* (UCWIISER 1960), p. 23.

102 *Daily Telegraph*, 3 April 1980.

103 *Daily Mirror*, 3 March 1981.

104 John Brown, 'Cranfield and policing', *Police Review*, vol. 89, no. 4603 (24 April 1981), and 'The function of communities in police strategy', *Police Studies* (Spring 1981).

105 *New Standard*, 23 April 1981.

106 *The Sunday Times*, 24 May 1981.

107   Ex-Superintendent D. Webb, 'Policing a multi-racial community', unpublished paper, West Midlands Police, Handsworth.

108   BBC Radio 4, 'World at One', 13 April 1981, and *The Times*, 13 April 1981.

109   *Daily Telegraph*, 10 August 1981; see also *Daily Telegraph*, 1 July and 11 August 1981.

110   John Brown, 'Policing by multi-racial consent', *Police Review* (31 July 1981), and Brown, 'The function of communities'.

111   *Birmingham Evening Mail*, 13 December 1977, and 'Lozells project background and objectives', undated unpublished paper, West Midlands Police, Handsworth. See also *Observer*, 18 October 1981.

112   Cain, *Society and the Policeman's Role*.

113   Simon Holdaway, 'Changes in urban policing', *British Journal of Sociology*, vol. 28, no. 2 (June 1977), and 'The reality of police race relations: towards an effective community relations policy', *New Community*, vol. 6, no. 3 (Summer 1978).

114   (title of Royal Commission on the Police), Cmnd 1728 (HMSO 1962).

115   Holdaway, 'Changes in urban policing'.

116   Holdaway, 'The reality of police race relations'.

117   Superintendent Lawrence Roach, 'The Metropolitan Police community relations branch', *Police Studies*, vol. 1, no. 3 (1978).

118   ibid., p. 18.

119   'Note by the Home Office' for 'Workshop on young people in the ethnic minorities and their relationship with the police', University of Birmingham, 1981, p. 5.

120   G. J. Dear, 'The future development of police organisation', in Brown and Howes (eds.), p. 32.

121   Doreen McBarnett, 'The police and the state: arrest, legality and the law', in Littlejohn *et al.*, *Power and the State* (Croom Helm 1978).

122   Holdaway, 'The reality of police race relations', p. 262.

123   Metropolitan Police evidence to Select Committee on race relations and immigration, 25 March 1976, p. 182.

124   Roach, p. 18.

125   Critchley, *A History of the Police*, p. 329.

126   Commander Peter Marshall quoted by Critchley, *A History of the Police*, p. 328.

127   Bob Jessop, 'Capitalism and democracy – the best possible shell?', in Littlejohn *et al.* (eds.), p. 11.

128   Antonio Gramsci, *Selections from the Prison Notebooks* (Lawrence and Wishart 1971), p. 210.

129   Martin Kettle, 'The politics of policing and the policing of politics', in P. Hain (ed.), *Policing the Police*, vol. 2 (John Calder 1980).

130   Roach, p. 18.

131   Thompson, *Writing by Candlelight*, p. 200.

132   T. Bunyan and M. Kettle, 'The police force of the future is now here', *New Society* (21 August 1980).

133   *The Times*, 13 April 1980.

134   Jim Jardine, quoted on BBC Radio 4, 'International Assignment', 22 May 1981:

It's very nice down in Devon and Cornwall, I don't know when they had a riot down in Devon and Cornwall. I haven't seen Mr Alderson leading the riot squads down in Devon and Cornwall. I agree that out there it's very, very nice indeed, but you try it in Brixton, that's an impossibility . . . it just doesn't work in certain areas.

See also Tony Judge's 'Alderson's law: who's out of line', in *Police* (October 1981).

135 J. C. Alderson, *Annual Report* (Devon and Cornwall Police 1980), p. 6.
136 *State Research Bulletin* no. 1 (October 1977).
137 Alderson to Janke (22 June 1972), *Searchlight* (November 1976).
138 Janke, 'Report', *Searchlight* (November 1976).
139 Quoted by Bob Willis, 'The ideology of British counter-insurgency and its reverberations', unpublished MA thesis, University of Birmingham, 1978.
140 Alderson, 'People, government and the police', p. 7.
141 The Toynbee scenario is jargon for a regimented and authoritarian society, see Alderson, 'People, government and the police', p. 13.
142 Clarke and Hough, p. 7. See also M. Punch and T. Naylor, 'The police: a social service', *New Society* (17 May 1973).
143 J. C. Alderson, *Policing Freedom* (Macdonald and Evans 1979).
144 G. L. Kelling, 'Police services and crime prevention – the presumed effects of a capacity', *Crime and Delinquency*, vol. 24 (1978).
145 William Whitelaw, 'James Smart Memorial Lecture', *Police Review* (26 September 1980.
146 R. V. G. Clarke and K. H. Heal, 'Police effectiveness in dealing with crime: some current British research', *Police Journal*, vol. 52, no. 1 (January–March 1979).
147 Clarke and Hough, p. 9.
148 ibid., p. 3.
149 David J. Farmer, 'Out of hugger-mugger: the case of police field services', in Clarke and Hough (eds.).
150 Clarke and Heal, p. 36; see also W. G. Skogan, 'Public policy and public evaluations of criminal justice system performance', in J. S. Gardiner and M. A. Mulkey, *Crime and Criminal Justice: Issues in Public Policy Analysis* (Lexington Books 1975).
151 London Borough of Lambeth, *Report* (1981).
152 *Police Review* (7 March 1980); *Evening Mail*, 3 December 1977.
153 *Police Review* (1 May 1981).
154 *Police Review* (7 March 1980).
155 Duncan Campbell, 'Society under surveillance', in Hain (ed.), pp. 109–17.
156 Poulantzas, p. 187.
157 Gordon Brooke-Shepherd, *Sunday Telegraph*, 19 April 1981.
158 Poulantzas, p. 187.
159 *New Statesman*, 17 July 1981; *Race and Class*, special issue, vol. 23, nos. 2–3 (Winter–Spring 1982).
160 *Guardian*, 12 May 1981.
161 Brown, 'The social compact', p. 95, and Alderson, 'People, government and the police', p. 11.
162 *Police Review* (7 March 1980).
163 Webb, 'Policing a multi-racial community', p. 3.

164   P. Schlesinger, 'On the shape and scope of counter insurgency thought', in Littlejohn *et al.* (eds.).
165   ibid., p. 98.
166   Frank Kitson, *Low Intensity Operations* (Faber 1971).
167   Alderson, *Policing Freedom*, p. 79.
168   Kitson, p. 3.
169   ibid., p. 69.
170   ibid., pp. 30-1 and 188-91.
171   ibid., pp. 49-63.
172   C. Ackroyd *et al.*, *The Technology of Political Control*, 2nd edn (Pluto Press 1980).
173   ibid., p. 104.
174   *Army Quarterly*, vol. 107, no. 2 (April 1977). Thank you Bob Willis.
175   Superintendent Alan Lievesley, *Police Review* (7 March 1980).
176   Webb, 'Policing a multi-racial community', p. 13.
177   *The Times*, 21 September 1981.
178   ibid.
179   *Daily Telegraph*, 12 July 1981; *Sun*, 17 August 1981; *Sunday Mirror*, 23 August 1981; *The Times*, 21 September 1981.
180   *Police* (October 1981).
181   *Sun*, 17 August 1981.
182   ITV 'News at Ten', 13 April 1981.
183   For an explication of these concepts, see S. Lukes, *Power: A Radical View* (Macmillan 1975), and Mathew Crenson, *The Unpolitics of Air Pollution* (Johns Hopkins University Press 1971).
184   James Anderton's *Annual Report* (Devon and Cornwall Police 1979):

   The work of the branch . . .includes . . . assistance in the execution of deportation orders . . . and, because of *specialised knowledge* in the field, investigation into matters relating to illegal immigration. (my emphasis)

185   J. C. Alderson, 'The case for community policing', evidence to Lord Scarman's enquiry 1981', p. xii.
186   Manchester Law Centre, *Immigration Handbook* no. 5 (1981).
187   Brent Community Health Council, *Black People and the Health Council* (BCHC 1981).
188   E. B. Pashukanis, *Law and Marxism* (Ink Links 1978).

5   Schooling in Babylon

Hazel V. Carby

Emancipate yourselves from mental slavery
None but ourselves can free our minds.

BOB MARLEY

The educational response to the presence of black students in the British school
system has been framed in terms of the 'problems' for the system that these
students pose. Since the sixties, educational theory has located these 'problems' in
the black child, his or her educational 'failure' being explained through the
application of common-sense racist assumptions outlined in Chapter 2: black students' language structures are inadequate and inhibit learning processes, or, as
individuals and as a group, black students suffer from identity crises, negative
self-images or culture shock. Having thus situated 'failure' in the individual black
student, educational theories trace the causes, or roots, of these 'problems' to a
cycle of pathology within the black communities: excessively patriarchal or
matrifocal family structures, self-determined ghettoization, or generational crises
precipitated by the repressive measures of black parents. This cycle of pathology
arises in this scenario, from the need to force their children to conform to social
and cultural practices increasingly alien to sons and daughters born into, or maturing
in, a society unquestioningly assumed to be more 'enlightened' or 'progressive' than
that of the black parents' origin. From these examples or theoretical positions that
mobilize a racist common sense, educational policies have been recommended or
implemented that elaborate this common sense into an ideological system which
justifies an exclusive focus on the black child in certain educational practices:
practices which are remedial, compensatory or coercive.

This chapter will examine theories, policies and practices which have addressed
the black child in school. An understanding of the relationship between the
function of schooling as institution, and issues of race, is crucial to an understanding
of the ways in which state intervention in schooling has become (and is becoming)
more direct, overt and authoritarian. We will examine the race relations discourse
emanating from local authorities, the Department of Education and Science (DES),
Select Committee Reports, Education Bills and the MSC. Black communities have
been engaged in a struggle to redefine what constitutes education and have condemned the consequences of schooling in Britain for black students. Their actions,
in defiance of dominant definitions of the practices and function of schooling,

have profound implications for the whole of the British working class *vis-à-vis* its relation to the aims, objectives and achievements of the formal education system. The politics of white working-class subcultures have been the subject of much academic research.[1] Paul Willis in *Learning to Labour* refers to what he calls 'patterns of racial culture'[2] and describes racism as present at the 'formal' as well as the 'informal' levels of school culture.

Both 'lads' and staff do share . . . resentment for the disconcerting intruder. For racism amongst the 'lads' it provides a double support for hostile attitudes. The informal was, for once, backed up by at least the ghost of the formal.[3]

We will argue, in the terms in which we have conceptualized class fractions in Chapter 8, that the material interests of black students and the structure of social relationships, in which these interests are embedded, are distinct from those of white students. However, in being distinct (a struggle that is different to their white peers), we cannot view the struggles of black students in schools as struggles of school students only. These forms of resistance must be understood within the wider context of the struggles of the whole of the black community: students practising forms of resistance as members of the black fraction of the working class. As we shall illustrate, the requirements of white working-class parents of the formal schooling system have differed from the demands of black parents, and in fact the two have often appeared to be incompatible. The history of the transformation of the 'popular' interests of the white working class into the formal mechanisms of the representation of 'popular' interests through the Labour Party has been dealt with elsewhere.[4] Social-democratic initiatives in the field of education have always displayed profound contradictions, notably in the attempt to balance the perceived needs of the working class and the demands of capital. One attempt at a resolution of these conflicting interests is the construction of a 'national interest'. This resolution is apparent only, disguising conflict in its attempt to win consent. However, this consent has been won through the creation of a 'national interest' that has been mobilized against and which excludes the black community.

Black struggles over educational processes and practices have occurred auto-nomously, outside of the formal mechanisms of representation. The expectations of what schooling in Britain would mean for the black community were shattered by the end of the sixties. The social-democratic rallying cry of 'equality of opportunity' became demonstrably bankrupt. The research of Bernard Coard into the over-representation of black children in Educationally Sub-Normal (ESN) schools presented what many black parents were already experiencing – formal schooling was not going to provide an alternative future for their children.

Numbers, language and the weather

We can characterize initial educational policy as embodying the philosophy of assimilation. Schools were viewed as the primary site for successful assimilation. Black parents were referred to only as potential, or actual, inhibitors of this process. In common-sense terms the system was seen as capable of absorbing black children; 'race problems' would literally die away with the older generations. The Commonwealth Immigrants Advisory Council reported that,

a national system of education must aim at producing citizens who can take their place in a society properly equipped to exercise rights and perform duties which are the same as other citizens . . . a national system cannot be expected to perpetuate the different values of immigrant groups.[5]

A year later, in 1965, the DES echoed this approach, defining the task of education as 'the successful assimilation of immigrant children'.[6] No adjustments in the system were seen to be necessary, all adjustments were to be made by the students. Attention was focused upon language and numbers as these were seen to be the major inhibitors to successful assimilation.

The first official reactions were in terms of numbers. In 1964 the Commonwealth Immigration Economist Intelligence Unit reported that there were 38,000 pupils in London schools of overseas origin compared to 8000 in 1956. Four reports issued from the Home Office between 1963 and 1965: on Housing (Cmnd 2119, Cmnd 2796), on the Education of Commonwealth Immigrants (Cmnd 2766) and on Immigrant School Leavers (Cmnd 2458). The concern with numbers and their accuracy culminated in the Home Office White Paper of 1965 (Cmnd 2739) which instituted a quota system and formally acceded to increasing racist hostility against black people. Events in Nottingham and Notting Hill were interpreted as being the result of increasing numbers of immigrants and of their concentration in urban areas. The Commonwealth Immigration Act, which had met with Labour Party opposition in 1962, was approved for renewal by Labour in 1964. A consensus was reached that numbers were the 'problem' and restriction the 'solution'.

The concentration of immigrants in significant numbers was seen by the DES to undermine the process of assimilation:

as the proportion of immigrant children in a school or classes increases, the problems will become more difficult to solve and the chances of assimilation more remote.[7]

Numbers and white hostility were also equated in educational policy and it was the black children that were constructed as the threat, threatening to disrupt the education progress of white pupils.

in areas of high immigration density, immigrant children can form large percentages in some schools. . . . This may cause racial tension, since parents are afraid that their children will be affected by the apparent lower standards of the immigrant children as the latter numbers increase.[8]

These policy documents express the widespread, common-sense notion that racism is imported into Britain with the black immigrant. This consensus was described in the seventies by Stuart Hall:

Neither side can nowadays bring themselves to refer to Britain's imperial and colonial past, even as a contributory factor to the present situation. The slate has been wiped clean. Racism is not endemic to the British social formation. . . . It is not part of the English culture, which now has to be indeed protected against pollution – it does not belong to the 'English ideology'. It's an external virus somehow injected into the body politic and it's a matter of *policy* whether we can deal with it or not – it's not a matter of *politics*.[9] (original emphasis)

Assimilationist policy laid the ideological basis for practices designed to protect the indigenous population. Hostility, for example, was not conceived as being perpetrated upon black communities in the form of racist attacks and racist street corner politics, nor was it seen that it was the black community who needed protection. Rather hostility was seen to be the result of whites' *justifiable* fear of the very presence of blacks. In schools the situation for black students was an extension of the situation that their whole community faced. Their existence was a threat to their white counterparts. The Ministry of Education pamphlet N.43, 1963, outlined 'administrative procedure' to deal with 'this sudden influx into schools' whilst at the same time admitting that its advice to local authorities was not based upon research 'since research evidence [was] not available'. Bussing began in Southall in 1963. Though there was recognition that the institution of a quota system and dispersal were controversial, the DES continued to recommend in their Circular 7/65 that 'the proportion of immigrant children in any one school should not be unduly high'.

The ideological foundation was laid for policies and practices that would necessarily construct opposing material interests of the black and white working class. Powellism, as opposed to the individual pronouncements of Powell which were formally rejected, became implicitly embodied in policies which seemed to promise that race problems would have a conclusive end (returning whence they came) and protect white interests in the process. The black community, on the other hand, organized around specific issues, such as bussing and testing in education, but from the common basis in the wider struggle of the right to stay. What has been referred to as a 'structured antagonism' would characterize the relation between politics and race.[10]

Educational testing in the mid-sixties was taken to 'prove' the educational inferiority of the black child. The National Foundation for Educational Research (NFER) acknowledged that 'the existence of colour prejudice and other social pressures may affect intelligence test scores as a result of differences in emotional and motivational climate'.[11] Contemporary research, however, argued not for an examination of the 'social pressures' in Britain, but on the contrary saw educational performance as a product of the conditions of the countries of origin, and concluded that if that performance was considered to be low the answer lay within the black community itself.

Vernon compared his study of West Indian boys made in 1961 with a study of English schoolboys made in 1965 and argued that 'the factors which handicapped the children's environment' were previous 'defective education', 'family instability' and the 'cultural level of the home'. Children from 'non-technical cultures', he stated, 'are seriously handicapped in picture and performance tests as well'. Vernon in 1966 concluded 'that the whole pattern of a culture determines the educational and vocational potential and combines to reduce the effective intelligence'.[12]

Consistent with a colonialist and imperialist reasoning 'the natives' were being condemned as 'uncivilized' and, with a missionary zeal, the acquisition of the English language was seized upon as the key to successful assimilation. The only impediment was the language the child had already acquired. The intention was not just to teach a language but to rectify cultural and intellectual backwardness. To distinguish this process from processes of learning other languages, complicated systems of cataloguing were devised to 'explain' the deficiencies of immigrant language structures. The findings of Alleyne were relied upon. The three categories he used were:

1. Total language deficiency; to describe the acquisition of a foreign language but no script.
2. Partial language deficiency; to describe the acquisition of a foreign language, some English and a script which may or may not be a western alphabet, and
3. Dialect impediments; where English may be fluent but dialect or 'pidgin' English was spoken. West Indian Creole was seen to be the cause of problems of listening, interpreting and later reading and writing.[13]

A black child speaking a language from a black country was seen as backward not as actually or potentially bilingual. In fact the 'greatest danger' Alleyne discerned 'was that the child learns the language for a certain segment of the environment in which he [*sic*] will operate and another language for specific situations'.[14] Assimilation through language was seen to be necessarily total; alternative languages were not to survive. The ability of black students to use language as a form of resistance can be seen in the teachers' fear of being excluded from communication between pupils; this has always been regarded as an unacceptable loss of authority. Black pupils using their own language is often referred to by teachers with the derisory comment 'jabbering'. In 1963 Jones outlined the conclusions of the Conference Commission on Communication by saying,

The dialect or Creole English is an immature language which is clearly inadequate for expressing the complexities of present day life, for complete understanding of human motivation and behaviour.[15]

This statement outlines quite clearly the evolutionary notions behind these language theories and attitudes towards black cultures. Western societies were felt to be more advanced, not just technologically, but also intellectually, and language was the index of the stage of civilization reached. In terms of the total and partial language deficiency categories outlined above, speaking an Asian or African language didn't really count as having a language at all.

The two major strands, language and numbers, came together in a project sponsored by the Schools Council and conducted by Derrick, initiated in 1966. The aim was

to establish the number of immigrant children born overseas *or here* who have not been brought up with English as their first language, and the number of West Indian children and of children of other immigrant groups; and to find out the arrangements, made by the local authorities to teach them.[16] (our emphasis)

Language became the most obvious indication, in educational terms, of the black child's inferior intelligence, and confirmed the paucity, or complete lack, of a culture. In order to 'work' as a theory assimilationist concepts had to deny the existence of a viable culture in those to be assimilated. In the words of the NFER

It appears, therefore, that language is one major factor in this culturally induced backwardness of immigrant children and affects assessment of ability and actual school performance.[17]

Black children were perceived and treated as retarded. However, around the language issue gravitated other common-sense, racist notions to reaffirm the inferiority of blacks in general, and the pathology of their family structures.

Many of the surveys listed indicate that of the three ethnic groups now settling in Britain . . . it is the West Indian group which appear to illustrate our difficulties most vividly. Linguistically, they seem to have an advantage over the other two groups, but it is their partial mastery of English, and their use of dialect which seems to be a major barrier to educational motivation and achievement. They also appear to be more susceptible to the climate, in terms of health, and pose difficulties for the host community because of the high incidence of broken families or children of varied parentage.[18]

The pathology of the black family has been discussed in a previous chapter. At this point we wish to indicate the pivotal significance that climate has gained in the determination of other cultural and social characteristics. The economic relations of exploitation have been effectively disguised through the presentation of the Caribbean as a tropical paradise in which live a happy, smiling, though simple people – it becomes incomprehensible that they should ever wish to leave. At this point we can see clearly the transference of ideas from educational research into textbooks designed for use in teacher training. Moving from apparently 'objective' educational surveys that attempt to naturalize social relations of exploitation, we find a more developed and sophisticated ideological use of 'nature' as the determinant in the shaping of a social system, in handbooks that attempt to construct a sociological approach to teaching black children. In Ivor Morrish's *The Background of Immigrant Children*, we find the following paragraph.

Life in the West Indies is, for the most part, a life spent in the open air in a warm, sunny and friendly climate; and the warmth of the atmosphere is translated also in terms of human relationships. In the Caribbean people live together in crowded kin-group communities, and they share one another's hopes, fears, joys, sorrows, troubles and all family occasions. When they come here they find a climate which is cold, wet and highly unpredictable; they have to live most of their lives indoors, and there is no common 'yard' where all the street can congregate and engage in idle chatter. They begin to experience a pace of life which is greatly removed from the *dolce far niente* of the tropical Caribbean; its speed and unchanging, incessant routine are at first strange, and to some quite terrifying. If *we* suffer from 'colour shock', they suffer from climate and culture shock.[19] (original emphasis)

Racism becomes naturalized through the use of Sheila Patterson's concept of 'colour shock', offering reassurance to the student teachers, for whom the book was intended, that their distaste for black skin is only natural. The reference to 'crowded communities' acts as a naturalizing mechanism in relation to the explanation offered for the existence of ghettos later in Morrish's chapter. The weather as an unquestioned natural, biological force is used as the cause and justification for the existence of the concepts surrounding numbers and language that we have discussed. Blacks 'naturally' crowd together, their language is 'chatter' and, because it is 'idle', it explains why they are culturally, intellectually and technologically 'backward'.

'Special problems need special treatment'

A recognition that assimilationist policies and practices had failed and could not hope to succeed emerges during the last half of the sixties. It is impossible to present a strictly chronological account of precisely when assimilation as a philosophy dies and integration in a pluralistic form becomes the dominant ideology. Theories of assimilation have been associated with the period of optimism and economic expansion of the fifties and early sixties, and their disappearance with the 'profound social, cultural and political polarization' evident in 1968.

It is when the great consensus of the 50s and early 60s comes apart, when the 'politics of the centre' dissolves and reveals the contradictions and social antagonisms which are gathering beneath.[20]

The formal education system had undergone an unprecedented period of expansion and experimentation with 'progressive' teaching methods. However, within the wider context of a perceived threat to the social order from excessive permissiveness, schooling became linked to the 'youth crisis' and a loss of traditional standards. Liberal concepts of education for 'equality of opportunity' came under attack and stories of 'blackboard jungles' and the abdication of authority by teachers well popularized in the press. It is within this atmosphere of a crisis in social relations that we must situate the significance of the ideological shift from assimilation to integration through cultural pluralism. That this period also marks a more general shift in race relations policy and is punctuated by a crisis of race has been commented upon in Chapter 1. Though there is often a disjuncture between official policy recommendations and the implementation of policy, official statements do reflect a transition from indirect to more direct control over the schooling of black children.

An illustration of this shift is the move from a predominant concern with language to the construction of categories of the 'complex disabilities' of the black pupil. Language does not disappear as a problem but becomes incorporated into a complex which also includes 'culture shock', 'cultural conflict' and 'generational conflict'. The concern with cultural factors contrasts with the previous denial of culture but many characterizations of the structure of black communities remain, though granted greater significance as disabling factors to integration. At the axis of many of these disabilities was placed the black family, constituted as a pathological family structure, outlined in Chapter 2. The black family, it is argued, is unable to provide the conditions for, or acts as an inhibitor to, the successful educational progress of the black child. Most frequently, in educational reports, the focus is placed upon the black mother.

The report from the Select Committee on Race Relations, 1968–1969, hypothesised a generational conflict existing within the black communities which would hinder integration. The committee asked,

Should the young Pakistani retain the clothes and manners of his [sic] parents or adopt those of his [sic] white contemporaries with whom he [sic] spends most of his [sic] time? The mother, in particular, usually at home and mixing little in British society, may object to her daughter in a mini-skirt.[21]

It has been around black women that pathological notions of the black family and the responsibility for the failure, or inability, to integrate have been secured. Common-sense constructions of the passive Indian or Pakistani wife and mother, speaking no English and never leaving the home, have been elaborated alongside constructions of the dominating Afro-Caribbean wife and mother, who is always out working and therefore never at home, into ideologies that justify increased state intervention into school and home. The report condemned the lack of contact between schools and black parents which they saw as existing because,

many Asian parents, *particularly mothers*, speak less English than their children. *Many West Indian mothers* work during school-hours and cannot get to school meetings.[22] (our emphasis)

Black children were labelled 'disadvantaged' or 'disabled' either because their
mothers worked or because they didn't. The position of Asian women in the labour
force (see Chapter 7) has been ignored and common-sense conceptions of their
passivity reinforced. Alternatively, it has been precisely the Afro-Caribbean woman's
position in the labour force that has been used to imply the neglect of her children's
interests. Hypothetical situations such as that over clothes, cited above, are used in
an explanation of the failure of black and white youth to integrate. The report
also refers to the 'more rigid discipline' of Asian and Afro-Caribbean parents which
is described as being a contributory factor in a 'conflict of culture and customs',
a 'barrier to would-be social integration in youth clubs and their neighbourhood'.
The portrayal of black parents as deficient, unable to equip their children to
compete equally with white youth, has been used to justify increased state intervention to compensate for this supposed 'failure' on the part of black parents.

In particular recommendations for action the Select Committee stressed the
importance of intervention in the home. It suggested that social workers be appointed to 'liaise with immigrant parents' and that special attention be paid to attempting 'to overcome the language deficiencies of the parents of immigrant children –
especially Indian and Pakistani mothers' (our emphasis). This represents a significant
shift from policies of assimilation which concentrated on the school/child relationship, towards an increasingly direct interventionist approach which links the social
services, teachers and, most recently, the police in the schooling of black students.
Direct intervention by the careers service was also recommended in the report to
compensate for a perceived lack of parental guidance. 'Much careers teaching'
was seen by the committee to be 'uninformative about life on the factory floor'
but, they argued

White boys and girls may learn from their fathers, relatives and friends. For the
coloured immigrant the change from school to work may be more bewildering. He
[*sic*] may therefore need particular advice and help.[23]

There was no discussion of how black parents managed to find their way onto the
factory floor, into the transport services and into the National Health Service;
intervention was perhaps more to ensure that the state established the mechanisms
for the control of black youth.

This Select Committee report responded directly to the actuality and poten-
tiality of black organization, resistance and rebellion. In its initial pages the
'existence of sympathy to . . ."black power" policies' is noted and concern is
expressed that the 'second generation may be less patient in surmounting difficulties
that confront them than their parents have been'.[24] Written against the background
of the 'youth crisis' of the sixties, the increased visibility of white male subcultures,
gangs and social unrest on the streets, the anxiety of the committee members
about future 'alienated' black youth can clearly be felt. Whilst they attempt a tone
of optimism there is also recognition, of prophetic proportions, that the optimism
may be ill-founded; 'we have assumed there will be no widespread and sustained

shortage of employment in this country'.[25]

In relation to policing the report is at pains to indicate a 'much lower level of crime and juvenile delinquency among coloured people than white'. The criminalization of black youth is discussed in Chapter 4 but here it is important to indicate that the report recognized the potential for 'trouble' and the need for 'monitoring' black youth.

In general terms the Committee laid the groundwork for policies to focus exclusively on the black student in school and during the transition to work. In comparison with the physically and mentally disabled, black youth were seen as disabled because they were black:

'equal opportunity' for coloured school-leavers does not flourish naturally in the crowded areas of our towns and cities. Many of them have special problems, whether because of their upbringing in another country or from discrimination, that handicap them in entering adult life. White school-leavers do not suffer the same handicaps.

In terms of policy, however, it was not the conditions of towns and cities that were under scrutiny but the black youth for whom separate, special provision should be made.

Equality of opportunity does not always mean treating everyone in exactly the same way. . . . Special problems need special treatment.[26]

The Committee argued that this special treatment should be seen in the same light as that given to backward children and the special assistance provided for the physically handicapped in both education and employment. This correlation between being backward and being physically handicapped has remained and is enshrined in the extension of 'special needs' and 'special provision' in the Education Bill 1981.

In summary we argue that towards the end of the sixties an ideological shift to more direct forms of social control can be perceived in race relations policy. First, through increased monitoring (the Committee favoured the keeping of statistics on black youth); second, through direct intervention by the state into the home and school, under the guise of compensating for the inadequacies of black parents.

Alongside the establishment of mechanisms that would allow for more effective means of social control grew a sociology of race relations that was to concern itself with culture and ethnicity. Roy Jenkins had defined integration, in 1966, as 'not the flattening process of assimilation but an equal opportunity accompanied by cultural diversity in an atmosphere of mutual tolerance'. Around this doctrine, as Jenny Bourne has pointed out, was formed a

school of thinking . . . which held that if racialism, seen as the cultural intolerance underlying and giving rise to racial discrimination, was educated away, equal opportunity would begin to flourish. This could be achieved not least through anti-discriminatory legislation which their guru Jenkins had promised. They approached race relations, then, in terms of cultural relations (like the earlier assimilationists) and not in terms of power relations, least of all state power.[27]

The development of the sociology of race relations has been criticized elsewhere, by Jenny Bourne and in Chapter 3 of this book, but it is important to note two dimensions that have implications for schooling in this shift from assimilation to cultural pluralism. The first is the central role given to education, and the second is the close relationship between the investigations of the sociology of race relations and policy making. As Deakin said in *Colour and Citizenship* (1970), a central text in the formation of a race relations discourse,

Any proposals for the amelioration of relationships between minority and majority – and this book is intended principally as a constructive contribution towards policy making in this field – must be justified in purely practical terms.[28]

These two dimensions come together in the development of educational theories which used the findings of the sociology of race relations to formulate educational processes and practices. The pluralistic model acknowledged the existence of different cultures, different 'ways of life', but ignored the way in which these cultures were produced and existed in social relations of power, of dominance and subordination. It was clear, from the first teacher training handbooks that argued for the adoption of cultural pluralism, which cultural factors were to be encouraged 'to contribute to the enrichment of our society and its culture' and which were viewed as threatening to the British social fabric.

Ivor Morrish complained that 'the isolation of immigrants in certain areas of our large cities will tend to encourage the retention of their own social systems rather than accommodation to those of their hosts'. What this meant was that black family structures were not accepted in notions of cultural diversity. Morrish stressed that the 'danger of the ghetto is the perpetuation of Caribbean familial concepts and values in the new society', that 'the very forces which make for Sikh solidarity are at the same time the forces which prevent assimilation or integration', and that for Pakistanis Britain would offer 'liberation from the narrowing limitations of an ancient, but parochial and stifling, hierarchical system'.[29]

Cultures do not exist in egalitarian diversity and, therefore, cultural pluralism had to be 'managed'. One of the principal sites in which this managing has occurred is through the formal education system. Concepts of the white, nuclear family were to remain as indices of the 'pathology' of black family structures. The responsibility for the transmission of black cultural forms was to be removed from the black family and undertaken by schools: interpreted, digested and made safe for consumption. Just as the sociology of race relations was to ignore the implications of increasingly militant black political consciousness, so educational theory advocated avoidance, at all costs, of 'black power' politics.

Most thinkers would perhaps agree that the concept of negritude, which involves 'the awareness, defence, and development of African cultural values' . . . is a misguided one if applied to West Indian immigrants in our society. There is no common West Indian culture to which West Indian children in this country may turn; leaders such as Neville Maxwell . . . have, it is true, referred to 'our original African culture' and its suppression by the acquisitive whites, but this is more in the nature of an *emotional appeal* than an anthropological statement. There are, and there have been, African 'cultures', many of them; but no single, or original, African culture. Nor is the West Indian immigrant child likely to discover one, unless some new Ras Tafari movement should develop in our midst and create a pseudo-African culture'.[30] (our emphasis)

The concepts of a multicultural, multiracial or multiethnic society that grew from this pluralistic model assumed that equality could be achieved through cultural diversity and thus removed from the realm of politics. Race relations became totally absorbed with issues of black ethnicity at the expense of examining institutionalized racism. The educational philosophy of multiculturalism followed the sociologists of race relations in the reinterpretation of ethnic cultural forms for the classroom. In the words of the Select Committee on Race Relations 'much can also be done . . . to create better understanding of the national and cultural background of immigrants'. It advocated

specific teaching about the countries from which the immigrants in any particular town come. Here material direct from those countries can be displayed in the classroom by immigrant children. Children in primary schools in Hackney or Brixton, for example, could be taught West Indian songs, or children in Wolverhampton be shown Indian art, jewellery and costumes. This would help bring the immigrant children into the life of the school.[31]

Two aspects should be discerned in this approach. First, this implies that racial prejudice and racial discrimination would come to an end through an education in cultural diversity; racism was thus merely a matter of individual ignorance. Second, the articulation by black movements of the need for an awareness of black history and culture, formed in the struggles against imperialism and colonialism, and essential in the struggle against contemporary forms of racism, was turned by the state into a superficial gesture in an attempt to control the rising level of politicized black consciousness. The multicultural curriculum was from its inception part of state strategies of social control. Black culture and history were what the schools said they were. The state recognized the danger of the demand for black studies and determined to exercise control over what black students were taught. In 1973 the Select Committee on Race Relations and Immigration stated:

The demand for Black Studies has arisen because the content of eduation in Britain is seen as Anglocentric and biased against black people. We can understand this. *But we doubt whether Black Studies in the narrow sense would make a contribution to*

wider education and better race relations and we are not attracted by the idea of
black teachers teaching pupils in separate classes or establishments. But the history,
geography and cultures of the large minorities which now form a part of British
society are worthy of study and appreciation, not least by indigenous children.
We are certainly not suggesting that curricula be turned upside down.[32] (our
emphasis)

A critique of multicultural curricula has been made elsewhere and we will not
repeat that analysis here.[33] It has not only been irrelevant to the black struggle in
Britain but has also failed to address any of the crucial aspects of the relation
between race and education. A recent Schools Council report[34] confirms that the
multicultural curriculum, even in its limited approach to black cultures, has had very
little impact on schools in Britain. The *Guardian*, in a review of the report, stated
that most white schools 'have carried on teaching as though multi-ethnic Britain
never happened' and seemed surprised that white local education authorities
'invariably replied that they thought a multi-ethnic society was not a matter which
concerned them . . .'

Three quarters of schools with few or no minority ethnic group pupils expressed
similar views; most of those that did report including relevant teaching said that
this was limited to R.E.[35]

On the contrary, this limited application of multiculturalism should not be surprising because, as we have argued, it had been conceived and applied as a method
of social control over black children. The ways in which the curriculum content
innovations were originally conceived, as an integral part of an overall strategy
which was developing towards black youth, were neglected by teachers, their
professional organizations and unions. The 'progressive' boom in the industry of
multiracial, multiethnic and multicultural teaching materials, journals, departments
and organizations was doomed to be myopic, failing to address the issues around
which blacks themselves were to organize.

From containment to policing

In 1971, Bernard Coard published the results of his research that exploded the
myth of education for 'equality of opportunity'. He revealed the practices implicit
in theories of the deficiencies and disabilities of black children.

Thus the one way to ensure no changes in the social hierarchy and abundant unskilled labour is to adopt and adapt the educational system to meet the needs of
the situation: to prepare our children for the society's future unskilled and ill-paid
jobs. It is in this perspective that we can come to appreciate why so many of our
black children are being dumped in E.S.N. schools, secondary moderns, the lowest
streams of the comprehensive schools, and 'Bussed' and 'Banded ' about the school
system.[36]

This book, published for the Caribbean Education and Community Workers Association, made an intervention in educational debate and gave many black parents an understanding of what was happening to their children in British schools. Until then many black parents had been led to believe, by head teachers and local education authorities, that special education was 'special' in the sense of giving their children additional educational advantages to succeed.

Many white, liberal teachers were shocked by the results of Coard's research and the early seventies saw a rapid increase in the production of research projects, reports, policy documents and teaching materials focusing upon the black child. Concern with language and numbers remained whilst approaches to a multicultural content in curricula expanded in number. It is beyond the scope of this chapter to include an inventory of all policy documents and reports concerning the black child in school but we will indicate the general trends and concerns and discuss any significant shifts or consolidations of policy and practice.

The National Association for Multiracial Education (NAME) was formed and issued its first journal *Multiracial Schools* in the autumn of 1971, indicating a commitment to concepts of cultural pluralism in its move from being the journal of the Association for the Education of Pupils from Overseas (ATEPO).

A Schools Council project on 'Teaching English to West Indian children' based at Birmingham University was tested during 1971–72 and published in the summer of 1972, with units designed to deal with the 'problems' arising specifically from West Indian dialect. The Schools Council Working Paper on Religious Education recognized a 'multifaith context' and two years later working paper no. 50 concentrated on curricular changes for a multiracial education.[37] The NFER undertook three major research projects: into the provisions made by local education authorities for immigrant pupils in England, in 1971; an investigation of 'the opinions of teachers as to the need for development of materials' and an identification of 'existing innovations', started in 1972; and, in response to a joint proposal of ATEPO, the NUT and NFER, research into education for a multiracial society, scheduled to last from April 1973–December 1976.[38]

The DES continued to be preoccupied with numbers, publishing the figures of New Commonwealth immigrant children in London and County Boroughs on 1 January 1970, in January 1971, and became increasingly concerned with forms of assessment. In the same year the DES Education Survey no. 10[39] tried to assess 'potential and progress in a second culture' but, because of Coard's work, also recognized that the practices of assessment were a contentious area in the acknowledgement of the 'currently highly sensitive issue of West Indian children inappropriately placed in E.S.N. Schools'.[40]

Completing the second phase of a three-phase research project for the DES, located at the NFER and entitled 'Educational arrangements in schools with immigrant pupils', Townsend and Brittain complained of the inaction of education authorities and schools in the face of the 'disturbing number of immigrant children underachieving'.[41] Judith Hayes was also located at the NFER researching into the 'educational assessment of immigrant pupils'.

What would seem to be a move from a concern with 'immigrants', as a distinct group, to a concentration on the wider aspects of a multiracial society was not, in fact, the significant change it appeared to be. We can see that a concern with language and assessment was shared by all the bodies participating in the above research. Though those preoccupied with developing multicultural curricular content expressed disquiet at culturally biased testing, the major concern was still the performance of the black child. Innovations in content were conceived as enabling the black child to improve his, or her, performance in ways that could be assessed. The social relations of power that sustained institutionalized racism and which are reproduced in the classroom were not seen as open to investigation. Content innovation concerned itself with 'ethnic' cultural forms only, or with the removal of racist stereotyping from school textbooks. Multiculturalism has reacted to racism as if it were limited to a struggle over forms of representation – a struggle over images – in an attempt to disguise the social relations of domination and subordination in which it is situated and which it reproduces. In place of an analysis of schooling as a mechanism for increasing direct social control over black communities, those who advocated the adoption of 'progressive methods' of teaching saw changes towards a multicultural curricular content as being the catalyst that would reverse the 'underachievement' of black school children.

It is necessary, here, to indicate the background against which 'progressive' support for the drive for the multicultural curriculum occurred. In 1960 the Albemarle Report on the Youth Service in England and Wales had associated a crime problem with a youth problem. In education the reaction to the 'youth crisis' of the sixties was to increasingly associate delinquency with 'educational failure' and, in turn, with the family and neighbourhood culture of the working class.[42] Two Central Advisory Committee reports, Crowther and Newsom, emphasized the influence of home background on children's performance in school and a third, the Plowden Report, recommended the diversion of extra resources to the deprived and disadvantaged.[43] The latter report endorsed 'progressive' teaching methods and advocated the creation of educational priority areas. However, in the process, remedial or compensatory strategies still placed the 'cause' of failure in the child and its family, in particular focusing upon inadequate mothering. We have already seen how the black mother was specifically addressed, as schools moved towards the kind of 'client' relationship towards the working class of the other social services.[44] As schools moved in between children and the working-class family, 'progressive' or child-centred methods were seen to be part of the strategy of compensation. Schools, it was suggested, should be part of their 'community', and should aim at involving the working-class mother to teach her state-approved methods of mothering and thus break the 'cycle of deprivation'. However, in relation to the white working-class family this type of intervention by the state was viewed as an interruption in the process of social reproduction not as a disruption of this process. The white working-class family was seen as a unit capable of reproducing required labour power with some modification. As we have already argued the black family was not, and has not been, considered a viable or desirable unit for social and cultural reproduction and, therefore, the state response has not been one of transformation but of negation. Changes in the immigration laws from immigrant to migrant status and the denial of black motherhood as constituting motherhood attest to this.

Thus, in arguing for the relevance of a multicultural curriculum to black children, 'progressive' supporters were an integral part of an interventionist approach. Liberal and progressive teachers were reluctant to acknowledge their role in the wider aspects of social control, but, in the face of increasing classroom resistance by black students, the introduction of a multicultural syllabus was an attempt to pacify the recalcitrant. Curriculum development was an essential part of trying to streamline the school curriculum to meet the needs of industry[45] but multiculturalism did not question the nature of the relation between black students in the classroom and their future position as labour. 'Progressive' teachers also failed to make the connections between their role, in what we have referred to as the management of the transmission of black culture, and the process *Unpopular Education* (1981) describes as 'the general manageability of labour' which 'could only be strengthened through a heightened manageability of and through education'.[46] Educational disadvantage was a waste of potential talent to industry, and educational disadvantage became more and more associated with black students.

In 1974, a White Paper, 'Educational disadvantage and the educational needs of immigrants', was published by the DES in direct response to the Select Committee on Race Relations's recommendations that ways be found to identify and prevent the growth of educational disadvantage. This report clearly illustrates ways in which state control over education and the curriculum was to be increased. Three units were to be established: an information centre, the Centre for Educational Disadvantage; an administrative sector, the Educational Disadvantage Unit; but most importantly, the Assessment of Performance Unit as a branch of the DES. This latter unit was to:

Promote the development of methods of assessing and monitoring the achievement of children at school and to seek to identify the incidence of underachievement.[47]

All black school children were identified as in need of increased centralized monitoring and assessment. This form of direct DES intervention contradicted the previous 'power sharing' role with local education authorities. It also confronted teacher professionalism which had tried to establish autonomy of control over curricular innovation. The multicultural curriculum came to be used as the last bastion of control that teachers had over curriculum innovations.[48] But so defensive was the battle against encroachment on the territory of professionalism that the links between direct centralized control and schooling for industry was ignored by teachers, some of whom were busily being 'multicultural' whilst really protecting the grounds for their own autonomy.

Teachers involved in multicultural teaching maintained that they were improving the self-concepts of black children, providing positive images and alleviating disadvantage. This role confirmed the importance of the autonomy of their position, their need to be professionals, and displays a liberal moral conscience of messianic proportions.

Self-concept research is saying to the teacher: you are the backbone of the educational system, not the social scientist or the armies of advisers and petty officialdom. The teacher is a force in the classroom and in the field of self-concept he [*sic*] is a force for good, given he [*sic*] has the will to experiment and succeed. Teachers can enhance self-concept through the provision of special curriculum materials . . . through developing experimental curriculum projects designed to enhance self-worth in children and in general through becoming more person-oriented in the classroom.[49]

The parallels with missionaries following in the wake of the armies of colonialism are more than metaphorical. Like missionaries these teachers have not examined their own racism in their preoccupation with their own spiritual regeneration through 'doing good' to black youth. Neither have they examined their own positions as agents of the state in a hierarchy of relationships in which they are in a position of control and ultimate authority in the classroom. It is in the lack of this form of analysis that 'anti-racist' teaching has become a mere substitute for political action.

The Bullock Report[50] of 1975 reinforced earlier recommendations that the role of the teacher and social worker be interrelated through its encouragement to teachers to visit the parents of children in their home. The 1976 Great Debate on Education formalized the parameters for debate upon the relation school/industry and the crucial role for the new assessment procedures.

In addition to establishing basic skills, the curriculum should enable children, as part of their essential general education, to understand the society of which they are a part, including the economics of everyday life and the role of industry and commerce in sustaining our standard of living.[51]

The application of the education/industry equation to schooling has been underestimated. Stuart Hall, in describing the 'major restructuring of the state apparatus' during this period, argued that

The D.E.S. has been set aside, and new state apparatuses capable of realising the equation in more immediate and practical forms, have moved into a central position in the field.[52]

The Great Debate, however, did re-emphasize the necessity for increased centralized control over the curriculum, through the DES and its new assessment units. The 1977 Green Paper, the product of this 'debate', outlined the tasks that schools were expected to undertake in the reproduction of a future, disciplined workforce in its advocacy of the core curriculum.

In addition to their responsibility for the academic curriculum, schools must prepare their pupils for the transition to adult and working life. Young people need to be equipped with a basic understanding of the functioning of our democratic political system, of the mixed economy and the industrial activities, especially manufacturing, which create our national wealth.[53]

What is actually involved in constituting 'life skills' will be discussed later, but it is important to note how ambivalent the notion of 'skills' becomes. Basic skills had previously been defined as the acquisition of the 3 Rs but has now been extended to include an understanding of the 'necessity' of capitalist modes of production and the importance of the reproduction of labour in a stratified form:

Young people need to reach maturity with a basic understanding of the economy and the activities, especially manufacturing activities, which are necessary for the creation of Britain's national wealth. It is an important task of secondary schools to develop this understanding, and opportunities for its development should be offered to pupils of all abilities.[54]

Teachers' autonomy over the curriculum was to give way to 'industry, the trades unions and commerce [who] should be involved in curriculum planning processes'.[55] Also recognized was the need for the collection of statistical knowledge 'essential for any effective policy' designed to meet 'the special needs of ethnic minorities'.[56]

The Green Paper, and the Great Debate which heralded it, were the last attempt at a 'corporatist' solution to the schooling/industry relation in 'crisis'. This shift towards a more direct relation between schooling and industry has allowed for the disciplining into the wage relation of a large sector of unemployed youth. During the present economic recession the education system has had to adopt this role in the absence of employment which had previously been the site in which this disciplining would take place.

The Select Committee on Race Relations, 1975-6, was concerned about black youth who seemed to be escaping this process of disciplining. It noted the 'reluctance of young West Indians' to use the services of the Manpower Services Commission (MSC) and the Careers Service because of what was termed 'alienation'. The Committee requested further information about this group 'which would be of help to the agencies in ensuring that their market arrangements are such as to meet their special needs'. The possibility of a group of youth who may escape the disciplining into the wage relation field obviously represents a threat to the state agencies of social control. And, we would argue, in relation to black youth it is increasingly becoming a priority that this disciplining occurs before they leave school and refuse to register as unemployed. Here, again, we see expressed the need for the increased monitoring of black youth. As well as statistical information the Select Committee suggested the need for 'intensive counselling', a process that was intended to follow the strategy of entering in between black youth and the black family.

Young West Indians even though they have been born and educated in this country, may be handicapped to the extent that the advice and information about employment opportunities available to them from their family, relatives and friends which is one of the main sources of finding jobs, will often be less complete than that available to other young people.[57]

It is not a lack of knowledge but the form of knowledge held within the black communities about the state of the labour market which is really threatening to the smooth reproduction of the black labour force. Older brothers and sisters are increasingly likely to have more information about unemployment than about employment. It is precisely to disrupt the flow of this sort of information within the black communities that the state finds it necessary to intervene under the guise of intensive counselling in an attempt to counter strategies for survival and the ways and means of resisting.

Concurrent with the staging of the Great Debate and public discussion of the aims and objectives of schooling, new practices of training were being established in the schooling/industry relation. Intervention was felt to be necessary in the period of transition from school to work. The Manpower Services Commission (MSC) through its Training Services Agency (TSA) expanded from training schemes in its own skill centres into massive representation in further education. The history of the formation of these agencies and courses and their relation to the phenomenon of growing youth unemployment has been thoroughly analysed elsewhere.[58] We do not intend to re-present those arguments here but to concentrate only upon the implications and consequences of these training practices for black youth.

As Dan Finn has emphasized in *Unpopular Education*, the MSC

in no way sees itself as engaged in a struggle against existing forms of class, sexual or racial privilege. Indeed, its activities to date simply reproduce and reinforce these fundamental distinctions emanating from the 'world of work'.

However, most research, so far, has concentrated upon the ways in which TSA (and later, YOP) training schemes transformed the role of further education, reproducing the class position of the youth enrolled. This research has ignored the gendered and racialized aspects of this training. Sheridan Welsh has exposed the ways in which research on the young unemployed has neglected the position of girls. She has pointed to 'the invisibility of unemployed young women who tend to be isolated in the home'. The MSC, Welsh feels, has only

paid lip service to women as a source of potential and untapped labour . . . the focus has been on the potential dangers of a large male unemployed population.[59]

Unemployment itself, argues Welsh, is generally regarded as a male 'problem' 'to the extent that the very term "the unemployed" has masculine overtones'.[60]

The aptitudes and capabilities that unemployed youth are seen to lack and the skills which are to be provided by Youth Opportunity Training Schemes are, in their very conception, sexually and racially specific. Very rarely do MSC or YOP reports specifically refer to black male youth or black or white young women. The discourse of their official documents abstracts a generalized category of unemployed youth. But this discourse already references common-sense divisions within the category, not only in terms of gender as Welsh indicates but also in terms of race. This form of training is not immune to the forms of common-sense racism which pervade society and which operate throughout the education system to structure its policies and practices. It would be naive to conclude that because the official discourse is abstract that in practice the experience of YOP's courses are the same for black and white, male and female youth. As we have seen above, 'the unemployed' has predominantly masculine connotations but within this wider categorization racialized divisions will function with consequences for the practices of being trained for industry/work. In terms of future careers Asian male youth are frequently categorized as holding unrealistically high aspirations. A training scheme consisting predominantly of this group will, as part of its function, attempt to make their aspirations 'more realistic'. The 'life-skills' that Asian young women are seen to need are usually considered to be minimal as it is assumed that they will disappear into wifehood and motherhood at a very young age, literally vanishing into their homes from which it is thought they will rarely emerge. In the careers service West Indian young women are thought to be most suitable for occupations as orderlies in the National Health Service and thus are encouraged to train for such jobs, the chosen few being channelled towards SEN nursing. Black youth are associated with low-paid, low-skilled jobs, jobs that their parents were encouraged to migrate to Britain to do. In common-sense terms, the relation has become 'naturalized'; shit-work is all that the sons and daughters of those who fill those positions now, can, will or want to do. A refusal to consent to this form of subordination is interpreted as a refusal to contemplate any type of labour.

The central contradiction remains. The MSC has predicated its courses on the assumption that an entry into the labour market will follow for its students. However, this is less and less the case and YOP's courses have to manage the potential and actual disaffection from the economic, political and social order that can arise from prolonged, structural unemployment. The 'skills' that it is necessary for these courses to inculcate, therefore, are not purely vocational. They also incorporate the instilling of what Dan Finn has called 'work socialization'.[61] This socialization process includes work disciplines: time-keeping, respect for work-place hierarchies and behaviour modifications.

Attempts to alter behaviour are thought to be particularly necessary for black youth, both male and female, but especially in the case of West Indian male youth. As was described in Chapter 2, they are thought to lack discipline of any sort and have a history of a lack of regard for authority. They are, therefore, key targets for attempts at behaviour modification. A study that was produced from Liverpool University reported that,

In Wolverhampton and Manchester, blacks had markedly better qualifications than their white peers. More that two-thirds had some qualifications on leaving school, compared with about one third of whites, and almost three times as many had some further education. Yet they had greater difficulty finding and keeping work.[62]

The reason offered to explain this dilemma is that black, particularly West Indian youth, have attitudes which are not attractive to potential or actual employers. We are offered yet more 'proof' that West Indian youth 'fail' to function in ways which could guarantee success. These attitudes become a prime cause of failing to achieve and, therefore, must be changed to make West Indian youth more acceptable to employers. YOP's courses thus become involved in the changing of these attitudes and attempt to mould black youth into an acceptance of their position at the bottom of the very hierarchy that rejects them. It would appear that it is the behaviour of black youth, the attitudes of defiance and resistance, that have come to be regarded as the least acceptable of the modes of behaviour of any sector of youth. It is precisely this group that have transformed their position of wagelessness from being one of subordination and complete demoralization into the basis for new forms of politicization: a questioning of the basis of the social formation itself.

The consequences of black youth unemployment for the social, political and economic order, are feared. Throughout MSC documents the 'alienation', work-refusal and non-registration of black youth is described as a potential and actual threat to the social fabric. The depth of this fear needs to be understood in the context of the entirety of black youth culture, which has been developed in the struggle against the demands of capital for certain forms of labour, being categorized as rebellious, anarchic and threatening. It is not an individual but a collective struggle and the fear is not fear of individual black youths whose mode of dress, style or way of talking are unacceptable to the status quo. Attempts to transform the behaviour and attitudes of black youth is a part of the rejection of their culture as a whole. Young adolescent West Indian women, for example, are frequently regarded by teachers as 'unfeminine'. Accused of being 'too loud', of 'flaunting' their sexuality as opposed to being demure but tempting, and of 'talking back' when they are being repressed, they 'fail' to reach Western standards of femininity. In practice, in relation to careers or job opportunities, West Indian girls are not regarded as suitable for work where an overt but malleable display of sexuality is required. These conditions apply to many office jobs where women are expected to display yet subordinate their sexuality, to flatter and amuse; to pamper a white, middle-aged male. Qualities thought desirable in racist ideologies of illicit sexuality and processed in the commodification of black female sexuality in international iconography, are deemed unsuitable for the glass-domed reception area of a merchant bank in the City of London (the black women will usually be found in the post room). Pratibha Parmar has outlined instances of racialized gender differentiation in MSC programmes.

Schemes under the Youth Opportunities Programmes . . . are another area in which

Asian girls are seen as 'problems'. Unemployment for Black school leavers is three times higher for young Black women than men. The prevalence of sex role stereotyping existing in the wider context of society is reflected in YOP schemes through gender appropriate training courses such as community service, sewing and typing for the young female trainees and building maintenance, carpentry and painting and decorating for the young male trainees. This gender ascribed job training is compounded by specific cultural and racial features in the case of Asian girls. One YOP scheme in Yorkshire trained the predominantly Muslim female trainees by taking them out to the park for walks, and their work placement consisted of them watching male trainees dig up old people's gardens.[63]

The MSC sustains the mythological reason for its existence; it aims to correct the disparity between the aptitudes of young employees and the demands of employers. Politically it cannot afford to acknowledge the contradiction underlying the organization of provision for the young unemployed; namely that it is not the failings of youth that determine the distribution and availability of jobs. Consequently, neither the MSC nor the YOP schemes question the gender, racial or class ascriptions that structure their courses. It is the labour force itself, not the British economic structure, that is seen to be the 'problem' and in need of transformation.

　　If, however, we posit the reverse of this formulation, we can argue that

An understanding of the differentiation of groups within the labour market, and of the relationships between these groups, is possible only through an examination of the forces which operate in the labour market. An understanding of the labour markets which exist must precede an explanation of the circulation of individuals within these markets.[64]

Certain practices of MSC training programmes can be seen to operate in line with theories that claim the existence of a dual labour market in Britain. Within this theoretical framework YOPs training could be seen to be a mechanism for the maintenance of the majority of blacks in the secondary labour market.

They are not chosen [trained?] for primary sector jobs because they are associated with secondary sector employee characteristics such as unreliability or low aspirations or because of anticipated hostility to them from other workers. By relegating them to secondary sector employment, the labelling becomes self-fulfilling.[65]

The training programmes themselves need to be investigated for the ways in which they reproduce and maintain a dual labour market and base their practices upon accepted social divisions of labour which are racist. Alternatively the application of the 'reserve army of labour' thesis can be revealing when applied to the MSC. In this case it can be seen as a direct intervention by a state agency to discipline youth into the wage relation, outside of actual employment. This would mean that the programmes were a part of an attempt to reproduce a transformed labour force, one that would be disciplined for future protracted periods of structural unemployment, and deskilled and available for use in possible future economic expansion.

Both these theoretical positions illuminate different aspects of MSC policies and practices and could be utilized in research that is needed into the reproduction of racially constituted gender roles through these training programmes.

The 1981 Youthaid review of the Youth Opportunities Programme recommended that

Black organisations should be encouraged to establish YOP projects so that young blacks whose pride and self image has been damaged by the experience of discrimination can work with black people in positions of leadership and authority. Such projects would also help to attract 'alienated' young blacks into the Programme.[66]

It would appear that the Youthaid review body have completely missed the point. Their suggestion sounds all too familiar, yet another 'encouragement to black people to acquiesce in their own exploitation'.[67] Whose interests do these YOPs courses serve? Is it, in fact, in the black communities' interests to participate in them at all? The forms of resistances of black youth that these schemes have been attempting to manage and control are not about merely entering a hierarchy and leaving it untouched, but transforming that hierarchy and the sets of social relations that are oppressive.

Conclusion

In 1980 the Inner London Education Authority (ILEA) launched a £1.6 m programme to provide disruptive units. Over fifty 'sanctuaries' had been established within schools for disruptive children, and fifty off-site centres were being established to cater for approximately 2000 pupils. In January 1981 a survey was demanded to establish the 'ethnic origins of children in units for disruptive children' because of their use as a ' "dumping ground" for blacks'.[68] Concerted action by black parents in Haringey led the local education authority to abandon its programme of establishing further disruptive units for the present.

Contemporary debate is still locked into a framework of assessing the educational 'failure' of the black child. Under-achievement is assumed and then tested to be proven. A general consensus appears to exist that testing will provide the 'evidence' needed to be able to make 'compensatory provision'; argument occurs only over how this testing is to be implemented. Black parents dissent and argue that their children now in school were born here and should no longer be treated as an alien sector of the school population. However, as we have seen, educational policy and practice actually constitutes black children as an alien group that present 'problems' that are external to 'normal' schooling. A recent report from the Assessment of Performance Unit recommends the testing of children of 'Afro-Caribbean' origin, 95 per cent of whom the report says were born here.

Though the unit's report gives no clue about which pupils would be included, it is understood that teachers would be expected to pick out such pupils by their appearance and on the basis of what they already know about their family. . . . West Indian children of Asian or Chinese extraction would be excluded and the unit has suggested that black African children can be distinguished by their names. Children of mixed marriages would be included if one of their parents was of West Indian origin.[69]

It was felt by the APU that such figures, however absurd the process of identification, would be useful to the Rampton Committee investigation into the 'Education of children from ethnic minority groups'.

The Rampton Committee was set up in 1979 in order to look at 'the educational needs and attainments of children from ethnic minority groups taking account, as necessary, of factors outside the formal education system relevant to school performance, including influences in early childhood and prospects for school leavers'.[70] In practice, however, its terms of reference in no way suggested that racism itself had to be analysed in order to explain the 'underachievement' of black pupils. In its submission to the Committee the Institute of Race Relations pointed out that:

Your terms of reference are concerned with the 'educational needs and attainments of children from all ethnic minority groups', particularly West Indian children. We feel, however, that an ethnic or cultural approach to the educational needs and attainments of racial minorities evades the fundamental reasons for their disabilities – which are the racialist attitudes and the racist practices in the larger society and in the educational system itself.[71]

The first interim report of the Committee was published in June 1981, under the title 'West Indian children in our schools'.[72] By then, however, the Chairman had been replaced by a person thought more amenable to routine policy analysis, and the Government had made it clear that social and political questions were not the main concern of the revamped Committee. These changes were a response to attempts by black members of the Committee to consider the place of racism as central to its considerations.

This is no place to consider the impact of the Rampton report, or the forthcoming Swann reports on the Asian communities, in policy and practice. The early signs are that the main result will be a reworking of the multiculturalist ideology and its further institutionalization in the educational system.[73] There is little likelihood, however, that governments are going to take seriously the view of blacks themselves that racism *is* the central issue. At one point in the Rampton report we find the following statement:

Many West Indians insisted to us that the major reason for the underachievement of their children at school was racism (racial prejudice and discrimination), and its effects both in schools and in society generally. Many other people who gave evidence mentioned racism as a contributory factor.[74]

But such ideas are not discussed in the body of the report itself, and they seem to have had little impact on the formulation of policy alternatives. By implication the report seems to be saying that with increased special provision and more multi-culturalism the problem of racism will disappear, at least from schools. In addition, by locating the source of racism in schools in the attitudes of teachers, Rampton failed to face up to the thorny problems of looking at the racism inherent in all state institutions.

Meanwhile – through an extension of the concept of 'community' (noted earlier) used in conjunction with more direct control and the linking of educational services with social services – the police are in the classroom with black students. Under the Birmingham Inner City Partnership Programme (1979–82) the sum of £30,000, subsequently raised to £50,000, per annum for three years, was provided to be used exclusively with the jointly supported 'Lozells Project'. The original area of the project was modified to include the Holte School and the Wallace Lawler Centre. The objectives were seen as follows

1. to enable the police to develop closer links with the community;
2. to encourage local residents to participate with statutory agencies in the solving of community problems;
3. to reduce crime and vandalism in the Project area.[75]

The policing of black communities has already been discussed. What we wish to point to here, is the close liaison between the police, the social services and the schools and to the association with the disciplining of black youth. It is interesting that modifications were made to include the Holte school, 80 per cent of whose pupils are black, in the light of police intentions. The police 'with the support of teaching staff, will seek to assist within the schools in developing law-abiding young people'.[76] The construction of the 'fear' of crime by black youth is used as a justification to police them in schools. Policing them in the classroom also aids with identifying and monitoring black youth on the streets.

The Lozells Project is not an exceptional instance but an illustration of the direct control being exerted through the practice of 'community relations'. The reaction of the police to a hoax telephone call describing a 'riot' at Archway School in London was to send six police cars and a helicopter! When the headmistress complained to the head of the juvenile bureau of the local police, she informed him that this police reaction had 'totally destroyed much of the good community relations work *you and I* have been doing through the school in the last 18 months months'.[77]

Community relations, or what is often referred to as a 'soft-centred' form of control, has replaced notions of integration.

The state, the police, the media and race relations experts ascribe to young blacks certain objective qualities, e.g. alienated, vicious little criminals, muggers, disen-chanted unemployed, unmarried mothers, truants, classroom wreckers etc. The youth workers, community workers, counsellors (teachers) and the rest start with these objective qualities as given, and intervene on the basis that through their operations they could render young blacks subjectively different, and make them people to whom those objective qualities could no longer be applied. When this is done in collaboration with control agents themselves, as in police–community liaison schemes, or instances in which professional blacks collaborate with schools in blaming black kids for their 'failure', it is interpreted as progress towards 'good community relations'.[78]

Multiculturalists had visions of classrooms as microcosms of a race relations paradise. Proponents of community policing strategies are concerned to reap a harvest of information from the seed-beds of schools and youth clubs. Meanwhile, black youth recognize liberal dreamers and the police for what they are and act. They determine the terrain on which the next struggle will be fought - the street, the day. Intensive policing of all areas of black life, domestic, public, social and educational testifies to the political strength and resilience of black culture. Black communities as a whole have withdrawn their consent to being governed in an increasingly authoritarian and racist way. Black youth have led the way in the redefinition of who's got the problem.

Acknowledgements

I wish to thank Valerie Amos for hours of fruitful discussion in the shaping of the ideas for this chapter and for being not only a friend but a sister. Andy Green also gave up much of his time debating with me the hotly contested issue of the role of multicultural and anti-racist teaching practices. I am sorry that I have not been able to do justice to his arguments but this chapter had to concentrate on our brothers and sisters struggling in the classrooms and outside rather than on the struggle of teachers. That story should appear somewhere – I hope he will write it.

Notes and references

1   Phil Cohen, 'Subcultural conflict and working class community', in Hall, Hobson, Lowe and Willis (eds.), *Culture, Media, Language* (Hutchinson 1980); S. Hall and T. Jefferson (eds.), *Resistance Through Rituals* (Hutchinson 1975); Angela McRobbie, 'Working class girls and the culture of femininity', in CCCS, *Women Take Issue* (Hutchinson 1975); Angela McRobbie, 'Settling accounts with subcultures', in *Screen Education*, no. 34 (Spring 1980); Paul Willis, *Learning to Labour* (Saxon House 1977).
2   Willis, p. 47.
3   Willis, p. 49.
4   CCCS Education Group, *Unpopular Education* (Hutchinson 1981).
5   Commonwealth Immigrants Advisory Council, *Second Report*, Cmnd 2266 (HMSO 1964).
6   DES, *The Education of Immigrants*, Circular 7/65, 14 June 1965.
7   ibid.

8   National Foundation for Educational Research, *Coloured Immigrant Children: A Survey of Research, Studies and Literature on Their Educational Problems and Potential in Britain* (NFER 1966), p. 167.
9   Stuart Hall, 'Racism and reaction', in *Five Views of Multi-Racial Britain* (CRE 1978), p. 24.
10   ibid., p. 28.
11   NFER, p. 171.
12   ibid., pp. 171–2.
13   ibid., p. 173.
14   ibid.
15   ibid., p. 174.
16   ibid., p. 169.
17   ibid., p. 173.
18   ibid., p. 177.
19   Ivor Morrish, *The Background of Immigrant Children* (Unwin 1971). See also: Sheila Patterson, *Dark Strangers* (Penguin 1965).
20   Stuart Hall, p. 29.
21   Select Committee on Race Relations and Immigration, 1968–9, *The Problems of Coloured School-Leavers* (HMSO 1969), p. 16.
22   ibid., p. 17.
23   ibid., p. 45.
24   ibid., p. 6–7
25   ibid., p. 10.
26   ibid., p. 10.
27   Jenny Bourne, 'The sociology of race relations in Britain', *Race and Class*, vol. XXI, no. 4 (Spring 1980), p. 336. Jenny, at this point in her article, elaborates upon the work of Deakin *et al.* and a mode of thought that informed the research of the Institute of Race Relations during this period.
28   N. Deakin, *Colour and Citizenship and British Society* (IRR 1970).
29   Ivor Morrish, pp. 87, 164 and 232.
30   Ivor Morrish, p. 90.
31   Select Committee on Race Relations and Immigration, p. 41.
32   Select Committee on Race Relations and Immigration, *Education Report* (HMSO 1973).
33   See H. V. Carby, 'Multiculturalism', *Screen Education*, no. 34 (Spring 1980), pp. 62–70; H. V. Carby, *Multicultural Fictions*, occasional stencilled paper no. 58, CCCS, Birmingham University (1980).
34   Alan Little and Richard Willey, *Multi-Ethnic Education: The Way Forward*, Schools Council Pamphlet no. 18 (1981).
35   Education Guardian, 'The mixture as before', *Guardian*, 10 March 1981.
36   Bernard Coard, *How the West Indian Child is made Educationally Subnormal in the British School System* (New Beacon Books 1971).
37   Schools Council Working Papers: no. 36, *Religious Education in Secondary Schools* (Evans/Methuen 1971); no. 50, *Multiracial Education: Need and Innovation* (Evans/Methuen 1973).
38   H. E. R. Townsend, *Immigrant Pupils in England: The LEA Response* (NFER 1971); Schools Council Working Paper no. 50; Schools Council, *Education for a Multiracial Society* (1976).

39   DES, 'Potential and progress in a second culture', *Education Survey 10* (HMSO 1971).

40   NAME, *Multiracial Schools*, vol. 1, no. 1 (1971).

41   ibid., vol. 3, no. 1 (1972).

42   CCCS Education Group.

43   Central Advisory Council for Education (CACE), *15 to 18*, Crowther Report (HMSO 1959); CACE, *Half our Future*, Newsom Report (HMSO 1963); CACE, *Children and their Primary Schools*, Plowden Report (HMSO 1967).

44   CCCS Education Group.

45   Miriam David, *The State, The Family and Education* (Routledge and Kegan Paul 1980), pp. 170–8.

46   CCCS Education Group.

47   DES, *Educational Disadvantage and the Educational Needs of Immigrants*, Cmnd 5720 (HMSO 1974).

48   Clara Mulhern, 'Multicultural education and the fight against racism in schools', in *Teaching and Racism* (ALTARF 1979).

49   Quoted in: Maureen Stone, *The Education of the Black Child in Britain: The Myth of Multiracial Education* (Fontana 1981).

50   DES Committee of Enquiry, *A Language for Life*, Bullock Report (HMSO 1975).

51   DES, *Educating our Children: Four Subjects for Debate* (DES 1976).

52   S. Hall, 'The great moving right show', *Marxism Today* (January 1979).

53   DES, *Education in Schools: A Consultative Document*, Green Paper, Cmnd 6869 (HMSO 1977), p. 41:18.

54   ibid., p. 22:5.2.

55   ibid., p. 35:7.5.

56   ibid., p. 44:10.41.

57   Select Committee on Race Relations and Immigration, *The West Indian Community* (HMSO 1976).

58   Merilyn Moos, *Government Youth Training Policy and its Impact on Further Education*, General Series: SP no. 57, CCCS, University of Birmingham; Dann Finn and Simon Frith, 'Education and the labouring market', in *The State and the Politics of Education*, Open University Educational Studies, E353, Block 1, Part 2, Unit 4 (Open University Press 1981); Dan Finn, 'The rise of manpower servicedom', in CCCS Education Group; Simon Frith, 'Education, training and the labour process', in Cole and Skelton (eds.), *Blind Alley* (Hesketh 1980); British Youth Council, *Youth Unemployment: Causes and Cures* (BYC 1977).

59   Sheridan Welsh, 'Unemployment in the transition from school to marriage of working class girls in the East End of London', in *Schooling and Culture: Gender and Education*, no. 8 (1980), p. 20.

60   ibid.

61   Dan Finn.

62   Diana Geddes, 'Young blacks' attitudes: a factor in lack of jobs', *The Times*, 11 August 1980.

63   Pratibha Parmar, 'Young Asian women: a critique of the pathological approach', in *Multiracial Education*, vol. 9, no. 3 (Summer 1981), p. 27.

64   M. D. A. Freeman and Sarah Spencer, 'Immigration control, black workers

and the economy', in *British Journal of Law and Society*, vol. 6, no. 1 (Summer 1979).

65 ibid.

66 'Quality or collapse', *Report of the Youthaid Review of the Youth Opportunities Programme* (Youthaid 1981).

67 Gus John, *In the Service of Black Youth: A Study of the Political Culture of Youth and Community Work with Black People in English Cities* (NAYC 1981).

68 *Guardian*, 2 January 1981.

69 *The Times Educational Supplement*, 16 January 1981.

70 Committee of Inquiry into the Education of Children from Ethnic Minority Groups, *Press Notice*, 14 July 1981.

71 IRR, 'Anti-racist not multicultural education', *Race and Class*, vol. XXII, no. 1 (Summer 1980), pp. 81–2.

72 *West Indian Children in Our Schools*. Interim Report of the Committee of Inquiry into the Education of Children from Ethnic Minority Groups, Cmnd 8273 (Chairman: Anthony Rampton) (HMSO 1981).

73 DES, *The Education of Children from Ethnic Minority Groups: Consultative Document* (HMSO 1981). A one-day conference on the Interim Report held in November 1981 seems to indicate a further watering down of some of Rampton's more critical arguments.

74 *West Indian Children in Our Schools*, p. 12.

75 West Midlands Police, 'Lozells Project: background and objectives', unpublished document, 1980.

76 ibid.

77 *Guardian*, 19 March 1981.

78 Gus John, p. 155.

6 White woman listen! Black feminism and the boundaries of sisterhood

Hazel V. Carby

I'm leaving evidence. And you got to leave evidence too. And your children got to leave evidence. . . . They burned all the documents. . . . We got to burn out what they put in our minds, like you burn out a wound. Except we got to keep what we need to bear witness. That scar that's left to bear witness. We got to keep it as visible as our blood.[1]

The black women's critique of *his*tory has not only involved us in coming to terms with 'absences'; we have also been outraged by the ways in which it has made us visible, when it has chosen to see us. *His*tory has constructed our sexuality and our femininity as deviating from those qualities with which white women, as the prize objects of the Western world, have been endowed. We have also been defined in less than human terms.[2] Our continuing struggle with *his*tory began with its 'discovery' of us. However, this chapter will be concerned with herstory rather than *his*tory. We wish to address questions to the feminist theories which have been developed during the last decade; a decade in which black women have been fighting, in the streets, in the schools, through the courts, inside and outside the wage relation. The significance of these struggles ought to inform the writing of the herstory of women in Britain. It is fundamental to the development of a feminist theory and practice that is meaningful for black women. We cannot hope to reconstitute ourselves in all our absences, or to rectify the ill-conceived presences that invade herstory from *his*tory, but we do wish to bear witness to our own herstories. The connections between these and the herstories of white women will be made and remade in struggle. Black women have come from Africa, Asia and the Caribbean and we cannot do justice to all their herstories in a single chapter. Neither can we represent the voices of all black women in Britain, our herstories are too numerous and too varied. What we will do is to offer ways in which the 'triple' oppression of gender, race and class can be understood, in their specificity, and also as they determine the lives of black women.

Much contemporary debate has posed the question of the relation between race and gender, in terms which attempt to parallel race and gender divisions. It can be argued that as processes, racism and sexism are similar. Ideologically for example, they both construct common sense through reference to 'natural' and 'biological' differences. It has also been argued that the categories of race and gender are both socially constructed and that, therefore, they have little internal coherence as concepts. Furthermore, it is possible to parallel racialized and gendered divisions in the sense that the possibilities of amelioration through legislation appear to be equally ineffectual in both cases. Michèle Barrett, however, has pointed out that it is not possible to argue for parallels because as soon as historical analysis is made, it becomes obvious that the institutions which have to be analysed are different, as are the forms of analysis needed.[3] We would agree that the construction of such parallels is fruitless and often proves to be little more than a mere academic exercise; but there are other reasons for our dismissal of these kinds of debate. The experience of black women does not enter the parameters of parallelism. The fact that black women are subject to the *simultaneous* oppression of patriarchy, class and 'race' is the prime reason for not employing parallels that render their position and experience not only marginal but also invisible.

In arguing that most contemporary feminist theory does not begin to adequately account for the experience of black women we also have to acknowledge that it is not a simple question of their absence, consequently the task is not one of rendering their visibility. On the contrary we will have to argue that the process of accounting for their historical and contemporary position does, in itself, challenge the use of some of the central categories and assumptions of recent mainstream feminist thought. We can point to no single source for our oppression. When white feminists emphasize patriarchy alone, we want to redefine the term and make it a more complex concept. Racism ensures that black men do not have the same relations to patriarchal/capitalist hierarchies as white men. In the words of the Combahee River Collective:

We believe that sexual politics under patriarchy is as pervasive in Black women's lives as are the politics of class and race. We also often find it difficult to separate race from class from sex oppression because in our lives they are most often experienced simultaneously. We know that there is such a thing as racial–sexual oppression which is neither solely racial nor solely sexual e.g. the history of rape of Black women by white men as a weapon of political repression.

Although we are feminists and lesbians, we feel solidarity with progressive Black men and do not advocate the fractionalisation that white women who are separatists demand. Our situation as Black people necessitates that we have solidarity around the fact of race, which white women of course do not need to have with white men, unless it is their negative solidarity as racial oppressors. We struggle together with Black men against racism, while we also struggle with Black men about sexism.[4]

It is only in the writings by black feminists that we can find attempts to theorize the interconnection of class gender and race as it occurs in our lives and it has only been in the autonomous organizations of black women that we have been able to express and act upon the experiences consequent upon these determinants. Many black women had been alienated by the non-recognition of their lives, experiences and herstories in the WLM. Black feminists have been, and are still, demanding that the existence of racism must be acknowledged as a structuring feature of our relationships with white women. Both white feminist theory and practice have to recognize that white women stand in a power relation as oppressors of black women. This compromises any feminist theory and practice founded on the notion of simple equality.

Three concepts which are central to feminist theory become problematic in their application to black women's lives: 'the family', 'patriarchy' and 'reproduction'. When used they are placed in a context of the herstory of white (frequently middle-class) women and become contradictory when applied to the lives and experiences of black women. In a recent comprehensive survey of contemporary feminist theory, *Women's Oppression Today*, Michèle Barrett sees the contemporary family (effectively the family under capitalism) as the source of oppression of women:

It is difficult to argue that the present structure of the family-household is anything other than oppressive for women. Feminists have consistently, and rightly, seen the family as a central site of women's oppression in contemporary society. The reasons for this lie both in the material structure of the household, by which women are by and large financially dependent on men, and in the ideology of the family, through which women are confined to a primary concern with domesticity and motherhood. This situation underwrites the disadvantages women experience at work, and lies at the root of the exploitation of female sexuality endemic in our society. The concept of 'dependence' is perhaps, the link between the material organisation of the household, and the ideology of femininity: an assumption of women's dependence on men structures both of these areas.[5]

The immediate problem for black feminists is whether this framework can be applied at all to analyse our herstory of oppression and struggle. We would not wish to deny that the family can be a source of oppression for us but we also wish to examine how the black family has functioned as a prime source of resistance to oppression. We need to recognize that during slavery, periods of colonialism and under the present authoritarian state, the black family has been a site of political and cultural resistance to racism. Furthermore, we cannot easily separate the two forms of oppression because racist theory and practice is frequently gender-specific. Ideologies of black female sexuality do not stem primarily from the black family. The way the gender of black women is constructed differs from constructions of white femininity because it is also subject to racism. Black feminists have been explaining this since the last century when Sojourner Truth pointed to the ways in which 'womanhood' was denied the black woman.

That man over there says women need to be helped into carriages, and lifted over ditches, and to have the best place everywhere. Nobody ever helps me into carriages, and lifted over ditches, or over mud-puddles, or gives me any best place! And aint I a woman? Look at me! Look at my arm! I have ploughed, and planted, and gathered into barns, and no man could head me! And aint I a woman? I could work as much and eat as much as a man – when I could get it – and bear the lash as well!

And aint I a woman? I have borne thirteen children, and seen most all sold off to slavery, and when I cried with my mother's grief, none but Jesus heard me! And aint I a woman?[6]

In our earlier examination of common sense we indicated the racist nature of ideologies of black female sexuality. Black women are constantly challenging these ideologies in their day-to-day struggles. Asian girls in schools, for example, are fighting back to destroy the racist mythology of their femininity. As Pratibha Parmar has pointed out, careers officers do not offer them the same interviews and job opportunities as white girls. This is because they believe that Asian girls will be forced into marriage immediately after leaving school. The common-sense logic of this racism dictates that a career for Asian girls is thought to be a waste of time. But the struggle in schools is not just against the racism of the careers service:

'Yes, and then there are some racist students who are always picking on us. Recently, we had a fight in our school between us and some white girls. We really showed them we were not going to stand for their rubbish.'
Sangeeta and Wahida's statements reflect a growing confidence and awareness amongst young Asian girls about themselves and their situations in a climate of increased racist attacks on black people generally.
Many Asian girls strongly resent being stereotyped as weak, passive, quiet girls, who would not dare lift a finger in their own defence. They want to challenge the idea people have of them as girls 'who do not want to stand out or cause trouble but to tip-toe about hoping nobody will notice them'.[7]

The use of the concept of 'dependency' is also a problem for black feminists. It has been argued that this concept provides the link between the 'material organisation of the household, and the ideology of femininity'. How then can we account for situations in which black women maybe heads of households, or where, because of an economic system which structures high black male unemployment, they are not financially dependent upon a black man? This condition exists in both colonial and metropolitan situations. Ideologies of black female domesticity and motherhood have been constructed, through their employment (or chattel position) as domestics and surrogate mothers to white families rather than in relation to their own families. West Indian women still migrate to the United States and Canada as domestics and in Britain are seen to be suitable as office cleaners, National Health Service domestics, etc. In colonial situations Asian women have frequently been forced into prostitution to sexually service the white male invaders, whether in the form of armies of occupation or employees and guests of multinational corporations. How then, in view of all this, can it be argued that black male dominance exists in the same forms as white male dominance? Systems of slavery, colonialism, imperialism, have systematically denied positions in the white male hierarchy to black men and have used specific forms of terror to oppress them.

Black family structures have been seen as pathological by the state and are in the process of being constructed as pathological within white feminist theory. Here, ironically, the Western nuclear family structure and related ideologies of 'romantic love' formed under capitalism, are seen as more 'progressive' than black family structures. An unquestioned common-sense racism constructs Asian girls and women as having absolutely no freedom, whereas English girls are thought to be in a more 'liberated' society and culture. However, one Asian schoolgirl points out:

Where is the freedom in going to a disco, frightened in case no boy fancies you, or no one asks you to dance, or your friends are walked home with boys and you have to walk home in the dark alone?[8]

The media's 'horror stories' about Asian girls and arranged marriages bear very little relation to their experience. The 'feminist' version of this ideology presents Asian women as being in need of liberation, not in terms of their own herstory and needs, but *into* the 'progressive' social mores and customs of the metropolitan West. The actual struggles that Asian women are involved in are ignored in favour of applying theories from the point of view of a more 'advanced', more 'progressive' outside observer. In fact, as has been seen in Chapter 2, it is very easy for this ideology to be taken up and used by the state in furtherance of their racist and sexist practices. The way in which the issue of arranged marriages has been used by the government to legitimate increased restrictions on immigration from the sub-continent is one example of this process.

Too often concepts of historical progress are invoked by the left and feminists alike, to create a sliding scale of 'civilized liberties'. When barbarous sexual practices are to be described the 'Third World' is placed on display and compared to the 'First World' which is seen as more 'enlightened' or 'progressive'. The metropolitan centres of the West define the questions to be asked of other social systems and, at the same time, provide the measure against which all 'foreign' practices are gauged. In a peculiar combination of Marxism and feminism, capitalism becomes the vehicle for reforms which allow for progress towards the emancipation of women. The 'Third World', on the other hand, is viewed as retaining pre-capitalist forms expressed at the cultural level by traditions which are more oppressive to women. For example, in an article comparing socialist societies, Maxine Molyneux falls straight into this trap of 'Third Worldism' as 'backwardness'.

A second major problem facing Third World post-revolutionary states is the weight of conservative ideologies and practices; this is often subsumed in official literature under the categories of 'traditionalism' or 'feudal residues'. The impact and nature of 'traditionalism' is subject to considerable variation between countries but where it retains any force it may constitute an obstacle to economic and social development which has to be overcome in the formation of a new society. In some societies customary practices tend to bear especially heavily on women. Institutions such as polygyny, the brideprice, child marriages, seclusion, and forms of mutilation such as footbinding or female 'circumcision' are woven into the very fabric of pre-capitalist societies. They often survive in Third World countries long after they have been made illegal and despite the overall changes that have occurred.[9]

Maxine Molyneux sees 'systems of inheritance and arranged marriages' as being one of the central ways 'by which forms of pre-capitalist property and social relations are maintained'.

One immediate problem with this approach is that it is extraordinarily general. The level of generality applied to the 'Third World' would be dismissed as too vague to be informative if applied to Western industrialized nations. However, Molyneux implies that since 'Third World' women are outside of capitalist relations of production, entering capitalist relations is, necessarily, an emancipating move.

> There can be little doubt that on balance the position of women within imperialist, i.e. advanced capitalist societies is, for all its limitations, more advanced than in the less developed capitalist and non-capitalist societies. In this sense the changes brought by imperialism to Third World societies may, in some circumstances, have been historically progressive.[10]

This view of imperialism will be addressed in more detail later in the chapter. At this point we wish to indicate that the use of such theories reinforces the view that when black women enter Britain they are moving into a more liberated or enlightened or emancipated society than the one from which they have come. Nancy Foner saw the embodiment of West Indian women's increased freedom and liberation in Britain in the fact that they learned to drive cars![11] Different herstories, different struggles of black women against systems that oppress them are buried beneath Eurocentric conceptions of their position. Black family structures are seen as being produced by less advanced economic systems and their extended kinship networks are assumed to be more oppressive to women. The model of the white nuclear family, which rarely applies to black women's situation, is the measure by which they are pathologized and stands as a more progressive structure to the one in which they live.

It can be seen from this brief discussion of the use of the concept 'the family' that the terms 'patriarchy' and 'reproduction' also become more complex in their application. It bears repetition that black men have not held the same patriarchal positions of power that the white males have established. Michèle Barrett argues that the term patriarchy has lost all analytic or explanatory power and has been reduced to a synonym for male dominance. She tries therefore to limit its use to a specific type of male dominance that could be located historically.

> I would not . . . want to argue that the concept of patriarchy should be jettisoned. I would favour retaining it for use in contexts where male domination is expressed through the power of the father over women and over younger men. . . . Hence I would argue for a more precise and specific use of the concept of patriarchy, rather than one which expands it to cover all expressions of male domination and thereby attempts to construe a descriptive term as a systematic explanatory theory.[12]

Barrett is not thinking of capitalist social organization. But if we try to apply this more 'classic' and limited definition of patriarchy to the slave systems of the Americas and the Caribbean, we find that even this refined use of the concept cannot adequately account for the fact that both slaves and manumitted males did not have this type of patriarchal power. Alternatively, if we take patriarchy and apply it to various colonial situations it is equally unsatisfactory because it is unable to explain why black males have not enjoyed the benefits of white patriarchy. There are very obvious power structures in both colonial and slave social formations and they are predominantly patriarchal. However, the historically specific forms of racism force us to modify or alter the application of the term 'patriarchy' to black men. Black women have been dominated 'patriarchally' in different ways by men of different 'colours'.

In questioning the application of the concepts of 'the family' and 'patriarchy' we also need to problematize the use of the concept of 'reproduction'. In using this concept in relation to the domestic labour of black women we find that in spite of its apparent simplicity it must be dismantled. What does the concept of reproduction mean in a situation where black women have done domestic labour outside of their own homes in the servicing of white families? In this example they lie outside of the industrial wage relation but in a situation where they are providing for the reproduction of black labour in their own domestic sphere, simultaneously ensuring the reproduction of white labour power in the 'white' household. The concept, in fact, is unable to explain exactly what the relations are that need to be revealed. What needs to be understood is, first, precisely *how* the black woman's role in a rural, industrial or domestic labour force affects the construction of ideologies of black female sexuality which are different from, and often constructed in opposition to, white female sexuality; and second, how this role relates to the black woman's struggle for control over her own sexuality.[13]

If we examine the recent herstory of women in post-war Britain we can see the ways in which the inclusion of black women creates problems for hasty generalization. In pointing to the contradiction between 'home-making as a career' and the campaign to recruit women into the labour force during post-war reconstruction, Elizabeth Wilson fails to perceive migration of black women to Britain as the solution to these contradictory needs. The Economic Survey for 1947 is cited as an example of the ways in which women were seen to form 'the only large reserve of labour left'; yet, as we know, there was a rather large pool of labour in the colonies that had been mobilized previously to fight in World War II. The industries that the survey listed as in dire need of labour included those that were filled by both male and female black workers, though Elizabeth Wilson does not differentiate them.

The survey gave a list of the industries and services where labour was most urgently required. The boot and shoe industry, clothing, textiles, iron and steel, all required female workers, as did hospitals, domestic service, transport, and the women's land army. There was also a shortage of shorthand typists, and a dire shortage of nurses and midwives.[14]

This tells us nothing about why black women were recruited more heavily into some of these areas than others; perhaps we are given a clue when the author goes on to point out that women were welcomed into the labour force in a 'circumscribed way',

as temporary workers at a period of crisis, as part-time workers, and as not disturbing the traditional division of labour in industry along sex lines – the Survey reflected the view which was still dominant, that married women would not naturally wish to work.[15]

Not all black women were subject to this process: Afro-Caribbean women, for example, were encouraged and chose to come to Britain precisely to work. Ideologically they were seen as 'naturally' suitable for the lowest paid, most menial jobs. Elizabeth Wilson goes on to explain that 'work and marriage were still understood as alternatives . . . two kinds of women . . . a wife and a mother or a single career woman'. Yet black women bridged this division. They were viewed simultaneously as workers and as wives and mothers. Elizabeth Wilson stresses that the post-war debate over the entry of women into the labour force occurred within the parameters of the question of possible effects on family life. She argues that 'wives and mothers were granted entry into paid work only so long as this did not harm the family'. Yet women from Britain's reserve army of labour in the colonies were recruited into the labour force far beyond any such considerations. Rather than a concern to protect or preserve the black family in Britain, the state reproduced common-sense notions of its inherent pathology: black women were seen to fail as mothers precisely because of their position as workers.

One important struggle, rooted in these different ideological mechanisms, which determine racially differentiated representations of gender, has been the black woman's battle to gain control over her own sexuality in the face of racist experimentation with the contraceptive Depo-Provera and enforced sterilizations.[16]

It is not just our herstory before we came to Britain that has been ignored by white feminists, our experiences and struggles here have also been ignored. These struggles and experiences, because they have been structured by racism, have been different to those of white women. Black feminists decry the non-recognition of the specificities of black women's sexuality and femininity, both in the ways these are constructed and also as they are addressed through practices which oppress black women in a gender-specific but nonetheless racist way.

This non-recognition is typified by a very interesting article on women in Third World manufacturing by Diane Elson and Ruth Pearson. In analysing the employment of Third World women in world market factories they quote from an investment brochure designed to attract foreign firms:

The manual dexterity of the oriental female is famous the world over. Her hands are small and she works fast with extreme care. Who, therefore, could be better qualified by *nature and inheritance* to contribute to the efficiency of a bench-assembly production line than the oriental girl?[17] (original emphasis)

The authors, however, analyse only the naturalization of gender and ignore the specificity signalled by the inclusion of the adjective 'oriental', as if it didn't matter. The fact that the sexuality of the 'oriental' woman is being differentiated, is not commented upon and remains implicit rather than explicit as in the following remarks.

It is in the context of the subordination of women as a gender that we must analyse the supposed docility, subservience and consequent suitability for tedious, monotonous work of young women in the Third World.[18]

In concentrating an analysis upon gender only, Elson and Pearson do not see the relation between the situation they are examining in the periphery and the women who have migrated to the metropole. This last description is part of the common-sense racism that we have described as being applied to Asian women in Britain to channel them into 'tedious, monotonous work'. Elson and Pearson discuss this ascription of docility and passivity and compare it to Frantz Fanon's analysis of colonized people, without putting together the ways in which the women who are their objects of study have been oppressed not by gender subordination alone but also by colonization. The 'oriental' sexuality referred to in the advertising brochure is one of many constructions of exotic sexual dexterity promised to Western male tourists to South East Asia. This ideology of 'Eastern promise' links the material practice of the move from the bench – making microchips – to the bed, in which multinational corporate executives are serviced by prostitutes. This transition is described by Elson and Pearson but not understood as a process which illustrates an example of racially demarcated patriarchal power.

If a woman loses her job in a world market factory after she has re-shaped her life on the basis of a wage income, the only way she may have of surviving is by selling her body. There are reports from South Korea, for instance, that many former electronics workers have no alternative but to become prostitutes. . . . A growing market for such services is provided by the way in which the tourist industry has developed, especially in South East Asia.[19]

The photographs accompanying the article are of anonymous black women. This anonymity and the tendency to generalize into meaninglessness, the oppression of an amorphous category called 'Third World women', are symptomatic of the ways in which the specificity of our experiences and oppression are subsumed under inapplicable concepts and theories. Black feminists in the US have complained of the ignorance, in the white women's movement, of black women's lives.

The force that allows white feminist authors to make no reference to racial identity in their books about 'women' that are in actuality about white women, is the same one that would compel any author writing exclusively on black women to refer explicitly to their racial identity. That force is racism. . . . It is the dominant race that can make it seem that their experience is representative.[20]

In Britain too it is as if we don't exist.

There is a growing body of black feminist criticism of white feminist theory and practice, for its incipient racism and lack of relevance to black women's lives.[21] The dialogues that have been attempted[22] have concentrated more upon visible, empirical differences that affect black and white women's lives than upon developing a feminist theoretical approach that would enable a feminist understanding of the basis of these differences. The accusation that racism in the women's movement acted so as to exclude the participation of black women, has led to an explosion of debate in the USA.

from a black female perspective, if white women are denying the existence of black women, writing 'feminist' scholarship as if black women are not a part of the collective group American women, or discriminating against black women, then it matters less that North America was colonised by white patriarchal *men* who institutionalised a racially imperialist social order, than that white women who purport to be feminists support and actively perpetuate anti-black racism.[23]

What little reaction there has been in Britain has been more akin to lighting a damp squib, than an explosion. US black feminist criticism has no more been listened to than indigenous black feminist criticism. Yet, Bell Hooks's powerful critique has considerable relevance to British feminists. White women in the British WLM are extraordinarily reluctant to see themselves in the situations of being oppressors, as they feel that this will be at the expense of concentrating upon being oppressed. Consequently the involvement of British women in imperialism and colonialism is repressed and the benefits that they – as whites – gained from the oppression of black people ignored. Forms of imperialism are simply identified as aspects of an all embracing patriarchy rather than as sets of social relations in which white women hold positions of power by virtue of their 'race'.

Had feminists chosen to make explicit comparisons between . . . the status of black women and white women, it would have been more than obvious that the two groups do not share an identical oppression. It would have been obvious that similarities between the status of women under patriarchy and that of any slave or colonized person do not necessarily exist in a society that is both racially and sexually imperialistic. In such a society, the woman who is seen as inferior because of her sex can also be seen as superior because of her race, even in relationship to men of another race.[24]

The benefits of a white skin did not just apply to a handful of cotton, tea or sugar plantation mistresses; all women in Britain benefited – in varying degrees – from the economic exploitation of the colonies. The pro-imperialist attitudes of many nineteenth- and early-twentieth-century feminists and suffragists have yet to be acknowledged for their racist implications. However, apart from this herstorical work, the exploration of contemporary racism within the white feminist movement in Britain has yet to begin.

Feminist theory in Britain is almost wholly Eurocentric and, when it is not ignoring the experience of black women 'at home', it is trundling 'Third World women' onto the stage only to perform as victims of 'barbarous', 'primitive' practices in 'barbarous', 'primitive' societies.

It should be noted that much feminist work suffers from the assumption that it is only through the development of a Western-style industrial capitalism and the resultant entry of women into waged labour that the potential for the liberation of women can increase. For example, foot-binding, clitoridectomy, female 'circumcision' and other forms of mutilation of the female body have been described as 'feudal residues', existing in economically 'backward' or 'underdeveloped' nations (i.e. not the industrialized West). Arranged marriages, polygamy and these forms of mutilation are linked in reductionist ways to a lack of technological development.

However, theories of 'feudal residues' or of 'traditionalism' cannot explain the appearance of female 'circumcision' and clitoridectomy in the United States at the same moment as the growth and expansion of industrial capital. Between the establishment of industrial capitalism and the transformation to monopoly capitalism, the United States, under the influence of English biological science, saw the control of medical practice shift from the hands of women into the hands of men. This is normally regarded as a 'progressive' technological advance, though this newly established medical science was founded on the control and manipulation of the female body. This was the period in which links were formed between hysteria and hysterectomy in the rationalization of the 'psychology of the ovary'.

In the second half of the [nineteenth] century ... fumbling experiments with the female interior gave way to the more decisive technique of surgery – aimed increasingly at the control of female personality disorders. ... The last clitoridectomy we know of in the United States was performed in 1948 on a child of five, as a cure for masturbation.
The most common form of surgical intervention in the female personality was ovariotomy, removal of the ovaries – or 'female castration'. In 1906 a leading gynecological surgeon estimated that there were 150,000 women in the United States who had lost their ovaries under the knife. Some doctors boasted that they had removed from fifteen hundred to two thousand ovaries apiece. ... it should not be imagined that poor women were spared the gynecologist's exotic catalog of tortures simply because they couldn't pay. The pioneering work in gynecological surgery had been performed by Marion Sims on black female slaves he kept for the sole purpose of surgical experimentation. He operated on one of them thirty times in four years.[25]

These operations are hardly rituals left over from a pre-capitalist mode of production. On the contrary, they have to be seen as part of the 'technological' advance in what is now commonly regarded as the most 'advanced' capitalist economy in the world. Both in the USA and in Britain, black women still have a 'role' – as in the use of Depo-Provera on them – in medical experimentation. Outside of the metropoles, black women are at the mercy of the multinational drug companies, whose quest for profit is second only to the cause of 'advancing' Western science and medical knowledge.

The herstory of black women is interwoven with that of white women but this does not mean that they are the same story. Nor do we need white feminists to write our herstory for us, we can and are doing that for ourselves. However, when they write their herstory and call it the story of women but ignore our lives and deny their relation to us, that is the moment in which they are acting within the relations of racism and writing *his*tory.

Constructing alternatives

It should be an imperative for feminist herstory and theory to avoid reproducing the structural inequalities that exist between the 'metropoles' and the 'peripheries', and within the 'metropoles' between black and white women, in the form of inappropriate polarizations between the 'First' and 'Third World', developed/ underdeveloped or advanced/backward. We have already argued that the generalizations made about women's lives across societies in the African and Asian continents, would be thought intolerable if applied to the lives of white women in Europe or North America. These are some of the reasons why concepts which allow for specificity, whilst at the same time providing cross-cultural reference points – not based in assumptions of inferiority – are urgently needed in feminist work. The work of Gayle Rubin and her use of discrete 'sex/gender systems' appears to provide such a potential, particularly in the possibility of applying the concept within as well as between societies. With regard to the problems with the concept of patriarchy discussed above, she has made the following assessment:

The term 'patriarchy' was introduced to distinguish the forces maintaining sexism from other social forces, such as capitalism. But the use of 'patriarchy' obscures other distinctions.[26]

In arguing for an alternative formulation Gayle Rubin stresses the importance of maintaining,

a distinction between the human capacity and necessity to create a sexual world, and the empirically oppressive ways in which sexual worlds have been organized. Patriarchy subsumes both meanings into the same term. Sex/gender system, on the other hand, is a neutral term which refers to the domain and indicates that oppression is not inevitable in that domain, but is the product of the specific social relations which organize it.[27]

This concept of sex/gender systems offers the opportunity to be historically and culturally specific but also points to the position of relative autonomy of the sexual realm. It enables the subordination of women to be seen as a 'product of the relationships by which sex and gender are organized and produced'.[28] Thus, in order to account for the development of specific forms of sex/gender systems, reference must be made not only to the mode of production but also to the complex totality of specific social formations within which each system develops. Gayle Rubin argues that kinship relations are visible, empirical forms of sex/gender systems. Kinship relations here is not limited to biological relatives but is rather a 'system of categories and statuses which often contradict actual genetic relationships'.

What are commonly referred to as 'arranged marriages' can, then, be viewed as the way in which a particular sex/gender system organizes the 'exchange of women'. Similarly, transformations of sex/gender systems brought about by colonial oppression, and the changes in kinship patterns which result from migration, must be assessed on their own terms, not just in comparative relation to other sex/gender systems. In this way patterns of subordination of women can be understood historically, rather than being dismissed as the inevitable product of pathological family structures.

At this point we can begin to make concrete the black feminist plea to white feminists to begin with our different herstories. Contact with white societies has not generally led to a more 'progressive' change in African and Asian sex/gender systems. Colonialism attempted to destroy kinship patterns that were not modelled on nuclear family structures, disrupting, in the process, female organizations that were based upon kinship systems which allowed more power and autonomy to women than those of the colonizing nation. Events that occurred in the Calabar and Owerri provinces of Southern Nigeria in the winter months of 1929 bear witness to this disruption and to the consequent weakening of women's position. As Judith Van Allen points out, these events are known in Western social science literature as the 'Aba Riots', a term which not only marginalizes the struggles themselves but which makes invisible the involvement of Igbo women. 'Riots' implies unsystematic and mindless violence and is a perfect example of the constructions of *history*. The Igbo people on the other hand remember this conflict as Ogu Umuniwanyi (the 'Women's War').[29]

In November of 1929, thousands of Igbo women . . . converged on the Native Administration centers. . . . The women chanted, danced, sang songs of ridicule, and demanded the caps of office (the official insignia) of the Warrant Chiefs, the Igbo chosen from each village by the British to sit as members of the Native Court. At a few locations the women broke into prisons and released prisoners. Sixteen Native Courts were attacked, and most of these were broken up or burned. The 'disturbed area' covered about 6000 square miles and contained about two million people. It is not known how many women were involved, but the figure was in tens of thousands. On two occasions, British District Officers called in police and troops, who fired on the women and left a total of more than 50 dead and 50 wounded. No one on the other side was seriously injured.[30]

Judith Van Allen examines in detail the women's organizations that ensured and regulated women's political, economic and religious role in traditional Igbo society. Although their role was not equal to that of men they did have 'a series of roles – despite the patrilineal organization of Igbo society'.[31] Two of the associations that Judith Van Allen finds relevant were the *inyemedi*, or wives of a lineage, and the *umuada* – daughters of a lineage. Meetings of the *umuada* would 'settle intralineage disputes among their 'brothers' as well as disputes between their natal and marital lineages'. Since these gatherings were held in rotation among the villages into which members had married, 'they formed an important part of the communication network of Igbo women'. *Inyemedi*, on the other hand, came together in villagewide gatherings called *mikri*, gatherings of women who were in common residence rather than from a common place of birth (*ogbo*).

The *mikri* appears to have performed the major role in the daily self-rule among women and to have articulated women's interests as opposed to those of men. *Mikri* provided women with a forum in which to develop their political talents and with a means for protecting their interests as traders, farmers, wives and mothers.[32]

Men recognized the legitimacy of the decisions and rules of the *mikri*, which not only settled disputes among women but also imposed rules and sanctions which directly affected men's behaviour. The *mikri* could impose fines for violations of their decisions, and if these were ignored, women would 'sit on' an offender or go on strike.

To 'sit on' or 'make war on' a man involved gathering at his compound at a previously agreed upon time, dancing, singing scurrilous songs detailing the women's grievances against him (and often insulting him along the way by calling his manhood into question), banging on his hut with pestles for pounding yams, and in extreme cases, tearing up his hut (which usually meant pulling the roof off).[33]

A strike, on the other hand, 'might involve refusing to cook, to take care of small children or to have sexual relations with their husbands'.[34]

British colonizers in Nigeria dismissed all traditional forms of social organization that they found as 'organized anarchy', and promptly imposed a system of administration that ignored female political structures and denied Igbo women any means of representation, leave alone any decision-making or rule instituting power. Coming from sex/gender systems of Britain in the 1920s these colonial males could not conceive of the type of autonomy that Igbo women claimed. When the women demanded that they should serve on the Native Courts, be appointed to positions as District Officers, and further that 'all white men should go to their own country', they were scoffed at by the British who thought they acted under the influence of 'savage passions'. Their demands were viewed as totally irrational. The war waged by Igbo women against the British was a concerted organized mobilization of their political traditions. The fruits of colonialism were the imposition of class and gender relations which resulted in the concentration of national, economic and political power in the hands of a small, wealthy elite. We have quoted at length this example from the herstory of Igbo women, in order to illustrate the ways in which an unquestioning application of liberal doses of Eurocentricity can completely distort and transform herstory into *history*. Colonialism was not limited to the imposition of economic, political and religious systems. More subtly, though just as effectively, it sedimented racist and sexist norms into traditional sex/gender systems. Far from introducing more 'progressive' or liberating sex/gender social relations, the colonizing powers as:

class societies tend to socialize the work of men and domesticate that of women. This creates the material and organizational foundations for denying that women are adults and allows the ruling classes to define them as wards of men.[35]

Karen Sacks, in her essay 'Engels revisited', examines the ways in which these class societies have domesticated the field of activity for women to the extent that 'through their labour men are social adults; women are domestic wards'.[36] Although this work agrees with much white feminist theory, which has focused on the isolation of women within the nuclear family as a prime source of oppression in Western sex/gender systems, it does not necessarily follow that women living in kinship relations organized in different sex/gender systems are not oppressed. What it does mean is that analysis has to be specific and is not to be deduced from European systems. She goes on to explain that in India,

in Untouchable tenant-farming and village-service castes or classes, where women work today for village communities . . . they 'have greater sexual freedom, power of divorce, authority to speak and witness in caste assemblies, authority over children, ability to dispose of their own belongings, rights to indemnity for wrongs done to them, rights to have disputes settled outside the domestic sphere, and representation in public rituals'. In short, women who perform social labour have a higher status *vis-à-vis* men of their own class than do women who labor only in the domestic sphere or do no labor.[37]

Unfortunately feminist research has neglected to examine the basis of its Eurocentric (and often racist) framework. In the words of Achola O. Pala:

Like the educational systems inherited from the colonial days, the research industry has continued to use the African environment as a testing ground for ideas and hypotheses the locus of which is to be found in Paris, London, New York or Amsterdam.[38]

Throughout much of this work, what is thought to be important is decided on the basis of what happens to be politically significant in the metropoles, not on what is important to the women who are under observation. Thus, from her own experience, Achola Pala relates how the major concerns of women are totally neglected by the researcher.

I have visited villages where, at a time when the village women are asking for better health facilities and lower infant mortality rates, they are presented with questionnaires on family planning. In some instances, when the women would like to have piped water in the village, they may be at the same time faced with a researcher interested in investigating power and powerlessness in the household. In yet another situation, when women are asking for access to agricultural credit, a researcher on the scene may be conducting a study on female circumcision.[39]

The non-comprehension of the struggles and concerns of the African women, which Pala talks about, is indicative of the ways in which much Euro-American feminism has approached the lives of black women. It has attempted to force them into patterns which do not apply and in the process has labelled many of them deviant.

Another problem emerges from the frequently unqualified use of terms such as 'pre-capitalist' and 'feudal' to denote differences between the point of view of the researcher and her object of study. What is being indicated are differences in the modes of production. This distinction is subsequently used to explain observable differences in the position of women. However, the deployment of the concept sex/gender system interrupts this 'logical progression' and reveals that the articulation of relations of production to sex/gender systems is much more complex. 'Pre-capitalist' and 'feudal' are often redundant and non-explanatory categories which rest on underestimations of the scope and power of capitalist economic systems. Immanuel Wallerstein, for example, has argued that the sixteenth century saw the creation of

a world-embracing commerce and a world-embracing market . . . the emergence of capitalism as the dominant mode of social organisation of the economy . . . the only mode in the sense that, once established, other 'modes of production' survived in function of how they fitted into a politico-socio framework deriving from capitalism.[40]

Wallerstein continues to dismiss the idea that feudal and capitalist forms of social organization could coexist by stressing that:

The world economy has one form or another. Once it is capitalist, relationships that bear certain formal relationships to feudal relationships are necessarily redefined in terms of the governing principals of a capitalist system.[41]

There are ways in which this economic penetration has transformed social organization to the detriment of women in particular. Work on sexual economics by Lisa Leghorn and Katherine Parker demonstrates that the monetary system and heavy taxation that European nations imposed on their colonies directly eroded the status of women.

In many nations the impact of the sudden need for cash was more devastating than the steep taxes themselves. Only two mechanisms for acquiring cash existed – producing the new export crops and working for wages – both of which were made available only to men. Men were forced to leave their villages and farms to work in mines, plantations or factories, at extremely low wages. Women were often left doing their own as well as the men's work, while most of the men's wages went to taxes and to support themselves at the higher standard of living in urban areas. As men who remained on the farms were taught how to cash crop, most technological aid and education went only to them, and women were left maintaining the subsistence agricultural economy that sustained themselves and their children. In Africa women still do 70% of the agricultural work while almost all the agricultural aid has gone to men.[42]

We need to counteract the tendency to reduce sex oppression to a mere 'reflex of economic forces'[43] whilst at the same time recognizing that:

sexual systems cannot, in the final analysis, be understood in complete isolation. A full-bodied analysis of women in a single society, or through out history, must take everything into account: the evolution of commodity forms in women, systems of land tenure, political arrangements, subsistence technology, etc.[44]

We can begin to see how these elements come together to affect the lives of black women under colonial oppression in ways that transform the sex/gender systems in which they live but that are also shaped by the sex/gender system of the colonizers. If we examine changes in land distribution we can see how capitalist notions of the private ownership of land (a primarily economic division) and ideas of male dominance (from the sex/gender system) work together against the colonized.

Another problem affecting women's agricultural work is that as land ownership shifts from the collective 'land-use rights' of traditional village life, in which women shared in the distribution of land, to the European concept of private ownership, it is usually only the men who have the necessary cash to pay for it (by virtue of their cash-cropping income). In addition, some men traditionally 'owned' the land, while women 'owned' the crops as in the Cameroons in West Africa. As land becomes increasingly scarce, men begin to rent and sell 'their' land, leaving women with no recourse but to pay for land or stop their agricultural work.[45]

It is impossible to argue that colonialism left pre-capitalist or feudal forms of organization untouched. If we look at the West Indies we can see that patterns of migration, for both men and women, have followed the dictates of capital.

When men migrated from the islands for work in plantations or building the Panama canal, women migrated from rural to urban areas. Both have migrated to labour in the 'core' capitalist nations. Domestic, marginal or temporary service work has sometimes been viewed as a great 'opportunity' for West Indian women to transform their lives. But as Shirley-Ann Hussein has shown,

Take the case of the domestic workers. A development institution should be involved in more than placing these women in domestic jobs as this makes no dent in the society. It merely rearranges the same order. Domestic labour will have to be done away with in any serious attempt at social and economic reorganisation.[46]

If, however, imperialism and colonialism have ensured the existence of a world market it still remains necessary to explain how it is in the interests of capitalism to maintain social relations of production that are non-capitalist – that is, forms that could not be described as feudal because that means pre-capitalist, but which are also not organized around the wage relation. If we return to the example of changes in ownership of land and in agricultural production, outlined above, it can be argued that:

the agricultural division of labor in the periphery – with male semi-proletarians and female agriculturalists – contributes to the maintenance of a low value of labor power for peripheral capital accumulation through the production of subsistence foodstuffs by the noncapitalist mode of production for the reproduction and maintenance of the labor force.[47]

In other words the work that the women do is a force which helps to keep wages low. To relegate 'women of colour' in the periphery to the position of being the victims of feudal relations is to aid in the masking of colonial relations of oppression. These relations of imperialism should not be denied. Truly feminist herstory should be able to acknowledge that:

Women's economic participation in the periphery of the world capitalist system, just as within center economies, has been conditioned by the requirements of capital accumulation . . . (but) the economic participation of women in the Third World differs significantly from women's economic participation within the center of the world capitalist system.[48]

Black women have been at the forefront of rebellions against land seizures and struggle over the rights of access to land in Africa, Latin America and the Caribbean. Adequate herstories of their roles in many of these uprisings remain to be written. The role of West Indian women in the rebellions preceding and during the disturbances in Jamaica in 1938, for example, though known to be significant has still not been thoroughly described. White feminist herstorians are therefore mistaken when they portray black women as passive recipients of colonial oppression. As Gail Omvedt has shown in her book *We Will Smash This Prison*,[49] women in India have a long and complex herstory of fighting oppression both in and out of the wage relation. It is clear that many women coming from India to Britain have a shared herstory of struggle, whether in rural areas as agricultural labourers or in urban districts as municipal employees. The organized struggles of Asian women in Britain need to be viewed in the light of this herstory. Their industrial battles, and struggles against immigration policy and practice, articulate the triple oppression of race, gender and class that have been present since the dawn of imperialist domination.

In concentrating solely upon the isolated position of white women in the Western nuclear family structure, feminist theory has necessarily neglected the very strong female support networks that exist in many black sex/gender systems. These have often been transformed by the march of technological 'progress' intended to relieve black women from aspects of their labour.

Throughout Africa, the digging of village wells has saved women enormous amounts of time which they formerly spent trekking long distances to obtain water. But it has often simultaneously destroyed their only chance to get together and share information and experiences. Technological advances such as household appliances do not free women from domestic drudgery in any society.[50]

Leghorn and Parker, in *Women's Worth*, attempt to create new categories to describe, in general terms, the diversity of male power across societies. Whilst they warn against the rigid application of these categories – few countries fit exactly the category applied to them – the work does represent an attempt to move away from Euro-American racist assumptions of superiority whether political, cultural or economic. The three classifications that they introduce are 'minimal', 'token' and 'negotiating power' societies. Interestingly, from the black women's point of view, the most salient factor in the categorization of a country has

usually been that of women's networks, because it is the existence, building or dissolution of these networks that determines women's status and potential for change in all areas of their lives.[51]

These categories cut through the usual divisions of First/Third World, advanced/ dependent, industrial/non-industrial in an attempt to find a mechanism that would 'free' thinking from these definitions. Space will not allow for a critical assessment of all three categories but it can be said that their application of 'negotiating power' does recognize as important the 'traditional' women's organizations to be found in West Africa, and described above in relation to the Igbo. Leghorn and Parker are careful to stress that 'negotiating power' is limited to the possibilities of negotiating, it is not an absolute category of power that is held *over* men by women. The two examples of societies given in their book, where women hold this negotiating position are the Ewe, in West Africa, and the Iroquois. Both of course, are also examples where contact with the whites has been for the worse. Many of the Ewe female institutions disintegrated under colonialism whilst the institutions that afforded Iroquois women power were destroyed by European intrusion. In contrast to feminist work that focuses upon the lack of technology and household mechanical aids in the lives of these women, Leghorn and Parker concentrate upon the aspects of labour that bring women together. Of the Ewe they note:

Women often work together in their own fields, or as family members preparing meals together, village women meeting at the stream to do the wash, or family, friends and neighbours, walking five to fifteen miles a day to market together, sitting near each other in the market, and setting the day's prices together. They share childcare, news, and looking after each other's market stalls. In addition to making the time more pleasant, this shared work enables women to share information and in fact serves as an integral and vital part of the village communications system. Consequently, they have a tremendous sense of solidarity when it comes to working in their collective interest.[52]

It is important not to romanticize the existence of such female support networks but they do provide a startling contrast to the isolated position of women in the Euro-American nuclear family structure.

In Britain, strong female support networks continue in both West Indian and Asian sex/gender systems, though these are ignored by sociological studies of migrant black women. This is not to say that these systems remain unchanged with migration. New circumstances require adaptation and new survival strategies have to be found.

Even childcare in a metropolitan area is a big problem. If you live in a village in an extended family, you know that if your child's outside somewhere, someone will be looking out for her. If your child is out on the street and your neighbour down the road sees your child in some mess, that woman is going to take responsibility of dealing with that child. But in Brooklyn or in London, you're stuck in that apartment. You're there with that kid, you can't expect that child to be out on the street and be taken care of. You know the day care situation is lousy, you're not in that extended family, so you have a big problem on your hands. So when they talk about the reduction of house-work, we know by now that that's a lie.[53]

However, the transformations that occur are not merely adaptive, neither is the black family destroyed in the process of change. Female networks mean that black women are key figures in the development of survival strategies, both in the past, through periods of slavery and colonialism, and now, facing a racist and authoritarian state.

There is considerable evidence that women – and families – do not . . . simply accept the isolation, loss of status, and cultural devaluation involved in the migration. Networks are re-formed, if need be with non-kin or on the basis of an extended definition of kinship, by strong, active, and resourceful women. . . . Cultures of resistance are not simple adaptive mechanisms; they embody important alternative ways of organizing production and reproduction and value systems critical of the oppressor. Recognition of the special position of families in these cultures and social structures can lead to new forms of struggle, new goals.[54]

In arguing that feminism must take account of the lives, herstories and experiences of black women we are not advocating that teams of white feminists should descend upon Brixton, Southall, Bristol or Liverpool to take black women as objects of study in modes of resistance. We don't need that kind of intrusion on top of all the other information-gathering forces that the state has mobilized in the interest of 'race relations'. White women have been used against black women in this way before and feminists must learn from history. After the Igbo riots described above, two women anthropologists were sent by the British to 'study the causes of the riot and to uncover the organisational base that permitted such spontaneity and solidarity among the women'.[55] The WLM, however, does need to listen to the work of black feminists and to take account of autonomous organizations like OWAAD (Organisation of Women of Asian and African Descent) who are helping to articulate the ways in which we are oppressed as black women.

In addition to this it is very important that white women in the women's movement examine the ways in which racism excludes many black women and prevents them from unconditionally aligning themselves with white women. Instead of taking black women as the objects of their research, white feminist researchers should try to uncover the gender-specific mechanisms of racism amongst white women. This more than any other factor disrupts the recognition of common interests of sisterhood.

In *Finding a Voice*, by Amrit Wilson, Asian women describe many instances of racial oppression at work from white women. Asian women

are paid low salaries and everything is worse for them, they have to face the insults of supervisors. These supervisors are all English women. The trouble is that in Britain our women are expected to behave like servants and we are not used to behaving like servants and we can't. But if we behave normally . . . the supervisors start shouting and harassing us. . . . They complain about us Indians to the manager.[56]

Black women do not want to be grafted onto 'feminism' in a tokenistic manner as colourful diversions to 'real' problems. Feminism has to be transformed if it is to address us. Neither do we wish our words to be misused in generalities as if what each one of us utters represents the total experience of all black women. Audre Lourde's address to Mary Daly is perhaps the best conclusion.

I ask that you be aware of how this serves the destructive forces of racism and separation between women – the assumption that the herstory and myth of white women is the legitimate and sole herstory and myth of all women to call for power and background, and that non-white women and our herstories are note-worthy only as decorations, or examples of female victimisation. I ask that you be aware of the effect that this dismissal has upon the community of black women, and how it devalues your own words. . . . When patriarchy dismisses us, it encourages our murders. When radical lesbian feminist theory dismisses us, it encourages its own demise. This dismissal stands as a real block to communication between us. This block makes it far easier to turn away from you completely than attempt to understand the thinking behind your choices. Should the next step be war between us, or separation? Assimilation within a sole Western-European herstory is not acceptable.[57]

In other words, of white feminists we must ask, what exactly do you mean when you say 'WE'??

Acknowledgements

The debt I owe to my sisters, Valerie Amos and Pratihba Parmar, is enormous for the many hours we have spent discussing our experiences as black women and as feminists. Both contributed to the ideas in this chapter but any criticisms for inadequacies should be directed at me. To Paul, John and Errol, thank you for those transatlantic telephone calls – support and brotherly affection was regularly transmitted. To Susan Willis I owe especial thanks for her support and friendship in a new job and a new country. To faculty, staff and students at the Afro-American Studies Program at Yale and the Birmingham Centre for Contemporary Cultural Studies, thank you for your encouragement and enthusiasm for my work.

Notes and references

1   Gayle Jones, *Corregidora* (Random House 1975), pp. 14, 72.
2   Winthrop Jordan, *White Over Black* (Penguin 1969), pp. 238, 495, 500.
3   My thanks to Michèle Barrett who, in a talk given at the Social Science Research Council's Unit on Ethnic Relations, helped to clarify many of these attempted parallels.
4   Combahee River Collective, 'A black feminist statement', in Moraga and Anzaldúa (eds.), *This Bridge Called My Back: Writings by Radical Women of Color* (Persephone Press 1981), p. 213.
5   Michèle Barrett, *Women's Oppression Today* (Verso 1980), p. 214.
6   J. Loewenberg and R. Bogin (eds.), *Black Women in Nineteenth Century American Life* (Pennsylvania State University Press 1978), p. 235.
7   Pratibha Parmar and Nadira Mirza, 'Growing angry, growing strong', *Spare Rib*, no. 111 (October 1981).
8   ibid.
9   Maxine Molyneux, 'Socialist societies old and new: progress towards women's emancipation?', *Feminist Review*, no. 8 (Summer 1981), p. 3.

10   ibid., p. 4.
11   Nancy Foner, *Jamaica Farewell* (Routledge and Kegan Paul 1979). She also argues that:

> In rural Jamaica, most women do not smoke cigarettes; in London, many of the women I interviewed smoked, and when I commented on this they noted that such behaviour would not have been approved in Jamaica. Thus in England there is an enlargement of the women's world. (pp. 69–70)

12   Michèle Barrett.
13   See Chapter 7 for an elaboration of this point.
14   Elizabeth Wilson, *Only Halfway to Paradise: Women in Postwar Britain 1945–1968* (Tavistock 1980), pp. 43–4.
15   ibid.
16   OWAAD, *Fowaad*, no. 2 (1979).
17   Diane Elson and Ruth Pearson, 'Nimble fingers make cheap workers: an analysis of women's employment in Third World export manufacturing', *Feminist Review*, no. 7 (Spring 1981), p. 93.
18   ibid., p. 95.
19   ibid.
20   Bell Hooks, *Ain't I a Woman* (South End Press 1981), p. 138.
21   Much of this critical work has been written in America but is applicable to the WLM in Britain. Apart from the books cited in this chapter, interested readers should look out for essays and articles by Gloria Joseph, Audre Lourde, Barbara Smith and Gloria Watkins that represent a range of black feminist thought. In Britain, the very existence of the feminist Organisation of Women of Asian and African Descent (OWAAD) is a concrete expression of black feminists critical distance from 'white' feminism. See also: Valerie Amos and Pratibha Parmar, 'Resistances and responses: black girls in Britain', in A. McRobbie and T. McCabe (eds.), *Feminism For Girls: An Adventure Story* (Routledge and Kegan Paul 1982), who criticize the WLM for its irrelevance to the lives of black girls in Britain.
22   See: Gloria Joseph and Jill Lewis, *Common Differences: Conflicts in Black and White Feminist Perspectives* (Anchor 1981), for an attempt at a dialogue that shows just how difficult it is to maintain.
23   Bell Hooks, pp. 123–4.
24   ibid., p. 141.
25   Barbara Erenreich and Dierdre English, *For Her Own Good* (Doubleday Anchor 1979).
26   Gayle Rubin, p. 167.
27   ibid., p. 168.
28   ibid., p. 177.
29   Judith Van Allen, ' "Aba riots" or Igbo "women's war"? Ideology, stratification and the invisibility of women', in Nancy Hafkin and Edna Bay (eds.), *Women in Africa Studies in Social and Economic Change* (Stanford University Press 1976), p. 59.
30   ibid., p. 60.
31   ibid., p. 62.
32   ibid., p. 69.
33   ibid., p. 61.

34   ibid., p. 69.
35   Karen Sacks, 'Engels revisited: women, the organization of production, and private property', in Rayna R. Reiter (ed.), *Toward an Anthropology of Women* (Monthly Review Press 1975).
36   ibid., p. 231.
37   ibid., p. 233.
38   Achola O. Pala, 'Definitions of women and development: an African perspective', *Signs, Journal of Women in Culture and Society*, vol. 3, no. 1 (Autumn 1977).
39   ibid., p. 10.
40   Immanuel Wallerstein, *The Modern World System 1* (Academic Press 1974), p. 77.
41   ibid., p. 92.
42   Lisa Leghorn and Katherine Parker, *Women's Worth, Sexual Economics and the World of Women* (Routledge and Kegan Paul 1981), p. 44.
43   Gayle Rubin, p. 203.
44   ibid., p. 209.
45   Leghorn and Parker, p. 45.
46   Shirley-Ann Hussein, 'Four views on women in the struggle', in *Caribbean Women in the Struggle*, p. 29; quoted in Leghorn and Parker, p. 52.
47   Carmen Diane Deere, 'Rural women's subsistence production', in Robin Cohen *et al.* (eds.), *Peasants and Proletarians: The Struggles of Third World Women Workers* (Monthly Review 1979), p. 143.
48   ibid., p. 133.
49   Gail Omvedt, *We Will Smash this Prison* (Zed Press 1980).
50   Leghorn and Parker, p. 55.
51   ibid., p. 60.
52   ibid., p. 88.
53   Margaret Prescod-Roberts and Norma Steele, *Black Women: Bringing it all Back Home* (Falling Wall Press 1980), p. 28.
54   Mina Davis Caufield, 'Cultures of resistance', in *Socialist Revolution*, 20, vol. 4, no. 2, October 1974, pp. 81, 84.
55   Leis, 'Women in groups', quoted in Mina Davis Caufield.
56   Amrit Wilson, *Finding a Voice: Asian Women in Britain* (Virago 1978), p. 122.
57   Audre Lourde, 'An open letter of Mary Daly', in Moraga and Anzaldúa, p. 96.

7 Gender, race and class: Asian women in resistance

Pratibha Parmar

Introduction

Asian women have been at the forefront of numerous industrial, political and social struggles over the last decade. They have also been subjected to the full oppressive force of immigration legislation and institutional racism at all levels of British society. Yet, existing literature on black people in Britain has tended to ignore gender differences or to look at them through ethnocentric and pathological categories.[1] With the exception of a few recent studies,[2] there have been no serious attempts to analyse the role of women in the processes of migration and settlement, let alone the struggles against racism which have characterized the everyday lives of West Indian and Asian people in Britain.

The growth of the white women's liberation movement in the 1960s in Britain catapulted the question of women's subordination into the forefront of theoretical and political debates. But little attention has been given to the lives of black women and this is, in part, a reflection of the way in which black women have been either made invisible or marginalized in the theoretical and political spheres.

White feminist researchers have been correct in pointing to the 'disparity between the sophistication of analyses of the social formation in terms of class and the relative under-development of work on the structures of sex/gender'.[3] While there have been numerous attempts made to bridge this gap[4] there has been a glaring absence of an attempt to give race and racism any weight. It is totally inadequate for race to be merely tagged on by means of some colourful, cursory comparison with the structure of gender.[5] Furthermore, any attempts to address oneself to the complexities involved in the articulation of race, class and gender solely at a theoretical level yields very generalized observations which would be undermined by a lack of reference to specific instances. It is crucial that these observations are grounded in concrete and specific material situations. Attempts at outlining the concrete linkages between capital, patriarchy and race will serve not only to add theoretical clarity to some of the existing debates within Marxist and/or feminist discourse, but the political implications of such connections will hopefully give the political movements premised on any one of these determinations, insights into the particular oppression of black women.

The recent debate on 'the unhappy marriage between Marxism and feminism' has sprouted a significant amount of literature but as Joseph has correctly pointed out, 'the feminist question has never truly embraced "Black women", and that "incestuous child of patriarchy and capitalism", namely racism, is not acknowledged'. Therefore, it is necessary to appreciate that 'in a discussion of Marxism and the woman question, to speak of women, all women categorically, is to perpetuate white supremacy – white female supremacy – because it is white women to whom the comments are addressed and to whom the comments are most appropriate'.[6]

In the past the women's liberation movement has shown a tendency to ignore the struggles of black women, and, where visible, to treat them as simply another element of the campaigns in which white women are involved. They have thus failed to accommodate the specificity of black women's experiences of racism, which have been structured by *racially constructed gender roles*.

We have argued in the chapter on black women that any analysis of their social position in British society must operate at a number of levels, both inside and outside of work. It is important to look at employment, because of its central position in the reproduction of migrant workers. It is also important to look at how common-sense images of West Indian and Asian women have helped to socially construct certain roles for them in the labour market.

Chapter 2 has already developed the idea that the construction of common-sense ideas about black male and female sexuality plays a central role in reproducing racist ideologies, which in turn influence the kind of policies which the state pursues in the field of race relations. Here we want to take this argument further and show how these common-sense notions have particular effects on the ways in which the relation of Asian women to waged work is viewed.

The chapter is divided into three parts. First, there is a discussion of the interrelationship of class, race and gender in the political economy of black labour. Second, there is a historical account of the position of Asian women in the labour market, and a critique of culturalist explanations of their economic role. Third, there is a critique of certain common-sense images of Asian women through a historical account of some of the struggles and resistances they have organized in the last decade.

The political economy of migration and gender

The State takes on new tasks; first of all economically by regulating the ebb and flow of foreign labour power and then also politically by finding and carrying out new means of direct and indirect political oppression, and finally ideologically by trying to integrate, on a non-political basis, the immigrant workers selected to stay.[7]

Within advanced capitalist economies the migrant workers play an important economic role, particularly in the basic industries and in the service sectors. It is not surprising, therefore, that a huge volume of research has been carried out into various aspects of the role which migrant workers play, and on the political and social effects of large settlements of migrants in the major urban conurbations of most European countries.[8] In Britain this has taken the form of a sociology of 'race relations', with numerous studies of the housing, employment and educational implications of black workers entering Britain on a large scale during the fifties and sixties.[9] In both the European and British context there is a conspicuous absence of gender-specific studies which look seriously at migrant women in this whole process. There are numerous discussions of family life and culture which mention the existence of migrant women, but few serious *historical* accounts of their position.

As Nancy Foner comments in relation to West Indian women:

Those who are concerned about the manner in which urbanisation affects migrant women, have had to seek out those few pages or paragraphs in books and articles which explicitly analyse those women's experiences.[10]

Much of the recent race-relations literature uses categories which are gender-blind, or looks at women merely within the terms of a pathology of either West Indian or Asian family life. Although the impact of immigration legislation has important effects on black women it is still common to read accounts of the history of restrictions on the entry of black workers which totally ignore gender. More recently there have been a few notable attempts to develop critical analyses of the experiences of both Asian and West Indian women,[11] although these have had little impact on the main body of race-relations research.

The broad critique of pathological notions of the black family and culture developed in Chapter 2 can be applied more specifically in the case of attempts made by sociologists to look at the position of Asian women in Britain. In the work of authors such as Verity Khan we can find a sociology of Asian women which reproduces common-sense ideas about their passivity, the role of their husbands, and religious rules.[12] What these authors fail to do, however, is to look seriously at the ways in which the everyday and institutional racisms which permeate British society affect the position of Asian women.

The emphasis in the work of Khan and others is on the Asian communities themselves, rather than on the economic, political and ideological structures which reproduce Asian women as a specific class category. The hazards of this approach are that it becomes easy to blame cultural, religious and communal factors for the subordinate positions which Asian women occupy in the British social structure. It can, all too easily, become another variation on the theme of 'blaming the victim'.

Our concern in this chapter is to overcome the limits of this culturalist bias in existing research by looking at the roles of Asian women as waged workers, and how these are in turn determined by a racist patriarchal ideology based on common-sense ideas about Asian sexuality/feminity. It would be wrong, however, to see this as a simple assertion of the primacy of economic determinants over politico-ideological determinants. As we have argued in Chapters 1 and 8 the development of struggles around race and gender cannot be viewed as a simple epiphenomenon

of an immutable economic base. At the same time, we argue against traditional
sociological theories of race which locate racial/ethnic divisions in the labour
market as the result of discrimination, by firmly placing these divisions *within the
complex processes which produce and reproduce capitalist social relations*. Racial
and sexual divisions are not exogenous to the capitalist mode of production but
endogenous to it. As Stuart Hall argues:

One must start, then, from the concrete historical work which racism accomplishes
under specific historical conditions as a set of economic, political and ideological
practices, of a distinctive kind concretely articulated with other practices in a social
formation.

    These practices ascribe the positioning of different social groups in relation
to one another with respect to the elementary structures of society; they fix and
ascribe those positionings in on-going social practices; they legitimate the positions
so ascribed. In short, they are practices which secure the hegemony of a dominant
group over a series of subordinate ones, in such a way as to dominate the whole
social formation in a form favourable to the long-term development of the economic
productive base. Though the economic aspects are critical, as a way of beginning,
this form of hegemony cannot be understood as operating purely through
economic coercion.[13]

The value of this approach to racism need not be elaborated here for us to see that
the specific historical conditions of the last three decades should be the starting-
point of any analysis of the interconnections between race, class and gender.
Against Khan and the 'ethnicity school', therefore, the bulk of this chapter will
focus on the institutional power relations which oppress and exploit Asian women
and not on the specific socio-cultural features of Asian communities.

    The emphasis we place on locating racially constructed gender roles within the
broader structures of society should not be taken to mean that we see Asian women
as being at the mercy of these relations. It is also important to look seriously at
the resistance and struggles Asian women have participated in at their workplaces,
their communities, and households.

    Despite the force of racist stereotypes Asian women do not experience the
racism from which they suffer in a passive way. They have developed their own
forms of resistance, articulate their own ideas about British society, and rely on
their own historical cultural traditions as a means of support.

Migration and the state

The volume of migrant labour is not something to be taken as given but is created
and recreated by the State.[14]

The extent of immigration and the strategic role of immigration in the European
economy have to be explained, not in terms of the technical demands of production
but by the specific interests of capital in a particular phase of its development.[15]

One cannot look at the political economy of black labour without considering the role of the state in regulating labour power through the politico-legal mechanisms of immigration legislation. Without entering into the debate about the nature of the state it is sufficient for the present purpose to point to the role the state performs in maintaining conditions conducive to capital accumulation. One must guard against viewing immigration legislation purely as a control mechanism for the regulation of labour power thereby disregarding the political motivations for such controls. Nevertheless, it is crucial to consider two points – first, that there are specific ways in which immigration legislation has functioned in the interest of the accumulation of capital, and second, how legislation has affected Asian *women*'s lives. The importation of black labour in the post-war period was essential in trying to solve the labour shortage of the British economy.[16] This was parallel to the vigorous recruitment of women for sustaining the economy during World War II, when almost the entire population of adult women were drawn into wage labour.[17]

The position of black labour in this country has been substantially transformed since the fifties but it has always been the subject of specific types of political intervention. Although the model of the European migrant labour system, as typically represented in the experience of the German *gastarbeiter*, is not an exact replica of the system which has operated in Britain in various forms since the war, there are some similarities. But before discussing these, it is important to note some crucial differences. First, the group of workers who perform the economic function analogous to the European *gastarbeiter* are, in the main, black men.[18] Second, black migration to Britain up until 1974 was basically settler not migrant. This makes the unqualified use of the concept 'migrant labour' problematic. Its transitory connotations imply that black workers in Britain are in the same temporary position as the migrant workers in Europe, who do not have 'the right of abode' in the country where they work. It needs to be emphasized that black people in Britain are a settler community. Thus where we use the term 'migrant workers', it is as a conceptual tool only and *not* as a descriptive term for black workers in Britain. This distinction is particularly important given the racist implications of the idea that black people will eventually 'go back to their own countries'. Nevertheless, and despite our reservations, we feel that the comparison between the European system of 'contract' labour and the British system, is a vital one to make.

The argument that immigration legislation has been used as a form of control that would ensure a labour supply best matched to the needs of capital at different times has been developed succinctly by Sivanandan.[19] The legislation on immigration control culminating in the 1971 Act can be viewed as a progression towards a 'European' migrant labour system.[20] This has been demonstrated by Freeman and Spencer,[21] through a detailed chronology of the basis and effects of state interventions, beginning with the 1962 Commonwealth Citizens Act and ending with the 1981 Nationality Act. It was the 1971 Act, limiting the entry of non-patrial (i.e. black) Commonwealth immigrants only to do a specific job, in a specific place, for a specific length of time, which reduced the status of the black 'citizen', who came to Britain after 1971, to that of a migrant.[22] Whilst Sivanandan is correct to see the general drift of immigration controls as being towards a 'contract labour' model, his contention that each successive piece of legislation exactly matched the economic needs of capital is less supportable. In fact it seems more than likely that the results of the 1962 Act were far from beneficial to the economy. Ceri Peach points out[23] that primary immigration would probably have dropped in the early 1960s anyway as a result of the fall in labour demand. The fact that not all of the vouchers available, in the first few years following the Act, were taken up is an indication that the Act may not have been necessary.

Primary immigration was declining without the aid of controls. The threat of controls caused a wave of panic immigration to 'beat the ban', which was far from in the interest of capital, as it would not be so easy to put whole families to profit. In this period many Pakistani and Indian women and children from the Indian subcontinent came to Britain to join their husbands and fathers. In contrast to West Indian women[24] the majority of Asian women came to Britain as the dependants of male workers. Asian women were never drawn into the metropolis as wage labourers. They were not recruited directly as cheap labourers as were Asian men, whose migration to Britain from the subcontinent was closely linked to the postwar economic boom.[25] Thus the forces and motivations behind Asian women's migration to Britain were different and their entry was circumscribed by different state policies and strategies. On the other hand, the East African Asian men and women who came to Britain in 1967 were nearly all British passport holders, who were forced out of East Africa when the former British colonies gained independence. In 1968 the British Government moved in very quickly to try and control this new source of immigration to Britain, by altering their legal rights of entry. A voucher system was introduced whereby vouchers were issued to heads of households, normally males, for themselves and certain categories of dependants. Here, the dependent status of women was clear. Women holding British passports had great difficulty in proving they were heads of households; though widowed, divorced and deserted women as well as those with dependent husbands, came into this category. Thus from the very beginning Asian women have been discriminated against not only because they are black but also as women in terms of their legal rights of entry and settlement. Later on, we consider some of the ways in which state legislation has been responsible for the breakup of Asian families and the way in which Asian female sexuality has been abused and controlled through state practices.

Cheap labour?

A common strand in discussions of both black labour and female labour is that both groups of labour are cheap. In relation to women, Beechey has argued[26] that women, particularly married women, are a preferred source of the reserve army of labour because they do not rely wholly on their own wages for the reproduction of their labour power. In relation to male migrant workers, Castles and Kosack[27] argue that discrimination on the basis of racism enables heightened exploitation of black 'immigrants' and thus enhances profits, and second that capital has not had to bear the cost of educating and training 'immigrant' labour.

Through criticisms of both these analyses, we wish to pose some issues not hitherto considered.

Central to both is the concept of 'reproduction'. In the chapter on black women, we have subjected this concept to a critique through a consideration of historical and social factors. Alongside this, we would like to take up some specifically economic aspects of this critique.

Beechey's theorization had, until recently, been widely accepted as being unproblematic. However, Anthias has offered an interesting, and in parts, convincing critique of Beechey's analysis which she describes as being both economistic and functionalist; 'economistic because it explains women's employment with reference to its *economic* advantages to capital; functionalist because it argues that it is these advantages that actually determine women's employment'.[28] She argues correctly that 'There have been legal and ideological changes, state activity, changes in the family structure and so on that need to be taken into account' and 'any of these wider issues involved in the feminist problematic are not touched by Beechey'.[29]

By depicting women simply as a reserve army of labour, subject to the economic needs of capital, her analysis obscures and marginalizes the relative autonomy of the ideological and political structures that operate to determine when, where and how women workers will be employed. During the post-war years the reasons why women were drawn into production were different and contradictory. Bland *et al.* argue 'at least for the post-war period it was principally the production of household commodities – "labour saving" devices for the home, together with cheap subsistence commodities previously produced as use values in the home – which contradictorily drew women into social production'.[30] Although women were to be found working in the labour-intensive industries such as clothing, the machinery increasingly used in these sectors needed to be operated on a twenty-four-hour basis for the maximum profit to be extracted. In turn, this needed a labour force which would be more suitable to work the unsocial hours required, in some cases to work the permanent night shifts.[31] It is necessary to look at what role the wider historical and ideological structures play in the process, whereby 'particular groups of human subjects, with certain characteristics (whether sex or race) fill particular places in society and specifically in the labour process'.[32] The history of colonialism, the role of racist ideologies – in particular the common-sense racist perception of the 'naive, passive, and subservient coolie' – need to be considered.

Similarly, in the case of women workers, the patriarchal ideology of women's 'natural' place in the home, servicing not only the needs of capital through regenerating the male labourer and reproducing future workers but also being subjugated and controlled by an individual man, needs to be examined in this way. On the basis of the characteristics of migrant labour, as outlined by Castles and Kosack, it has been accepted that black workers have a potential for providing greater surplus value. This easy acceptance of the assertion that black labour is cheap has been disputed by Burawoy on several counts. He challenges Wolpe (1972), Castells (1975) and Castles and Kosack by arguing 'that the assessment of the costs and benefits of migrant labour and of its effects on the rate of profit is far more complicated than these writers have indicated and requires considerably more substantiation'.[33]

By defining a system of migrant labour by its institutional forms rather than economic terms, he points out three difficulties with the thesis that migrant labour is cheap. First, the question of 'cheap for whom' is not asked; second, the writers do not adequately examine which aspects of the costs of the reproduction of labour power are reduced; and third, while it is true that migrant labour does lead to some economic savings for the employing state, none of the writers consider the economic and above all political costs of the reproduction of a system of migrant labour. Burawoy concludes that to 'merely point to the existence of "excessive exploitation" and the externalization of costs of labour power renewal is not the same as demonstrating the existence of cheap labour'.[34] His criticisms are based partly on the conceptual distinction he makes between two distinct processes in the reproduction of labour power, namely, maintenance and renewal. The organization of migrant labour makes this dual characteristic very clear because 'it is defined by the separation of the processes of maintenance from those of renewal', they take place in geographically separate locations.[35]

It is the renewal aspect of his distinction that needs to be looked at further, in relation to the situation of migrant women. Burawoy uses the concept of reproduction in a very limited way, and a discussion of domestic labour and the family introduces another dimension to the concept which he does not consider.

In capitalist societies the family is the site for the reproduction of labour power. There, the woman's domestic labour is essential to the rearing of future workers and the day-to-day sustenance and maintenance of the male productive worker. Little significance had been given to the contribution domestic labour makes to the processes of maintenance and renewal until both Marxists and feminists began to debate the question of whether domestic labour contributes to the value of labour power and therefore indirectly to surplus value.[36] This attention to the importance of unpaid domestic labour, which goes into the daily 'production and reproduction' of male workers, has been important in bringing to visibility a whole area of women's subordination and oppression. But these discussions of 'domestic labour' and whether its contribution is direct or indirect to surplus value, have been Eurocentric in that they are premised on the significance and meaning of domestic work for women only in Western European countries.

Given the nature of uneven development of captialism internally within specific countries, it is often common for pre-capitalist forms of production to be simultaneously present alongside a capitalist mode of production.[37] Women might be found engaged in unpaid agricultural labour necessary to the maintenance of the family while the husband is working in the urban areas in the factories or mines. This historical advance of capital accumulation has initiated a process in which the peasant family as a productive unit is being slowly destroyed in Third World countries.[38] Nevertheless, most Third World women still play key roles in the running of the family's subsistence farm economies, and domestic labour for these women means grinding wheat, churning the milk, caring for the domestic animals, preparing the harvest, fetching water, and cutting podder in the fields. In fact women work longer hours than men.

Several case-studies of rural women in a wheat-growing area of Haryana have shown that the average working day for women, if all work is included, is between 15 and 16.5 hours. In households with only one adult woman she would be so over-worked that she would scarcely have time to nurse her baby. Old women also worked extremely hard. One 75 year old woman was still labouring 10 hours a day preparing food for sale. Men, on the other hand, had a much less strenuous work-load, and plenty of time to smoke and play cards.[39]

The value of domestic labour carried out by women in the Western industrialized countries has been calculated to be approximately one third of the gross national product.

If such a calculation were to be made in many peripheral countries, it would, no doubt, be much higher, not only because women in these countries are still largely responsible for subsistence production, but also because in the absence of social security and social welfare schemes they provide services like care for the ill, the old, and so on which are provided by the State in other countries.[40]

When looking at the advantages to metropolitan capital of importing exclusively male labour power (whereby there is a saving on the cost of reproduction) it is important to assess the role played by the wives and children of male immigrants in the maintenance and renewal of their families. Does the woman work to subsidize the costs of maintaining herself and her children? How is the money her husband sends them used? Is it saved to pay for their fares to come over to join him, or is it used in the renewal of educating and clothing the children? These questions render visible the activity of women in the reproduction and renewal processes in the Indian subcontinent even if their husbands work in the cities of Britain. Considering these questions necessarily challenges the narrow Eurocentric confines within which the 'domestic labour' debate has flourished. Without doubt the domestic labour of women in Third World countries 'greatly subsidises the costs of reproducing male labour in the cities, mines and other centres of production'.[41]

Patriarchal immigration legislation

We now turn to a discussion of the ways in which Asian families and Asian women in particular have been affected by racist and patriarchal immigration legislation. We do not intend to present a schematic or chronological analysis of all immigration legislation; instead, we have picked out some of the more overt illustrations of its repressive effects.

I think as far as most Black people are concerned, there has been a steady growth in state racism. Whereas before it was at the level of insensitivity – to use a euphemism – it has gradually become almost an intelligence unit in its own right against Black people. There has been a steady inter-linking and build-up of controls – immigration control, plus stopping people at the point of entry (into the country), plus control over people who are settled here.[42]

The abuse and humiliation to which the Asian community is submitted by immigration officials has been documented elsewhere.[43] Yet Asian women are exposed to British racism even before they arrive in Britain. To gain entry permission they have had to go through long and rigorous interviews in the British Embassies in India, Pakistan and Bangladesh.

They have had to undergo the ordeal of answering absurd and very intimate questions about themselves, their husbands and their families. Questions such as 'How long did you spend with your husband on the wedding night?' are common, and if either partner makes the slightest misjudgement then entry permission is refused. In 1978, there was an exposé of the vaginal examinations carried out on Asian women to determine whether they were married or not, and to determine whether they were fiancées of men already settled in England. This was not a new phenomenon; complaints had previously been lodged against the Home Office but without any results. It was only when the liberal press had taken it up as a moral and sensational issue that there was some publicity. Examinations to 'prove' whether a woman is a virgin can only be seen as acts of violence and intimidation against black women by the British state:

one cannot prove virginity by poking a finger up a vagina – not every woman has a hymen. Secondly, even if one could, then not being a virgin does not mean that you are married.[45]

This 'testing' is based on the racist and sexist assumption that Asian women from the subcontinent are always virgins before they get married and that it is 'not in their culture for women to engage in sexual activity before marriage'. This kind of absurd generalization is based on the same stereotype of the submissive, meek and tradition-bound Asian woman.

Many Asian people are also given chest X-rays before they enter the country to 'ensure that they are not carrying any serious and contagious disease'. These are also used to prove the identity of people wishing to settle in Britain. X-rays on pregnant Asian women have been carried out by untrained entry clearance officers in Dacca. X-rays are only ever carried out on pregnant women in 'exceptional circumstances when either the child or the mother's life is believed to be at risk'. The fact that the immigration officers administer them quite haphazardly on pregnant Asian women is only one example of the racism not only of individual officers but also the structural and institutional racism of the British state. Such practices also indicate the direct control the state is attempting to have on Asian women's sexuality.

One of the effects of the 1971 Immigration Act and subsequent legislation has been the break-up of Asian families.[45] The 1981 Nationality Act put further constraints on the right of dependants to join their families in Britain. One of the most obvious threats posed by this was to the future of black families and black culture. This trend can be traced back to the 1978 parliamentary Select Committee. One of its recommendations was that children over 12 years born abroad to those settled here, would not be allowed to join their parents. The report states,

we believe that the members of those minorities should themselves pay greater regard to the mores of their country of adoption and indeed, also to their traditional pattern of the bride joining the husband's family.[46]

This effectively meant that Asian women from India, Pakistan and Bangladesh, who have either grown up in Britain or were born here, were being denied the right to choose to live in Britain if their husbands came from these countries.[47]

These are just a few instances of how Asian women and Asian families have been affected by state legislation. More detailed and comprehensive analysis has been documented elsewhere.[48]

Asian women in employment

In Britain, women are a significant part of the national labour force. The 1971 census showed that women between 15 and 45 years of age formed 22 per cent of the total population at work; in other words, these working women form 51 per cent of the total female population between the age of 15 and 45.[49]

The proportion of women in the workforce has risen throughout the post-war years. By 1980 there were over 9 million women in paid employment compared to 13 million men.[50] 'Three quarters of all women workers are found in service industries, compared to just a fifth in manufacturing industry.' Over half of all female manual workers are in catering, cleaning, hairdressing and other personal services, and more than half of the non-manual women are in clerical and related occupations. Almost two million women work in occupations that are almost entirely (over 90 per cent) done by women – typists, secretaries, maids, nurses, canteen assistants, sewing machinists.

Within this concentration, there are regional and racial variations whereby Asian women are confined to even more specific sections of the labour market. They are over-represented in the low paid unskilled and semi-skilled sector, where most Asian women are to be found working as machinists in the clothing industry, in laundries, light engineering factories, the hosiery industry, in canteens, as cleaners and also as homeworkers.[51]

According to the 1971 census figures, 40.8 per cent of women from India were engaged in waged labour and 20.7 per cent of women from Pakistan. Regionally Indian women in the South East (which includes Greater London) almost approach the regional average for employment. Within the Muslim community, over a quarter of women between 15 and 45 are at work in the South East and South West, whereas in Yorkshire and West Midlands there is a very low rate of Pakistani women going out of the house to work. Reasons for these variations are not clear, but it would be wrong to assume the primacy of cultural/religious factors in hindering Asian women's involvement in wage labour. Factors such as the employment opportunities within each region must play some part in determining their entry into the labour market.

With the entry of Uganda Asians in 1972, the situation altered significantly. The rate of economic participation for women aged 15 and over born in East Africa is 52 per cent. A more detailed picture is presented in the Runnymede Trust Census Project which studied four 'coloured' [*sic*] communities in Bradford, Leicester, Manchester and Wolverhampton.[52] This estimated from 1971 Census data that 85 per cent of black mothers of children under 5 are at work in Leicester, 71 per cent in Manchester, 44 per cent in Bradford, 41 per cent in Wolverhampton. This project confirmed that, nationally, a higher percentage of black men are employed as unskilled labourers than white men, and therefore, they have lower incomes. It also found that, on average, the black household was larger than the white one and therefore it was inevitable that there would be a greater economic need for women from these households to work in order to contribute to the household income. This situation has led to one in two of all black women of working ages going out to work in full time jobs.[53] Other data confirms that a high percentage of married black women are to be found in full time employment. The Unit of Manpower Studies findings show that women born overseas are more likely to be full-time workers than those born in the UK. Married women in the age group 30–44 are more likely than single women to be part-timers, but while 43 per cent of married women born in the UK of this age group were full timers, 74 per cent of those born overseas in the same age group were working full-time.

Just as many Asian women as West Indian women are to be found in full-time work. Lomas's findings show the hours of work of married women from India and Pakistan compared to the women born in the UK in the same age groups (see Table 1).

The reasons why Asian women are engaged in wage labour are primarily economic: Uberoi,[54] Dahya[55] and Khan's[56] studies have shown that high mortgage repayments, high rents and the increasing cost of living are the reasons most

Table 1   *Hours of work of married women born in India and Pakistan compared to married women born in the UK*

		Place of birth		
Age group	Hours worked	India	Pakistan	UK
20–34	Less than 30	18.4	25.3	40.5
	30+	77.5	70.0	56.9
35–49	Less than 30	29.6	29.9	52.4
	30+	67.0	60.6	44.5

Based on Table 4.3 in G. B. Gillian Lomas and Elizabeth Monck, *Employment and Economic Activity* (Runnymede Trust 1971).

frequently given by Asian women workers.

Our own study shows that a combination of the increase in cost of living, desire for a better environment for the children, high rent and/or mortgage repayments and the desire to have independent means were all cited as reasons for women doing paid work either in the home or outside where childcare facilities and other factors permitted it.

D. J. Smith has concluded that

Women are already discriminated against as women, and this tends to restrict them to more junior and less well paid jobs: they are therefore not regarded as a threat, and there is less need for employers to discriminate against them on the ground of colour as well in order to keep them in a subordinate position.[57]

We would be wary of accepting these comments uncritically as some authors have done.[58] Black women are subject not only to sexual discrimination at work, but also to racial oppression. It is not always possible to give primacy to sexual discrimination – as, for instance, when black women workers face greater obstacles with regard to childminding than do white women. A report on working mothers and childminding in 'ethnic' minority communities[59] confirmed that Asian and West Indian women face a particular disadvantage in this sphere. This was partly due to a greater degree of need, since a greater proportion of black women with children under five are at work, for longer hours than comparable white women.

This study presented a number of other factors. First, black women are less able to get access to the day-care provision they most desired than were white mothers. Second, they had less access to subsidized or free services, i.e. day nurseries and nursery schools. Third, they had greater difficulty finding childminders near their home. And finally, some white minders refused to take black children. All these point to the force of racism in conditioning the lives of black women.

Having outlined the composition of the labour market and pinpointed the particular distribution of Asian women within it, it is important to point to the historical forces which brought about this distribution. Up until the late 1960s, few Asian women worked outside home but with the end of male immigration in the 1970s, many were recruited into factory production. In the early 1970s the Government introduced a series of 'socialisation programmes' – language classes, child care education, health education etc., all of which were geared to teaching Asian women English habits which would help them to become 'more integrated' into British society. A closer look at these programmes reveals not so much a desire to make a section of their 'Commonwealth cousins' [sic] more welcome in Britain, but rather the realization that here was a new section of the migrant community who could be easily prepared to enter wage labour. 'New to the labour market they needed to be both trained and disciplined.'[60] Asian women were a section whose exploitation the state wrongly presumed would meet with little or no resistance.

In 1975, the London Council of Social Services report *The Inner City* not only confirmed the growing number of Asian women being drawn into wage labour and the economic necessity of this, but also expressed specific patriarchal racist ideas about Asian female domesticity. This was related to fear of the Asian family becoming unstable as a result of its women going out to work.

A working man's pay packet will no longer of itself support a family in London, an assumption on which so much of our fiscal and social policies have been based. Asian families may find themselves the most vulnerable in this situation. Many Asian men suffer from under employment. They have qualifications for jobs which are not recognised or accepted here and find themselves, therefore, typically in low paid employment. The normal pattern would be for the wife to work to supplement the family income, but this runs contrary to the whole Asian pattern of female domesticity. Either they adhere to tradition, the wife does not work and the result is a significant degree of poverty or the wife breaks the normal cultural patterns and goes out to work, whether as a second wage earner or even, in some cases, where there are vacancies only for women workers, as the sole bread-winner. The result of this on the stability of the family within this community can only be guessed at but it is likely to have severe consequences.[61]

The assumptions about 'patterns of Asian female domesticity' and 'the normal cultural patterns' which were made are without any foundation whatsoever. In reality, a majority of these women come from societies where a large number of women are involved in work both outside and inside the home. What is new about their situation in Britain is that they have not worked in an *industrial* situation. It was the experience of working outside the home in a non-agrarian industrial capitalist enterprise that was different rather than the experience of working to subsidize the family.

Development researchers and funding agencies are also imbued with the illusion that Third World women who are involved in subsistence work, which involves long hours and arduous work, do not really 'work'.

Women are relegated to the unpaid 'family labour' category which is itself very

inadequately measured, if at all. . . . If there is one broad generalization that one
can make about rural women, it is their 'non-farm' work is strenuous, takes enormous amounts of time, and is absolutely essential to the survival of the family
concerned.

The division between farm and non-farm activities is a very unhelpful one in
terms of measuring the contribution to subsistence made by women and men
respectively, particularly with regard to the most basic need of all – food
production.[62]

These assumptions which have serious implications in development planning
programmes and the allocation of funding, are carried over and perpetuated when
Asian women come to the centres of Western capitalist countries.

The image of Asian female domesticity and its related 'cultural patterns', which
is popular with the social services agencies, is 'theoretically' expounded by a
number of sociologists, anthropologists and journalists. The specific literature on
Asian women conceptualizes them as non-working wives and mothers, whose problems are that they do not speak English, hardly ever leave the house, and find
British norms and values ever more threatening as their children become more
'integrated' into the new surroundings. Their lives are limited to the kitchen, the
children and the religious rituals, and they are both emotionally and economically
dependent upon their husbands.[63] The title of one early article was 'Pakistani
wives [sic] in Britain'.[64] Here, the author persistently refers to Pakistani women as
Pakistani wives and the descriptions of the women are obsessively preoccupied with
the ways in which purdah circumscribes their children's and husbands' lives. Although the women's experiences of isolation and loneliness are mentioned, the
women are denied the status of individuals capable of manipulating and negotiating
the environment to their own benefit.

A more recent version of this conceptualization is provided by V. S. Khan
'Purdah in the British situation'.[65] Khan's analysis is based on fieldwork which
involved her in 'becoming more Pakistani than a Pakistani girl' (albeit with a white
skin), and 'observing a modified form of purdah' over a period of 6 months in
a Mirpuri household in Bradford.[66] Khan's detailed anthropological descriptions of
purdah as practised in Pakistan and its modifications in the British situation
reiterate many of the points raised by Dahya eleven years earlier even though her
analysis is within a more sophisticated sociological framework. Despite this seeming
'elevation', she stereotypes these women as passive, static, and incapable of change,
and ends up making gross generalizations: 'to the Asian . . . freedom is not
identified with self-assertion', and 'it is arguable, I think, that Asians do not see the
status of men and women as comparable, and thus not in competition or conflict'.[67]
We have already subjected such 'ethnicity'-based studies to a vigorous critique in
Chapter 3. These crudities illustrate the deep-rooted ethnocentrism of a white
anthropologist studying a different culture and presumptuously making proclam-
ations on its behalf.[68] Khan's statements also reveal a tendency in the literature in
this field to obscure the religious, linguistic, regional and cultural *differences*
within the Asian community in Britain. This pervasive assumption of homogeneity

ignores the fact that the Asian population in Britain originate not only from the Indian subcontinent, i.e. India, Pakistan and Bangladesh, but also from East Africa.

Particular journalists have become expert writers on Asian and Afro-Caribbean communities and in the process produced volumes of material on black people and their cultures. One example of such a journalistic adventure was a four-part story about a fictitious Azad Kashmiri family based in Bradford, a town where a community of real Azad Kashmiris have been living and working for the past two decades.[69] The first part of this project is about 'the fears of a lonely mother', Zarina Begum, and illustrates popular racist misconceptions of Asian women. Zarina comes across as an adolescent child whose depressions, worries, tantrums and suspicions have to be 'tolerated'. Her fears are treated with condescension; for instance, she never walks more than 20 yards in Bradford after dark because 'she fears that all sorts of terrible things happen at night'. Of course, she is quite right not to walk alone after dark because 'terrible things' do happen at night: things like blacks being assaulted and beaten up by gangs of racists, and women being assaulted and raped; things which should be given some publicity 'instead of being dismissed as the idle fears of a lonely Asian mother'.[70]

However, the stereotype of the 'passive' and 'helpless victim' is not confined to Asian women alone – migrant women in Europe have also been subject to this representation, although often in more sophisticated ways. The recent book *Migrant Women Speak* is composed of personal accounts which range from North African women in Marseilles talking about their work conditions, to Moroccan women relating their experiences of organizing around issues like racial attacks and murders, and the consequent effect on their personal and political lives. The authors are earnest in their approach: 'instead of producing analyses, statements and explanations about migration, we shall hear what the women migrants themselves have to say about it, the floor is theirs'.[71]

Unfortunately, instead of letting the women have their say and leaving them or the reader to draw the conclusions, the personal accounts are interspersed with interpretative analyses of their experiences and formulations of policies for change. We would not say that an analysis of these accounts is unjustified, but the framework within which this analysis operates detracts from an otherwise valuable book. It attempts to redress the balance between statistically orientated, empirical treatises on migrant workers and more vivid, experiential documentation of the feelings of first-generation migrant women. However, despite their awareness of the shortcomings of existing approaches to the study of migrants, the authors reveal their own biases and assumptions, and fall thus into the very trap they seek to evade:

Only in rare cases do these people who are the victims of the alien world into which they have come to live and work in such difficult material and psychological conditions realise for themselves why their lives are as they are in a society they are unable to understand and where they constantly meet with arrogance, ignorance and even violence, on the part of the local inhabitants.[72]

Once again migrant women are passive 'victims of an alien world'. A picture is painted whereby they appear totally helpless, oppressing themselves and their families with their onerous traditions and cultures, illiterates who must be helped to develop a 'critical faculty' and who remain totally passive in the face of changes imposed on them. In short, wide-eyed peasant women, finding it extremely diffi-cult to negotiate their way around the big, bad concrete metropolis.[73]

It is very often in the country to which she has emigrated that she first has a chance to form her own ideas on subjects that theoretically do not belong to her province.[74]

What must be done to make a much greater number of women abandon their passive attitude and adopt a more dynamic approach to the challenges and opportunities of a new situation?[75]

Migrant women, be they from the Caribbean, Ghana, the Indian subcontinent or southern Europe, have all had experience of fighting the hostile forces of imperial-ism in one form or another. Women from the Caribbean have a long history of struggle which goes back to the days of slavery; and many Portuguese women went through revolutionary struggles before coming to Western Europe. For the authors to assume that these women have no history of struggle and are only politically 'born' when they arrive in the metropolis, is to deny their historical experience of fighting back, and to devalue anti-imperialist struggles as a whole.

In Britain, the publication of Wilson's *Finding a Voice* was applauded by a wide audience of social workers, academics, community workers and white feminists. The book is about the experiences and lives of Asian women in Britain, though interviews and subjective accounts are presented without any explicit political and economic framework. The significance of this absence is brought out by the fact that a common response to the book was, 'I had to put it down, half way through reading it, because it made me cry'.

While not denying the reality of the hardships and isolation of a lot of Asian women's lives as brought out in the book, it is important to be careful about providing further fodder for the liberal racist whose reading of the book can all too easily reinforce ideas of Asian men being more sexist than white men and Asian families being particularly barbaric and tyrannical.[76] Given that existing concep-tualizations of Asian women are one-sided, and that the day-to-day resistances and militancy of Asian women are often presented as an afterthought or an excep-tion, it is inevitable that the subjective accounts in Wilson do little to challenge the dominant view. Mala Dhondy points out,

The weakness of the interviews, all of them, is that they give the impression that Asian women have begun waking up to the reality of their oppression only since they landed in Britain.[77]

This is an unfortunate omission in a book which is otherwise an important departure from previous writings about Asian women. It goes some way towards breaking down the ideology of Asian women as helpless creatures.

Ideologies of motherhood and domesticity have often been used to explain the predominance of women in part-time employment. Purcell has challenged the idea that it is because women perceive their main job as wife and mother they they are relegated to low paid, part-time work with no career prospects. She points out 'women's insistence on part-time jobs may well reflect a home-centred approach to life, but it might more plausibly reflect a lack of alternative childcare facilities'.[78] She correctly points to the lack of choice women have in deciding when, how and where they enter the labour market. Even though ideologies of motherhood and consequent ideas of what constitutes appropriate employment for women have many cultural variations, there is a tendency to simply attribute Asian women's predominance as homeworkers to their apparent domesticity and 'peculiar' cultural norms and values. Khan states, 'the majority of Pakistani women of rural origin do not go out to work because it is unacceptable for cultural religious reasons'.[79] Homeworking cannot be adequately explained by reference to this single cause, and Khan's generalization does not take into account a whole host of other determinations which could explain why large numbers of Asian women are involved in homeworking. Dependent children, lack of access to childcare facilities, or indeed of alternative employment, as well as the structure of the local labour market, are some key factors that need to be considered.[80] Even where cultural and religious norms do have a more decisive influence than the lack of access to appropriate jobs outside the home, to ignore other structural constraints leads to a crude, mono-causal explanation which is also mystifying, in that, it conceals the complexity which shapes these women's lives.

A study carried out by Hope, Kennedy and de Winter (of homeworkers from a variety of cultural and racial backgrounds in North London) established that one of the main considerations for the women was childcare responsibilities. Apart from family responsibilities some women are forced into homeworking in the absence of any other employment. For example, a study of Asian women who had been made redundant in West Yorkshire, followed up twenty women after six months.[81] It was found that seven women were still unemployed although they had been actively seeking employment, six were homeworkers, two had stopped looking for a job and three had part-time jobs while only two had any success in securing full-time jobs. The six homeworkers stated their main reason for working at home as being unable to find employment outside of the home and they had therefore been left with no alternative but to take up homeworking which was the only employment available to them.

There is an urgent need to look carefully at the way women are being pushed out of the visible areas of the economy as an effect of the recession. Expansion of the 'informal economy' is inevitable in the present economic climate. One of the effects of unemployment is that in a substantial number of households, the woman's income is more important than ever before in maintaining the family.[82]

Historical realities

One of the primary reasons for the one-sided and incomplete images of Asian women's experiences can be attributed to a lack of history in the sociological and journalistic accounts which we have criticized.[83] The historical features of Asian women's lives, particularly their social relations and economic positions in their countries of origin, are a crucial consideration in an analysis of their lives in Britain.

Historical specificity demands assessment of the circumstances which governed and shaped Asian women's lives prior to migration, and gives their experiences subsequent to migration more continuity. We will, therefore, look briefly at the rates of economic activity for Asian women in the subcontinent. This will destroy the illusion that Asian women in Britain came from societies where women are not to be found in paid employment, and reveal the reality behind their apparent domesticity.

In fact, a close examination of the situation of women workers in the Indian subcontinent reveals many similarities with the situation of female, waged workers in the Western, capitalist countries. The sexual division of labour, the concentration of women in low paid, unskilled, non-unionized sectors of the economy, the use of female labour to undercut male wages, the threat of new technology to traditionally female jobs and the patriarchal ideology of women's roles as being primarily that of a wife and a mother are also central to the experience of female workers in the subcontinent.

The majority of Asian women who originate from the Indian subcontinent come from a rural socio-economic background in the Punjab, Gujarat and Pakistan. At some point in their lives, most of them have played key roles in running the family's subsistence economies through caring for the domestic animals, preparing the harvest, fetching water and cutting podder in the fields. These women do not always appear in the official statistics because often they fall outside the extremely limited official criteria for who constitutes a 'worker'. It was only in 1961 that for the first time the Indian Census classified the total population into workers and non-workers and working women appeared in the category of workers in their own right. Even then, the Committee studying the status of women in India in 1975 pointed out that the Census categories were not adequate in making a proper assessment either of the nature and extent of women's participation in the economy or of their problems and disabilities.[84] They therefore classified women workers into two broad categories, the unorganized and the organized sectors. 'The real difference between them lies in the organization of productive relations, the degree of state control and regulation, and recognition by data-collecting agencies and scientific investigators'.[85] Of women workers in India, 94 per cent are to be found in the unorganized sector and only 6 per cent in the organized sector.[86]

Agriculture

As is typical of most Third World countries, the largest percentage – 83 per cent –

of the female labour force in India is employed in the agrarian sector. In 1971, out of the 25.7 million women working in agriculture, 9.7 million were cultivators whereas the rest were agricultural labourers. Agricultural labourers work for wages in cash or kind and cultivators work on family-owned land.

Table 2 *Distribution of cultivators and agricultural labourers (in millions)*

	1961 Census		1971 Census	
	Cultivators	*Agri. lab.*	*Cultivators*	*Agri. lab.*
Male	66.416	17.323	68.996	31.313
Female	33.112	14.196	9.714	15.992
Total	99.528	31.519	78.707	47.305

Table 2 illustrates that although both men and women have increasingly been squeezed out of their roles as cultivators, it is the women who are bearing the brunt of this.[87]

Even as agricultural labourers the opportunity for women to participate in productive activity is more limited than it is for men, because of the pattern of division of labour, apart from the seasonal nature of their employment. As agricultural labourers, men find employment for 208 days while women do so for only 178 days.[88]

In non-agricultural occupations in the unorganized sector there are estimated to be 4 million women in areas such as construction, various forms of sweated industries, such as the *bidi* industry, and garment workers, sweepers, and domestic servants. The *bidi* industry is one of the most notorious of the sweated industries in India. 'In the factories women work from 9.00 a.m. to mid-night or later with minimal breaks, working without face masks to protect them from the deadening tobacco particles in the air . . . and the work is carried on without ventilation.'[89] The mining, tea, coffee, rubber, textiles, engineering, electrical and telecommunications industries all employ women. These industries come under the organized sector of work where 6 per cent of workers are women. 45 per cent of the women were in industry and 55 per cent in the services and professions.

On close examination of some of the conditions of work for women in the organized sector, it becomes quite clear that they are deprived of benefits, protection and rights supposedly accruing to them by virtue of being in the organized sector.

The telecommunications industry presents an illustration of some of the harsh conditions under which women are forced to work. Women telephone operators are forced to work on a daily wages basis for 6 or 7 years and are completely at the mercy of higher officers who can sack them at a moment's notice. The women work on seven and half hour shifts with minimal breaks and are forced to do night duty. The wages are extremely low. The evening shift ends at 8.00 p.m. at which hour no transport is provided and women who travel long distances to return home are vulnerable to attacks and assaults. The unions which are supposed to represent the workers' demands do nothing for the women and in some cases actively work against them, as in the case of one woman telephone operator who was sexually harassed by her supervisor who was also her trade union boss.[90] These conditions of work are not uncommon in other sections of the organized sector of industry.

There are few statistical and empirical studies available on the proportion of women working in Pakistan, but it is nevertheless possible to challenge the assumption that Muslim women are totally restricted in their movement by the practice of purdah, and therefore are not engaged in productive work. In 1961 only 9 per cent out of the 43 million women in Pakistan were classified as in the labour force, compared to 48 per cent classified as housewives.[92]

This empirical evidence is particularly difficult to accept when the methodology and the criteria used is challenged. As Rogers observes,

It is significant that outside observers would simply not see the work being done by most of the women, since it is inside the compound where male strangers are not admitted; but being literally invisible to men does not render this work any the less vital for family subsistence. The problem of subsistence work being done by women out of sight of male researchers is one which is common to many countries, such as those in the Middle East and North Africa, where purdah is observed to some degree. What is surprising is that the existence or otherwise of purdah seems to make relatively little difference in terms of the measurement of women's work; this is almost always ignored regardless of whether or not it can be seen.[92]

Despite these problems, official statistics give some indication of the rise in the number of women working in the non-agricultural sector. Over 80 per cent of women in paid employment worked in agriculture in 1961, but the non-agricultural sector showed a continuing increase. By 1964, almost 8 million women were working in non-agricultural activities and by 1966 a survey of establishments employing twenty workers or more recorded an increase of 25.2 per cent over the previous year in the number of women workers.[93]

The degree to which purdah circumscribes Muslim women's participation not only in economic activity but also in the political sphere has been challenged by several studies. Minault[94] argues that purdah has not been as restrictive to women taking an active part in the political process as previous observers have indicated. In fact the observance and interpretation of purdah varies as much according to locale and social class as it does according to degrees of religious orthodoxy.[95] In tribal societies, women may move about unveiled with relative freedom. Out of economic necessity, in many villages, the poorer women who work in the fields will also not observe purdah.[96] It is often claimed that in the rural areas of Pakistan, 'a woman's life is household activities, gossip, grooming, visits to female relatives or shrines and religious festivals'.[97] However, a study compiled by questioning the men in the North-West Frontier Province of Pakistan, shows that women are doing a wide range of essential work. This involves particularly the post-harvest processing of grains and the maintenance of livestock. Their work was probably underestimated 'as [male] farmers do not readily volunteer information about women or their families'.[98] In general, there is no difference in the participation by women in farm work and food processing inside the compound, according to ethnic group and the degree of purdah practised.[99]

In Bangladesh, where there is a considerable degree of purdah, one study has stressed that women's work in food production is very important, particularly in fruit and vegetables which form an important part of the diet; their work is seen as directly related to the variety as well as the quantity of food available to the family. Women also process the staple paddy after the harvest. A few women are involved in fish-breeding and fishing, while others produce important medicinal herbs.[100] One study stresses that not only do Bangladeshi women work extremely hard at a variety of productive activities, including the production of rice, livestock, fruit and vegetables but that they are being drawn increasingly into field work, including irrigation and work on new crops. Since the war of liberation, large numbers of women have become the sole source of support for their families.[101] Even strict purdah is no barrier to their familiarity with the details of field work.[102]

There are many complexities involved in understanding how far Islamic norms and values, in particular the practice of purdah, determine the participation of Muslim women in economic and political activity.

In light of the above evidence, it is clear that Khan's statement that 'the majority of Pakistani women of rural origin do not go out to work because it is unacceptable for cultural/religious reasons'[103] is a crude generalization based more on commonsense ideas about Muslim women than any empirical evidence. We conclude this section by emphasizing that although a direct correspondence between the women in the Indian subcontinent and Asian women in Britain is not being made, it is crucial to outline the historical, political and socio-economic features of the societies from which they come. Without an understanding and knowledge of such features an analysis of Asian women's experiences in Britain would exist in a vacuum.

Patriarchal racism and resistances

Those old women would like to be at work tomorrow. It is their old men who are forcing them to go on strike. Asian women are easily dominated. They do what their men tell them.

> Dennis Rose, the manager at Chix factory

Let him wait and see, we'll show him who is easily dominated. It was we who decided to strike. But our men are supporting us and our community is supporting us. Why shouldn't they?

> Asian women on the picket line at Chix factory[104]

We want to argue two points in this section; first, that the ways in which patriarchal relations affect Asian women in the work place take a distinct form that is determined by a *racist* patriarchal ideology based on common-sense ideas of Asian sexuality/femininity; and second, that these differing modes of femininity are manipulated by the women to their own advantage (albeit limited). They give rise to specific forms of resistance in the workplace.

We have girls here because they have less energy, and are more disciplined and are easier to control.

Our starting-point is the recognition that the sale of women's labour power is mediated by particular patriarchal ideological structures. Whereas no obvious contradiction exists for male wage workers between their roles as fathers and husbands and as waged workers, women who enter into wage labour face a contradiction and conflict between their position as wives and mothers in the family and their position as waged workers.

In so far as we sell our commodity, labour power, for a wage as do men, femininity plays no part. Nevertheless, the conditions of that sale differ; we are not able to 'freely' sell our labour power on the market because we are not 'the untrammelled owner of our capacity to labour', i.e. of our person.[105]

Women's sale of their labour is structured through particular patriarchal relationships and these are carried over into the workplace, where women are controlled. However, patriarchal control over women in the workplace takes many forms and is culturally and racially specific. Women are defined differently according to their 'race'. Women perform predominantly 'feminine' jobs which replicate and/or contain features of their roles as mothers/wives on the one hand and as 'sexual' objects on the other.

Women are concentrated in the service and catering industries where in the same way as they perform domestic service in the home, in paid work they serve 'consumers' in hospitals and canteens. Jobs such as secretaries, receptionists, sales assistants, models, etc. require women to look and conform to the prevalent stereotype of an attractive woman, and in such instances women are forced to sell their sexuality. The ideology of femininity is contradictorily constructed for women and as Bland *et al*. point out,

We have to consider two aspects of the construction of femininity; while we are mothers who serve our husbands and children we are also the desirable 'sexual' objects for men.[106]

When we break down these two aspects of the construction of femininity for black women, it becomes clear that not only the market-place value of black and white women is different, but also that ideas about their femininity are racially specific. Those jobs which are seen as more 'glamorous' such as secretarial work, telephone/ receptionist work, hairdressing and 'beauty therapy' present women as *visibly* attractive to men.[107] It is precisely these jobs from which black women are excluded because in such instances it is white femininity which is required to be visible. Griffin cites an example of a woman administrator, working in local further education provision, who engaged a young Afro-Caribbean woman as a secretary, and who had purposely practised 'positive discrimination' because of young black women's doubly 'disadvantaged' position in the local labour market. She had been astounded at the reactions of her white colleagues and visitors. On hearing 'Yvonne' answer the phone, or seeing her in the office, visitors would assume that she was the *cleaner* – simply due to the pervasiveness of race-specific and racist assumptions about young black women's position in employment.[108]

Nursing is considered an appropriate 'caring profession' for all women, but it has distinct connotations for black women and a particular history rooted in their experience of slavery and colonialism.

No woman is more identified with service work than black women. The relation-ship between the black woman and nursing of other people's children and other people's husbands and wives, dates from before any National Health Service, whether working in hospitals as auxiliaries, SEN or SRN, in the head of the black nurse from the Caribbean is the echo of slavery, in the head of the Asian nurse is the servitude to Sahibs and Memsahibs.[109]

The images that exist for black women at work are those of nurses, cooks, domes-tics and machinists. The servicing role that black women perform is often invisible; as cleaners they enter offices after dark, as cooks they remain 'belowstairs'. Even their sexuality is hidden, whereas images of white women's sexuality are on display through advertising. Here, the ideal woman is a white middle-class woman, blonde or brunette, sensual, sexual or virginal. Black women's sexuality becomes relevant in very different places.[110] Women of Asian origin range from being seen as sexually exotic creatures, 'full of Eastern promise', to being seen as oppressed wives and mothers completely dominated by their menfolk, having little or no control in their families. The most familiar image of Asian women is one of a passive woman walking three steps behind her domineering and sometimes brutal 'lord and master'. This passivity is presented as both natural and cultural – the Asian woman is thought to have been socialized into learning appropriate ways of using her 'natural' attri-butes to please, serve and accommodate her future husband. On the other hand, the cultural dimension is focused around the issue of marriage. It becomes dominant where immigration laws call the status of Asian marriages into question, or become the means of protecting 'the second generation' from the excessive alienness of their parents' traditional ideas about marriage. For it would appear that the point at which 'passivity' is abandoned is also the point at which Britishness is acquired. However, Asian women in industrial conflict have demonstrated that this is not the case.

Another aspect of the common-sense construction of Asian women's sexuality is, as we have indicated, contextualized within an ideology of 'Eastern promise'.

The international tourist industry and visiting executives of multinational companies are offered the services of exotic and sexually dexterous Asian women, as part of their package holiday trips.[111]

Our concern here is to illustrate how these ideological constructions of Asian women's femininity articulate with wage relations of capital. The image of passive and docile Asian women has been used by employers, first to manipulate and control the women in their workplaces, and second to harass and intimidate them when they withdraw their labour. Although a long way from home, R. Grossman's study of women workers in the electronics industry in South East Asia[112] shows in similar terms how management are able to invoke a passive and 'oriental' life-style and a 'culture' of the workplace in order to increase productivity, providing a framework for control and discipline of the women which forestalls any collective action against the employers. The beauty contests she mentions are just one stark example of the way in which they manipulate the transition from traditional concepts of femininity and gender roles to their modern counterparts.

The plant manager usually an American presents himself as a kindly but nonetheless demanding father figure, playing basketball with the team, kissing the beauty contest winners, eating in the factory canteen.[113]

The myth of the cheap, passive and compliant Asian female is also used by Asian governments to obtain and attract foreign investment; glossy brochures describe the attractiveness of Asian female labour in the following way:

The manual dexterity of the oriental female is famous the world over. Her hands are small and she works fast with extreme care; who, therefore, could be better qualified by nature and inheritance to contribute to the efficiency of a bench assembly production line than the oriental girl.[114]

Certain characteristics and structures of patriarchal power relations in the family and in society generally are reproduced in the workplace as a means of controlling the female workforce. It is in these instances that one can begin to see 'how the ways in which the wider subordination of women as it arises in the family sets the transferral of patriarchal relation and "femininity" into the workplace.[115]

Ethnographic studies of women workers in South East Asia have shown very clearly how the multinational companies have manipulated the Asian patriarchal relations which involve a special status and reverence accorded to the father as well as the importance attached to doing one's duty to one's parents and the country.

In addition to male supervisors insulting, belittling and sexually assaulting them at work, some of the women have to live in company controlled dormitories, and are subjected to management, party and union officials' speeches about the female virtue of hard work for one's parents and country.[116]

Such stark illustrations of patriarchal control in the workplace have their counterparts in the experiences of Asian women in England. Grunwick, a factory processing films in North West London, came to the public attention when on 20 August 1977 the predominantly female Asian workforce came out on strike. The reasons for striking and the ensuing long struggle have been adequately covered elsewhere[117] and it is unnecessary to rehearse them here. What we do need to do is point to the ways in which there has been little significance attached to the fact that most of the strikers were Asian women subject to particularized forms of racial and sexual oppression. Levidow,[118] while correct in recognizing that the control over labour power at Grunwick was rooted in sexual as well as racial oppression, incorrectly problematizes the particular forms in which these oppressions of Asian women are articulated. He hastily generalizes that 'though threats of ostracism to wayward women come ultimately from the men, the norms of behaviour are enforced by women in the home. This burden weakens women's collective power in the same factory'.[119]

Women, like the strike leader, Jayaben Desai, come from a generation which engaged in and supported the massive Ghandian demonstrations in India against British rule and many of these women were beaten by British troops with lathies and often also imprisoned and/or locked up. The younger unmarried women in the factory were affected to a larger extent by the fear of ostracism and of being gossiped about in the community and it was primarily this group against whom the manager, George Ward, used the threat of spreading rumours about the strikers as 'loose women'. He manipulated and used his distorted and exaggerated understandings of certain Asian cultural ideas about the role of Asian women.

An illustration of George Ward's use of this knowledge is revealed in the following statement from Mrs Jayaben Desai;

He would come to the picket line and try to mock us and insult us. One day he said 'Mrs Desai, you can't win in a sari, I want to see you in a mini'. I said 'Mrs Gandhi, she wears a sari and she is ruling a vast country'. I spat at him. 'I have my husband behind me and I'll wear what he wants me to.' He was very angry and he started referring to me as a big mouth. On my second encounter with Ward he said, 'Mrs Desai I'll tell the whole Patel community that you are a loose woman'. I said, 'I am here with this placard, look, I am showing all England that you are a bad man. You are going to tell only the Patel community but I am going to tell all of England'. Then he realised that I would not weaken and he tried to get at the younger girls. About one girl he started spreading the story that she had come out only to join her boyfriend. He did this because he knew that if it got to her parents they would force her to go back in. You see he knows about Indian society and he is using it. Even for those inside he has found for each one an individual weakness, to frighten some and to shame others. He knows that Indian women are often easily shamed.[120]

Ward's hold over the workforce came in the case of the Asian women, not from 'a culturally sanctioned docility which could now be exploited by capital as the women began to work outside their families for the very first time',[121] but rather from the ways in which he attempted to reproduce some features of the

Asian patriarchal ideology. This was guided by his understanding of Asian sexuality and femininity. The explanation for the ways in which a particular labour force, i.e. Asian women, were able to be controlled and consequently exploited in particular ways is not to be found in archaic and sexist practices within the Asian cultures, but in the process by which these patriarchal features are transformed by a patriarchal ideology invoking common-sense racist ideas about Asian women.

Elsewhere younger Asian women are often subject to particular forms of sexual harassment at their places of work. They are often subjected to comments from white supervisors alluding to their supposed sexual prowess and expertise. 'I bet you can show a fella a thing or two. Your lot know how to please a man. No need to be shy with me, luv.' Comments about dress also carry sexual innuendos. 'It must be very convenient for your man, with you in a sari. You don't need to wear anything underneath, now do you.' Such comments are followed by laughter and often made in front of other male workers. The shame and humiliation these women experience is great and creates a lot of resentment. In some instances young women had been propositioned by male supervisors and managers in exchange for a raise or promotion to another department.

One young woman had this to say about her particular experience:

There weren't many Asians working in my factory. It was mostly older white women and one or two older Asian women. I had just left college and couldn't get a job anywhere else, so I was working in this sewing factory. I think I was the only young woman in my floor. The foreman was a young English boy, he was married but he was trying to flirt with me as soon as I started work there. I tried not to take notice of him. He started getting really persistent with me, you know, always asking me to take lunch with him at his house. He said his wife worked so we would be alone and not have to worry about anything. I told him I didn't want to and to stop talking to me all the time. Because I knew the other Asian women were watching and I didn't want them to get the wrong idea. This went on for months. I used to get so miserable. One day he said to me, 'Listen, you must want to move on, you are too clever to be at that machine all day, how would you like to have a go at working in the office upstairs'. I was really pleased because that's what I had wanted to do in the first place. I said yes to him but he really shocked me because then he said, 'See, I can do you a favour, now it's your turn to pay me back. How about going out with me'. I was so angry and I told him that I would complain about him if he didn't stop pestering me. Anyway after that he made my life at work so miserable, being really nasty and saying all sorts of things in front of other workers. I decided to leave after that.

The ways in which patriarchal ideological structures are reproduced in the workplace take very similar forms for Asian women who work in South East Asia, in the microelectronics industry and other industries run by multinational companies, and their Asian sisters who work in England. Not only do they have similar cultural backgrounds but they are also racially distinct from those who employ them and have similar experiences of imperialism and neo-colonial rule. Other Third World women living in metropolitan cities (as in the case of Mexican women in North America) are found in industries which are both capital and labour intensive, a common feature of the microelectronics industry in South East Asia.[122] As already stated, Asian women in England are also to be found in labour-intensive industries such as light engineering, laundries and small scale sweatshops.

It is possible to begin to explain why these similarities exist between the experiences of Asian women in England and South East Asian women in relation to wage labour, by pointing to capital's perpetual search for cheaper labour power. One of the crucial features of the uneven development inherent in the capitalist mode of production is the tendency for both European and American capital to move from a policy of labour importation to one of capital export whereby labour-intensive industries are relocated in the periphery. The growth of free trade zones in countries of South East Asia, such as the Philippines and Malaysia offer great opportunities for profit. The incentives for firms to relocate in these areas are limitless. Higher productivity is achieved through low wages; greater intensity of work; unfavourable work conditions; limited social security and fringe benefits; and a greater control over the workforce, which is usually made up of young women, through limited opportunities for trade union organization often compounded by the existence of authoritarian regimes.[123]

So far we have argued that the specific ways in which patriarchal relations affect Asian women in the workplace take different forms to that of white women, but it is necessary to repeat that this exploration has to be contextualized within a discussion about the dynamics of the capitalist labour process and the specific forms of authority capital must establish over labour within production.[124]

We would now like to turn to a brief discussion about the ways in which Asian women in Britain and in the subcontinent have responded to their oppression and exploitation. We argue that Asian women bring with them a rich and varied tradition of resistance and struggle and the forms which these struggles take are culturally, racially and gender specific. We argue against the analysis and criteria of struggle as offered by writers such as Miles and Phizacklea who impose inappropriate and Eurocentric conceptualizations of struggle and political organization when looking at the situation of black workers in Britain. They 'consider the extent of class consciousness amongst black workers' by collecting data about 'joining a trade union and participation in industrial action'. They attempt to quantify political consciousness through the use of questionnaires and thus totally ignore the fact that there have been many instances where black workers have drawn support from the black community as a whole[125] in their struggles at the work place. Furthermore, they discount black workers' racist experiences of trade union and labour movements both in Britain and in their countries of origin, where there has been a history of such organizations being turned into instruments of management. During and after the independence struggles in the Caribbean and in India, many trade unions and other working-class organizations emerged, but they and their leaders became the 'labour' arm of the management and the state. From Alexander Bustamante (Jamaica) to George Fernandes (India), the pattern is more or less the same, and at present, union control is, with very few exceptions, now part and parcel of management and state control. Black workers' experience of trade unions in Britain is also bitter and has been documented comprehensively elsewhere.[126] The Asian community in Britain has used its community cohesiveness as a major weapon in their industrial battles.

In Britain in the 1960s and 1970s Asian workers throughout the country became increasingly organized in their resistance in small textile factories and in the foundries and most assembly and engineering works as well as in the labouring and servicing industries.[127] Asian women have been at the forefront of some of these key industrial struggles in the last decade.

For example, the Imperial Typewriters strike of 1974 in Leicester in the Midlands was one of the first major strikes that Asian workers initiated in Britain. The struggle at Imperial was strengthened by the fact that the workers across the shop floor inside the factory comprised a network of friends and relatives, which made for solidarity both inside and outside the factory and provided material and moral support to the strikers and their families. These workers were in the main women from Uganda.

The strike started from a gut feeling of economic wrong-doing and racial exploitation. It developed into an all out battle against the management, the agencies of the state which attempted to mediate and the TGWU, which denied support to the strikers and attempted to assist the management in defeating them.[128]

The distinctive feature of this strike was that in the absence of union recognition and support for its three-month duration, the strikers relied solely on the resources of their own community. Financial assistance was given by local shopkeepers and businessmen and community groups organized fund-raising events. This source of community-based power was recognized in 1967, in an official report produced by Barbara Castle's Commission on Industrial Relations, which states:

Management's employment policies have led to the reinforcement of this cohesion [between Punjabi workers] because managers allow their existing Punjabi workers to suggest recruits. In terms of numbers this was a successful policy, but it had the effect of transferring to groups of workers, the power to determine their own composition, because workers put forward those with whom they had ties within the wider community. The effect of this policy was to create groups which are held together by a powerful set of mutual obligations.[129]

Such sources of power are culturally specific and Asian women, in particular, have a tradition of struggle where they have used and converted their so called 'weaknesses' into strengths and developed gender and culturally specific forms of resistances.

Language is one specific cultural form of resistance. One common-sense image of Asian women is that they do not speak English and it is frequently used as an excuse to explain their low position within the labour market and their low participation in trade unions. Many Asian women are well aware that there is always an assumption made that they are dumb because they cannot speak English. As one woman put it,

Our supervisor, who is a white woman, told my friend off because we were speaking in Gujarati. We think she didn't like it because she thought we were saying things about her. Well, we were, but not always. She knew some of us didn't speak very good English so she would go so fast and tell us to do things under her breath. She did it deliberately. Well, we didn't always understand so we had to ask her to say it again. She was really nasty about it. So we started to say things to each other in Gujarati and that really made her go angry. We would get so bored so we would talk about the Indian films we had seen, sometimes we would even sing our songs. We didn't care what she thought. She couldn't stop us, now, could she?

Many Asian women whom we have interviewed have a good grasp of English and can understand it well. Yet, because they are usually expected not to utter more than a few words and are spoken to by management in a patronizing manner, they deliberately let them believe that they don't understand very well. They often pretended that they hadn't understood what they were told to do, so they would ask for instructions to be repeated several times; a delaying tactic. Other times, if they had made mistakes in their work, for instance sewed two pieces of material the wrong way around, they would apologize and blame it on their lack of under-standing English. In such instances, the women are using management's precon-ceived ideas of Asian women as being illiterate and dumb and not understanding English, to their own advantage within the workplace and thereby turning their apparent disadvantage to a form of resistance.

In India, during the last decade, a powerful movement against excessive drinking has drawn active support from women and given collective expression to their wishes. During the Independence movement, women had been active in the picket-ing of illicit liquor shops, and more recently on 20 November 1971, more than 10,000 women of India's most poverty-stricken district, Tehri Garhwal, staged a massive demonstration against drunkenness. Despite the fact that fifty-six women were arrested and jailed for picketing outside a liquor shop, the agitation continued until drunkenness was well under control in the area.[130] In many hill villages, women have organized in Mahila Mandals (women's groups) to keep an eye on drunkards and their dens. When the Mahila Mandal in one particular village came to know of such a den in their village, they surrounded the house of the liquor distiller, caught hold of him and tied him to the buffalo pole. They then walked for miles to the nearest town to call the police. This is just one instance of such an action. The anti-liquor campaign was not and is not a moral issue; *daru* or 'country liquor' had once been a simple part of tribal culture and ceremonial life until it spread and became a social evil for poor and working-class people. As Gail Omvedt observed,

The fact that among the poor, faced with unemployment and misery, it was primarily the men who could escape into drink; women, always more mindful of domestic responsibilities, did so much more rarely. And when people are at the economic margin, the men literally drink up the food money, and then come home to beat their wives. So an anti-alcohol campaign was always popular with women.[131]

In South Korea, women have been at the forefront of initiating protests against the terrible working conditions imposed by multinational companies. Lenz argues that 'it was women who began to build a grassroots trade union movement, thus coming into violent conflict with the employers, the police and Korean CIA . . . and a male dominated and bureaucratic trade union movement backed by the State'. She concludes that 'this movement has exposed as a myth the image of cheap compliant female labour, a myth which Asian governments have been using to obtain foreign investment.[132]

Through a strategy of a high turnover and absenteeism, women workers have developed systems of what she calls 'passive resistance'. Women have had to struggle for worker and union rights and then have had to struggle within the unions themselves. For example, in 1976, the management bribed male union delegates with drink, male candidates offered two months' salary as a bribe to a woman worker, and they locked women in their dormitories; all in an effort to oust the woman union president and get a man elected. The following day 800 of the 1000 women workers began a sitdown strike, 400 of them remaining almost without food and drink for three days. When police were called in to clear the occupation, the women stripped to their underclothes to shame them. Lenz argues that in this instance when the women workers undressed 'they expressed without words a renunciation of the sexist concept of the naked passive woman as an object for men'.[133]

In Malaysia, women workers have regularly shut down factories for hours and even days at a time with spontaneous outbreaks of possession by spirits affecting hundreds of workers. 'Mass possessions in the factories usually occur during times of high production pressures, changes in the production process or other generally recognised tension. Incidents commonly begin with one worker seeing a spirit in her microscope, often that of her mother. The vision sweeps through the factory floor and suddenly several hundred women are hysterically weeping and writhing. Though management personnel try to remove the affected women from the floor immediately, the outbreaks frequently close the factory down in a subconscious wildcat strike'.[134] In Malay culture, where expressions of anger and strong emotions by women are not condoned, seeing spirits becomes an acceptable form of social protest.

In Britain, the Grunwick strike was one of the major and most publicized strikes of the 1970s. It drew the support of thousands of white workers, who attended the many mass pickets organized by the strike committee. The issue they had come to support was of 'defending the trades union movement'. The Grunwick struggle became symbolic of the fundamental right of a worker to belong to a union. The fact that most of the strikers were Asian women was seen as incidental to the struggle for workers' rights to belong to a union, and this negation of the race and gender of the strikers was exemplified in one miner saying 'we are right behind the lads here, they have our full support'.[135]

The traditions and cultural forms of resistance that Asian workers have brought with them were denied and subsumed in the fourteen-month strike at Grunwick. The only time that the Grunwick strikers drew on their history was when, in a desperate last effort, a two-day hunger strike was staged outside the headquarters of the Transport and General Workers Union. The action failed but historically the method of a hunger strike in struggles against the British colonials in India has been widely and successfully used. Whereas at Imperial Typewriters the struggle drew on the support of the wider black community, the Grunwick struggle did not make any concerted effort to involve the wider Asian community in its struggle. Although the same pattern of employment of relatives and friends existed in Grunwick[136] as at Imperial, this source of power was not tapped. 'From the outset of the Grunwick walk-out, its strikers have been led to believe that mobilising white workers had to be their primary purpose, that only this could deliver them from the jaws of bondage.'[137]

A similar situation existed at Chix bubblegum factory in Slough where 96 Asian women went on strike on 10 October 1980. The conditions at Chix were bad when the strike began. The wages were 95p per hour for Asian women and £1.10 per hour for white women. One hundred and twenty workers had to share four toilets. The day shift workers were allowed 5 minutes for washing and the night shift workers weren't allowed any time to wash on the premises. One of the older women describes the working conditions at the factory:

The work is very dirty and heavy. I have been working on the belts for years. It is very hard. They constantly want more and more output and it is very difficult particularly at my age. There is a lot of discrimination. In fact discrimination had always been present ever since I started working here thirteen years ago, on three shillings a week. We get different pay rates from the white women working with us and harassment from the supervisors, who have always been white since my days at the factory.[138]

No security existed and no medical facilities such as a sick room were provided. In fact women were penalized if they had to take time off to go to the doctor. 'If ever we were late because we went to the doctor, on arriving we were given our cards and commanded "out". This meant we were sent home and instead of losing an hour's pay, we would lose the whole day's. We had to put up with a lot of indignities.'[139]

Things came to a head when one woman asked the management to allocate her a lighter job because she was pregnant. The management refused and consequently she lost her baby. The majority of the workers decided that they were no longer prepared to put up with the harsh conditions of their work and 107 workers out of a total of 120 joined the General and Municipal Workers Union. They approached

Dennis Rose, the manager, who refused to recognize their union. So they decided to go on strike.

But, as at Grunwick, the trade union bureaucracy dragged its feet. The regional secretary of the union GMWU said,

We've been playing it very low key because there has been very little response from other unions. Maybe we'll have to change our tactics.[140]

Yet again, the fact that these were predominantly Asian women who were on strike was being ignored. One white trade union official said at one of the pickets, 'This is not a strike about Asian women or women's rights'. As Southall Black Sisters who actively supported the strike by attending the pickets, pertinently commented:

such a statement refuses to recognise that it is because they are women and black, that they are at the bottom of the ladder in terms of wages, long hours, and unsafe work conditions. Why are there not any Asian women on the strike committee? Why is it always men who speak for the Chix strikers at public rallies? The excuse that the women did not speak English is a very poor one.

They go on to say:

Asian women strikers at Chix have found that their experience and interests are being subsumed under the general issue of the struggle for union recognition. To make the class issue the only one is to ignore the racist and sexist situation which has given rise to the struggle of Asian women at Chix.[141]

While there are some bitter lessons to be learnt from the struggles at Grunwick and Chix, in terms of the strategy and tactics that Asian workers should or should not rely on, the strike at Grunwick in particular demonstrated the powerful determination of Asian women workers to resist exploitation and unfair treatment. As Mrs Jayaben Desai of the Grunwick strikers said in 1977, 'The treatment we got was worse than the slaves in *Roots*'.[142]

A more long-term and positive effect of the strike has been the impetus it has given other Asian workers, particularly the women, to make more demands at their workplaces. Mrs Jayaben Desai, the strike leader, comments:

Already Asian ladies from other factories are approaching us and asking us what they should do. I met a woman the other day who said in their factory they only had two sinks to wash up after work and that took them an extra half hour. Their management is always making problems for them. They should not do that washing in their time. Management have to give them more time and more sinks. It is little things like this, but every day we have something new. They will not work in these conditions for ever. They cannot. That's why she came to see us. Now she is going to call all of those ladies to a meeting with us. Another time, two Asian men came to the picket line. They were printing something in their factory — 20 men from India and Pakistan. They had no union and very bad pay. They wanted us to ask

APEX to take them in the union. I realized they were new and did not know very much. I told them APEX is not for you, you have to join a printer's union. I took them to one of our own meetings so they could see how we organise. This gave them some ideas and now they are joining (SOGAT) Society of Graphical and Allied Trades. Their management has to accept that.[143]

The reverberations of Grunwick are still being felt by Asian women workers throughout Britain, and being expressed in strikes such as at Chix sweet factory at Slough and at Fritters in North London.

Asian women have not only been active at their workplaces but have also been involved in struggles and campaigns against other forms of oppression and repression. Asian women's groups, with a strong and culturally specific form of feminism, have emerged and actively campaigned against virginity testing, the use of Depo-provera, immigration legislation, racist attacks in schools, for better housing, against the racist practices of DHSS and the NHS, and in every other area of their lives.

The ways in which capital, patriarchy and race structure Asian women's oppression and exploitation does not make it possible or desirable to separate out the primary cause of oppression; all three factors are intrinsic to the day-to-day experiences of Asian women. The stereotypes and myths that exist about Asian women are being constantly challenged through the militant actions that many of them have taken in the past and will continue to take in the future. The collective actions that they have taken have sometimes been alongside their white sisters and at other times they have struggled alongside their black brothers. They have learnt that while it is necessary for them as black women to struggle with white women on issues of mutual concern and with black men against their common oppression as black people, they have to do this from a position of strength and power as organized black women. As black women they are successfully defining their own experiences of oppression and developing their own framework for struggling against it.

Acknowledgements

My many thanks to Paul Gilroy and John Solomos who gave me much needed support through their criticisms, comments and suggestions in the painstaking task of rewriting. Outside the group, thanks to Chris Griffin, Gail Lewis and Maureen McNeil for their comments and discussions and for their sisterly encouragement. Finally, an acknowledgement to my mother whose experiences of fighting British colonialism in India and her subsequent migration to East Africa and Britain has inspired me to write about Asian women. She has worked for a number of years as a machinist in a factory and as a homeworker.

Notes and references

1   See: Zaynab Dahya, 'Pakistani wives in Britain', *Race*, vol. VI no. 4 (1965);

Narinder Uberoi, 'Sikh women in Southall', *Race*, vol. VI (1965); and V. Khan, 'Purdah in the British situation', in Diane Leonard Barker and Sheila Allen (eds.), *Dependence and Exploitation in Work and Marriage* (Longman 1976).

2   A. Wilson, *Finding a Voice: Asian Women in Britain* (Virago 1978); M. Prescod-Roberts and N. Steele, *Black Women, Bringing It All Back Home* (Falling Wall Press 1980).

3   CCCS, *Women Take Issue – Aspects of Women's Subordination* (Hutchinson 1975).

4   The more recent efforts in this area are contained in: Lydia Sargent (ed.), *The Unhappy Marriage of Marxism and Feminism, A Debate on Class and Patriarchy* (Pluto Press 1981).

5   See Chapter 6 for a critique of such approaches.

6   Gloria Joseph, 'The imcompatible ménage à trois: Marxism, feminism and racism', in Lydia Sargent, pp. 92–3.

7   G. Carchedi, 'Authority and foreign labour: some notes on a late capitalist form of capital accumulation and state intervention', *Studies in Political Economy*, no. 2 (1979), p. 48.

8   For instance, B. Cohen and P. Jenner, 'The employment of immigrants: a case study within the wool industry', *Race*, vol. X, no. 1 (July 1968); B. Hepple, *The Position of Coloured Workers in British Industry*, Report prepared for the Conference on Racial Equality in Employment (National Committee for Commonwealth Immigrants 1967); S. Patterson, *Dark Strangers: A Sociological Study of the Absorption of a Recent West Indian Migrant Group in Brixton, South London* (Tavistock 1963); P. L. Wright, *The Coloured Worker in British Industry, with Special Reference to the Midlands and North of England* (Oxford University Press/Institute of Race Relations 1968); and J. Rex and R. Moore, *Race, Community and Conflict: a Study of Sparkbrook* (Oxford University Press/Institute of Race Relations 1968).

9   See J. Bourne, 'Cheerleaders and ombudsmen: the sociology of race relations in Britain', *Race and Class*, vol. XXI, no. 4, for a critique of this body of research.

10 Nancy Foner, 'Women, work and migration: Jamaicans in London', *New Community*, vol. V, nos. 1–2 (Summer 1976).

11 Wilson; and Prescod-Roberts and Steele.

12 Khan.

13 S. Hall, 'Race, articulation and societies structured in dominance', in *Sociological Theories, Race and Colonialism* (UNESCO 1981), p. 328.

14 M. Castells, 'Immigrant workers and class struggles in advanced capitalism: the Western European experience', *Politics and Society*, vol. 5, no. 1 (1975).

15 Michael Burawoy, 'Migrant labour in South Africa and the United States', in Theo Nichols (ed.), *Capital and Labour: A Marxist Primer* (Fontana 1980).

16 C. Peach, *West Indian Migration to Britain* (Oxford University Press/Institute of Race Relations 1968).

17 P. Summerfield, 'Women workers in Britain in the Second World War', *Capital and Class*, no. 1 (Spring 1977).

18 In the main, West Indian women migrated to Britain as workers. For example,

Davison's study carried out in Jamaica in 1961 shows that there were an equal number of women and men migrating. The main reason given by the women for migrating was to seek employment. R. B. Davison, *West Indian Migrants* (Oxford University Press/Institute of Race Relations 1962).

19   See: A. Sivanandan, *Race, Class and The State: The Black Experience in Britain. Race and Class* pamphlet no. 1 (1976).

20   ibid.

21   Freeman and Spencer, 'Immigration control, black workers and the economy', *British Journal of Law and Society*, vol. 6, no. 1 (Summer 1979).

22   Sivanandan.

23   Peach.

24   Davison.

25   See: Eric Butterworth, 'Immigrants in West Yorkshire; social conditions and the lives of Pakistanis, Indians and West Indians', Institute of Race Relations, Special Series (1967).

26   V. Beechey, 'Some notes on female wage labour', *Capital and Class*, no. 3 (1977).

27   S. Castles and G. Kosack, *Immigrant Workers and Class Structure in Western Europe* (Oxford University Press 1973).

28   See in particular: Floya Anthias, 'Women and the reserve army of labour: a critique of Veronica Beechey', in *Capital and Class*, Theory and Politics special issue 10 (Spring 1980).

29   ibid., p. 55.

30   L. Bland *et al.*, 'Inside and outside the relations of production', in *Women Take Issue*.

31   For instance, in a study of the distribution of thirty-five clothing workplaces in West Yorkshire, it was found that the majority of those doing permanent night-shift work were Pakistani men. The study also showed the stresses that night work brought upon the wives of these men.

Many of the wives felt frightened being alone in the house at nights, and made themselves anxious, trying to keep the house quiet while their husbands were asleep in the day; avoiding the use of their vacuum cleaners, trying to hush the children and rushing to the door if anyone rang to stop it happening twice. Cooking also took longer when meals had to be prepared for husbands and children at different times.

See: M. D. Still, 'Turnover of Asian immigrant labour in the wool textile industry of Bradford', unpublished MSc dissertation, University of Bradford, 1976.

32   Anthias, p. 55.

33   Burawoy, p. 141.

34   ibid., p. 142.

35   ibid., p. 168.

36   See: Eva Kaluzynska, 'Wiping the floor with theory, a survey of writings on housework', *Feminist Review*, no. 6 (1980). for an interesting and stimulating discussion of the different positions and perspectives on the domestic labour debate.

37   'Women and class struggle', *Latin American Perspectives*, vol. iv, joint nos. 12 and 13 (1977).

38   ibid.

39   Barbara Rogers, *The Domestication of Women: Discrimination in Developing Societies* (Kogan Page 1980).

40   Newsletter of *International Labour Studies*, no. 7 (July 1981), special theme, 'Women and wage labour', p. 1.

41   ibid.

42   See: N. N. Murray, C. Cockburn and J. Mitchell, 'The state as we know it', part of which is an interview with Lena and Parita (two black women) in *Spare Rib*, no. 107 (1981).

43   See back copies of *Race Today*. Also: T. Wallace and R. Moore, *Slamming The Door* (Martin Robertson 1975).

44   See: *Spare Rib*, no. 107.

45   Many campaigns have been mounted where children have been refused entry to join their families in Britain. The most successful and well-publicized case was that of Anwar Ditta.

46   See: 'Asian women stand firm', *Bradford Black* (1978), where one Asian woman had this to say:

> I have two children still in India and I am really worried that they won't be allowed to come and join me here. All these different immigration laws have separated quite a lot of families that I know. It's created so much hardship and suffering. It's not right that families are split up like this. Children and other close relatives should be given priority. It takes two or three years, sometimes much longer, before they are given permission to join their families. All these difficulties we people have to go through just because they don't want any more blacks in this country.

47   V. Amos and P. Parmar, 'Resistances and responses: black girls in Britain', in A. McRobbie and T. McCabe (eds.), *Feminism for Girls: An Adventure Story* (Routledge and Kegan Paul 1982).

48   See: Kum Kum Bhavani, 'Racist acts; racism, racialism in Britain in the 1980s', *Spare Rib*, no. 115 (1982).

49   Counter Information Services, special report on *Women in the 80s* (1981).

50   ibid., p. 9.

51   For descriptions and details of the situation of Asian women employed as cleaners at Heathrow Airport, London, see: 'Low pay, long hours and a small flame of rebellion', *Race Today*, vol. 6, no. 5 (May 1974).

52   G. B. Gillian Lomas, Census 1971, *The Coloured Population of Great Britain* (Runnymede Trust 1973).

53   ibid.

54   Uberoi,

55   Dahya.

56   Khan.

57   D. J. Smith, *Racial Disadvantage: The PEP Report* (Penguin 1977).

58   A. Phizacklea and R. Miles, *Labour and Racism* (Routledge and Kegan Paul 1981), p. 9.

59   *Who Minds*, Report on working mothers and childminding in 'ethnic' minority communities (Community Relations Council 1975).

60   *Race Today* (July 1974).

61   Quoted in ibid. It is interesting to note the overt reference to the concept of the 'family wage' at the beginning of the quote. For a discussion of this

concept see articles by: Hilary Land, 'The family wage', *Feminist Review*, no. 6, and Michèle Barrett and Mary McIntosh, 'The family wage: some problems for socialists and feminists', *Capital and Class*, no. 11 (Summer 1980).

62   Rogers.

63   See: V. Khan, 'Pakistani women in Britain', *New Community*, vol. V, nos. 1–2 (Summer 1976).

64   Dahya.

65   Khan, 'Purdah in the British situation'.

66   ibid., p. 242.

67   Khan, 'Purdah in the British situation'.

68   This point is developed by Achola Pala, who illustrates through graphic examples how Western anthropologists are often completely unaware of the realities and immediate practical concerns of the people they set out to study.

69   J. Salmon, 'The fears of a lonely mother'; 'The hard fact: walls are not lined with gold'; 'Why Ayesha cried after her arranged marriage'; 'An appalling barrier for Maruf and his English girl'. A series of four feature articles, the *Telegraph and Argus*, Bradford, 12–15 July 1978.

70   See a review of these articles, *Bradford Black* (July 1978).

71   'Migrant women speak', published for the Churches Committee in *Migrant Workers*, by Search Press Ltd (World Council of Churches 1978), p. 2.

72   ibid., p. 3.

73   See a review of this book in *Race Today* (November–December 1978).

74   'Migrant women speak', p. 145.

75   ibid., p. 145.

76   See: Mala Dhondy, 'Voices already heard', *Race Today* (January 1979).

77   ibid.

78   Kate Purcell, 'Working women, women's work and the occupational sociology of being a woman', *Women's Studies International Quarterly*, vol. 1 (1968), pp. 153–63.

79   Khan, 'Purdah in the British situation'.

80   See: V. Goddard, 'Domestic industry in Naples', *Critique of Anthropology*, no. 9 (1977), where she points out that:

It is hoped that the research will show that the proliferation of home work in Naples cannot be explained in terms of single causes, but that it is due to the interconnection of a set of causes of a different nature: the economic structure of Naples, the conditions of the working class, the form of political domination that has governed Naples for the last twenty years, the role of the family in society, the division of labour within the family, and the ideology of male dominance.

81   E. Hope, M. Kennedy, and A. A. de Winter, 'Homeworkers in North London', in Barker and Allen.

82   This study is part of postgraduate research I am doing at CCCS on Asian women and the relations of waged work.

83   See pages 238–9 and 250–3 above.

84   *The Status of Women in India*, a synopsis of the report of the National Committee (Allied Publishers Ltd 1975).

85   ibid.

86   ibid.
87   Increasing landlessness is associated with the increased penetration of capitalist relations of production in some areas which had previously been left in more feudal relations of production (although still linked to capital through the world market system) and in India in particular, this occurred as a result of the 'green revolution'. See: C. Bettleheim, *India Independent*, (Monthly Review Press 1968). See also: K. Gough and H. P. Sharma (eds.), *Imperialism and Revolution*, (Monthly Review Press 1973). It is also interesting to note the effects of these changes, on the sexual division of labour in agriculture, both in terms of the changes and entrenchments in women's roles and positions. See: *Social Scientist*, special number on women, nos. 40–41 (November–December 1975), a monthly Journal of the Indian School of Social Sciences.
88   *The Status of Women in India*.
89   See, 'Women roll bidis, factory owners roll in wealth', *Manushi*, no. 7 (1981).
90   'Women on the lowest rung – a report on the working conditions of telephone operators in Delhi', *Manushi*, no. 6 (July–August 1980), pp. 10–13.
91   *The Status of Women in India*.
92   Rogers.
93   ibid.
94   See: Gail Minault, 'Political change: Muslim women in conflict with parda [*sic*]: their role in the Indian nationalist movement', in Sylvia A. Chipp and Justin J. Green (eds.), *Asian Women in Transition* (Pennsylvania State University 1980).
95   See: S. A. Chipp, 'The modern Pakistani woman in a Muslim society', in Chipp and Green, pp. 204–26.
96   ibid.
97   Quoted by Rogers, p. 160.
98   ibid.
99   ibid.
100   ibid.
101   ibid.
102   ibid.
103   Khan, 'Purdah in the British situation'.
104   A. Wilson, 'White scabs, cold comfort', *New Statesman*, 28 February 1980.
105   Bland *et al*.
106   ibid.
107   Chris Griffin, *The Good, the Bad and the Ugly; Images of Young Women in the Labour Market* (CCCS 1981).
108   ibid.
109   *Race Today*.
110   See: Janice Winship, 'Handling sex', in S. Hall, D. Hobson, A. Lowe and P. Willis (eds.), *Media, Culture, Language* (Hutchinson 1980).
111   See: K. Thitsa, 'Tourist Thailand, women for sale', *Spare Rib*, no. 103 (1981).
112   R. Grossman.
113   ibid.
114   Quoted by Grossman.
115   J. Winship, *Thinking about women in paid work* (CCCS 1981).
116   See: Lenz, *International Labour Studies* (July 1981).

117 See: Les Levidow, 'Grunwick; the social contract meets the 20th century sweatshop', in CSE, *Technology and the Labour Process* (CSE 1981). See also: *Race Today* (April–May 1977; September–October 1977; November –December 1977; January 1978; August–September 1979).
118 Levidow.
119 ibid.
120 Wilson.
121 Levidow, p. 145.
122 See: 'Women and class struggle', *Latin American Perspectives,* vol. iv, joint nos. 12 and 13 (1977).
123 See: A. Sivanandan, 'Imperialism and disorganic development in the silicon age', *Race and Class*, vol. xxi, no. 2 (Autumn 1979).
124 See a discussion of the specific forms of authority capital establishes over the labour process in: 'The capitalist labour process', by the Brighton Labour Process Group, *Capital and Class*, no. 1 (1977).
125 Miles and Phizacklea.
126 See: Gupta.
127 See these documented in back copies of *Race Today*.
128 *Race Today*.
129 ibid.
130 Gail Omvedt.
131 ibid.
132 Lenz.
133 ibid.
134 Grossman.
135 Quoted in *Spare Rib*, no. 66.
136 Quote from Mrs Desai.
137 *Race Today*.
138 *Southall Black Sisters Newsletter*.
139 ibid.
140 Wilson.
141 *Southall Black Sisters Newsletter*.
142 *Race Today*.
143 ibid.

8 Steppin' out of Babylon - race, class and autonomy

Paul Gilroy

The communists have a long time ahead of them before they can do anything for themselves in this country. When they get there we will be for them. But meantime we are for ourselves.

MARCUS GARVEY

Socialism is not a fixed unchanging doctrine. As the world develops, people's insight increases and as new relations come into being, there arise new methods of achieving our goal.

ANTON PANNEKOEK

Even as moribund socialist and Eurocommunist parties cultivate the populist potential in national chauvinism as the answer to their growing marginality,[1] there is a positive side to the political crisis of the European workers' movement. It exists in the diverse attempts to explore the relation between socialism and democracy, to break with reductionist understandings of class relations, and to establish a perspective on social transformation which gives a primary place to the insights and demands of feminism. They are also fruits of that crisis. In place of the totalizing 'zero-sum' view of classes in struggle, which has become an albatross around the neck of socialists who will not turn and face the future, these advances substitute a new dialectic of 'people' and 'power bloc'. Its value is in an understanding of power relations capable of relating political developments in the workplace to those in the home, the neighbourhood and the queue for social security payments. This involves giving due weight to cultural factors, understood neither as purely autonomous nor as epiphenomena of economic determinations. This concluding chapter focuses on the cultural politics of 'black' people in this country, and the implications of their struggles for the institutions and practices of the British workers' movement. It is about *class* struggle. Our premise is therefore the problem of relating 'race' to class, not for sociological theory, but for socialist politics. We will explore the idea that no simple separation of race and class consciousness can be made. Our starting-point is Stuart Hall's observation that in contemporary Britain:

The class relations which inscribe the black fractions of the working class function as race relations. The two are inseparable. Race is the modality in which class relations are experienced.[2]

Race and class struggle - the eurocommunist version

Unlike the sociologists we looked at in Chapter 2, the British left has been reluctant to approach the Pandora's box of racial politics. They have remained largely un-affected by over sixty years of black critical dialogue with Marxism presented most notably in the work of Garvey, Padmore, James, Wright, Fanon and Cox. The simplistic reduction of 'race' to class, which has guided their practice for so many years, has been thrown into confusion by intense and visible *black* struggles; and, at a different level, by the revival of interest in Marxist theory which has followed Althusser's reading of *Capital*.[3] Recently in a commendable if overdue attempt to confront the specificities of racial politics, sections of the left have reached out to the analyses of independent black political groupings only to dismiss them with a few fashionable insults.[4] These would-be architects of a national 'third way'[5] to democratic socialism, armed with a fervour for cultural politics derived from their idiosyncratic reading of Gramsci,[6] have begun to grapple with the political prob-lems of constructing their version of working-class hegemony over the strategic alliances which their predilection for 'popular democratic' struggle has placed on the historical agenda. Forced back from relating gender to class by the resolutely autonomous politics of women who will not subsume feminism to an unmodified version of socialism,[7] these theorists have made 'race' a prime site on which to establish the value of their break from Stalinist tradition. Race has become impor-tant at last, not because of black suffering, but because it can be used to demon-strate the distance Marxists have travelled from economism. Unfortunately, the analysts of 'race' in this influential tendency have expounded the popular and democratic qualities of the struggle for black liberation to the point where its class character has escaped them:

The struggle for racial equality and racial justice . . . needs to be seen *primarily* as a popular-democratic struggle.[8] (my emphasis)

Though widespread on the left, this position has been most systematically advocated by Gideon Ben-Tovim and John Gabriel,[9] who have acknowledged that it owes a great debt to the important theoretical contributions of Ernesto Laclau.[10] Some comment on their application of Laclau's theses to the theorization of racist ideology and politics is therefore required. His complex positions cannot be rehearsed here in any detail but the basic argument is that the ideological elements, which interpolate individuals and constitute them as subjects in discourse, are not ascribed by class. Discourses, which are not the intrinsic property of any particular class, become articulated to and by conflicting class practices in ideological struggle. They can serve a variety of political ends. His principal examples are the discourses of nationalism and democracy, both of which are particularly pertinent to the study of racial politics and structuration in late capitalist conditions. Drawing his illustration from the debate about the relation of socialism and nationalism in the KPD,[11] Laclau argues that the discourse of 'the nation' may be articulated into struggles where working-class interests are hegemonic, without antagonistic contradiction.[12] Non-economistic socialism becomes compatible with nationalism. He distinguishes thus between the German and British social formations as part of his argument against a necessarily negative character to popular nationalism in the working-class movement:

In the British case, for example, the nationalist element is far less present – indeed the universalist element is predominant in democratic ideology.[13]

This statement betrays regrettable ignorance of the unwholesome power of nationalism in British politics.[14] It will take far more than the will to create a 'pluralist national identity' to prise the jaws of the bulldog of British nationalism free from the flesh of the labour movement. It is precisely because the discourses of the British Nation and the British People are *racially exclusive* that a contradiction around race becomes a grave problem for those who adopt Laclau's framework. It may be that the benefits of imperialism have determined that 'the people' will always tend towards 'the race' in this country,[15] at any rate 'The British Nation' and 'The Island Race' have historically failed to, and cannot at present, incorporate black people. Indeed their alienness and externality to all things British and beautiful make it hard to imagine any such discourse which could accommodate their presence in a positive manner and retain its popular character. The popular discourse of the nation operates across the formal lines of class, and has been constructed *against* blacks.

If increasing segments of the nation come to feel that neither church establishment nor unions care for their sentiments and distress, where may they not turn? The results could be catastrophic for all, not least for the minorities.[16]

It should be clear that the authoritarian statism that signals the transformation of social democracy in this country has been secured on the basis of popular consent. For us, the racist interpellation of 'the nation' is a prime example of 'social democracy having provided authoritarian populism with popular contradictions on which to operate'.[17] Laclau explains that 'popular-democratic' discourses are constructed on the basis of opposition between 'The People' and 'The Power Bloc'. However, his followers remain unable to face the fact that for Britain in crisis, 'The People' are articulated into a racially specific discourse which has distinctly undemocratic consequences for the blacks whom it excludes. For example, where they follow the Fascist dictum and 'blame the bosses for the blacks', the 'white people' confront an ill-conceived vision of the power bloc, alone in racial purity and for the wrong reasons. This has serious implications for anti-racist practice, as we shall see; it is a concrete illustration of a theoretical point made elegantly by Nicos Mouzellis:

Certain ideological themes (whether popular or not) can be so incongruent with the structural and *organisational* realities of a class that they cannot become dominant in its discourse. In other terms, if there is no one to one correspondence between classes and ideological themes, neither is there a completely arbitrary relationship between the two. . . . once an ideological discourse takes a specific place and form within a concrete social formation, then it too becomes organised and fixed within limits imposed both by *the internal organisation of a class and by the overall socio-political context.*[18] (my emphasis)

This realization transposes the argument onto the historical plane of the social formation, from where it should be easier to see that the white working class of Great Britain was formed, and has matured, in evolving conditions of imperialist dominance. This historical perspective is yet more important because racial fragmentation is not a permanent or eternal fact. We shall argue later that the politics of working-class youth cultures offers the possibility that 'race', as a source of segmentation, may recede. This must be considered seriously in the wake of recent rioting where black and white youth stood shoulder to shoulder against the police.

Like Laclau, Gabriel and Ben-Tovim move from considering abstract, structural contradictions to examine ideological struggles. They scarcely pause over the concrete reality of the class institutions and organizational forms that comprise the 'mode of class struggle'[19] in which the subsequent articulation and disarticulation of interpellations takes place. They have attempted to address this weakness in recent work on anti-racist struggle and the democratization of the local state,[20] but merely replicate it by failing to come to terms with the lack of accountability and representativeness which they discovered in the 'race relations' agencies of Liverpool and Wolverhampton. What is valuable in their account is deformed by an idealism which cites 'lack of political will' as an adequate explanation of the government's failure to eliminate racial discrimination. It carries the unquestioned assumption that the problem of racial oppression is open to solutions at the level of policy rather than the level of politics. As the institutions of the social-democratic state change, forms of political action predicated on their continued existence must be subjected to rigorous criticism. The expectations which Gabriel, Ben-Tovim *et al.* have of such structures are puzzling, as is their view of them as unproblematically open to infusions of meaningful democratic, anti-racist practice, particularly in the light of the evidence they themselves produce to the contrary. Invoking a concept of democracy in general 'as if it were an ahistorical essence defined by its attributes',[21] they argue for the 'democratization' of these bodies without sensing the obligation to show *why* this has so far failed to develop. For example, it is difficult to disagree with their opinion that poor co-ordination and insufficient integration of the Commission for Racial Equality with other local state agencies has curtailed its efficiency. But the marginal relation of these institutions to the political lives of black communities, and their ubiquitous failure to tackle the problems of racial oppression cannot be seen as an unfortunate accident which can be rectified easily by an injection of ethereal accountability. It need not be reductionist or conspiratorial to enquire whether the popular and structural bases of racism in the 1980s are within the capacity of such agencies to resolve at all. The CRE/CRC complex does not have to be viewed as homogeneous or monolithic for it to be considered essentially irrelevant and intermittently obstructive. We should not be understood to be advocating abstention from these structures which may have valuable, if limited, local roles to play.

The true question at issue is not the necessity of struggling for the democratisation of the state, both within and outside its limitations, but the scope, modalities and limits of such a struggle.[22]

We are forced to argue that the authors have muddled the distinction between 'people's democratic rights and freedoms and the institutions of the bourgeois democratic state',[23] and further, that their position is only tenable at the cost of understanding race exclusively as an ideological or cultural issue, shorn of structural determinacy, which only 'subsequently intervenes at the level of the economy'.[24] It is secured by several assertions which fly in the face of historical and political reality.

The authors persistently invoke the possibility of 'broad based political struggles' and 'broad democratic alliances' against racism, though these have failed to materialise on cue. They ignore the inhibitions to the development of political breadth in this area which have crystallised around the pole of nationalism, but more importantly, also fail to examine the character of groups which *have* become involved in large-scale anti-racist mobilizations. Here the most glaring omission is their failure to take account of the experience of white youth and the Rock Against Racism initiative, which leaves a considerable gap in their analysis. However, if the reader is tempted to endorse their convenient vision in spite of these failings, it is well to recall the havoc wrought on the black movement in the United States by the 1935 'popular front' period which is the antecedent of this 'Euro-communist' intervention.[25] There must be serious debate over whether this broad orientation is desirable or appropriate to the struggle against racism. It should not be emphasized at the expense of a refusal to consider the historic appeal of racist ideologies to the white working class.

Finally, the authors look into the political institutions of the black communities for the mirrored images of their own limited conceptions of political organization.[26] They simply assert that 'Third World ideologies' are 'relatively insignificant in Liverpool' and do not see any need to situate the culture of young Afro-Caribbean people on political terrain. It may be that black youth on Merseyside do not listen to reggae, build sound systems, or wear headwraps, tams and dreadlocks like their sisters and brothers in other parts of the country, but the authors shirk the obligation to make explicit their anxieties over the political limits of these ideologies. Gabriel and Ben-Tovim prefer to discuss the 'black para-professionals' who constitute the locally born black 'leadership', though they never explain who or what this group actually lead. If, as they explain, 'the form of organisation in fact depends on the context and the issue at stake', they give no idea of the issues which have generated an identifiable leadership of the type they have written about. Carchedi's observation that 'immigrant workers . . . have not only participated in existing forms of struggle: they have invented new ones'[27] means that serious analysis cannot take the *forms* of political struggle and organization for granted. The social formation, in which the different political traditions of immigrants and their children confront those of the British labour movement, has constructed the arena of politics on ground overshadowed by centuries of metropolitan capitalist development. But the dominance of these specific institutions and political forms should not be allowed to disrupt assessment of political traditions born elsewhere.

The other influential position that we must note before we proceed, is presented in the sociologistic pseudo-Marxism of Annie Phizacklea and Robert Miles.[28] Here, having advanced a social stratification problematic, the authors argue for a rigid separation of race and class consciousness which they claim to be able to quantify on the basis of questionnaire material. Though we must object to their conceptualization of autonomous black politics as a threat to the working-class movement comparable to that posed by organized Fascism,[29] we will not engage in a detailed critique of their work here because the remainder of this chapter presents our objections in a constructive rather than negative mode. We will attempt to tread a different path from the sociologism of their approach, and the idealism of Gabriel and Ben-Tovim. This involves taking explicit distance from 'race relations'. One or two general remarks about the way we conceive of 'race' and racism are therefore in order.

We are fully aware that the ideological status of the concept 'race' qualifies its analytic use. It is precisely this meaninglessness which persistently refers us to the construction, mobilization and pertinence of different forms of racist ideology and structuration in *specific historical circumstances*. We must examine the role of these ideologies in the complex articulation of classes in a social formation, and strive to discover the conditions of existence which permit the constitution of 'black' people in politics, ideology and economic life. Thus there can be no general theory of 'race' or 'race relations situations', only the historical resonance of racist ideologies and a specific ideological struggle by means of which real structural phenomena are misrecognised and distorted in the prisms of 'race'.[30]

Race, struggle and class formation

The impact of the feminist movement has recently ensured that the status of struggles against patriarchal oppression[31] has been raised as a political and theoretical problem for the versions of 'Marxism' which are also our targets here.[32] We must be wary of overemphasizing parallels between oppression by means of 'race' and oppression grounded in gender difference, yet racist and patriarchal ideologies both 'discover what other ideologies have to construct' in the natural differences they reference. The struggles against the forms of domination they structure suffer a common marginalization by 'sex and race blind' Marxist 'science', which has either ignored or provided reductionist accounts of racial and gender conflict. The way in which racism involves the control of fertility[33] as well as the control of labour power is one of several approaches to thinking about similarities between these forms of oppression. Yet the relation between the ways oppressions work must not be confused with the possibility of political alliances between the movements which struggle to end them. The liberation which these struggles anticipate does not exist in competition with the economic emancipation which may be its precon-dition, but political organization in these areas can only be built on an understand-ing of the primacy of racial and sexual determinations in the development of political consciousness, a point well made in a particular context by Richard Wright:

Negro writers must accept the nationalist implications of their lives, not in order to encourage them, but in order to change and transcend them. They must accept the concept of nationalism because in order to transcend it they must possess and understand it . . . it means a nationalism that knows its origins, its limitations; and is aware of the dangers in its position.[34]

In acknowledgement of this point and armed with a view of the social formation as a contradictory but complex *unity*, our approach seeks to demonstrate the correspondences, connections, ruptures and breaks between capital, patriarchy and their racial structures. It would be wrong to deduce that the recognition of this unity compels its simple transfer into politics. The opposite is true, since our view of the complexity of these relations is such that the autonomy of different political forces in struggle is our premise.

Relations between patriarchal oppression and racisms are most clearly visible where each attempts to ground social differences in a spurious conception of nature. The structures of patriarchy are established in material conditions of a qualitatively different order from the subjugation of peoples who do not have 'white' skin, because political 'races' have no relation to the biology of 'racial characteristics', but we follow Timpanaro[35] in arguing that meaningful materialism must recognize that both have a biological dimension. This resides in the relation of biological determinations to the social construction of their significance. The fact that racisms have often comprised a struggle to establish biological relevance at group level, should not blind us to the 'conspicuous weight (of the biological level) in the determination of individual characteristics'.[36] Skin 'colour' is genetically deter-mined no matter how biologically irrelevant we know it to be. Kate Soper's formulation of 'relatively autonomous biological determinations' sheds some light on a notoriously difficult problem:

There may be a considerable degree of difference in the extent to which the effects of biological determinations are dominant or subordinate in their 'impor-tance' for the person relative to the effects of other social or less directly biological determinations. . . . one might want to suggest that they would be relatively dominant for most women and black persons today.[37]

Discussion of the 'reality' of these differences can rapidly degenerate into an academic issue at odds with materialist explanation, they are clearly real enough to be necessary though not sufficient conditions of existence for the emergence of racist ideologies which are always biologically reductionist. Racist pseudo-materialism must be fought with a scientifically founded materialism.[38]

The significance of these differences is contested in ideological struggle made possible by the contradictory nature of signs themselves, what Volosinov has termed their multi-accentuality:

in fact each living ideological sign has two faces like janus. Any current curse word can become a word of praise, any current truth must inevitably sound to many other peoples the greatest lie.[39]

He argues that this 'inner dialectic quality of the sign . . .comes out fully into the open only in times of social crisis or revolutionary change' but we want to suggest that this quality is also foregrounded in the struggle to make 'race' meaningful. This should be obvious where anti-racism challenges the status of visible differences designated racial, but is more important where the oppressed negate the very categories of their oppression, revealing that these categories mark sites and boundaries of class struggle in ideology, where they create cultures of resistance.

Thus black musicians, for instance, had earlier subverted the word bad into its dialectical opposite, a term of approbation' 'Man, that cat is *bad*!' In its jazz usage, funky, obviously enough represented an extension of this tradition. To describe a musician as funky – i.e. unwashed, repellent – meant he was *worse* (that is, better) than just *bad* – he was . . . *funky*.[40]

This is one small illustration of Volosinov's view of ideological struggle.

Existence reflected in the sign is not merely reflected but refracted. How is this refraction of existence in the ideological sign determined? *By an intersecting of differently oriented social interests within one and the same sign community, i.e. by the class struggle.*[41]

In this case we are confronted by a class struggle in and through 'race'. The move from 'race' to class becomes crucial at this point because 'The division of humanity into social classes explains its history infinitely better than its division into races or peoples'.[42] However, it cannot be accomplished without reconceptualizing class in opposition to a Marxist orthodoxy which views the working class as a continuous historical subject[43] which, once formed, develops in a linear manner as a political actor. The class character of 'black' struggles in the present conjuncture will remain elusive until the following questions have been answered:

What brings the particular conflict about? what led the participants to be organised in the particular form? what are the potential outcomes? what are the consequences of these outcomes for future development?[44]

Prezworski continues:

All these questions concern objective conditions: the conditions which made the emergence of a particular conflict possible, the conditions which made the particular organisations, ideology, relation of forces possible, the conditions which make particular outcomes plausible or implausible; and finally, but importantly, the conditions which may be created as the result of a particular conflict.

This way of conceptualizing class must be located as part of an attempt to give class struggle a degree of determinacy which it has relinquished in much recent Marxist writing.[45]

Following these methodological guidelines we will establish the boundaries of our concept of class struggle so that it includes the relentless processes by which classes are constituted – organized and disorganized – in politics, as well as the struggles between them once formed. In this way their synchronized movement, no longer pre-given in an ontology of classes, becomes a goal of class struggles themselves. The recent history of the racial segmentation of the British working class[46] readily demonstrates the instability of any view of that class as a continuous or homogeneous subject of history. We have found the idea of 'discontinuous but related histories' a useful way of illustrating the relation of 'black' to 'white' workers, who, though structurally related, were not always geographically proximate.

If their blood has not mingled extensively with yours, their labour power has long since entered your economic blood stream. It is the sugar you stir, it is in the sinews of the infamous British sweet tooth, it is the tea leaves at the bottom of the British cuppa.[47]

We will also speak of blacks as racially demarcated class fractions in recognition of their power to constitute themselves as an autonomous social force in politics.[48]

In opposition to theorists who reduce race to custom or ethnicity as part of their own parochial battle to maintain the 'sociology of ethnic relations', we must locate racist and anti-racist ideology as well as the struggle for black liberation in a perspective on culture as a terrain of class conflicts. Space does not permit the detailed reproduction of Richard Johnson's important contribution to the theorization of working-class culture,[49] but it indicates the direction of our own enterprise:

From this viewpoint 'working class' culture is the form in which labour is reproduced. . . . This process of reproduction, then, is always a contested transformation. Working class culture is formed in the struggle between capital's demand for particular forms of labour power and the search for a secure location within this relationship of dependency. The outcomes of such necessary struggles depend on what ideological and political forces are in play, and ultimately on the existence of socialist organisation with an integral relation to proletarian conditions and working class cultural forms.

Having said this, we must be immediately wary of simply tinting Johnson's argument a different shade, by tacking race on beyond the commas of class, and gender. The internalization of blacks by the working class is such that it requires more than that their presence is noted and the multicultural tones of metropolitan class struggle registered accordingly, though this may have polemical value. Marx's famous remark that 'the traditions of all dead generations weighs like a nightmare on the brains of the living' acquires new poignancy as the great grandchildren of martyred slaves and indentured labourers set up home in the land of those who had tormented their progenitors. The mass of black people who arrived here recently as fugitives from colonial underdevelopment, brought with them legacies of their political, ideological and economic struggles in Africa, the Caribbean and the Indian subcontinent, as well as the scars of imperialist violence.

Far from being fixed or unchanging, the accumulated histories of their far-flung resistance have brought a distinct quality to struggle at the cultural level in their new metropolitan home. For as Cabral points out:

If imperialist domination has the vital need to practise cultural oppression, national liberation is necessarily an act of culture.[50]

Sivanandan has argued that a disorganic articulation of capitalist relations of production with vestigial political and ideological forms tends to generate a contradiction between:

The political regime and the people, with culture as the expression of resistance. And it is cultural resistance which . . . takes on new forms . . . in order fully to contest foreign domination. But culture in the periphery is not equally developed in all sectors of society. . . . it does have a mass character . . . at the economic level, different exploitations in the different modes confuse the formal lines of class struggle but the common denominators of political oppression make for a mass movement. Hence the revolutions in these countries are not necessarily class, socialist revolutions – they do not begin as such anyway. They are not even nationalist revolutions as we know them. They are mass movements with national and revolutionary components – sometimes religious, sometimes secular, often both, but always against the repressive state and its imperial backers.[51]

This passage has been quoted at length not only because it refers us to the people/ power-bloc contradiction we shall explore below, but because it hints at the political traditions which the blacks who arrived here since World War II brought with them. The process Sivanandan describes is the dying embers of the furnace in which their now-transplanted political consciousness was forged. They and their British-born children have preserved organic links with it, in their kitchens and temples – in their *communities*. Though their new struggles at the centre are diffused throughout a different structure in dominance, the lingering bile of slavery, indenture and colonialism remains – not in the supposedly pathological forms in which black households are organized, but in the forms of struggle, political philosophy, and revolutionary perspectives of non-European radical traditions, and the 'good sense' of their practical ideologies.

Working-class black communities

Localized struggles over education, racial violence and police practices continually reveal how black people have made use of notions of community to provide the axis along which to organize themselves. The concept of community is central to the view of class struggle presented here. It links distinct cultural and political traditions with a territorial dimension, to collective actions and consciousness[52] within the relation of 'economic patterns, political authority and uses of space'.[53] The idea of a racially demarcated collectivity of this type underlines the fact that community cannot be viewed as either static or given by some essential character-istics of the class or class fractions which come to constitute it. The cultural institutions which specify community have not been a continual feature of working-class life. The history of working-class communities, into which we will introduce the particular experiences of post-war immigrants and their children, is entwined with the processes of industrialization and social discipline[54] which established the city as a site of unique political conflicts. The form and relevance of community have therefore fluctuated with the changing social character of capitalist production which has accorded black labour a specific place, highlighting the means by which 'the dissociation of the upper and lower classes achieves form in the city itself'.[55] Even while the modern proletariat remained immature, the attempt to chart com-munity necessarily required attention to the dynamics of class formation and political organization. The histories of the Minters, the Costermongers, the Scuttlers and their Molls[56] all present the working class organized on the basis of community in urban struggles long before blacks were concentrated as a replacement population in areas which, 'despite the demand for labour power . . . failed to attract sufficient white population'.[57] In an influential discussion which anticipates the direction of our work here, Gareth Stedman-Jones has pointed to a growing separation of the workplace from the domestic sphere as an important determination of the cultural and political patterns of urban workers in late-nineteenth-century London.[58] His example of the disruption of community illustrates how the concept can be useful in the connection of waged and domestic labour space. It is valuable not only where leisure practices impinge on the labour process,[59] but also where political organization forged outside the immediate processes of production (for blacks, with juridico-political apparatuses, organized racists or profiteering ghetto land-lords) has effects on the struggle at work, and vice versa.

The making of classes at work is *complemented* by the making of classes where people live; in both places, adaptive and rebellious responses to the class situation are inevitably closely intertwined.[60]

Used to cover this connection, the concept denies the hasty separation of the social formation into purified instances. The struggle to construct community in the face of domination makes Eurocentric conceptualizations of 'the political' or 'the economic' hazardous if not misguided. To speak of community is to address complex articulated interests which blur these distinctions. It is to confront the materiality of hegemony and power, not in the abstract but evidenced in definite institutions and structures.

When I think of the mechanics of power, I have in mind its capillary form of existence, at the point where power returns into the very grain of individuals, touches their gestures and attitudes, their discourses, apprenticeships and daily lives.[61]

Though primarily concerned with the labour-process end of the equation, Michael Burawoy has argued for a reformulation of the relation of politics in production to those outside, on ground afforded by the concept of hegemony.[62] The example of 'homeworking' discussed in Chapter 7 is an illustration of how the experiences of the black communities can make his point in acute form. 'The production of objects is simultaneously the production of relations',[63] and the significant political processes he has discovered in production assume racially specific form. They become articulated to racially bounded struggles, in ways which defy orthodox Marxist wisdom, even as front rooms are daily transformed into machine shops. The interrelation of production and the political space in which community develops is not satisfactorily understood at the level of production's immediate processes. In order to periodize class struggle and relate it to phases of accumulation, it must be remembered that capitalist production necessarily generates surplus labour power. The form in which this labour power appears in social formations is not determined mechanistically by accumulation, but directly by political struggles.

Processes of formation of workers into a class are inextricably fused with the processes of organisation of surplus labour.[64]

The place of community in this process will be illuminated in the discussion of black culture which follows, but it should be obvious that the move from full employment to structural unemployment heralds fundamental changes in the way surplus labour power appears as surplus population. We saw in Chapters 4 and 5 that new problems of social control and surveillance have been posed by this development and its context of crisis. It must be understood that the political traditions of black people, expressed in the solidarity and political strength of their communities, have determined a specific *territorialization* of social control; a general tendency noted by Dario Melossi[65] and elaborated in the British context by Lee Bridges[66] in his important analysis of urban social policy. Melossi points out that:

At this point the discussion of social control becomes the discussion of the state, given that the hegemonic apparatus of the state is the most fundamental vehicle of social control. The struggle for hegemony, therefore, is not a question of more struggle within the institutions or in the localities, generically understood, but the construction . . . of real vehicles of hegemony.

Community is just such a vehicle.

We wish to locate the competing definitions of community, which occur in the struggle to create localized equivalents of the people/power-bloc contradiction, in this context. Community policing initiatives recognize the political opportunities here in their attempt to organize ideological elements so that community is counterposed to crime, rather than to the police themselves. It should be appreciated that this is an overdue response to the fact that working-class communities have traditionally viewed the officers of the law as representatives of the power bloc.[67] The territorial dimension to social control of urban black communities is presented with startling clarity by the use of 'sus' laws to confine black youth to particular neighbourhoods[68] and by particularly brutal police operations which have become acceptable for black areas.[69] These give credence to the designation of black residential communities as 'colony areas' in which law and order techniques refined overseas can be applied with gusto and impunity.[70]

Ira Katznelson[71] and more recently John Lea[72] have elaborated the patterns of state intervention designed to secure the integration of blacks into the tripartite[72] political apparatuses of the social-democratic state. Their useful accounts are incomplete without some attention to the forms of struggle, organization and political ideology which made this corporatist relation possible. Above all, this requires consideration of the ideology of self-help which fused political representation and state intervention, disorganizing black discontent and channelling it into 'quasicolonial institutional structures . . . (which would) deal with the issue of race outside traditional political arenas'.[74] If the political consensus over containing the black problem owed something to the colonial period, the black organizations which struggled with it on the terrain of community made this connection increasingly explicit – unfortunately, often in forms which drew the most unhelpful parallels with the situation in the Third World.[75] In a nationalist framework which could do little more than present an inverted image of the oppressor's power, the issue of black control of self-help projects sometimes obscured the nature of the schemes themselves. By restricting their analysis to racial parameters, the nationalist self-help groups became easy meat for state institutions already placing a premium on self-help 'as a response to the threat posed by alienated black youth'.[76] The Community Relations Commission's self-help report for 1976 spells out the limits of their approach:

Some of the leaders of self-help groups have strong political views particularly with regard to the struggles for freedom for blacks in the USA and Africa. These do not, however, appear to have any significant effect on the work of these organisations.[77]

In both black communities generational conflict expressed deeper debates over political responses, rather than aberrant familial practices. Such conflicts were always premised on the fundamental unity of the community, and conducted within the repertoire of its political traditions, both of organization and ideology. Tension between Asian Youth Movements and the IWA organizations is the clearest example of this process, posing the distinction between corporate and autonomous modes of class struggle in complex fashion, overdetermined by the peasant political traditions from which both have sprouted.[78]

Black people, the power bloc and cultural politics

Though parallel arguments could be constructed from the experience of Asian blacks from Africa and the Indian subcontinent, the remainder of this chapter is focused around the popular culture and politics of Britons of Afro-Caribbean descent. Through their experience we will demonstrate that the mass of blacks in this country are engaged in a complex political and ideological struggle. This is organized through the collective refusal of capitalist domination which they experience in the form of racial oppression. We will explore the basis for a view of their struggles as processes of class struggle, here constituted by and through the dialectical experience of racism. By this, we refer to popular and theoretical racist ideologies, racialist practices and, most importantly, the struggles of the oppressed to contest and transform the categories of their oppression into a source of political strength: their collective refusal of racial domination.

It is necessary to account for the cultural dimension to the political struggles of 'black' people. This involves realizing that the politics of black liberation is necessarily a cultural politics. Coons, Pakis, Nig-nogs, Sambos and Wogs are social constructions *in culture*. Marx's 'On the Jewish question'[79] is relevant to this theme. Towards the end of this notoriously oblique text he attempts to explore the connection between 'Judaism', which for him is the ideology of civil society *not* of the Jews themselves – 'civil society ceaselessly begets the Jew from its own entrails' – and Germany, which requires the 'Jew' at a particular stage of its development. The difficult, and not entirely consistent usage of the term 'Jew', points to the way oppressed people have to locate the ideologies which oppress them historically as the first step to their transcendence. Cedric Robinson[80] has extended Marx's line of thought and demonstrated its applicability to the construction of 'the Negro' in nineteenth-century America. Drawing on C. L. R. James's view[81] of voodoo as the ideology of the Haitian revolution, he speculates that Marx's essay provides a useful means of understanding the complex negation of ideas and images which characterizes the cultural struggles of colonized people. This, if it is to be successful, must move beyond a simple nationalist mirror-image of the colonizer's conquering vision. This nationalist reaction, which has an important place in the recent racial politics of this country, is only a partial and unsatisfactory response to racial domination. Following Robinson, we shall focus on a more profound negation of 'race' and of Europe to be found at the core of the cultural politics of

British blacks. It is the key to understanding the relatively recent supersession of nationalist politics by an international revolutionary movement of black people, the most visible manifestations of which are organized popular currents in the Caribbean, America and Britain which have been identified by the dominant ideology as 'Ethiopianism' or 'Rastafarianism'. Horace Campbell[82] and Sebastian Clarke[83] have delivered timely reminders that 'Ethiopianism' is no recent development. There is no space here to consider how the same profound comprehension of the need 'to reverse the ideas, to reverse the values, to reverse even the conceptualisations of movement, causality, forces'[84] links mass organization of African peoples from Chilembwe to Garvey, from Njama and Mwiarma to Omulú.[85] Contemporary Britain is neither Africa nor the Caribbean, but the distinct political traditions of African people must be borne in mind. Contrary to the views of sociologists of 'acculturation' they are present in the practice of black movements today.[86]

This brings us to an examination of what sociological orthodoxy now defines as 'the Rastafarian movement'.[87] Our own view of these phenomena involves considerable redefinition of their contours, boundaries and supposed aims. The critique of sociological theories is set out in Chapter 3; however, it is important to emphasize that we do not consider the sociology of religion as an adequate starting-point for analysis, not least because the pan-Africanist philosophy which characterizes the movement has been in an elliptical and sometimes reluctant dialogue with revolutionary Marxism since the days of Garvey and Randolph.[88] We must also challenge the idea of simple correspondences between the movement in Britain and its forms elsewhere. Though wherever it has taken root,

Rastafari culture remains an indelible link between the resistance of the maroons, the pan-africanist appeal of Marcus Garvey, the materialist and historical analysis of Walter Rodney and the defiance of reggae.[89]

We must be careful not to fudge the differences between its political and ideological complexions in Grenada, Dominica and Jamaica let alone amidst the relation of forces in this country where the pertinence of racial politics shifts Rasta struggle into an altogether different mode. The relatively small number of black people here places an immediate limit on the populist appeal of these ideas. The impact of Afro-Caribbean culture in general, and through reggae, Rastafarianism in particular, on the lives and politics of white working-class youth is too often overlooked, but it is the mass character of the movement in the black communities which provides our starting-point.

This means that we take issue with any tendency to define the movement in a crude empirical manner by offering a number of dogmatic tenets to which 'cultists' are subsequently found to subscribe.[90] Instead, we locate the symbols of 'dread', by which researchers have so far identified cult-affiliates, at one end of a broad continuum of belief which spans both age and gender difference. At this extreme, an open signification of 'dreadness' – the wearing of headwraps, hats, dreadlocks, long skirts and Ethiopian colours – merely transposes the *difference* already immanent in the unacceptable attribute of dark skin into open semiotic struggle characteristic of youth subculture.[91] In this case the struggle is against categories associated with the whole racial group. These symbols consolidate the group's collective identity, and become meaningful to those who do not signify their political philosophy in such overt ways. The growing of dreadlocks which draws attention to that least acceptable attribute of 'blackness' – woolly hair – must be seen as superseding the 'afros' and 'naturals' which, once a focus for the redefinition of black as beautiful, faded into the commonplace from the front page of Ebony:

I and I grow dreadlocks, i.e. uncut and uncombed locks as a symbol of cultural rebellion, since I and I as Africans must establish our own standards of beauty, niceness and discipline.[92]

Thus the confrontation in style acts as a focal point for dread and baldhead alike, and the scope of the movement must not be underestimated by dwelling on the stylized defiance of its younger and more flamboyant adherents. The second problem with any attempt to approach these struggles through a 'youth subculture' problematic, is its inherent masculinism.[93] Few analysts have perceived that there are female Rastafari. Even fewer discuss their specific relation to the movement. Ernest Cashmore views 'Rasta patriarchy' as a revolt against the supposed matriarchy of the 'normal' West Indian family. For him, as with Dick Hebdidge, it appears that youth subculture has provided the perch from which he has been able to engage the young locksmen in conversation. The ideology of the 'queen' in Rasta discourse represents the space from which Rasta women have begun to wage their distinct form of feminist struggle. The cultural offensive represented by reggae music is so central to the political development of the movement that it would be surprising if this trend were not represented at that level. One small but interesting example of the struggle taking place is to be found in the record 'Black Woman' released by Judy Mowatt in the summer of 1979. It formed the basis of several 'Black Woman Experience' stage presentations,[94] and proved so popular during the following eighteen months that a major white-owned record company stepped in to provide a British release for the disc, which had previously only been available through comparatively restricted outlets in black areas. Changes in the packaging and design of the subsequent re-released version are evidence of the impact of the images on the original record sleeve. Mowatt had made 'the queen' the starting point for a redefinition of the Rasta woman, establishing her in an activist role waging struggles distinct from but complementary to those of her brethren. The front was a star of Israel on which a red, gold and green cross had been superimposed. This was divided into five equal squares; in each of the surrounding four was a picture of Mowatt attired as an African queen. In the central square was a very different portrait of her in the male and militant uniform of dread, seemingly prepared to do battle with the forces of Babylon. On the back was a full face view of her, this time with her hair uncovered in explicit defiance of the taboo which some more theologically inclined Rastas have placed on females. The contrasting images posed an explicit challenge to male domination, but in a context which emphasized the continuity of Rasta ideology. The repackaged version disrupted all this with a large 'glamorous' picture of her conventionally attired. Her songs 'Strength To Go Through', 'Slave Queen' and 'Black Woman' were the basis of the record's great popularity at the grass-roots, but it was in 'Sisters' Chant' that Mowatt made her straightforward demand for the validity of 'feminist' Rastafari in language which recalled the nineteenth-century feminists who distinguished between 'man' and 'god'.[95]

Once dread style has been set aside as the essential qualification for 'cult membership', it becomes clear that many older black people share the movement's pan-Africanist sentiments and take pride in its refusal of racial domination. It is often forgotten that blacks arrived here bearing traditions of anti-colonial struggle wherever they set out from. Older West Indians have encountered the discourse of Rasta before, and though sometimes critical of it, many of the first generation we interviewed in preparing this volume were happy to recount tales of their contact with the Garveyites 'at home'. Their sympathy with the movement should be no surprise; the solidarity it provides the whole community appears to offer a refuge from the new pressures of *popular* racism. The formation of parents' groups and defence organizations in both black communities confirms that a high level of state harassment has effected the consolidation of black households across generational lines. Whole families have been drawn into conflict on the basis of immigration laws and police practices which do not differentiate on age lines, but construct black households as special objects of state policy.[96]

The breadth of the Rastas' cultural intervention is also important here. Like the 'Bop' players of the sixties who absorbed black nationalism and Elijah Mohammed alike, reggae musicians have been converted to Rasta in such numbers that it has become impossible to discuss one without the other. Though there are certain styles which appeal more to older people, the universal popularity of Bob Marley is a good illustration of how these different preferences have been spanned. In the West Indian orientation to leisure, the raw material of white youth cultures becomes the background music to an old age pensioner's night out. Closure of shebeens has meant that a growing number of pubs in black areas have opened their doors to reggae music at the weekend. Though these 'hi-fis' are no match for the powerful sound systems of the second generation, they are in many ways a counterpart, catering for the taste of their parents with a selection of 'lovers' ' reggae, soca and the occasional soul record. The popularity of communalist ideology and its implicit politics may also be gauged by the widespread use of Rasta concepts and speech patterns by those who do not wish to express their affiliation or interests more overtly. Such language is able to convey commitment in a selective or intermittent manner, and its racially exclusive mode invites speakers to appropriate the ideas which appeal to them without being pigeon-holed by the oppressor. It is not only that young black people devoid of locks address each other habitually as

'Rasta', though such a group does exist and is far too large to be explained away by Ken Pryce's rather puzzling view of them as 'inbetweeners'.[97] Neither stigmas attached to the wearing of long hair nor the barrier supposedly created by participation in waged labour explain very much. We must resist the equation of Rasta politics with work refusal. Mass unemployment affects dread and baldhead alike, blurring the edges of any simple assessment. (There may be a connection with the reluctance to register with statutory services, but that is an altogether different political struggle.) In truth, the operation of a shared language, far more than the colours and vestimentary codes of dread style, marks the frontiers of a discursive community in which deep disagreement is possible without condemnation or schism. Here, racial interpellations predominate and the contradictions which arise remain in non-antagonistic form. This is a partial explanation of the avowed Rasta's insistence that all black people are Rasta whether they know it or not. This has been a difficult point for some sociologists to digest as the cohesion it invokes contradicts the dominant view of the dreads as a minority within a minority, suffering the resentment of their own people in addition to racial subjugation. This view, which separates the visible Rasta from the whole community, ignores the links forged in sharing language at its cost, a point acutely observed by Joseph Owens:

It may not always be possible to tell a rasta by his [*sic*] appearance, but in the absence of other signs his speech will frequently reveal his identity. Once two rastas told me that they had been forced out of a job because they were rastas. As they had no locks and could not be visibly identified as rastas, I enquired how the employer knew. They replied: 'By I and I argument. Man know I and I by I and I argument'.[98]

Within this linguistic community the introduction of specifically Rasta concepts is an attempt to bring order to the practical ideology and 'good sense' of the black community. This is:

not the result of any systematic educational activity on the part of an already conscious leading group, but (has) been formed through the everyday experience illuminated by 'common sense', i.e. by the practical popular conception of the world – what is unimaginatively called 'instinct', although it is in fact a primitive and elementary historical acquisition.[99]

The analytic tendency of Rasta concepts is in opposition to blind acceptance of the world as it appears and the body of ideas which maintain it: 'ism and schism'. Rastas are critical. Coherent explanation that operates at deeper levels is required, and Rastas strive towards a historical theorization of social dynamics – 'overstanding', 'truth and rights' – which is the result of collective processes of dialectical enquiry aptly named 'reasoning'. The Rastas' refusal of complicity with the world creates a distance from which these operations are possible. The philosophical contours of their view of the world are determined by a realism – 'burning all illusions' – and an anthropocentric materialism which not only identifies the present state of oppression as a cohesive human creation – Babylon *system* – but simultaneously acknowledges the potential power of working people to transform it.

is one ting I say about *any* ghetto, is one ting can solve all ghetto prablem. Togedaness. If de people jus know dat all of us comin off de poorer side a town mus stick togeda as poor people, we mash up anyting.[100] (my emphasis)

This same anthropocentrism points to the conclusion that we are not dealing with a religious movement, but with sophisticated criticism of an oppressed people's paralysing encounter with religion.

Most people think great god will come from the sky
take away everything, make everybody feel high
but if you know what life is worth
you will look for yours on earth
now you see the light, you stand up for your rights.[101]

The fact that this criticism appears partially in vestigial religious form should not encourage us to underestimate the extent of the rupture it represents.

When I look at the photograph of Selassie I, I am not looking at God, nor if I look at Eyesus Christus, these are merely representations for God is I and I and has always been.[102]

This denial of God, and the rasta insistence that heaven is on earth and nowhere else are the kindling of the process in which,

The criticism of heaven turns into the criticism of earth, the criticism of religion into the criticism of law, and the criticism of theology into the criticism of politics.[103]

Even the minority of Rastafari who openly proclaim the divinity of Haile Selassie I are not making simple religious statements. The most theological amongst them will still affirm the primacy of struggle for liberation in the present. Religion has always been a site of struggle for the colonized downtrodden and enslaved. Writing of slave revolts Genovese points out that:

Until the nineteenth century, and even then albeit with altered content, religion provided the ideological rallying point for revolt. In the Caribbean and in South America religious leaders – Obeahmen, Myalmen, Vodun priests, Nanigos, muslim teachers – led, inspired or provided vital sanction for one revolt after another.[104]

Here, religion became a central pillar in the refusal of servitude rather than 'the sigh of the oppressed creature'. Closer to home, Stephen Yeo has recently demonstrated that the radical potential of religious ideology is not the sole property of African and Asian traditions.[105]

The 1880s and 1890s were . . . a time of great organisational creativity. This was particularly manifest in the religion of socialism area. Not only was there a Labour Church, but a large number of 'allied social movements' – including Socialist Churches, the Labour Brotherhood, Brotherhood Churches and The Labour Army. . . . Groups gathered to follow prophets – Whitmanites in Bolton, Tolstoyans in Purleigh, Ruskinians in Liverpool – giving a grounding in reality to Katherine Conway's purple vision of a socialist guru in her 'The Religion of Socialism'.

The 'primary semantic function' of the bible in the popular culture of the Caribbean has facilitated an extremely selective and partisan appropriation of it by Rastas mindful of the long and bitter struggles master and slave fought across its pages. The sociologists we looked at in Chapter 3 who view 'religion' as a brake on the development of political consciousness, have not explained the Rastas' disinterest in the New Testament gospels, or their predilection for Psalms, Revelation, and the history of the Children of Israel.

Youth culture and the crisis

The popular character of Rasta politics leads us to the role of music in its dissemination and development. In Britain, the sphere of leisure no less than that of work has hosted the extraordinary encounter between the political traditions of disorganic development in the periphery and the urban working class at the centre. Youth culture has also created an important space for dialogue between black youth from the different communities. Asian youth movements have been inspired by the combativity of Afro-Caribbean young people which has received spectacular press coverage while their own equally tenacious defence of their communities remains concealed behind a stereotype of passivity. At a confrontation in Coventry in May 1981 which was under-reported for this very reason, young Asians chanted 'Brixton, Brixton' as they charged the police ranks.[106] The youth movements' support for the Chapeltown Rasta Defence Organisation (Leeds) campaign for the reinstatement of Rasta school students suspended for refusing to cut their hair, is a concrete example of how common oppression can generate united black struggle.[107]

The transformation of politics in post-war Britain – the welfare state and changes in production in particular – presaged new kinds of political organization and new sites of struggle. The arrival of black settlers proved to be both catalyst and inspiration to the grandchildren of jingoism who were quick to ape, absorb and adapt the styles and cultural practices which were black relics of a distant colonial engagement with their foreparents. Dick Hebdige has established the connection between white youth cultures and the presence of a black citizenry:

We can watch played out on the loaded surfaces of the British working-class youth cultures a phantom history of race relations since the war.[108]

By extending his argument, we can begin to see the fundamental class character of black cultural struggles in a different light, as well as the articulation of 'race' around the contradiction between capital and labour in ways that the dominance of corporatist political representation has obscured. The reification of pleasure in youth cultures has contradictory effects in the struggle for political space and cultural power. The mass mobilizations of white youth it spawned, though always both cultural and political, have not always been anti-racist. There are no guarantees of progressive outcomes even in the fact that neo-Fascists and nationalist interventions in this field identify the political power of black culture as the prime obstacle to success.

Britain's Youth have had imposed on them, nigger music, nigger culture, jungle standards and jungle culture.[109]

Regardless of the ultimate direction of the popular struggle of white youth, there are grounds to argue that its form has been prefigured in the resistances of the black communities, in much the same way that the movement of black Americans in the 1960s determined the patterns of autonomous protest which followed it:

Without Black Brotherhood, there would have been no sisterhood; without Black Power and Black Pride there would have been no Gay Power and Gay Pride. The movement against the abuse of powers of the state . . . derived much of its strength and purpose from the exposure of the F.B.I.'s surveillance and harassment of the Black Panthers and Black Muslims . . . .Only the Environmental Movement did not have the Black Movement as a central organisational fact or as a defining political metaphor and inspiration.[110]

Premised on the now-fading affluence of the teenage consumer and the mass-communications aspect of the leisure industries, the mechanisms of white youth culture provided the means to popularize oppositional ideas forged in the powerlessness of youth.[111] Since the incorporation of reggae into the subcultural repertoire in the late sixties, political themes have begun to displace moral and generational conflict as the raw material of young people's cultural expression. The shift between The Who's 'My Generation', The Sex Pistols' 'Anarchy in the U.K.' and The Beat's 'Stand Down Margaret' exemplifies this process, which has been fuelled at each stage by youth's own perception of economic crisis and the consequent crisis of social relations. It was in 'punk' subculture that youth's marginality came face to face with these crises. In the realization that 'there's no future, and England's dreaming' the relation of white to black youth took on its most complex form. Hebdige has described this phase as the self-conscious construction of a white 'ethnicity'. The 'disavowal of Britishness' and 'symbolic treason' implicit in 'God Save The Queen', as well as the punks' iconoclastic use of the Union Jack and the Queen's face, are interpreted as a 'white translation' of black subcultural style which the nationalist momentum of Rastafarian self-assertion had placed out of reach. The post-Rasta denial of access to the always-preferable black music, style and leisure pursuits was a severe shock; blacks were not going to lose reggae as they had lost soul to the mods.

The themes of Back to Africa and Ethiopianism celebrated in reggae made no concessions to the sensibilities of a white audience. Reggae's blackness was proscriptive. It was an alien essence, a foreign body which implicitly threatened mainstream British culture from within, and as such it resonated with punk's adopted values – anarchy, surrender and decline.[112]

This relationship, made concrete in the alliance of punk and reggae musicians under the banner of 'Rock Against Racism', was short-lived. There were contradictions in the nationalist symbols which punks had attempted to subvert, and the decisively working-class character of their movement harked back to an earlier subcultural style from which it had emerged.[113] The realization that black youth would insist on the particularity of their oppression no matter how much the whites identified with Rastafari, precisely because white interest was a threat to the autonomy of the movement, returned white youth to the drab horizons of the skinhead cult with particular bitterness. The familiar 'Crombie' coat and denim jacket returned, this time with Union Jacks and even swastikas stitched neatly onto breast pockets. This is the point at which white youths' culture intersects with the politics of organized Fascism, which acknowledging their experience and their potential power in their own language, speaks to their predicament with a hollow promise of 'jobs for white workers'. The white youth who could accept the racial limitations Rasta placed on their engagement with black culture came to constitute the core of the 'two-tone' subculture which synthesized punk and reggae. Those who were unable to make this adjustment retained their love of reggae – visible in their updating of the sixties skinhead 'ska' cult, constructing a white power ideology from common-sense racism to match the black power which intimidated them. The steady appeal of reggae to white youth throughout the sixties culminated in the skinheads' mass migration to Wembley in the summer of 1969. The success of the Reggae Festival there signified to the leisure industry the promise of mass marketing the music to whites. The independent distributors of reggae had expanded their business on the profits from the inevitably restricted black market to which white companies had little access.[114] They were keen to expand further. The growth of local radio with minority appeal music programming in the 1970-2 period consolidated the black market – once again, making the music available to the white youths, excluded from the clubs they had shared with the 'rudies' three years earlier by their own Powellism and the rhetoric of black power which had crossed the Atlantic to confront it to the strains of 'Young, Gifted and Black'.

The link between the multinational entertainment corporation and the purveyors of reggae to the ghettoes of Britain was secured by a Jamaican exile whose company 'Island Records' is now an appendage of EMI.[115] Island knew that they would have to find the right star to take black music to the white pop fan. Their prototype was Jimmy Cliff, a Jamaican former child star with a substantial following at the roots. Music alone could not transcend the racial hostility that narrowed the market. The company devised a plan to package Cliff and reggae music in an individualistic and romanticized vision of black life in the Caribbean, which posed no threat to the white consumers and was well inside the racist image of blacks as violent, licentious and primitive. The film 'The Harder They Come' starred Cliff as a 'rude-boy' musician turned gunman. The strategy of using film to circumvent the racial hostility of white fans has been an ongoing feature of Island's marketing. 'Exodus' – a film of Bob Marley on stage – and the more contradictory 'Rockers' made filmed live performances available to whites who had neither the inclination nor the opportunity to attend the actual concert hall. The film's initially unsuccessful release in 1972 ironically marks the beginning of the mass movement of black British youth towards Rastafari. It was not Cliff's dated and hopeless hero who captured the imagination of black crowds at The Ace, The Rio and The Kilburn State, but the studied philosophical cool of his dread co-star Ras Daniel Hartman, a well-known artist and poet. The film did not dwell on Rasta, but Hartman's performance whetted the appetites of young black people still hungry from their frustrating encounter with the British black power movement. The leap towards mass internalization of Rasta was not completed until the following year when the activity of 'religiously' inclined Rasta organizations in London formed the backdrop to the release of two LP records by The Wailers. Island pushed 'Catch a Fire' and 'Burning' through both roots and pop distributive networks. Cashmore is correct to situate Bob Marley at the centre of the Rasta movement's growth but the Marley who cranked this historical machinery was not the leather-jacketed pop star who crooned 'No Woman No Cry' two years later. He was the roots politician of these earlier recordings.

We gonna be burnin' and a lootin' tonight
(to survive, yeah)
burnin' and a lootin' tonight
(save your babies lives)
burning all pollution tonight
burning all illusions tonight [116]

These records presented a compulsive unity of populist anti-imperialist politics and Rasta themes which, though lost on the hoped-for white fans, set the black community aflame. Island Records' attempt to build a new market for reggae while retaining contact with roots distributors tempted other companies to try and connect markets. Unsuccessful promotion to whites was a common feature of a crop of releases which only fanned the flames that The Wailers had sparked. [117] When 'The Harder They Come' was relaunched in 1973 the blacks flocked to see it and the whites stayed away. The Wailers were unable to dislodge Johnny Nash from the pop chart, and their dread lyricism remained unpalatable to the white fans. Marley's eventual breakthrough was achieved after the original band had broken up, and he had returned to London as a solo star in the wake of 'Natty Dread'. His transformation from Wailer to superstar was accomplished at the expense of much of his support among the youth. As his long-term project for the internationalism of Rasta took shape, he worked to recover the respect of his first audience. The trail he made has been followed by other performers more skilled in the pedagogy of popular Rasta politics. Their historical researches and political abstractions brought maturity to the new Ethiopianism, simultaneously polarizing the politics of white youth culture.

Bass culture

Many commentators have remained curiously mute on the subject of the music of the black culture they scrutinize. Others who have heard a voice of 'protest' interpret it with bizarre insensitivity. Cashmore contends that the expression of discontent in reggae

acted to slough off any latent militancy in the black working-class, by translating the hostility into musical form rather than converting it into programmatic proposals.[118]

He is unable to understand that:

Committed art in the proper sense is not intended to generate ameliorative measures, legislative acts or practical institutions . . . but to work at the level of fundamental attitudes.[119]

Barry Troyna, whose contemptible methodology has not prevented him from soliciting 'differential commitment to ethnic identity' from the black youth he has 'sampled', believes that the social and political orientations of young blacks may be read off from their musical preferences.[120] His position has been influential and merits detailed examination. The typology of personalities he has adapted from Ken Pryce, is problematic enough, but even this pales into insignificance beside the misconceptions and distortions of black culture which inform his all-too-cosy model. Like Cashmore he locates the 'oppositional element' in reggae at the level of its lyrics, but goes on to divide the music into 'heavy' and 'sweet' categories as a result of the differences he claims to discern in them.Thus on the rare occasion that his 'compromisers' try 'heavy' reggae they are only interested in the music, whereas the 'rejectors' rather conveniently 'insist that the lyrics and not the music form the most important constituent of a record'. Troyna explains that:

The Rastafarian inspired lyrics inform and help structure their particular perspectives and provide them with their own distinctive and impenetrable group argot.

While reggae music may be subdivided into 'lovers' and 'roots' styles which echo Troyna's categories, this distinction *does not apply at the level of lyrics*. The contrast relates to different dance styles and the overlapping social relations in which they appear. Roots records usually belong to sexually segregated dancing, and lovers' rock is more often the accompaniment to couples dancing together.[121] The form of reggae music spans the extremities that these styles represent. A particularly resonant lyric or melody may draw temporary attention to one or the other, but this does not alter the need to approach each recording as a complex unity of words and music in its own right. The inept attempt to cast Burning Spear in the role of Joan Baez to the Rasta protest movement closes off the discussion of form and ignores the fact that the dominant form of reggae is Dub.[122] Dub is not a style of music as such, it is a process of enrichment in which music is deconstructed and the meaning of its lyrics transformed and expanded. The Dub process is applied to 'sweet' and 'heavy' reggae alike. The Dub experience is an intrinsic element of the social relations in which *all* reggae reveals its power – in the lounge bar of a pub on Sunday night, or in the heat of a sound-system competition. Only the few reggae records which are aimed exclusively at the white pop market lack a Dubbed version of the same tune on their 'B' side.

In the social context, these two different versions would be played as a pair, the Dub following the un-Dubbed version and forcing the listeners into a critical position by its dismantling of the former piece. A few fragments of the original lyric will have been left intact in the Dub version; these are a springboard for the disc-jockey's own improvised comments on its theme. Thus new meanings are created and the initial meanings modified in a process of selection and transform-ation which becomes a key source of pleasure for the dancing crowd. The sounds of the instruments in the Dub version are modified by modern sound processing techniques and skilful editing of the tape on which it was recorded. Phasers, Flangers, Delay Lines, Echo, Reverb and the addition of sound effects in particular gunfire, explosions, birdsong, sirens, animals, or even scratches and tape sounds which remind the audience they are listening to a recording, all play their part. Focusing on both the processed and natural sounds of each instrument in turn, and then in a variety of combinations with sound effects mixed in, the Dub engineer is able to expose the musical anatomy of the piece, showing how each layer of instrumentation complements the others to form a complex whole. For example, in the Dub version of the song 'General Penitentiary' by Black Uhuru an insistent syndrum becomes a cell door repeatedly slamming shut, and the only phrase left intact is the line 'down in this dark cell'. A slightly more complex example is furnished by the Wailing Souls whose 'Kingdom Rise and Kingdom Fall' is at the top of the chart as I write. Here, the word 'economy' in the phrase

Economy has got them in desperation
Poverty is causing dangerous political tension.

is transformed into the word 'army' by use of an analog delay device.

It is tempting to view the process which lays bare the structure beneath the unified exterior of the whole unmodified version as an expressive homology for the Rasta view of the world.[123] It is certainly articulated to the critical distance from the world of appearances which is the initial impetus for Rasta politics and there are many clues to understanding this in the relation of black music to political struggle all over the new world. The examples of Bebop and Samba generate the

most immediate comparisons.[124] This is certainly a long way from musical 'preferences' distinguished by the content of lyrics à la Troyna. Though they may
introduce an analytic coherence, political lyrics must be regarded as secondary to
the issues implicit in the form of reggae and its consequent exploration in Dub.
This may be a difficult point to grasp, but Dubbing is a feature of overtly commited
and apparently unpolitical recordings alike. Dub is a bridge between them rooted
in their form. This has been explicated eloquently by leading reggae drummer
Leroy 'Horsemouth' Wallace.

I man haffe start play my music in a militant way so we can relate to de people. Cos
you can't play a quiet and peaceful music in war time yunno, an dat won serve no
purpose because war is going on outside an yu play a lickle quiet violin music! Yu
haffe tell de people de right ting whey a gwan inna dem time ya now. Yu ave fe
mek *de music* so dread dat a man understan. Until my bredda dem and my sista
dem stop suffa me naw go really stop play roots *music*. When me see suffaration
stop pan black people me might start play some nice quiet peaceful music. But
right now Rasta, a juss some natty music me play as far as me see dis bizniz ya. A
de trute deh Iya. Caa tings too dread fe a man out deh now yaa Rasta, fe a man
play quiet music.[125]

Wallace's statement illustrates a point made by Armand Mattelart which should
serve as a reminder to the Eurocentric sociologist:

Acquiring and developing class consciousness does not mean obligatory boredom.
It is a question of transforming what used to be used exclusively for pleasure and
leisure into a means of instruction.[126]

Reggae is far more than the lullaby of a beleaguered population. In displacing the
lyric's 'message' into a secondary place, the Dub movement avoids a trap set for all
singers of political songs forced to contend with their art being packaged and sold
as commodities. This ensures that:

for the sake of political commitment political reality is trivialised, which then
reduces the political effect.[127]

Rasta discourse consigns hasty statements of commitment to the realm of 'ism
and schism' – the merely 'politrickal' ideologies which suffer by comparison to the
total processes of human emancipation involved in social revolution. Many years
ago, against Brecht, Adorno argued for the political efficacy of 'atelic, hermetic
works of art' in capitalist relations of cultural production. It is on this ground that
we have attempted to explore Dub music. Its creators,

By dismantling appearance explode from within the art which committed proclam-
ation sub-jugates from without, and hence only in appearance. The inescapability
of the work compels the change of attitude which committed works merely
demand.[128]

This music has been dealt with in detail not simply because it is a prime site of

cultural struggle by blacks. The popularity of Rasta ideology is in part an unfore-
seen consequence of the cycles and machinations of the popular music industry.
Like the politicization of youth subcultures, permitted by their importation of
black styles and forms, which has occurred beyond the limits of any corporatist
definition of 'the political', it is one of many new forms of struggle appropriate
to new historical conditions: organic crisis at the meeting point of Fordism and
neo-Fordism.[129]

Autonomous class struggle

It remains for us to show that black struggles are not merely political in the
broadest sense, but approach the task of social transformation not from a transplanted disorganic politics alone, but in ways which relate directly to the historical
conjuncture in which they have developed. We focused on Rastafari as one
sophisticated expression of the critical consciousness which informs those
struggles, commenting on society and state, and extending into an analysis of
the post-colonial scene as a whole.

Africans a bear the most pressure, because you find that the people that are
controlling them are the white people them. They try to be superior over black
people. Not all of them, but certain of them ones as is gods and seat up in high
places; All those system, you just see them big notches who a control. Certain of
them captains and them big pirates from long time is them family. Some of them
people really have the world in their hands, so them keep up various kinds of isms
now. Them stop slaving the Africans alone, but them slaving everyone else still.
Is the people them to come and unite now, that's the only way.[130]

We cannot accept that the consciousness of exploitation provoked in the
experience of racial oppression, both inside and outside production, typified by
this quote, is only some preliminary phase in the development of a mythically
complete class consciousness sometime in the future.[131] Though for the social
analyst 'race' and class are necessarily abstractions at different levels, black
consciousness of race and class cannot be empirically separated. The class character
of black struggles is not a result of the fact that blacks are predominantly
proletarian, though this is true. It is established in the fact that their struggles for
civil rights, freedom from state harassment, or as waged workers, are instances of
the process by which the working class is constituted politically, organized in
politics. We have distanced ourselves from the view of classes as continuous
subjects of history, they are made and remade in a continual struggle. We must also
reject the ancient heresy of economistic Marxism which stipulates that the
relations of commodity production alone determine class relations. The Marxist
concept of class refers primarily but not exclusively to the location of groups in
production relations. Capitalism's tendency to generate surplus population
structurally excluded from productive employment by the revolutions in the
labour process and changes in accumulation should emphasize this point. The

composition of this population and the ways it becomes organized politically are determined by class struggles which are not reducible to the objective conditions which delineate the range of possible outcomes. The political organization of surplus population is particularly salient to class segmentation, and therefore to racial politics in the era of structural unemployment. It serves to remind us that the privileged place of economic classes in the Marxist theory of history is not to be equated with an a priori assertion of their political primacy in every historical moment.

We cannot conceive of the class struggle as if classes were simply and homogeneously constituted at the level of the economic and only then fractured at the level of the political. The political level is dependent – determinate – because its raw materials are given by the mode of production as a whole.[132]

Marx makes it clear that there are periods in which the proletariat is unable to constitute itself as a class in politics even though 'the domination of capital has created for this mass a common situation, common interests'.[133] Recognizing the problems in the effective entry of classes into politics is the first step towards understanding Prezworski's instruction:

Classes must be viewed as the effects of struggles structured by objective conditions, that are simultaneously economic, political and ideological.[134]

These objective conditions change, and the unity between the 'economic movement and political action' of the working class is not the same in 1981 as it was in 1871. The working class is different.

The advent of Fascism, Fordism and Roosevelt's attempt to resolve the 1929 Crash in a Keynesian 'New Deal' all prompted Gramsci to raise the question of whether 'Americanism' could be seen as a new epoch based in capital's passive revolutions, an 'ethical' state and a recomposition of the working class itself: an epoch of social capital.

In America rationalisation has determined the need to elaborate a new type of man suited to a new type of productive process. This elaboration is still only in its initial phase . . . up to the present there has not been, except perhaps sporadically, any flowering of the 'superstructure'; in other words the question of hegemony has *not yet* been posed.[135] (my emphasis)

The years since Gramsci wrote these words have seen the question posed with increasing intensity. In these novel conditions the struggle for hegemony cannot be reduced to economic determinations or vulgarized to refer to solely cultural phenomena, and class analysis cannot be restricted to those positioned in the immediate processes of production.

The indeterminacy introduced by a view of class formation as an effect of heterogeneous struggles perhaps premised on different communalities – linguistic, sexual, regional, ecological and 'racial' – is a useful tool against reductionism. It is also a place at which a historical and non-essentialist theory of human needs can be worked into the practice of class politics. The latter is a pressing task, particularly if we understand Fordism to be 'the principle of an articulation between process of production and mode of consumption':[136]

It is because [the] interaction between needs and products is complex and bilateral, and bears the mark of many determinations other than those stemming directly from economic production and its particular distribution relations, that consumption is both specific to any stage of social development and contradictory in that specificity. The vitality of socialist politics depends on the extent to which it can distinguish between the unnecessary contradiction inherent to a social production that determines use value on the basis of exchange value, and the necessary contradiction inherent to any society that has to *plan* to meet needs. Neither contradiction should be seen as an opposition between a brute nature and the manipulations of production; but one is the effect of the dominance of the economic laws of capital accumulation, and the other is the benign index of the dominance of political decision; the latter is not a contradiction to be resolved but rather to be lived.[137]

The politics of need is to the fore in movements for black liberation, as in many of the other autonomous political forces in the ascendant during the last fifteen years.[138]

In our view of class formation, the racist ideologies and practices of the white working class and the consequent differentiation of 'the blacks' are ways in which the class as a whole is disorganized. The struggles of black people to refuse and transform their subjugation are no simple antidote to class segmentation, but they are processes which attempt to constitute the class politically across racial divisions – 'that is which represent it against capitalism against racism'.[139] Like feminist struggles against patriarchal oppression, which have also had side effects on the political formation of classes in the recent period, these struggles do not derive their meaning from the political failures of the classically conceived, white, male, working class. In both cases it appears that autonomous organization has enabled blacks and women to 'leap-frog' over their fellow workers into direct confrontations with the state in the interest of the class as a whole. Responsive and accountable health care raised by the struggle for abortion rights, or democratic and locally controlled police practices demanded by black organization against state harassment are small illustrations of this.[140] The more eruptive forms these struggles sometimes take are not the substitute for a disciplined and tactical war of position, neither are they irreconcilable to one. Both moments have their place in the long struggle to transform society.

The strategy of 'war of position' (which moreover in no way rules out moments of frontal attack and rupture, if we are not to fall into the most flaccid parliamentary gradualism) is the response to a historical phase marked by a dual tendency: towards the expansion of the state, and towards the passive revolutions of capital.[141]

The crisis in which this confrontation takes place is not yet a crisis of the state form and we must be careful not 'to mistake the appearance for the substance of state power'.[142] The strengthening of repressive apparatuses and functions does not require fundamental change in the institutional structures of the state, which constitute the legitimate arena of politics in relation to their own material existence. The struggles of the dominated masses are now more than ever present inside and outside the state framework, 'whose strategic configuration they map out'.[143] The strategy of 'broad democratic alliances' which perverts Gramsci does have a single virtue in its insistence that the ahistorical fetishization of organizational forms created in previous conjunctures is now a fetter on political progress.[144] These factors, together with the emphasis we have placed on the heterogeneity of class struggle, raise the issue of political organization. This must be considered historically and measured against the tasks of the period in which each specific form arises. In Gramsci's steps we learn that the historical epoch born in the thirties requires new forms of politics and strategy. His 'totalizing' view of the political party's role is rather at odds with this conclusion. It is certainly unsuited to British conditions in which the organization of the working class in politics has a peculiar history of entanglement with the different project of mobilizing electoral support for the Labour Party. Electoral abstention and disinterest are no longer confined to the wards where blacks are a majority, yet the disinterest in 'politics' which they signify is undiscussed from the point of view of left strategy.[145] Organic crisis and the microprocessor revolution demand reassessment of the institutions of political representation. Posing the problem of political organization in direct form is a means to separate corporatist modes of struggle from the diverse attempts to repoliticize the process of class formation in the face of a new imposition of authority, the ideologies of the crisis and the mobilization of the law. Corporatism should be understood as:

A political structure within advanced capitalism which integrates organized socio-economic producer groups through a system of representation and cooperative mutual interaction at the leadership level and mobilisation and social control at the mass level. Corporatism is understood here as *an actual political structure, not merely an ideology*.[146] (my emphasis)

We have seen how black political traditions fall outside the 'contradictory unity' of corporatism/parliamentarism. There is also overwhelming evidence to support the view that the institutions of the white working class have failed to represent the interests of black workers abroad[147] and at home, where black rank-and-file organization has challenged local and national union bureaucracy since the day the 'Empire Windrush' docked.[148] We are disinclined to the pretence that these institutions represent the class *as a class* at all. Nor are blacks alone in the marginalization they suffer. The experiences of female, young, unemployed or even unskilled workers present parallel examples,[149] while the growth of rank-and-file organization, and of conflict between shop stewards and the higher echelons of union bureaucracy only hint at the complexity of workplace struggle. The failures of these institutions must be compared to the rapid growth of new movements with an autonomy from capitalist command as well as from the constricting political repertoire of the 'labour movement'. Mass pan-Africanist communalism is but one place among many where the patient listener will discern:

The dialogue . . . between a young social movement, still searching for its identity, and the movement which preceded it but which is now growing old, dying, or being converted into its own antithesis by becoming an agent of the authorities.[150]

The tendency in the Marxist movement, best known for its early critique of the articulation of capitalist planning and Soviet statism,[151] is also the place in which a sustained critique of organizational forms has been developed hand in hand with confidence in the capacity of oppressed and exploited people to organize themselves without the mediation of a 'vanguard' on the Leninist model.[152] Though this position has been dismissed by invocation of a mutual exclusion between the concepts of organization and spontaneity, its distinguished advocate C. L. R. James has demonstrated their interrelation and unity.

You know nothing about organisation unless at every step you relate it to its opposite – spontaneity. It is meaningless without that correlative, its other tied to it, each developing the other.[153]

James is careful not to oppose organization *per se*; his target is a politics which cannot see beyond 'organisation as we have known it' which 'is now at an end'. For James, the changes Gramsci identified introduced a period in which the recognition of the proletariat's autonomous power would be the basis from which organization would develop. In its prime the working class would find its own methods and forms of organization just as it had done in its infancy.

New organisations will come as Lilburne's Leveller party came, as the sections and popular societies of Paris in 1793, as the commune in 1871 and the Soviets in 1905, with not a single soul having any concrete ideas about them until they appeared.[154]

Some of the dangers in this position emerge from critical discussion of the practice of the Italian Autonomists,[155] but none the less it provides a perspective in which we can usefully understand the double articulation of black politico-cultural struggle. This is simultaneously 'disorganic development' come home to roost, and an aspect of autonomous class struggle. Those who doubt that struggles which appear to be organized on the basis of communalities other than class can have effects on the processes of class formation or believe they are unable to transcend a defensive mode, should study the politicization of roots culture, no less than the auto-reduction movements of Turin.[156]

Those who clamour too quickly for 'unified counterhegemonic strategies' under working-class leadership should note that the political discourses of the powerless are subject to connotative resonance, and like the supposedly marginal groups they interpellate, overlap significantly. How *are* we to explain Gay participation in the 'Race Riots' at Brixton?[157] There are many young black women who will make their own struggles against patriarchy and capital which oppress them in racially specific ways. The class consciousness of our epoch is not the sole prerogative of male, white, productive labourers. It remains to be constructed from the potential complementarity of diverse political struggles which constitute the class politically at different levels. It provides a promise of unity which may only be apparent in the rarest moments of revolutionary rupture, where we may catch a fleeting glimpse of the class for itself.

Acknowledgements

Valerie Amos wrote the first draft of one section of this chapter. I would like to say 'thank you' to the various people outside our group who gave detailed and helpful comments during the process of preparation: Veronica Ware, Stuart Hall, Colin Prescod, Sue MacIntosh, Richard Johnson and Bob Lumley. Special thanks to John Solomos.

Notes and references

1   Cathie Lloyd, 'What is the French C.P. up to?', *Race and Class* (Spring 1980). the nationalist bent of The Alternative Economic Strategy is also relevant.
2   S. Hall *et al.*, *Policing the Crisis* (Macmillan 1978), p. 394.
3   S. Hall, 'Race, articulation and societies structured in dominance', in *Sociological Theories: Race and Colonialism* (UNESCO 1980).
4   There is a résumé of the contrasting positions of *The Black Liberator* and *Race Today* in the final chapter of *Policing the Crisis*. The disparaging remarks refer to writings by Gideon Ben-Tovim and John Gabriel listed below.
5   See: Colin Mercer, 'Revolutions, reforms or reformulations? Marxist discourse on democracy', in A. Hunt (ed.), *Marxism and Democracy* (Lawrence and Wishart 1980). For an historical account see: Fernando Claudin, *Eurocommunism and Socialism* (New Left Books 1978).
6   Compare: Chantal Mouffe, 'Hegemony and ideology in Gramsci', in Mouffe (ed.), *Gramsci and Marxist Theory* (Routledge and Kegan Paul 1979), with : Henri Weber, 'In the beginning was Gramsci', *Semiotext(e)*, vol. III, no. 3 (1980), *Autonomia Post Political Politics*, and also: Christine Buci-Glucksmann, *Gramsci and the State* (Lawrence and Wishart 1980).
7   Fran Bennett, Beatrix Campbell and Rosalind Coward, 'Feminists: the degenerates of the social', in Adlam *et al.* (eds.), *Politics and Power 3* (Routledge and Kegan Paul 1981).
8   G. Ben-Tovim *et al.*, 'Race, left strategies and the state'; also in *Politics and Power 3* (1981).
9   G. Ben-Tovim, 'The struggle against racism: theoretical and strategic perspectives', *Marxism Today* (July 1978). J. Gabriel and G. Ben-Tovim, 'Marxism and the concept of racism', *Economy and Society*, vol. 7, no. 2 (1978).
10   Ernesto Laclau, *Politics and Ideology in Marxist Theory* (New Left Books

1977); and 'Populist rupture and discourse', *Screen Education*, no. 34 (Spring 1980). The epistemological position from which my critique proceeds has been outlined with the greatest clarity by: Jose Nun, *Latin America Research Unit Studies*, vol. III, no. 2–3 (1980), pp. 85–145.

11   See: N. Poulantzas, *Fascism and Dictatorship* (New Left Books 1974), footnote on pp. 169–70; 'the error of the schlageter line lay elsewhere – to be precise, in the social chauvinist turn of the K.P.D., exploiting in a clearly nationalist way agitation against the Versailles treaty'. Also: Andrew Jenkins, 'Laclau on Fascism', *International*, vol. 5, no. 1 (Autumn 1979).

12   Laclau, *Politics and Ideology*, especially pp. 129–30.

13   ibid.

14   George Bennett (ed.), *The Concept of Empire: Burke to Attlee 1774–1947* (A. & C. Black 1962).

15   Laclau, *Politics and Ideology*, p. 120.

16   Alfred Sherman, *Daily Telegraph*, 9 November 1979.

17   Stuart Hall, 'The legacy of Nicos Poulantzas', *New Left Review*, no. 119 (1978).

18   Nicos Mouzellis, 'Ideology and class politics', *New Left Review*, no. 112 (1978).

19   See: G. Esping-Anderson *et al.*, 'Modes of class struggle and the capitalist state', *Kapitalistate*, no. 4 (Summer 1976), and also A. Markusen *et al.*, 'Typology and class struggle', *Kapitalistate*, no. 6 (1977).

20   Ben-Tovim *et al.*

21   Henri Weber, 'Eurocommunism, socialism, democracy', *New Left Review*, no. 110 (1978).

22   ibid., p. 9.

23   ibid., p. 8.

24   Gabriel and Ben-Tovim, p. 121.

25   Wilson Record, 'The Kremlin sociologists and the Black Republic', and 'Build the Negro People's United Front', in *The Negro and the Communist Party* (New York 1971), Chapters 3 and 4. See also: A. Gayle, *Richard Wright – Ordeal of a Native Son* (Anchor 1980); Claudin and S. Carillo, *Eurocommunism and the State* (1978), Chapter 5.

26   Anton Pannekoek, 'General remarks on the question of organisation', *Capital and Class*, no. 9 (1979), p. 127.

  The adherents of the old forms of organisation exalt democracy as the only right and just political form as against dictatorship, an unjust form. Marxism knows nothing of abstract right or justice, it explains the political forms in which mankind [sic] expresses its feelings of political right, as consequences of the economic structure of society.

27   G. Carchedi, 'Authority and foreign labour: some notes on a late capitalist form of capital accumulation and state intervention', *Studies in Political Economy*, no. 2 (1979), p. 50.

28   Annie Phizacklea and Robert Miles, *Labour and Racism* (Routledge and Kegan Paul 1980).

29   ibid., pp. 231–2.

30   See Dominique Lecourt's interesting discussion of this point: *Sociological Theories: Race and Colonialism* (UNESCO 1980), pp. 282–4.

31 Sally Alexander and Barbara Taylor, 'In defence of patriarchy', in R. Samuel (ed.), *People's History and Socialist Theory* (Routledge and Kegan Paul 1981). Veronica Beechey, 'On patriarchy, *Feminist Review*, no. 3 (1979).

32 Heidi Hartman, 'The unhappy marriage of Marxism and feminism', *Capital and Class*, no. 8 (1979).

33 Linda Gordon, 'The long struggle for reproductive rights', *Radical America*, vol. 15, nos. 1 and 2 (Spring 1981).

34 Richard Wright, 'Blueprint for negro writing', *Race and Class*, vol. xxi, no. 4 (Spring 1981).

35 Sebastiano Timpanaro, *On Materialism* (New Left Books 1975).

36 ibid., p. 45.

37 Kate Soper, 'Marxism, materialism and biology', in Mepham and Hillel-Ruben (ed.), *Issues in Marxist Philosophy*, vol. 2: *Materialism* (Harvester 1979).

38 Kate Soper, 'On materialisms', *Radical Philosophy*, no. 15 (Autumn 1976).

39 V. N. Volosinov, *Marxism and the Philosophy of Language* (Seminar Press 1973), p. 23.

40 Frank Kofsky, *Black Nationalism and the Revolution in Music* (Pathfinder 1970), p. 43.

41 Volosinov, p. 23.

42 Timpanaro, p. 43.

43 An important sociological critique of this position is provided by: Alain Touraine, *The Self-Production of Society* (Chicago University Press 1977), especially Chapters 3 and 7.

44 Adam Prezworski, 'Proletariat into a class: the process of class formation from Kautsky's "The Class Struggle" to recent controversies', *Politics and Society*, vol. 4, no. 7 (1977).

45 See Marx's letter to Weydemeyer, 5 March 1852. Though Althusser conceptualizes classes rather differently, he is absolutely correct to insist that:

> For reformists (even if they call themselves Marxists) it is not the class struggle that is in the front rank: it is simply the classes. Let us take a simple example, and suppose that we are dealing with just two classes. For reformists these classes exist *before* the class struggle, a bit like two football teams exist separately before the match. Each class exists in its own camp, lives according to its particular conditions of existence. One class may be exploiting another, but for reformism that is not the same thing as class struggle. One day the two classes come up against one another and come into conflict. It is only then that the class struggle begins . . . you will always find the same idea here: the classes exist *before* the class struggle, *independently* of the class struggle. The class struggle only exists *afterwards*. Revolutionaries on the other hand, consider that it is impossible to separate the classes from class struggle. The class struggle and the existence of classes are one and the same thing. In order for there to be classes in a 'society', the society has to be divided into classes: this division does not come *later in the story*; it is the exploitation of one class by another, it is therefore the class struggle, which constitutes the division into classes. For exploitation is already class struggle. You must therefore begin with class struggle if you want to understand class division, the existence and nature of classes. The class struggle must be put in the front rank.

Louis Althusser, 'Reply to John Lewis', in *Essays in Self-Criticism* (New Left Books 1976), pp. 49–50.

46 Robert Moore, *Racism and Black Resistance* (Pluto 1975); and A. X. Cambridge and C. Gutzmore, 'The industrial action of the black masses and the

class struggle in Britain', *The Black Liberator*, vol. 2, no. 3 (June–January 1974).

47   S. Hall, 'Race and moral panics in post-war Britain', in CRE (ed.), *Five Views of Multi-Racial Britain* (CRE 1978).

48   According to Poulantzas' original criteria of 'pertinent effects'. See: *Political Power and Social Classes* (New Left Books 1973).

49   Richard Johnson, 'Three problematics', in Critcher, Clark and Johnson (eds.), *Working Class Culture* (CCCS/Hutchinson 1979), p. 237.

50   Amilcar Cabral, *Return to the Source* (Monthly Review 1973), p. 43.

51   A. Sivanandan, 'Imperialism and disorganic development in the silicon age', *Race and Class*, vol. xxi, no. 2 (1979).

52   Phil Cohen, 'Subcultural conflict and working class community', *WPCS*, no. 2; reprinted in Hall *et al.* (eds.), *Culture, Media, Language* (CCCS/Hutchinson 1980).

53   Ira Katznelson, 'Community capitalist development and the emergence of class', *Politics and Society*, vol. 9, no. 2 (1979).

54   A. Gramsci, *Selections from the Prison Notebooks* (Lawrence and Wishart 1971), pp. 296–8.

55   Lewis Mumford, *The City in History* (Secker and Warburg 1961), p. 370.

56   R. Roberts, *The Classic Slum* (Manchester University Press 1971); E. P. Thompson, *Whigs and Hunters* (Penguin 1975); Henry Mayhew, *London Labour and London Poor*, vol. 1 (Frank Cass 1967).

57   Ceri Peach, *West Indian Migration to Britain* (Oxford University Press 1968), p. 62.

58   Gareth Stedman-Jones, 'Working class culture and working class politics in London 1870–1900', *Journal of Social History*, vol. vii, no. 4 (1974).

59   Paul Willis, *Learning to Labour* (Saxon Hall 1977).

60   Katznelson, p. 232.

61   Michel Foucault, interviews in *Radical Philosophy*, no. 16 (1977).

62   M. Burawoy, 'The politics of production and the production of politics', *Political Power and Social Theory*, vol. 1, no. 1 (1980). See also in the same volume: Adam Prezworski, 'Material bases of consent, economics and politics in a hegemonic system'.

63   Burawoy, p. 272.

64   Prezworski, 'Proletariat into a class', p. 344.

65   Dario Melossi, 'Institutions of social control and capitalist organisation of work', in NDC/CSE (ed.), *Capitalism and the Rule of Law* (Hutchinson 1979).

66   Lee Bridges, 'The Ministry of Internal Security: British urban social policy 1968–74', *Race and Class*, vol. xvi, no. 4 (1975).

67   Phil.Cohen, 'Policing the working class city', in *Capitalism and the Rule of Law*. Also: John R. Gillis, 'The evolution of juvenile delinquency in England 1890–1914', *Past and Present*, no. 67 (1975).

68   Clare Demuth, *Sus* (Runneymede Trust 1978), pp. 37–8.

69   *Report of the Unofficial Committee of Enquiry into Events in Southall 23.4.79* (NCCL 1980).

70   John Alderson, *Policing Freedom*, p. 43:

Colonial governments, never quite sure how the native population will react, equally require repressive police or military services if they are to stay in power against popular sentiment.

71   Ira Katznelson, *Black Men White Cities* (Oxford University Press 1973).

72   John Lea, 'The contradictions of the 60s race relations legislation', in NDC (ed.), *Permissiveness and Control* (Macmillan 1980).

73   Bob Jessop, 'Corporatism, parliamentarism and social democracy', in P. Schmitter and G. Lehmbruch (eds.), *Trends Towards Corporatist Intermediation* (Sage 1979).

74   Katznelson (1973), p. 178.

75   M. Marable, 'Black nationalism in the 1970s – through the prism of race and class', *Socialist Review*, no. 50/51 (1980).

76   Gus John, 'In the service of black youth: a study of the political culture of youth and community work with black people in English cities', National Association of Youth Clubs Special Report Series, *Special Report* no. 2 (March 1981).

77   ibid., p. 142.

78   Resham Sandhu, 'A tentative exploration of events on Saturday and Sunday following the death of Gurdip Singh Chaggar on the night of Friday 4th June 1976 in Southall West London', unpublished conference paper (1977).

79   Marx, *Early Writings* (Penguin 1975).

80   Cedric Robinson, 'Coming to terms: the Third World and the dialectic of imperialism', *Race and Class*, vol. xxii, no. 4 (1981).

81   C. L. R. James, *The Black Jacobins*.

82   Horace Campbell, 'Rastafari: culture of resistance', *Race and Class*, vol. xxii, no. 1 (1980).

83   Sebastian Clarke, *Jah Music* (Heinemann 1980).

84   Cedric Robinson, unpublished early draft of *Coming to Terms*.

85   Tony Martin, *Race First – The Ideological and Organisational Struggles of Marcus Garvey and the Universal Negro Improvement Association* (Greenwood 1976); Colin Henfrey, 'The hungry imagination: social formation, popular culture and ideology in Bahia', in S. Mitchell (ed.), *The Logic of Poverty* (Routledge and Kegan Paul 1981); Donald Barrett and Karari Njama, *Mau Mau from Within* (Monthly Review 1966); Richard Price (ed.), *Maroon Societies* (Anchor 1973).

86   David Dalby, 'Black through white: patterns of communication in Africa and the New World', and 'African survivals in the language and traditions of the Windward maroons of Jamaica', *African Language Studies*, no. 12 (1971). See also: T. Kochman (ed.), *Rappin' and Stylin' out: Communication in Urban Black America* (Chicago University Press 1972).

87   Ernest Cashmore, *Rastaman* (Allen and Unwin 1979); Robert Miles, 'Between two cultures? The case of Rastafarianism', *SSRC RUER Working Paper*, no. 10.

88   Martin, Chapter 10; Manning Marable, 'A. Phillip Randolph, a political assessment', in *From the Grassroots* (South End Press 1980); and Jeff Henderson, 'A. Phillip Randolph and the dilemmas of socialism and black nationalism in the United States', *Race and Class*, vol. xx, no. 2 (1978).

89   Campbell.

90   Cashmore, pp. 129–30.
91   D. Hebdige, *Subculture, the Meaning of Style* (Methuen 1979).
92   *Rastafari Universal Zion*, 18 February 1980.
93   Angela MacRobbie, 'Settling accounts with subculture', *Screen Education*, no. 34 (1980).
94   *Black Echoes*, 16 May 1981.
95   Angelina Grimke, 'Appeal to the Christian women of the south', in A. Rossi (ed.), *The Feminist Papers* (Bantam 1973).
96   London Borough of Lambeth, *Final Report of the Working Party into Community/Police Relations in Lambeth* (London Borough of Lambeth 1980), Section 2 (b).
97   Ken Pryce, *Endless Pressure* (Penguin 1979).
98   Joseph Owens, *Dread* (Sangster 1976), p. 64.
99   Gramsci, pp. 198–9.
100   Burning Spear, interviewed in *Jah Ugliman*, vol. 2 (September 1980).
101   The Wailers 'Get Up Stand Up', and The Congoes 'The Wrong Thing' are two of the best examples. There are many others.
102   E. Cashmore, p. 60.
103   Marx, *Introduction to the Critique of Hegel's Philosophy of Right*. Also in *Early Writings*.
104   E. Genovese, *From Rebellion to Revolution* (Baton Rouge 1979); V. Harding, 'Religion and resistance among ante-bellum negroes 1800–1860', in Meier and Rudwick (eds.), *The Making of Black America*, vol. 2 (Atheneum Publishers 1969); as well as R. Price, ibid.
105   S. Yeo, 'The religion of socialism in Britain 1883–1896', *History Workshop*, no. 4 (1977). We have yet to see how discussion of Rastafarianism is enlivened by comparison with the Owenite movement. In this connection see: J. F. C. Harrison, *Robert Owen and the Owenites in Britain and America* (Routledge and Kegan Paul 1969); and E. Yeo's contribution to Pollard and Salt (eds.), *Robert Owen, Prophet of the Poor* (Macmillan 1971). Logie Barrow's 'Socialism in eternity – the ideology of plebeian spiritualists, 1853–1913', *History Workshop*, no. 9 (1980) is also relevant.
106   Demonstration against racial violence in Coventry, 24 May 1981. See *The Observer, Sunday Times* and *News of the World*, 25 May 1981.
107   Kala Tara, paper of Bradford Asian Youth Movement, no. 1 (1979).
108   Hebdige, p. 46.
109   *British Tidings*, paper of the British Movement.
110   David Edgar, 'Reagan's hidden agenda: racism and the new American right', *Race and Class*, vol. xxii, no. 3 (1981).
111   S. Hall and T. Jefferson (eds.), *Resistance through Rituals* (CCCS/Hutchinson 1975).
112   Hebdige, p. 64.
113   Geoff Pearson, '"Paki-Bashing" in a North East Lancashire cotton town: a case study and its history', in Mungham and Pearson (eds.), *Working Class Youth Culture* (Routledge and Kegan Paul 1976). Also J. Clarke, 'Skinheads and the magical recovery of community', in Hall and Jefferson.
114   Sebastian Clarke, Chapter 7.
115   Island's director Chris Blackwell is a member of the family who own Crosse

and Blackwell.
116 The Wailers, 'Burning and Looting'.
117 Big Youth, 'Screaming Target' (TRLS61–1973). I. Roy, 'Presenting I Roy' (TRLS63–1973).
118 Cashmore, p. 104.
119 T. Adorno, 'Commitment', reprinted in Jameson (ed.), *Aesthetics and Politics* (New Left Books 1978).
120 Barry Troyna, 'Differential commitment to ethnic identity by black youths in Britain', *New Community*, vol. vii, no. 3 (1979).
121 *Black Echoes*, 13 December 1980.
122 See: Clarke, Chapter 6. A young Rasta with whom I discussed Troyna's analysis made the following comment: 'Cho, same way bass and drum carry the swing, bass and drum.'
123 Paul Willis's *Profane Culture* (Routledge and Kegan Paul 1978) presents the clearest exposition of this concept.
124 See: A. B. Spellman, *Four Lives in the Bebop Business* (Schocken 1971). On samba see: Marvin Harris, *Town and Country in Brasil* (Norton 1971); and sleeve notes to 'In Praise of Oxala and Other Gods Black Music of South America' (Nonesuch H72036), and 'Folklore e Bossa Nova do Brasil' (Polydor 583–710).
125 Interviewed in *JahUgliman*, vol. 2.
126 A. Mattelart, *Mass Media, Ideologies and the Revolutionary Movement* (Harvester 1980), p. 54.
127 Adorno, p. 185.
128 ibid., p. 191.
129 Michel Aglietta, *A Theory of Capitalist Regulation* (New Left Books 1979), pp. 111–15. Also C. Palloix, 'The labour process: from Fordism to neo-Fordism', in *The Labour Process and Class Strategies*, CSE Pamphlet no. 1 (CSE 1976); Mike Davis, ' "Fordism" in crisis', *Review*, vol. II, no. 2 (Fall 1978).
130 Hugh Mundell, *Black Echoes*, 8 November 1980.
131 Phizacklea and Miles, Chapter 7.
132 Stuart Hall, 'The political and the economic in Marx's theory of classes', in Hunt (ed.), *Class and Class Structure* (Lawrence and Wishart 1977).
133 Marx, *The Poverty of Philosophy* (Moscow 1976), p. 160.
134 Prezworski, 'Proletariat into a class', p. 344.
135 Gramsci, p. 286; M. Tronti, 'Social capital', *Telos*, no. 17, p. 197.
136 Aglietta, p. 117.
137 Kate Soper, 'Marxism, materialism and biology', p. 88.
138 Alain Touraine, *The Voice and the Eye: an Analysis of Social Movements* (Cambridge University Press 1981).
139 S. Hall, *Policing the Crisis*, p. 395.
140 See: Trotsky's April 1939 discussions with C. L. R. James in: Breitman (ed.), *Trotsky on Black Nationalism* (Monthly Review 1967).
141 Buci-Glucksmann, p. xii.
142 S. Bologna, 'The tribe of moles', in *Semiotext(e)* no. 9 (1980).
143 Nicos Poulantzas, *State, Power, Socialism* (New Left Books 1978).
144 C. Castoriadis, 'On the history of the workers' movement', *Telos*, no. 30

(Winter 1976–77); C. L. R. James, *Notes on Dialectics* (Allison and Busby 1980), p. 117; S. Rowbotham *et al.*, *Beyond the Fragments: Feminism and the Making of Socialism* (Newcastle Socialist Centre 1979).

145   I. Crewe *et al.*, 'Partisan de-alignment in Britain 1964–74', *British Journal of Political Science*, no. 7 (1976).

146   Leo Panitch, 'Trades unions and the state', *New Left Review*, no. 125 (1981); also 'The development of corporatism in Liberal democracies', *Comparative Political Studies*, vol. x, no. 1 (April 1977).

147   Partha Sarathi Gupta, *Imperialism and the British Labour Movement 1914–64* (Macmillan 1975); and D. Thompson and R. Larson, *Where were You, Brother? An Account of Trade Union Imperialism* (War on Want 1978).

148   R. Miles and A. Phizacklea, 'The TUC black workers and new commonwealth immigration 1954–73', *SSRC RUER Working Paper* no. 6 (1977); and 'The TUC and black workers 1974–76', *British Journal of Industrial Relations*, vol. xvi, no. 2 (1978). See also: *The Times*, 17 February 1954, and *Guardian*, 9 February 1954.

149   A. Coote and P. Kellner, 'Woman workers and union power', *New Statesman pamphlet* no. 1 (1980).

150   Alain Touraine, 'Political ecology: a demand to live differently now', *New Society*, 8 November 1979.

151   C. L. R. James, F. Forest and Ria Stone, *The Invading Socialist Society* (News and Letters Publications 1947; reprinted 1972).

152   Harry Cleaver, *Reading Capital Politically* (Harvester 1979).

153   *Notes on Dialectics*, p. 115.

154   C. L. R. James, *State Capitalism and World Revolution* (News and Letters Publications 1969).

155   Alberto Melucci, 'New movements, terrorism, and the political system: reflections on the Italian case', *Socialist Review 56*, vol. 11, no. 2 (March–April 1981). Bob Lumley, review of 'Working class autonomy and the crisis', *Capital and Class*, no. 12 (Winter 1980–1).

156   Eddy Cherki and Michel Wieviorka, 'Autoreduction movements in Turin', in *Semiotext(e)*, no. 9.

157   *Gay News*, no. 214 (30 April 1981).

Bibliography

Chapter 1   The organic crisis of British capitalism and race: the experience of the seventies

BUCI-GLUCKSMANN, C.,   *Gramsci and the State* (Lawrence and Wishart 1980)

BURTON, F. and CARLEN, P., *Official Discourse: On Discourse Analysis, Government Publications, Ideology and the State* (Routledge and Kegan Paul 1979)

CARCHEDI, C., 'Authority and foreign labour: some notes on a late capitalist form of capital accumulation and state intervention', *Studies in Political Economy*, no. 2 (Autumn 1979), pp. 37–74

CASTELLS, M., 'Immigrant workers and class struggles in advanced capitalism: the West European experience', in R. Cohen *et al.* (eds.), *Peasants and Proletarians* (Hutchinson 1979)

CASTLES, S. and KOSACK, C., *Immigrant Workers and Class Structure in Western Europe* (IRR/Oxford University Press 1973)

CLUTTERBUCK, R., *Britain in Agony* (Penguin 1978)

CONNOLLY, W., *The Terms of Political Discourse* (D. C. Heath 1974)

FREEMAN, G., *Immigrant Labour and Racial Conflict in Industrial Societies* (Princeton University Press 1979)

HALL, S., *et al.*, *Policing the Crisis* (Macmillan 1978)

JESSOP, B., 'The transformation of the state in post-war Britain', in R. Scase (ed.), *The State in Western Europe* (Croom Helm 1980)

KEANE, J., 'The legacy of political economy', *Canadian Journal of Political and Social Theory*, vol. 2, no. 3 (1978)

LECOURT, D. 'Marxism as a critique of sociological theories', in UNESCO, *Sociological Theories: Race and Colonialism* (Paris 1980)

LEYS, C., 'Neo-conservatism and the organic crisis in Britain', *Studies in Political Economy*, no. 4 (Autumn 1980), pp. 41–64

MELUCCI, A., 'The new social movements: a theoretical approach', *Social Science Information*, vol. 19, no. 2 (1980)

OFFE, C., 'Crises of crisis management: elements of a political crisis theory', *International Journal of Sociology*, vol. 6, no. 3 (1976), pp. 32–60

POULANTZAS, N. *Political Power and Social Classes* (New Left Books 1973)

PREZWORSKI, A., 'Material bases of consent: economics and politics in a hegemonic system', *Political Power and Social Theory*, vol. 1 (1980)

SIVANANDAN, A., 'Race, class and the state', *Race and Class*, vol. 17, no. 4 (1976), pp. 347–68

URRY, J.,   *The Anatomy of Capitalist Societies: The Economy, Civil Society and the State* (Macmillan 1981)
WRIGHT, E.,   *Class, Crisis and the State* (New Left Books 1978)

Chapter 2   Just plain common sense: the 'roots' of racism

BARKER, M.,   *The New Racism* (Junction Books 1981)
BALLHATCHET, K.,   *Race, Sex and Class under the Raj* (Weidenfeld and Nicolson 1980)
GRAMSCI, A.,   *Prison Notebooks* (Lawrence and Wishart 1971)
HENRIQUES, F.,   *Children of Conflict: A Study of Interracial Sex and Marriage* (E. P. Dutton 1975)
JORDAN, W. D.,   *White Over Black: American Attitudes Toward the Negro, 1550-1812* (Penguin 1969)
LORIMER, D.,   *Colour, Class and the Victorians: English Attitudes to the Negro in the Mid-Nineteenth Century* (Leicester University Press 1978)
RODNEY, W.,   *How Europe Underdeveloped Africa* (Bogle–L'Ouverture 1972)
ROGERS, J. A.,   *Sex and Race*, vols. 1-3 (New York 1940)
SHYLLON, F. O.,   *Black Slaves in Britain* (Oxford University Press 1974)
SHYLLON, F. O.,   *Black People in Britain* (Oxford University Press 1977)
WALVIN, J.,   *Black and White: A Study of the Negro and English Society, 1555-1945* (Allen Lane 1973)

Chapter 3   In the abundance of water the fool is thirsty: sociology and black 'pathology'

BARRETT, L.,   *The Sun and The Drum: African Roots in Jamaican Folk Tradition* (Heinemann 1976)
DAVIS, D. B.,   *The Problem of Slavery in Western Culture* (Cornell University Press 1966)
GENOVESE, E.,   *The Political Economy of Slavery* (Pantheon 1965)
HART, R.,   *Black Jamaicans' Struggle against Slavery* (Institute of Jamaica 1976)
JAMES, C. L. R.,   *The Black Jacobins: Toussaint L'Ouverture and the Saint Domingo Revolution* (Allison and Busby 1980)
KOCHMAN, T. (ed.),   *Rappin' n' Stylin' out: Communication in Urban Black America* (University of Illinois 1972)
LERNER, G. (ed.),   *Black Women in White America* (Pantheon 1972)
HURSTON, Z. N.,   *Mules and Men* (Indiana University Press 1978)
PRICE, R. (ed.),   *Maroon Societies* (Anchor Books 1973)
ROSE, P. I. (ed.),   *Slavery and Its Aftermath* (Atherton Press 1970)

Chapter 4   Police and thieves

ALDERSON, J. C.,   'Force is not enough . . .', *Sunday Telegraph*, 12 July 1981
ALDERSON, J. C.,   'Our Coppers', *Sun*, 17 August 1981

BALBUS, ISAAC D., *The Dialectics of Legal Repression* (Transaction Books 1973)

BOTTOMLEY, K. and COLEMAN, C., *Understanding Crime Rates* (Gower Press 1981)

CLARKE, R. V. G. and HOUGH, J. M., *The Effectiveness of Policing* (Gower Press 1980)

HAY, D. *et al.* (eds.), *Albion's Fatal Tree* (Allen Lane 1975)

HOLDAWAY, S. D., 'Changes in urban policing', *British Journal of Sociology*, vol. 28, no. 2 (1977)

KITSON, FRANK, *Low Intensity Operations* (Faber 1971)

LAMBERT, JOHN R., *Crime, Police, and Race Relations* (IRR/Oxford University Press 1970)

MOORE, COLIN and BROWN, JOHN, *Community Versus Crime* (Bedford Square Press 1981)

PLATT, TONY and TAKAGI, PAUL, (eds.), *Crime and Social Justice* (Macmillan 1981)

POPE, DAVID WATTS and WEINER, NORMAN L. (eds.), *Modern Policing* (Croom Helm 1981)

THOMPSON, E. P., *Whigs and Hunters* (Allen Lane 1975)

THOMPSON, F. P., *Writing by Candlelight* (Merlin 1980)

WEBB, SUPT. D., 'Policing a multi-racial community' unpublished paper, West Midlands Police, 1978

Chapter 5   Schooling in Babylon

CARBY, H. V., *Multicultural Fictions*, Occasional Stencilled Paper no. 58 (CCCS/Birmingham University 1980)

CARBY, H. V., 'Multiculturalism', *Screen Education*, no. 34 (Spring 1980), pp. 62–70

CCCS EDUCATION GROUP, *Unpopular Education* (CCCS/Hutchinson 1981)

COARD, B., *How the West Indian Child is made Educationally Subnormal in the British School System* (New Beacon Books 1971)

FINN, D. and FRITH, S., 'Education and the labour market', in *The State and the Politics of Education*, Open University Education Studies, E353, Block Part 2, Unit 4, Open University Press, 1981

JOHN, G., *In the Service of Black Youth: A Study of the Political Culture of Youth and Community Work with Black People in English Cities* (National Association of Youth Clubs 1981)

LITTLE, A. and WILLEY, R., *Multi-Ethnic Education: The Way Forward*, Schools Council Pamphlet no. 18, 1981

SELECT COMMITTEE ON RACE RELATIONS AND IMMIGRATION 1968–69, *The Problems of Coloured School Leavers* (HMSO 1969)

STONE, M., *The Education of the Black Child in Britain: The Myth of Multi-racial Education* (Fontana 1981)

WILLIS, P., *Learning to Labour* (Saxon House 1977)

Chapter 6   White woman listen! Black feminism and the boundaries of sisterhood

BARRETT, M.,   *Women's Oppression Today* (New Left Books 1980)
FONER, N.,   *Jamaica Farewell* (Routledge and Kegan Paul 1979)
HAFKIN, N. and RAY, E. (eds.),   *Women in Africa: Studies in Social and Economic Change* (Stanford University Press 1976)
HOOKS, B.,   *Ain't I a Woman?* (South End Press 1981)
JOSEPH, G. and LEWIS, J.,   *Common Differences – Conflicts in Black and White Feminist Perspectives* (Doubleday 1981)
LEGHORN, L. and PARKER, K.,   *Women's Worth. Sexual Economics and the Modern World* (Routledge and Kegan Paul 1981)
LOEWENBERG, J. and BOGIN, R. (eds.),   *Black Women in Nineteenth Century American Life* (Pennsylvania University Press 1978)
PRESCOD-ROBERTS, M. and STEELE, N.,   *Black Women: Bringing it all Back Home* (Falling Walls Press 1980)
REITER, R. (ed.),   *Toward an Anthropology of Women* (Monthly Review Press 1975)
RUBIN, G.,   'The traffic in women: notes on the political economy of sex', in R. Reiter (ed.), *Toward an Anthropology of Women* (Monthly Review Press 1975)
WILSON, A.,   *Finding a Voice: Asian Women in Britain* (Virago 1978)

Chapter 7   Gender, race and class: Asian women in resistance

OMVEDT, G.,   *We Will Smash This Prison: Indian Women in Struggle* (Zed Press 1980)
ROGERS, B.,   *The Domestication of Women: Discrimination in Developing Societies* (Kogan Page 1980)
LATIN AMERICAN PERSPECTIVES,   'Women and Class Struggle', vol. 114, nos. 1 and 2 (1977)
Migrant Women Speak, published for the Churches Committee by Search Press Ltd/ World Council of Churches 1978
Manushi – back copies
Social Scientist – special number on women, nos. 40–1 (November–December 1975) – a monthly journal of the Indian School of Social Sciences
MORAGA, C. and ANZALDUA, G. (eds.),   *Writings By Radical Women of Color* (Persephone Press 1981)

Chapter 8   Steppin' out of Babylon – race, class and autonomy

AGLIETTA, M.,   *A Theory of Capitalist Regulation* (New Left Books 1979)
BEN-TOVIM, G. *et al.*,   'Race, left strategies and the state', *Politics and Power*, no. 3 (Routledge and Kegan Paul 1981)
BURAWOY, M.,   'The politics of production and the production of politics', *Political Power and Social Theory*, vol. 1 (1980)
CASHMORE, E., *Rastaman* (Allen and Unwin 1979)

CLEAVER, H., *Reading Capital Politically* (Harvester 1979)

HALL, S., 'The political and the economic in Marx's theory of classes', in A. Hunt (ed.), *Class and Class Structure* (Lawrence and Wishart 1977)

HALL, S., 'Race, articulation and societies structured in dominance', in UNESCO, *Sociological Theories: Race and Colonialism* (Pan 1980)

HALL, S. and JEFFERSON, T. (eds.), *Resistance Through Rituals* (CCCS/ Hutchinson 1975)

HEBDIGE, D., *Subculture: The Meaning of Style* (Methuen 1979)

LACLAU, E., *Politics and Ideology in Marxist Theory* (New Left Books 1977)

MARABLE, M., *From the Grassroots* (South End Press 1980)

MARTIN, T., *Race First: The Ideological and Organisational Struggles of Marcus Garvey and the Universal Negro Improvement Association* (Greenwood 1975)

MELUCCI, A., 'New social movements, terrorism, and the political system: reflections on the Italian case', *Socialist Review*, no. 56 (1981), pp. 97–136.

OWENS, J., *Dread* (Sangster 1976)

PANITCH, L., 'Trade unions and the state', *New Left Review*, no. 125 (1981), pp. 21–44

PHIZACKLEA, A. and MILES, R., *Labour and Racism* (Routledge and Kegan Paul 1980)

POULANTZAS, N., *State, Power, Socialism* (New Left Books 1978)

PRZEWORSKI, A., 'Proletariat into a class: the process of class formation from Kautsky's *The Class Struggle* to recent controversies', *Politics and Society*, vol. 7, no. 4 (1977), pp. 343–401

ROBINSON, C., 'Coming to terms: the Third World and the dialectic of imperialism', *Race and Class*, vol. 22, no. 4 (1981), pp. 363–86

STEDMAN-JONES, C., 'Working class culture and working class politics in London 1870-1900', *Journal of Social History*, vol. 7, no. 4 (1974), pp. 460–507

TIMPANARO, S., *On Materialism* (New Left Books 1972)

TOURAINE, A., *The Self-Production of Society* (Chicago University Press 1977)

TOURAINE, A., *The Voice and the Eye: An Analysis of Social Movements* (Cambridge University Press 1981)

WILLIS, P., *Learning to Labour* (Saxon House 1977)

Index